Selected Prose of Christina Rossetti

Selected Prose of Christina Rossetti

Edited by
David A. Kent and P. G. Stanwood

St. Martin's Press
New York

Maude reproduced by permission of The Huntington Library, San Marino, California (item # HM6065).

Quotations from *Treasure Trove* reprinted by permission of the Syndics of the Fitzwilliam Museum to whom rights in this publication are assigned.

Quotations from Christina Rossetti's annotations to *Time Flies: A Reading Diary* and quotations from her manuscript of *Letter and Spirit* are used by permission of Mrs. Joan Rossetti and The Harry Ransom Humanities Research Center, The University of Texas at Austin.

Quotations from Christina Rossetti's "Notes for a new edition of *Time Flies*" in the Troxell Collection reprinted by permission of Princeton University Libraries.

ISBN 0-312-15903-X

Library of Congress Cataloging-in-Publication Data
Rossetti, Christina Georgina, 1830–1894.
   [Prose. Selections]
   Selected prose of Christina Rossetti / edited by David A. Kent and
Paul G. Stanwood.
      p.   cm.
   Includes bibliographical references and index.
   ISBN 0–312–15903–X
   I. Kent, David A., 1948–   . II. Stanwood, P. G. III. Title.
PR5237.A41998
828'.808—dc21   97-44885
                                                                          CIP

Internal design and typesetting by Letra Libre

First edition: May, 1998

10   9   8   7   6   5   4   3   2   1

PR5237
.A4
1998

For Margo and Dorothy

Contents

Acknowledgments

W e wish gratefully to acknowledge permission to consult or reprint material housed in a number of manuscript collections: The Harry Ransom Humanities Research Center, University of Texas at Austin, for access to its copy of *Time Flies* and Joan Rossetti for permission to reproduce some of Christina's annotations from this copy and to quote from the manuscript of *Seek and Find* at Texas; the Fitzwilliam Museum, Cambridge, for permission to reprint the variants of *Letter and Spirit* ("Treasure-Trove"); the Huntington Library for permission to publish the autograph manuscript of *Maude;* the Janet Camp Troxell Collection at Princeton University Library for the opportunity of consulting their rich collection of Rossetti materials; the Colbeck Collection (Special Collections) at the University of British Columbia for making available most of the printed texts and documents fundamental to this present volume. We wish also to acknowledge the most helpful staff of the University of Durham, the Bodleian Library, Oxford, the British Library, and the Society for Promoting Christian Knowledge (SPCK) in Marylebone, London.

We also wish to thank the University of British Columbia, which through its Humanities and Social Sciences Research funds, has generously supported this project. A number of individuals have provided timely help: Marlene Sherman for preparing early drafts of the manuscript; Diane D'Amico for helpful suggestions about our introduction; David Neelands, Roy Hoult, and Brian Freeland for identifying a number of fugitive references; Susan Plowden for her cooperation; Mary Ellen Henley for bibliographical assistance; Brent Whitted for collating printed texts and manuscripts; and colleagues Marguerite M. Chiarenza and W. E. Fredeman for readiness to assist with a number of perplexing questions.

D.A.K. and P.G.S.
Toronto and Vancouver
January 1998

List of Abbreviations

~~~~~

(Commonly cited in the Introduction and text)

AD	Christina Rossetti. *Annus Domini: A Prayer for each day of the year, founded on a text of Holy Scripture.* London: James Parker, 1874.
CGR	Christina Georgina Rossetti
Commonplace	Christina Rossetti. *Commonplace, and Other Short Stories.* London: Macmillan, 1870.
CS	Christina Rossetti. *Called to be Saints: The Minor Festivals Devotionally Studied.* London: SPCK, 1881.
FD	Christina Rossetti. *The Face of the Deep: A Devotional Commentary on the Apocalypse.* London: SPCK, 1892.
FL	*The Family Letters of Christina Georgina Rossetti, with Some Supplementary Letters and Appendices.* Ed. William Michael Rossetti. London: Brown, Langham, 1908.
LDGR	*The Letters of Dante Gabriel Rossetti.* Eds. Oswald Doughty and J. R. Wahl. 4 vols. Oxford: Clarendon Press, 1965–67.
Letters	*The Letters of Christina Rossetti.* Ed. Antony H. Harrison. 4 vols. Charlotte: University Press of Virginia, 1997–.
LS	Christina Rossetti. *Letter and Spirit: Notes on the Commandments.* London: SPCK, 1883.
Maude	*Maude: Prose & Verse by Christina Rossetti.* Ed. R. W. Crump. Hamden, Conn.: Archon Books, 1976.
Poems	*The Complete Poems of Christina Rossetti: A Variorum Edition.* Ed. R. W. Crump. 3 vols. Baton Rouge: Louisiana State University Press, 1979–1990.
PW	*The Poetical Works of Christina Georgina Rossetti.* Ed. William Michael Rossetti. London: Macmillan, 1904.
Reminiscences	*Some Reminiscences of William Michael Rossetti.* 2 vols. London: Brown, Langham, 1906; New York: AMS Press, 1970.

RM	*The Rossetti-Macmillan Letters.* Ed. Lona Mosk Packer. Berkeley: University of California Press, 1963.
RP	*Rossetti Papers.* Ed. William Michael Rossetti. London: Sands, 1903; New York: AMS Press, 1970.
SD	Maria Francesca Rossetti. *A Shadow of Dante: Being an Essay Towards Studying Himself, His World, and His Pilgrimage.* London: Longmans, Green, and Co., 1894.
SF	Christina Rossetti. *Seek and Find: A Double Series of Short Studies of the Benedicite.* London: SPCK, 1879.
SL	Christina Rossetti. *Speaking Likenesses.* London: Macmillan, 1874.
TF	Christina Rossetti. *Time Flies: A Reading Diary.* London: SPCK, 1885.
Verses	Christina Rossetti. *Verses.* London: SPCK, 1893.

A Note on the Texts

The copy texts of the selections that follow are described briefly at the beginning of each section. We have retained the spelling and other characteristics, including the retention of ligatures, of the original sources, even where Christina Rossetti appears to be inconsistent: for example, "connection" and "connexion" or "realize" and "realise" may appear on the same page. We have corrected obvious printer's errors and capitalized proper nouns; and we have normalized scriptural citations, using standard abbreviations and arabic numerals (Gen. 1.1). Where variant readings occur between manuscript and printed sources, or where textual information is given, we have in each case given the reading of the present text first, followed by a square bracket and the other (or variant) reading. Further details are given where necessary in the section headings of the notes. Typographical (or autograph) elements of the copy texts have generally been ignored, such as the typeface of titles, ornamental initials, and the like.

Introduction

C hristina Rossetti has emerged from comparative critical obscurity in the last two decades of the twentieth century as part of both the rediscovery of women writers and the continuing rehabilitation of Pre-Raphaelite writing and art. It seems unlikely that her reputation will again be quite so vulnerable to shifting critical preferences as it was during the forty-five year period that extends from 1930 to the 1970s. Since 1979, her complete poetry has been edited by Rebecca Crump in three volumes, she has been the subject of several biographies, and commentary on her poetry has steadily accumulated. In addition, her correspondence in four volumes, edited by Antony H. Harrison, has begun to appear, and more convenient, selected editions of her poetry are now being published.[1]

What remains conspicuously absent from readily available printed sources is a selection of her prose works, and it is that deficiency that the present volume seeks to address. Although there have been reprintings of several of Rossetti's prose works over the past twenty years, particularly her short fiction, these have been isolated publications often related to other purposes. *Speaking Likenesses*, for example, was reprinted in 1992, together with her short story "Nick," as two selections in an anthology, *Forbidden Journeys: Fairy Tales and Fantasies by Victorian Women Writers*. Rossetti's early novella, *Maude* (first published by William Michael Rossetti in 1897), was reprinted in 1976 by Rebecca Crump and then again in 1993, this latter time with two works by Dinah Mulock Craik, "On Sisterhoods" and *A Woman's Thoughts About Women*.[2] Rossetti's volumes of devotional prose, while not unacknowledged by commentators, have remained out of print since the early years of the century; yet those who have written about Rossetti as contributors to her reemergence often cite from these works to support their arguments. Furthermore, many of her religious poems originally appeared in the later devotional prose works, and their meanings are partially constituted and defined by these contexts. Making the prose works more accessible through care-ful selections marks another stage in efforts to provide reliable texts of Rossetti's writings and should foster obvious benefits for scholarship about her work.[3]

Christina Rossetti wrote prose all her life. Her first prose writings are fiction: a novella, *Maude* (which she never published), an unfinished epistolary novel ti-tled "Corrispondenzia Famigliare" ("Family Correspondence"), and some short stories.[4] Although in these early writings can be found elements of the didactic, exemplary impulse that would eventually dominate the devotional prose volumes in the final twenty years of her life, her first prose works are primarily concerned with issues important to her as a young woman coming to maturity in the mid-Victorian era. *Maude*, for instance, focuses on a devout late adolescent who writes poetry, in short a person apparently not far removed from Christina herself. Ros-setti's narrative revolves around matters of personal vocation, religious scruple, and pride. While her biographers tend to treat *Maude* as an index to Rossetti's early life experience and although feminist scholars have sometimes seized on Maude's fate as an implicit indictment of her patriarchal society, other critics have grown steadily more cautious about some of these assumptions and conclusions. Diane D'Amico, for example, sounded the warning about the "biographical fal-lacy" as early as 1981, and Sharon Smulders's recent analysis of the narrative in terms of its "triadic arrangements" makes a convincing case for the formal so-phistication of the narrative's design (D'Amico, 1981; Smulders, 1996, 24). Jan Marsh describes *Maude* as having been written "somewhat in the style of Char-lotte Yonge" (109), who was to write 150 books (about half being novels) and be-come the best-known Tractarian woman novelist, but how much Rossetti knew of Yonge's early writings in 1850 is uncertain.[5]

In contrast to *Maude*, many of the first stories Rossetti wrote are far removed from ordinary reality and belong to the world of the "tale."[6] Her early reading of gothic and romantic fiction and the novels of Charles Maturin, as well as her later acquaintance with the fairy tales of Anderson and Grimm, influences stories such as "Nick" and "Hero," although the apocalyptic imagination of Revelation is more obviously at work in the subsequent story, "Safe Investment" (Marsh, 30, 44, and 138). Similarly, the spiritual issues of Christian life are the focus of other later didactic stories like "Pros and Cons" and "The Waves of this Troublesome World" where the doctrinal imperatives become prominent. "The Lost Titian"—

with its effective evocation of Renaissance Italy and the competitive world of painters—is, however, often singled out as the most successful story in her collection, *Commonplace, and Other Short Stories.*

She returned to the novella form again after her second collection of poetry, *The Prince's Progress and Other Poems* (1866), was published and she felt she needed a longer narrative to complement her tales. *Commonplace* was written accordingly in 1869–70. It is, as her brother Dante Gabriel Rossetti wrote in a letter to Swinburne, decidedly in the "Austen vein" (*LDGR*, 2:297). The central theme of this narrative, pushing beyond the world of *Maude,* is marriage, and Rossetti's story—like a number of her poems in the 1850s and 1860s—presents three variants on a young woman's destiny: marrying for security and status, entering a convent, and marrying for love. Smulders, in fact, describes Rossetti's writings in the period from *Maude* to *Goblin Market* as an "exploration of sororal models of esthetic, social, and religious activity" in which she "records her resistance to Pre-Raphaelitism . . . and endeavours to overcome the discontinuities of her experience as a poet, a woman, and a Christian" (23). Another perspective on Rossetti's prose in *Commonplace* is provided by John Dixon Hunt, who singles out Rossetti's narrative as an example of Pre-Raphaelite realism and praises the "deliberately unheroic" tone and her concern with the "day-to-day lives of ordinary people." He cites stories such as "Vanna's Twins" and "The Waves of this Troublesome World" as containing other descriptive details that anticipate the bleak realism of fin de siècle prose. *Commonplace* has also evoked the admiration of Christopher Ricks who insists on taking her "instinctively corporeal" prose style seriously: "She believed in the Incarnation, and her words are acts of incarnation."[7]

One final attempt at success in the secular prose market came with her three interlocked stories for children, *Speaking Likenesses* (1874). On this occasion she imitated Lewis Carroll in an effort to win public favor and to build on the success she had had with her children's poetry, *Sing-Song* (1872).[8] Here again unsuspected complexities in the narrative have been disclosed. Furthermore, even in these stories for children, Rossetti is engaged in satire and parody of Victorian values, as, increasingly, in both poetry and prose, her priorities were shifting. The reference to Samuel Smiles's *Self-Help* (1859) in *Speaking Likenesses,* for example, leads Smulders to identify the second game in the opening section as a "savage satire of nineteenth-century entrepreneurship" (117).[9]

Whereas Linda Palazzo locates the turning point of Rossetti's career in the publication of *Annus Domini* (where her attention focuses on Scripture), Sharon

Smulders has identified the decisive turn from fictionality to spirituality as being signaled by the sonnet sequence "Monna Innominata" (included in the 1881 volume, *A Pageant and Other Poems*): "She moves from secular to devotional subjects, from death as an answer to the problem of carnal love as a necessary prelude to the consummation of spiritual love, and from the concept of the self bound in time to one of the self oriented to eternity" (128). This shift to religious concerns in her prose was probably underway by the mid 1860s when the later tales were written. No doubt her serious illness in 1871–72, coupled with the less than adulatory, mixed reviews of *Commonplace*, contributed to her decision to abandon prose fiction. While "The Lost Titian" was praised as "brilliant" and "excellent," there was general disapproval of the "three tracts" with their "narrow sectarianism" ("The Waves of this Troublesome World" is noted) and the author's strenuous efforts "to point a moral."[10] There is not much distance between such didactic fiction and the "themes of sober contemplation" that one reviewer identified as characteristic of *Time Flies* (1885), the second last of her six devotional works.[11]

Although Rossetti had always understood her vocation as that of a poet, she also saw herself as a professional writer earning her own way. She had managed to avoid becoming a governess, her attempt to become a nurse had been disappointed, and she rejected the marriage proposals of two suitors. And so, together with her brother William, she early took on the commission to write biographies of Italian writers for the *Imperial Dictionary of Universal Biography*. A decade later, she translated a short monograph on Italian architecture for John Murray.[12] Her other occasional prose includes two articles on Dante, a fictionalized description of her sister Maria's charitable work, printed in a parish newsletter, a "Harmony on Charity" for another church magazine (modified for inclusion in *Letter and Spirit*), and a brief description of her brother Dante Gabriel's house in Chelsea (all reprinted in this volume, with the exception of "Harmony"). She also seriously considered writing a monograph for the series *Eminent Women* (Adelaide Procter, Elizabeth Fry, Mary Lamb, Elizabeth Barrett Browning, and Ann Radcliffe were each considered [Marsh, 495–96]), and she is known to have destroyed at least one story when its moral influence was questioned.[13] Over the last two decades of her life, most of her writing energies were devoted to her six volumes of devotional prose, though these have been singularly neglected since her death.

To approach Rossetti's devotional prose receptively requires a reorientation in our own perspective. As part of her commentary on the Eighth Commandment in *Letter and Spirit: Notes on the Commandments* (1883), Rossetti makes one of her infrequent citations of source in her devotional prose—there are only two other footnotes in this text. Here she is discussing the Beatitude "Blessed are the poor in spirit." She suggests that "we are encouraged to love poverty whether we be rich or poor." She indicates that she owes this observation about "both literal poverty and a pious love of poverty" to Bishop George Moberly's sermon on this Beatitude.[14] Moberly understands the Beatitudes to describe "the main moral characters or traits which form the complete portraiture of the Christian man" (p. 1) and, on the matter of poverty of spirit, he defines this quality as follows: "It must be a willing poverty, of grace, not of nature, in the higher and spiritual part of man; not an outwardly imposed condition, nor an inward deficiency of force, but a willing and gracious selection and acquiescence by the spirit of a Christian man enlightened and enabled by the Holy Spirit of God, in a place, condition, desires, and the like, analogous to that which belongs to the outwardly and literally poor. . . . Blessed, then, is he who thus in his spirit, his higher spiritual nature, informed and illuminated by the Holy Spirit of God, is as a poor man among men upon this earth, not eager for its rewards or honours, nor ambitious of its first places, lowly, and unaffectedly content with lowliness!" (pps. 11–12). Poverty of spirit, an ideal that Christina Rossetti embraced and that she articulated in such well-known lyrics as "Give me the lowest place" (*Poems*, 1979–90, 1:187), helps to define that special quality of self-effacement—a refusal to put herself forward—that has inhibited critics from recognizing the full dimensions of her achievement as a writer since her death in 1894.

Even a brief excursion prompted by a citation such as the one noted here reconnects us with the Victorian religious mind and demonstrates several important features of Rossetti's devotional prose, undoubtedly the most inaccessible and, to contemporary readers, most alien portion of her writings. After her death, Bishop B. F. Westcott praised "the spiritual teachings of Miss Rossetti's poems" and described her as "pre-eminently the spiritual poet of our age" (Westcott, 21). But her devotional prose is equally consecrated to pious and earnest goals. In commenting on Scripture, describing a saint, or meditating on the natural world, Rossetti uses the Bible as her proof text for claims and as the warrant for assertions; and her understanding of the Bible is decidedly traditional. Yet ready access to her devotional prose is essential if we are to understand so many of the assumptions and premises of her religious poetry. Moberly himself was a conservative Christian, as is suggested by the preliminary essay in his book of sermons where he attacks *Essays and Reviews* (1859), the collection of essays that notoriously asserted liberalized opinions about such issues as the authority of Scripture and the question of eternal punishment in hell.[15] Moberly's Preface outlines the major themes of that book (xi–xxiii), comments on the "general disapprobation with which it has been received among church-people" (iii), and criticizes its critical spirit and the possible effects upon "young and unstable minds" (xxix). Rossetti presumably would have endorsed Moberly's attitudes. Indeed, she generally turns away from the new, higher criticism to assert traditional ideas about the "inspired" nature of the Bible (Moberly's Preface also endorses this approach).

A predecessor such as Isaac Williams or a contemporary like Richard Littledale (whom she knew) evidently express ideas with which she would have also agreed.[16] For example, Williams presumes the orderliness and meaningfulness of Scripture: "Revelation . . . is like Nature and Providence: for in these we doubt not that there is the perfection of exquisite order and arrangement; but it may appear to us in many respects otherwise, because we cannot comprehend the whole design. . . ." (Williams, 1876, 1.3). Exposition of Scripture cannot proceed as if the text were composed by human hands. It is, rather, a daunting, "awful and mysterious" (198) task predicated on a rigorously spiritual life and "opened" (153) by faith guided by the teaching of the Holy Spirit (198). To appreciate the "order, and variety, and distinctness of purpose" (77) in the revealed word of God (an order and variety analogous to the natural world), the interpreter, Williams insists, must go beyond "speculative reason" (153), "the critical skill and wisdom of the carnal mind" (184), which is more likely to lead to a common contemporary error, the suspicion of "imperfection" (3) in the Gospels.

Reading holy Scripture required a sense or understanding of how God wished to address human beings, and Rossetti shared the assumptions of Williams and also of John Keble about "Reserve" and "Analogy," ideas fundamental to Tractarianism and to Christina Rossetti's theological outlook and intellectual life. The idea of Reserve, first espoused by early church fathers such as Origen, urges that God is incomprehensible and can be known only in indirect, quiet, or secret ways. Truth may be revealed to us only in accordance with our capacity for understanding it. The principle of Analogy, also very ancient, teaches that Scripture (or indeed any and all parts of the created order) may be known through being figured or shadowed forth in innumerable types. Thus water (as in the baptism of Christ) is a figure of the Holy Spirit; dew of God's grace; wind the sign of God's unseen power; serpents of evil spirits. The sheep and goats represent (or analogize) our covenant with God, but the sheep are worthier than the goats; they may sit on God's right hand, but the goats must go to the left. The marriage feast of Cana represents the great feast prepared for us in Heaven, in the Kingdom to come.[17] One readily recognizes the compatibility of this kind of understanding throughout much of Rossetti's writing.

Christina Rossetti's attitudes, while dominantly conservative and deeply affected by the Tractarians (and later, the Oxford Movement) also have elements that some critics have gladly identified as radical and even "suffragette" in spirit. Trying to define her position with precision has become a major challenge. For example, Joel Westerholm rejects the inherited image of Rossetti as a "passive saint" (17) and believes that she "violated the restrictions . . . placed on women's devotional writing" (12). The church forbade women preachers, yet how else, he asks (11), are we to see and understand the majority of her works of devotional prose? In her "serious and scholarly biblical interpretation," she was "assuming a man's role according to standards of the time" (14) and was merely paying "lip service to men's superior position" (15).[18] Rossetti's connections with Anna Howitt, Barbara Smith (later Bodichon), and Bessie Parkes (women "in the vanguard of a new feminism," as Jan Marsh describes them) does support the position that Rossetti was fully aware of a variety of gender issues (153ff.). Similarly, Antony Harrison believes that Rossetti articulated a distinctive, antipatriarchal point of view in many of her devotional prose works by providing "a quietly comprehensive attack on the entire network of patriarchal values which even the most stringent social critics of her day normally accept without question. . . . By embracing religious values with a uniquely radical fervor . . . Rossetti's work undercuts the domestic ideology of middle and upper-class Victorians, and functions to subvert both the patriarchal values that governed Victorian England and their extension in industrial capitalism" ("The Sage Discourse," 89). The militantly renunciatory stance Rossetti adopts does undercut the "material assumptions upon which the stereotypical roles of middle-class women were based" (91), but this position, as Harrison demonstrates, may be more a function of her devout Anglo-Catholicism than an endorsement of the typical feminist issue of her day, universal suffrage. For if religious affiliation "traditionally complemented and served" the "social and material value systems" (95) of her culture, her fervent commitment realized many of the latent radical values of Christian social criticism. Furthermore, Anglo-Catholicism, with its rejection of pew rents, return to auricular confession, and encouragement of sisterhoods, among other departures from convention, was

regarded by many as "a radical movement" (96). It offered single women alternative forms of self-expression and its identification with the poor and marginalized
was also widely recognized.[19]

Against these arguments for Rossetti's incipient feminism, however, must be
placed her statements that assert men and women are different creatures, and that
the distinctions extended all the way back to Adam and Eve. Diane D'Amico observes the following about Rossetti's understanding of women's role: "In Rossetti's mind, because of 'Eve's lapse,' the woman's way to salvation differed from
that of man. Rossetti's helpmeet need not be a wife and mother, but she must be
humble and self-sacrificing, accepting her secondary status on earth. If woman
was too assertive and tried to compel action, for example, if she entered national
politics, her weak feminine nature could lead to destruction, literally to the loss of
her soul. . . ." (D'Amico, 1994, 27). Toward the close of her life, in 1889, she
signed "An Appeal Against Female Suffrage," which was written by Mrs.
Humphrey Ward and printed in *Nineteenth Century*. These signs of a more conservative attitude suggest that Rossetti's feminist tendencies were in uneasy ten-
sion with the tenets of her faith, and that she was not fully able to resolve the
conflict.[20]

As mentioned earlier, Christina only thought briefly of governessing (described
as "the family vocation" for women by William Michael Rossetti in his *Reminiscences*, 1:39), and that was at a time of severe financial worry for the family. Writing was her calling, and as she grew older she increasingly understood her gift as
consecrated to religious purposes. This "sense of vocation," Owen Chadwick has
observed, is one of the most characteristic features of Victorian religion, and "carried with it a powerful sense of the sacredness of time and the sin of wasting it.
They [Victorians] were the servants of God, under his eye, and their hands found
plenty to do in his cause" (2:466). By the end of her life, Rossetti's publications
had attracted a sizable audience—"an extensive following," "a large and appreciative audience" (observations by reviewers cited in Harrison, 1990, 88)—and this
audience was primarily, though not exclusively, female. The loyalty of this audience
was described by Theodore Watts-Dunton as he recalled the press reaction to her
death: "Yet that outburst was far from giving adequate expression to what was felt
by some of her readers—those between whom and herself there was a bond of
sympathy so sacred and so deep as to be something like a religion." What did Rossetti think her role was in relation to that audience to whom she was conscious of
speaking? The rector of Rossetti's Christ Church, H. W. Burrows, in one sermon

stressed the need for teachers of all kinds "to turn men to righteousness" and he included among them "writers in books." Elsewhere he regretted the misuse of "high poetic and imaginative power." A writer who has "the gift of feeling more accurately than others," he says, is potentially "fitted to be the mouthpiece of his time" who ought to "set forth . . . ideals of excellence," but too often the results are merely lewd or blasphemous. In her religious prose, Rossetti was evidently operating under these kinds of imperatives, and she identified both writing and reading as potentially forms of spiritual discipline.[21]

Take, for example, her massive final work, *The Face of the Deep: A Devotional Commentary on the Apocalypse* (1892). While this text nominally satisfies the definition of a commentary ("a book which discusses the biblical text chapter by chapter and verse by verse, lifting up noteworthy phrases and words for clarification" [Soulen, 39]), Rossetti's commentary is far from being conventionally academic (treating the historical, cultural, and linguistic contexts of Revelation). It is, rather, intended to arouse the reader's "devotional feeling," as George MacDonald describes religious poetry in a book of 1868.[22] A reviewer in *The Independent* perhaps expressed it best: "Veritably a poet's book; the work of a poet, and for poetic minds, but inspired by a faith that rises into the rhapsody of open vision."[23] Of course explicating the Bible was a "solemn" undertaking (*LS*, 158) since Rossetti followed the conservative theological premise in regarding Scripture as "the sure utterance of inspiration" (*Called to be Saints*, 25).[24] Studying the Bible is thereby a special kind of pilgrimage that requires the assistance of "Divine grace" (*FD*, 360, 114) and that involves both rewards and dangers for the reader. Rossetti's commentary would, she hoped, bring readers into "direct contact with God's Word" so that they might be "moulded and spiritualized" by it (*FD*, 12, 325).

Elsewhere in *The Face of the Deep*, Rossetti describes her commentary as the "surface study of an unfathomable depth" (365) whose "truths" (269) are elusive and sometimes inexplicable. Her commentary avoids "the interpretation of the sense" of words in favor of what she calls "simple meditation" (277). She also turns away from historical interpretations in order to give "typical" (195) or parabolic readings of passages. Her general approach can be contrasted with one work by Isaac Williams, whose *The Apocalypse, with Notes and Reflections* (1841, 1852) is dense with citations of authorities and with quotations from the early church fathers. He is interested in showing how Revelation encapsulates and sums up all Scripture, and he often delves into numerological symbolism and the Greek origins of important words. Writing for an audience of devout Victorian lay readers, Rossetti by contrast includes very few secondary allusions. She refers the reader to the accessible margins of ordinary Bibles and to such prominent writers as Augustine and, when an obscurity does arise, simply compares the Authorized and Revised versions.[25]

We get one of the only accounts available of her efforts to understand Scripture in a letter she wrote to Frederic Shields: "Our conversation of last evening gave me some subsequent thought and a wish to feel surer of my ground within such sacred precincts. So I turned to 2 commentaries we have at hand, and, though my search failed in great measure, I did light upon one passage in Scott's well-known work which I venture to extract and lay before you,—not as pretending to clash with your view, but simply as explaining why it seems to me that the promised 'desert of roses' blossomed not at the voice of St. John Baptist. I think so, of course, on other and wider grounds, and according to Mr. Scott the 'soldiers' form no exception to the rule" (*FL*, 71). One of the commentators referred to is Thomas Scott (1747–1821), whose *Commentary on the Bible* (issued weekly from 1788 to 1792) appears to have influenced Rossetti's practice as a commentator. Scott's work is known for its avoidance of historical explanations and for his inexhaustible collation of scriptural passages; he believed that Scripture is best understood by Scripture itself. He also endorses "the divine inspiration of the Holy Scriptures" and understands the Bible as "a divine revelation."[26] The other commentary she refers to in her letter to Shields may be the one also alluded to in *Called to be Saints* (pps. 319–20) where she is discussing St. Peter's comment about the church that is at Babylon: "Perhaps the most satisfactory, if tenable, solution is one put forward in (Taylor's edition of) Calmet's vast elucidatory work: that the Jews bestowed the name of Babylon on any place where any section of their nation had undergone captivity." The commentator in this case is Augustin Calmet (1672–1757) and the work is *Calmet's Dictionary of the Holy Bible* (in three volumes revised, corrected, and augmented under the direction of C. Taylor and printed several times during the nineteenth century). Rossetti's remark echoes her source almost exactly: "The Jews carry this notion still further, and give the name of Babylon to any place, whether in Babylonia Proper, or out of it, where any division of their nation had been held in a state of captivity" (p. 126). Identifying these works by Scott and Calmet adds additional contextual fields for understanding Rossetti's prose commentaries and, where poems form part of the commentary, another potential source for intertextual interpretation.

As a poet, Rossetti is often concerned with analyzing the "symbolical language accommodated to human apprehension" (*FD*, 23) found in Revelation. In focusing on the figurative significance of stories, images, and characters, she seeks to demonstrate the direct personal relevance of Scripture for her readers and to encourage them to turn their eyes "within" (396) in self-reflection. She explicates emblematic figures (462), comments on symbolism (for example, of left and right, 165–66, 275), and attends closely to colors (72) and typology (197, 433).[27] As with her other volumes of devotional prose, her commentary on Revelation attempts to disclose and assert a unity of purpose in the diversity of the Bible; she assumes that "a thread of perfect sequence runs throughout Divine Revelation, binding it into one sacred and flawless whole" (174). She therefore collates related biblical texts and uses of imagery, aiming to "harmonize" (403) themes and symbols to illustrate the inspired internal unity of the sacred text. Her own devotional works are usually characterized by an almost liturgical attention to form. They may be organized around the structure of the year (as in *Annus Domini* and *Time Flies*), particular biblical texts (Revelation in *The Face of the Deep*, the Benedicite in *Seek and Find*, or the Ten Commandments in *Letter and Spirit*), or a combination of features that systematically repeat themselves; *Called to be Saints* includes sections of scriptural excerpts, biographical details of saints' lives (associated traditions or legends), botanical digressions and descriptions of precious stones, and concluding prayers that stress a particular quality of the saint in question.

Accompanying Rossetti's limited exegetical goals is her awareness of the dangers involved in the whole enterprise of writing about the Bible, especially in an age of intense controversy over the interpretation of Scripture. As comments in several of her prose works reveal, she believed human beings to be extremely "vulnerable" to the powers of language (*LS*, 141).[28] Because Scripture (she states in *SF*, 125) "is so full of charm, so deep, so wide, so inexhaustibly suggestive," she recognized that readers might be tempted to look past the "main point" (*LS*, 85) of a passage in search of answers to abstruse or esoteric questions. Examples of imagination escaping its appropriate exercise are readings that seriously consider the "precise architecture of Noah's ark" or "the astronomy of Joshua's miracle" (*LS*, 86).[29] Any approach to the Bible that turns it into "a puzzle or riddle" (*FD*, 350) violates her sense of disciplined commentary; "pious exercise" is then, she holds, made into the kind of "curious investigation" (334) she associates with original sin: "To study the Apocalypse out of idle curiosity would turn it, so far as the student's self were concerned, into a branch of the Tree of the Knowledge of Good and Evil" (531).

Through the method of her commentary and the features of her other prose works, Rossetti wants to train readers to perceive the spiritual meaning of Scripture. Furthermore, by what she described as the supernaturalizing of the readers' eyes (116), she also hoped to help them read the text of everyday life to be filled with what in *Time Flies* she refers to as "spiritual lessons" and "heavenly meanings" (65). *Seek and Find* also provides numerous examples of how nature can speak of divine mercy to the devout observer: "Without adverting to spiritual analogues, a mere natural well has about it something religious if we make it a 'memoria technica' recalling to our minds many a merciful providence of olden times" (103). *Time Flies* contains numerous parables that she recognized in her own experience and that she recounts to foster "meditation" (138) and reflection about whatever happens "any day, any hour" (*FD*, 412). Such contemplative activity "fixes the spiritual eye on matters worthy of insight" (267). In effect, Rossetti seeks through her devotional prose writings to encourage devotional exercises.[30] Readers, she believed, can redeem their imaginations by storing them with sacred imagery and spiritual meanings. The supernaturalized imagination alive to biblical associations will see, for example, how a rainbow (since it is invariably linked with clouds) immediately suggests "an emblematic allusion to the Most High Spirit of God" (152). Similarly, "Sacred association" makes even animals (lambs, lions, sheep, doves, and eagles) "reverend to us" (157). The clearest statement of this view occurs in *Seek and Find*: "Common things continually at hand, wind or windfall or budding bough, acquire a sacred association, and cross our path under aspects at once familiar and transfigured, and preach to our spirits while they serve our bodies" (203). Rossetti here affirms the argument from design (deducing the "existence or qualities of God from a contemplation of nature" [Chadwick, 2:30]) and a sacramental mode of perception, endorsing a nineteenth-century version of reading the Book of the Creatures, as that tradition came down to her through such influences as Wordsworth, Keble, and Anglo-Catholicism. Her interpretive approach to Scripture is dominated by a "markedly typological" understanding of the Bible and, in works such as *Called to be Saints*, she applies the idea of correspondences in exploring matters as diverse as the popularized lives of saints and the botanical features of emblematic plants and precious stones.[31] Appropriately, the end for which she strives is to foster the Tractarian ideal of personal holiness she describes in *Letter and Spirit*: "Versed in such trains of thought the mind becomes reverential, composed, grave; the heart imbued with such associations becomes studied and ennobled; and out of the abundance of such a heart the mouth impulsively speaks that which is good and edifying" (132).

Christina Rossetti's reputation as a major English poet of the nineteenth century is now an accepted critical fact, but her real achievement as a writer will not have been fully recognized until the range and diversity of her prose writings are also taken into account. Her prose has been too easily dismissed by critics who have preferred to adhere to a more conventional image of the "poetess" of melancholy lyrics or by those who reduce the prose to statements of doctrine. It is true that much of her prose writing was driven by a deep sense of duty, the need to be of service, and the compulsion to make her writing gift an oblation of self. These motives do not mean, however, that her prose works lack power, imagination, or significance. This volume is intended to retrieve her prose writings from the periphery of critical attention precisely because there is much of inherent interest and artistry in them and also because they can assist substantially in the understanding of her poetry.[32]

Part 1

Fiction

Maude

~~~

Prose & Verse (1850)

The first of Christina Rossetti's works of fiction, *Maude* was completed shortly before the author turned twenty in 1850. The work first appeared posthumously in 1897 through the mediation of William Michael Rossetti, whose preface appeared with this first edition. He is rather apologetic over the literary merits of *Maude* (the poems excepted), but underlines the autobiographical significance of the work. The heroine, like Christina herself, is sensitive to the claims of art and religion, of poetry and faith. But the story offers far more than a fictionalized view of the young Christina Rossetti. Referring to the "Three Nuns," the poetic climax of the story, Rossetti wrote: "Whatever other merit it lacks, it possesses unity of purpose in a high degree" (*FL*, 6). For many readers, the story may seem to have unsatisfactory characterization and inadequate motivation; yet Rossetti constructs the story skillfully according to several triads: three parts, each further divided into three sections; three settings; three major characters (Agnes, Mary, and Maude). And there are interesting narrative shifts and modulations of style, from Maude's initial cheerfulness, to her acerbic wit and final melancholy. The point of view also changes meaningfully from the omniscient to the first person (through the exchange of letters). And the poetry is interspersed in such a way that we may better understand the changing mood of Maude and her friends and cousins.

The text follows the autograph manuscript in the Huntington Library (MS 6065), San Marino, California, with the addition of the "prefatory note," as it appeared in the first edition of 1897 (Chicago: Herbert S. Stone & Company), but we have also given in the notes original substantive readings that Christina Rossetti changed in the manuscript. The Chicago edition follows the corrected manuscript quite closely but often alters its punctuation and spelling. A second, English edition appeared also in 1897 (London: James Bowden), but it is much abridged and omits many of the poems; evidently William Michael Rossetti was having copyright difficulties. *Maude* was carefully edited by R. W. Crump (1976), who provides a detailed textual apparatus and an introduction that emphasizes biographical aspects. Like Crump, we have also presented a text that preserves the wording, spelling, punctuation, and paragraphing of the manuscript, the only authoritative version of the text. Crump also reprints all of the poetry in *Maude* in her Variorum Edition of the *Poems*, where she provides full textual and bibliographical information.

The Chicago edition of *Maude*, edited by Elaine Showalter, was recently reprinted along with two works by Dinah Mulock Craik (1826–87). The most recent and extended analysis of the novella is by Sharon Smulders, *Christina Rossetti Revisited* (New York: Twayne, 1996), 23–32.

Footnotes in this section are Rossetti's own.

MAUDE: *Prose & Verse*

Prefatory Note

This "Tale for Girls" (as I should be disposed to call it) was written out by Christina Rossetti, with her usual excessive neatness of calligraphy, in 1850. I suppose it may have been composed in that year, or a year or two earlier. In 1850, up to the 5th December, she was nineteen years of age. Of the rather numerous poems interspersed in the tale, all save two have, I think, been published ere now. They were all written without any intention of inserting them in any tale—except only the first two in the trio bouts-rimés sonnets. The MS. of the tale presents a few slight revisions, made at some much later date—perhaps about 1870, or 1875.

I daresay that Christina may, towards 1850, have offered the tale here or there for publication, but have no particular recollection as to that point. In now at last publishing it, I am not under any misapprehension regarding the degree of merit which it possesses. I allow it to be in all senses a juvenile performance; but I think it is agreeably written, and not without touches of genuine perception and discernment. Most of the poems I rate high. The literary reputation of Christina Rossetti is now sufficiently established to make what she wrote interesting to many persons—if not for the writing's own sake, then for the writer's. As such, I feel no qualms in giving publicity to *Maude*.

It appears to me that my sister's main object in delineating Maude was to exhibit what she regarded as defects in her own character, and in her attitude towards her social circle and her religious obligations. Maude's constantly weak health is also susceptible of a personal reference, no doubt intentional: even so minor a point as her designing the pattern of a sofa-pillow might apply to Christina herself. Maude is made the subject of many unfavourable comments, from herself and from her strict-minded authoress. The worst harm she appears to have done is, that when she had written a good poem, she felt it to be good. She was also guilty of the grave sin of preferring to forego the receiving of the eucharist when she supposed herself to be unworthy of it; and further, of attending the musical services at St. Andrew's Church (Wells Street, Oxford Street), instead of invariably frequenting her parish church. If some readers opine that all this shows Christina Rossetti's mind to have been at that date overburdened with conscientious scruples of an extreme and even a wire-drawn kind, I share their opinion. One can trace in this tale that she was already an adherent of the advanced High Church party in the Anglican communion, including conventual sisterhoods. So far as my own views of right and wrong go, I cannot see that the much-reprehended Maude commits a single serious fault from title-page to finis.

I fancy that Agnes and Mary Clifton may be, to some extent, limned from two young ladies, Alicia and Priscilla Townsend, whom my sister knew and liked in those years. The whole family emigrated—perhaps a year or two prior to 1850—to Canterbury Settlement, New Zealand. Some surnames introduced into the tale—such as Hunt, Deverell, and Potter—were highly familiar in our household. Towards the close is a sentence, "The locked book she never opened, but had it placed in Maude's coffin"; which is curious, as an unconscious prefigurement of a well-known and much-discussed incident in the life of Dante Gabriel Rossetti.[1]

With these few remarks I commit *Maude* to the reader. For its prose the "indulgent reader" (as our great-grandfathers used to phrase it) may be in requisition; for its verse the "discreet" reader will suffice.

W. M. Rossetti.
London, November, 1896.

MAUDE

Part 1st.

I.

"A penny for your thoughts," said Mrs Foster one bright July morning as she entered the sitting room with a bunch of roses in her hand, and an open letter: "A penny for your thoughts," said she addressing her daughter, who, surrounded by a chaos of stationery, was slipping out of sight some scrawled paper. This observation remaining unanswered, the Mother, only too much accustomed to inattention, continued: "Here is a note from your Aunt Letty; she wants us to go and pass a few days with them. You know Tuesday is Mary's birthday, so they mean to have some young people and cannot dispense with your company."

"Do you think of going?" said Maude at last, having locked her writing-book.

"Yes dear: even a short stay in the country may do you good, you have looked so pale lately. Don't you feel quite well? tell me."

"Oh yes; there is not much the matter, only I am tired and have a headache. Indeed there is nothing at all the matter; besides, the country may work wonders."

Half satisfied, half uneasy, Mrs Foster asked a few more questions, to have them all answered in the same style: vain questions, put to one who without telling lies was determined not to tell the truth.

When once more alone Maude resumed the occupation which her Mother's entrance had interrupted. Her writing-book was neither Common-Place Book, Album, Scrap-Book, nor Diary; it was a compound of all these; and contained original compositions not intended for the public eye, pet extracts, extraordinary little sketches and occasional tracts of journal. This choice collection she now proceeded to enrich with the following sonnet[2]:—

> Yes, I too could face death and never shrink:
> But it is harder to bear hated life;
> To strive with hands and knees weary of strife;
> To drag the heavy chain whose every link
> Galls to the bone; to stand upon the brink
> Of the deep grave, nor drowse, though it be rife
> With sleep; to hold with steady hand the knife
> Nor strike home: this is courage as I think.
> Surely to suffer is more than to do:
> To do is quickly done; to suffer is
> Longer and fuller of heart-sicknesses:
> Each day's experience testifies of this:
> Good deeds are many, but good lives[3] are few;
> Thousands taste the full cup; who drains the lees?—

having done which she yawned, leaned back in her chair, and wondered how she should fill up the time till dinner.[4]

Maude Foster was just fifteen. Small though not positively short, she might easily be overlooked but would not easily be forgotten. Her figure was slight and well-made, but appeared almost high-shouldered through a habitual shrugging stoop. Her features were regular and pleasing; as a child she had been very pretty; and might have continued so but for a fixed paleness, and an expression, not exactly of pain, but languid and preoccupied to a painful degree. Yet even now if at any time she became thoroughly aroused and interested, her sleepy eyes would light up with wonderful brilliancy, her cheeks glow with warm colour, her manner become animated, and drawing herself up to her full height she would look more beautiful than ever she did as a child. So Mrs Foster said, and so unhappily Maude knew. She also knew that people thought her clever, and that her little copies of verses were handed about and admired. Touching these same verses, it was the amazement of every one what could make her poetry so broken-hearted, as was mostly the case. Some pronounced that she wrote very foolishly about things she could not possibly understand; some wondered if she really had any secret source of uneasiness; while some simply set her down as affected. Perhaps there was a degree of truth in all these opinions. But I have said enough: the following pages will enable my readers to form their own estimate of Maude's character. Meanwhile let me transport them to another sitting room; but this time it will be in the country with a delightful garden look-out.

Mary Clifton was arranging her Mother's special nosegay[5] when that lady entered.

"Here my dear, I will finish doing the flowers. It is time for you to go to meet your Aunt and Cousin; indeed, if you do not make haste, you will be too late."

"Thank you, Mamma; the flowers are nearly done;" and Mary ran out of the room.

Before long she and her sister were hurrying beneath a burning sun towards the Railway Station. Through having delayed their start[6] to the very last moment, neither had found time to lay hands on a[7] parasol; but this was little heeded by two healthy girls, full of life and spirits, and longing moreover to spy out their friends. Mary wanted one day of fifteen; Agnes was almost a year older: both were well-grown and well-made, with fair hair, blue eyes and fresh complexions. So far they were alike: what differences existed in other respects remains to be seen.[8]

"How do you do, Aunt? How do you do, Maude?" cried Mary making a sudden dart forward as she discovered our friends, who having left the Station had already made some progress along the dusty road. Then relinquishing her Aunt to Agnes, she seized upon her cousin, and was soon deep in the description of all the pleasures planned for the auspicious morrow.

"We are to do what we like in the morning: I mean, nothing particular is arranged; so I shall initiate you into all the mysteries of the place; all the cats,

dogs, rabbits, pigeons, &c; above all I must introduce you to a pig, a special
protégé of mine:—that is, if you are inclined, for you look wretchedly pale;
aren't you well, dear?"

"Oh yes, quite well, and you must show me everything. But what are we
to do afterwards?"

"Oh! afterwards we are to be intensely grand. All our young friends are
coming and we are to play at round games, (you were always clever at round
games,) and I expect to have great fun. Besides, I have stipulated for unlim-
ited strawberries and cream; also, sundry tarts are in course of preparation.
By the way, I count on your introducing some new game among us benighted rustics; you who come from dissipated London."

"I fear I know nothing new, but will do my best. At any rate I can preside at your toilet and assist in making you irresistible."

Mary coloured and laughed; then thought no more of the pretty speech,
which sounded as if carefully prepared by her polite cousin. The two made
a strong contrast: one was occupied by a thousand shifting thoughts of herself, her friends, her plans, what she must do, what she would do; the other,
whatever might employ her tongue, and to a certain extent her mind, had
always an under-current of thought intent upon herself.

Arrived at the house, greetings were duly and cordially performed; also an
introduction to a new and very fat baby, who received Maude's advances
with a howl of intense dismay. The first day of a visit is often no very lively
affair: so perhaps all parties heard the clock announce bed-time without
much regret.

II.

The young people were assembled in Mary's room, deep in the mysteries of
the toilet.

"Here is your wreath, Maude; you must wear it for my sake, and forgive
a surreptitious sprig of bay which I have introduced;" said Agnes, adjusting
the last white rose, and looking affectionately at her sister and cousin.

Maude was arranging Mary's long fair hair with goodnatured anxiety to
display it to the utmost advantage.

"One more spray of fuchsia; I was always sure fuchsia would make a
beautiful head-dress. There; now you are perfection: only look; look
Agnes.—Oh, I beg your pardon; thank you; my wreath is very nice, only I
have not earned the bay." Still she did not remove it; and when placed on
her dark hair it well became the really intellectual character of her face. Her
dress was entirely white; simple, fresh and elegant. Neither she nor Agnes
would wear ornaments, but left them to Mary, in whose honour the entertainment was given, and who in all other respects was arrayed like her sister.

In the drawingroom[9] Mary proceeded to set in order[10] the presents received[11] that morning:—a handsomely[12] bound Bible from her Father, and a small Prayer-book with Cross and clasp from her Mother; a bracelet of Maude's hair from her Aunt; a cornelian heart[13] from Agnes, and a pocket bonbonnière from her Cousin, besides pretty trifles[14] from her little Brothers. In the midst of arrangements and re-arrangements[15] the servant entered with a large bunch of lilies from the village school-children, and the announcement that Mr and Mrs Savage were just arrived with their six daughters.

Gradually the guests assembled, young and old, pretty and plain; all alike seemingly bent on enjoying themselves: some with gifts, and all with cordial greetings for Mary; for she was a general favourite. There was slim Rosanna Hunt, her scarf arranged with artful negligence to hide a slight protrusion of one shoulder; and sweet Magdalen Ellis, habited as usual in quiet colours.[16] Then came Jane and Alice Deverell, twins so much alike[17] that few besides their parents knew them apart with any certainty; and their fair brother Alexis who, had he been a girl, would have increased the confusion. There was little Ellen Potter, with a round rosy face like an apple, looking as natural and goodhumoured as if, instead of a grand French Governess, she had had her own parents with her like most of the other children; and then came three rather haughty-looking Miss Stantons; and pale Hannah Lindley the orphan; and Harriet Eyre, a thought too showy in her dress.

Mary, all life and spirits, hastened to introduce the new-comers to Maude; who, perfectly unembarrassed, bowed and uttered little speeches with the manner of a practised woman of the world; while the genuine, unobtrusive courtesy of Agnes did more towards making their guests comfortable than the eager goodnature of her sister, or the correct breeding of her cousin.

At length the preliminaries were all accomplished, every one having found a seat, or being otherwise satisfactorily disposed of. The elders of the party were grouped here and there, talking and looking on: the very small children were accommodated in an adjoining apartment with a gigantic Noah's Ark: and the rest of the young people being at liberty to amuse themselves as fancy might prompt,[18] a general appeal was made to Miss Foster for some game, novel, entertaining and ingenious; or, as some of the more diffident hinted, easy.

"I really know nothing new;" said Maude: "you must have played at Proverbs, What's my thought like, How do you like it, and Magic music:— or stay, there is one thing we can try:—Bouts rimés."[19]

"What?" asked Mary.

"Bouts rimés: it is very easy. Some one gives rhymes, Mamma can do that, and then every one fills them up as they think fit. A sonnet is the best form to select; but, if you wish, we could try eight, or even four lines."

"But I am certain I could not make a couplet;" said Mary laughing. "Of course you would get on capitally, and Agnes might manage very well, and Magdalen can do anything; but it is quite beyond me: do pray think of something more suited to my capacity."

"Indeed I have nothing else to propose. This is very much better than mere common games; but if you will not try it, that ends the matter:" and Maude leaned back in her chair.

"I hope"—began Mary: but Agnes interposed:

"Suppose some of us attempt Bouts rimés; and you meanwhile can settle what we shall do afterwards. Who is ready to test her poetical powers?— What, no one?—Oh, Magdalen, pray join Maude and me."

This proposal met with universal approbation, and the three girls[20] retreated to a side table; Mary, who supplied the rhymes, exacting a promise that only one sonnet should be composed. Before the next game was fixed upon, the three following productions were submitted for judgement to the discerning public. The first was by Agnes:[21]

> "Would that I were a turnip white,
> Or raven black,
> Or miserable hack
>   Dragging a cab from left to right;
>   Or would I were the showman of a sight,
> Or weary donkey with a laden back,
> Or racer in a sack,
>   Or freezing traveller on an Alpine height;
> Or would I were straw catching as I drown,
>   (A wretched landsman I who cannot swim,)
>   Or watching a lone vessel sink,
>   Rather than writing: I would change my pink
> Gauze for a hideous yellow satin gown
>   With deep-cut scolloped edges and a rim."

"Indeed I had no idea of the sacrifice you were making;" observed Maude: "you did it with such heroic[22] equanimity. Might I however venture to hint that my sympathy with your sorrows would have been greater, had they been expressed in metre?"[23]

"There's gratitude for you," cried Agnes gaily: "What have you to expect, Magdalen?" and she went on to read her friend's sonnet:[24]

> "I fancy the good fairies dressed in white,
> Glancing like moon-beams through the shadows black;
> Without much work to do for king or hack.
>   Training perhaps some twisted branch aright;

Or sweeping faded Autumn leaves from sight
To foster embryo life; or binding back
Stray tendrils; or in ample bean-pod sack
   Bringing wild honey from the rocky height;
Or fishing for a[25] fly lest it should drown;
   Or teaching water-lily heads to swim,
Fearful that sudden rain might make them sink;
Or dyeing the pale rose a warmer pink;
Or wrapping lilies in their leafy gown,
   Yet letting the white peep beyond the rim."—

"Well, Maude?"

"Well, Agnes; Miss Ellis is too kind to feel gratified at hearing that her verses make me tremble for my own: but such as they are, listen:[26]

"Some ladies dress in muslin full and white,
Some gentlemen in cloth succinct and black;
Some patronise a dog-cart, some a hack,
   Some think a painted clarence only right.
   Youth is not always such a pleasing sight,
Witness a man with tassels on his back;
Or woman in a great-coat like a sack
   Towering above her sex with horrid height.
If all the world were water fit to drown
   There are some whom you would not teach to swim,
Rather enjoying if you saw them sink;
   Certain old ladies dressed in girlish pink,
With roses and geraniums on their gowns:—
   Go to the Bason, poke them o'er the rim."—

"What a very odd sonnet:" said Mary after a slight pause: "but surely men don't wear tassels."

Her cousin smiled: "You must allow for poetical licence; and I have literally seen a man in Regent Street wearing a sort of hooded cloak with one tassel. Of course every one will understand the Bason to mean the one in St. James' Park."

"With these explanations your sonnet is comprehensible," said Mary: and Magdalen added with unaffected pleasure: "And without them it was by far the best of the three."

Maude now exerted herself to amuse the party; and soon proved that ability was not lacking. Game after game was proposed and played at; and her fund seemed inexhaustible, for nothing was thought too nonsensical or too noisy for the occasion. Her goodhumour and animation were infectious:

Miss Stanton incurred forfeits with the blandest smile; Hannah Lindley blushed and dimpled as she had not done for many months; Rosanna never perceived the derangement of her scarf; little Ellen exulted in freedom from School-room trammels; the twins guessed each other's thoughts with marvellous facility; Magdalen laughed aloud; and even Harriet Eyre's dress looked scarcely too gay for such an entertainment. Well was it for Mrs Clifton that the strawberries, cream and tarts had been supplied with no niggard[27] hand: and very meagre was the remnant left when the party broke up at a late hour.

III.

Agnes and Mary were discussing the pleasures of the preceeding evening as they sat over the unusually late breakfast, when Maude joined them. Salutations being exchanged and refreshments supplied to the last comer, the conversation was renewed.[28]

"Who did you think was the prettiest girl in the room last night? our charming selves of course excepted," asked Mary: "Agnes and I cannot agree on this point."

"Yes," said her sister, "we quite agree as to mere prettiness; only I maintain that Magdalen is infinitely more attractive than half the handsome people one sees. There is so much sense in her face, and such[29] sweetness. Besides, her eyes are really beautiful."

"Miss Ellis has a characteristic countenance, but she appeared to me very far from the belle of the evening. Rosanna Hunt has much more regular features."

"Surely you don't think Rosanna prettier than Jane and Alice," interrupted Mary: "I suppose I never look at those two without fresh pleasure."

"They have good fair complexions, eyes and hair certainly;" and Maude glanced rather pointedly at her unconscious cousin: "but to me they have a wax-dollish air which is quite unpleasant. I think one of the handsomest faces in the room was Miss Stanton's."

"But she has such a disagreeable expression," rejoined Mary hastily: then colouring she half turned towards her sister, who looked grave, but did not speak.

A pause ensued; and then Agnes said, "I remember how prejudiced I felt against Miss Stanton when first she came to live here, for her appearance and manners are certainly[30] unattractive: and how ashamed of myself I was when we heard that last year, through all the bitterly cold weather, she rose at six, though she never has a fire in her room, that she might have time before breakfast to make clothes for some of the poorest people in the village. And[31] in the Spring, when the scarlet fever was about, her mother[32] would not let her go near[33] the sick children for fear of contagion; so she saved up all her pocket money to buy wine and soup and such things for them as they recovered."

"I dare say she is very good;" said Maude: "but that does not make her pleasing. Besides, the whole family have that disagreeable expression, and I suppose they are not all paragons.[34] But you have both finished breakfast, and make me ashamed by your diligence.[35] What is that beautiful piece of work?"

The sisters looked delighted: "I am so glad you like it, dear Maude. Mary and I are embroidering a cover for the lectern in our Church; but we feared you might think the ground dull."

"Not at all; I prefer[36] those quiet shades. Why, how well you do it: is it not very difficult?—Let me see if I understand the devices. There is the Cross and the Crown of Thorns; and those must be the keys of S. Peter, with, of course, the sword of S. Paul. Do the flowers mean anything?"

"I am the Rose of Sharon and the Lily of the Valleys," answered Agnes pointing: "That is balm of Gilead, at least it is what we call so; there are myrrh and hyssop, and that is a palm-branch. The border is to be vine-leaves and grapes; with fig-leaves at the corners, thanks to Mary's suggestions. Would you like to help us? there is plenty of room at the frame."

"No, I should not do it well enough, and have no time to learn, as we go home tomorrow. How I envy you;" she continued in a low voice as if speaking rather to herself than to her hearers: "you who live in the country, and are exactly what you appear, and never wish for what you do not possess. I am sick of display and poetry and acting."

"You do not act," replied Agnes warmly: "I never knew a more sincere person. One difference between us is that you are less healthy and far more clever than I am. And this reminds me: Miss Savage begged me to ask you for some verses to put in her Album. Would you be so very obliging? any that you have by you would do."

"She can have the sonnet I wrote last night."

Agnes hesitated: "I could not well offer her that, because—"

"Why? she does not tower. Oh! I suppose she has some reprehensible old lady in her family, and so might feel hurt at my Lynch-law.[37] I will find you something else then before I go."

And that evening, when Agnes went to her cousin's room to help her in packing, Maude consigned to her a neat copy of the following lines:—

> She sat and sang alway
> By the green margin of a stream,
> Watching the fishes leap and play
> Beneath the glad sun-beam.

> I sat and wept alway
> Beneath the moon's most shadowy beam,
> Watching the blossoms of the may
>   Weep leaves into the stream.

> I wept for memory;
> She sang for hope that is so fair;—
> My tears were swallowed by the sea;
>   Her songs died on the air.

Part 2nd.

I.

Rather more than a year had elapsed since Maude parted from her cousins; and now she was expecting their arrival in London every minute: for Mrs Clifton, unable to leave her young family, had gratefully availed herself of Mrs Foster's offer to receive Agnes and Mary during the early Winter months, that they might take music and dancing lessons with their cousin.

At length the rumbling of an approaching cab was heard; then a loud knock and ring. Maude started up: but instead of running out to meet her guests, began poking vigorously at the fire, which soon sent a warm, cheerful light through the apartment, enabling her, when they entered, to discern that Agnes had a more womanly air than at their last meeting, that Mary had outgrown her sister, and that both were remarkably good-looking.

"First let me show you your room, and then we can settle comfortably to tea; we are not to wait for Mamma. She thought you would not mind sleeping together, as our house is so small; and I have done my best to arrange things to your taste, for I know of old you have only one taste between you. Look, my room is next yours, so we can help each other very cosily: only pray don't think of unpacking now; there will be plenty of time this evening, and you must be famished: come."

But Agnes lingered still, eager to thank her cousin for the goodnatured forethought which had robbed her own apartment of flower-vases and inkstand for the accommodation of her guests. The calls of Mary's appetite were however imperious; and very soon the sisters were snugly settled on a sofa by the fire, while Maude in a neighbouring armchair made tea.[38]

"How long it seems since my birthday party;" said Mary, as soon as the eatables had in some measure restored her social powers:[39] "Why, Maude, you are grown quite a woman; but you look more delicate than ever, and very thin: do you still write verses?" Then without waiting for a reply:[40] "Those which you gave Miss Savage for her Album were very much admired; and Magdalen Ellis wished at the time for an autograph copy, only she had not the courage to trouble you. But perhaps you are not aware that poor Magdalen has done with Albums and such like, at least for the present: she has entered on her noviciate in the Sisterhood of Mercy established near our house."

"Why poor?" said Maude: "I think she is very happy."

"Surely you would not like such a life;" rejoined her cousin: "They have not proper clothes on their beds, and never go out without a thick veil, which must half blind them. All day long they are at prayers, or teaching children, or attending the sick, or making poor things, or something.[41] Is that to your taste?"

Maude half sighed; and then answered: "You cannot imagine me either fit or inclined for such a life; still, I can perceive that those are very happy who are. When I was preparing for Confirmation Mr Paulson offered me a district;[42] but I did not like the trouble, and Mamma thought me too unwell for regularity. I have regretted it since though: yet I don't fancy I ever could have talked to the poor people or done the slightest good.—Yes, I continue to write now and then as the humour seizes me; and if Miss Ellis"—

"Sister Magdalen," whispered Agnes.

"—If Sister Magdalen will accept it, I will try and find her something admissible even within Convent walls. But let us change the subject. On Thursday we are engaged to tea at Mrs Strawdy's. There will be no sort of party, so we need not dress or take any trouble."

"Will my Aunt go with us?" asked Agnes.

"No. Poor Mamma has been ailing for some time and is by no means strong; so as Mrs Strawdy is an old schoolfellow of hers[43] and a most estimable person, she thinks herself justified in consigning you to my guardianship. On Saturday we must go shopping, as Aunt Letty says you are to get[44] your Winter things[45] in London; and I can get[46] mine at the same time. On Sunday—or does either of you dislike Cathedral services?"

Agnes declared they were her delight; and Mary, who had never attended any, expressed great pleasure at the prospect of hearing what her sister preferred to all secular music.

"Very well," continued Maude: "we will go to St. Andrew's then, and you shall be introduced to a perfect service; or at any rate to perhaps the nearest English approach to vocal perfection.[47] But you know you are to be quite at home here; so we have not arranged any particular plans of amusement, but mean to treat you like ourselves. And now it is high time for you to retire. Here Agnes," handing to her cousin a folded paper, the result of a rummage[48] in her desk: "Will you enclose this to Sister Magdalen, and assure her that my verses are honoured even in my own eyes by her acceptance. You can read them if you like, and Mary too, of course; only please not in my presence."

They were as follows:

> Sweet sweet sound of distant waters falling
>   On a parched and thirsty plain;
> Sweet sweet song of soaring skylark, calling
>   On the sun to shine again;
> Perfume of the rose, only the fresher
>   For past fertilizing rain;
> Pearls amid the sea, a hidden treasure
>   For some daring hand to gain;—
>   Better, dearer than all these
>   Is the earth beneath the trees:
>   Of a much more priceless worth
>   Is the old, brown, common earth.
>
> Little snow-white lamb piteously bleating
>   For thy mother far away;
> Saddest, sweetest nightingale retreating
>   With thy sorrow from the day;
> Weary fawn whom night has overtaken,
>   From the herd gone quite astray;
> Dove whose nest was rifled and forsaken
>   In the budding month of May;—
>   Roost upon the leafy trees;
>   Lie on earth and take your ease:
>   Death is better far than birth,
>   You shall turn again to earth.
>
> Listen to the never pausing murmur
>   Of the waves that fret the shore;
> See the ancient pine that stands the firmer
>   For the storm-shock that it bore;
> And the moon her silver chalice filling
>   With light from the great sun's store;
> And the stars which deck our temple's ceiling
>   As the flowers deck its floor;
>   Look and hearken while you may,
>   For these things shall pass away:
>   All these things shall fail and cease;
>   Let us wait the end in peace.
>
> Let us wait the end in peace; for truly
>   That shall cease which was before:
> Let us see our lamps are lighted, duly
>   Fed with oil, nor wanting more:

> Let us pray while yet the Lord will hear us,
>   For the time is almost o'er;
> Yea, the end of all is very near us;
>   Yea, the Judge is at the door.
>   Let us pray now while we may;
>   It will be too late to pray
>   When the quick and dead shall all
>   Rise at the last trumpet call.

II.

When Thursday arrived Agnes and Mary were indisposed with colds; so Mrs Foster insisted on her daughter's making their excuses to Mrs Strawdy. In a dismal frame of mind Maude, assisted by her sympathizing cousins, performed her slight preliminary toilet.

"You have no notion of the utter dreariness of this kind of invitation: I counted on your helping me through the evening, and now you fail me. Thank you, Mary; I shall not waste eau de Cologne on my handkerchief. Goodnight both: mind you go to bed early and get up quite well tomorrow. Goodnight."

The weather was foggy and raw as Maude stepped into the street; and proved anything but soothing to a temper already fretted; so by the time that she had arrived at her destination, removed her walking things, saluted her hostess and apologized for her cousins, her countenance had assumed an expression neither pleased nor pleasing.

"Let me present my nieces to you, my dear," said Mrs Strawdy taking her young friend by the hand and leading her towards the fire: "This is Miss Mowbray, or, as you must call her, Annie; that is Caroline, and that Sophy. They have heard so much of you that any farther introduction is needless;" here Maude bowed rather stiffly: "But as we are early people you will excuse our commencing with tea, after which we shall have leisure for amusement."

There was something so genuinely kind and simple in Mrs Strawdy's manner, that even Maude felt mollified, and resolved on doing her best not only towards suppressing all appearance of yawns, but also towards bearing her part in the conversation.

"My cousins will regret their indisposition more than ever, when they learn of how much pleasure it has deprived them;" said she, civilly addressing Miss Mowbray.

A polite bend, smile and murmur formed the sole response: and once more a subject had to be started.

"Have you been very gay lately? I begin to acquire the reputation of an invalid, and so my privacy is respected."

Annie coloured and looked excessively embarrassed; at last she answered in a low hesitating voice: "We go out extremely little, partly because we never dance."

"Nor I either; it really is too fatiguing: yet a ball-room is no bad place for a mere spectator. Perhaps, though, you prefer the Theatre?"

"We never go to the play;" rejoined Miss Mowbray looking more and more uncomfortable.

Maude ran on: "Oh, I beg your pardon, you do not approve of such entertainments. I never go, but only for want of some one to take[49] me." Then addressing Mrs Mowbray: "I think you know my Aunt, Mrs Clifton?"

"I visited her years ago with your Mamma," was the answer: "when you were quite a little child. I hope she continues in good health. Pray remember me to her and to Mr Clifton when you write."

"With pleasure. She has a large family now, eight children."

"That is indeed a large family;" rejoined Mrs Strawdy, intent meanwhile on dissecting a cake with mathematical precision: "You must try a piece, it is Sophy's own manufacture."

Despairing of success in this quarter, Maude now directed her attention to Caroline, whose voice she had not heard once in the course of the evening.

"I hope you will favour us with some music after tea; in fact, I can take no denial. You look too blooming to plead a cold, and I feel certain you will not refuse to indulge my love for sweet sounds. Of your ability to do so I have heard elsewhere."

"I shall be most happy; only you must favour us in return."

"I will do my best," answered Maude somewhat encouraged: "but my own performances are very poor. Are you fond of German songs? they form my chief resource."

"Yes, I like them much."

Baffled in this quarter also, Miss Foster wanted courage to attack Sophy, whose countenance promised more cake than conversation. The meal seemed endless: she fidgetted under the table with her fingers; pushed about a stool on the noiselessly soft carpet until it came in contact with some one's foot; and at last fairly deprived Caroline of her third cup of coffee, by opening the piano and claiming the fulfillment of her promise.

The young lady complied with obliging readiness. She sang some simple airs, mostly religious, not indeed with much expression, but in a voice clear and warbling as a bird's. Maude felt consoled for all the contrarieties of the day; and was bargaining for one more song before taking Caroline's place at the instrument, when the door opened to admit Mrs and Miss Savage; who having only just reached town, and hearing from Mrs Foster that her daughter was at the house of a mutual friend, resolved on begging the hospitality of Mrs Strawdy, and renewing their acquaintance.

Poor Maude's misfortunes now came thick and fast. Seated between Miss Savage and Sophia Mowbray, she was attacked on either hand with questions concerning her verses. In the first place, did she continue to write? Yes. A flood of ecstatic compliments followed this admission: she was so young, so much admired, and, poor thing, looked so delicate. It was quite affecting to think of her lying awake at night meditating those sweet verses—("I sleep like a top," Maude put in dryly,)—which so delighted her friends, and would so charm the public, if only Miss Foster could be induced to publish. At last the bystanders were called upon to intercede for a recitation.

Maude coloured with displeasure; a hasty answer was rising to her lips, when the absurdity of her position flashed across her mind so forcibly that, almost unable to check a laugh in the midst of her annoyance, she put her handkerchief to her mouth. Miss Savage, impressed with a notion that her request was about to be complied with, raised her hand, imploring silence; and settled herself in a listening attitude.

"You will excuse me;" Maude at last said very coldly: "I could not think of monopolizing every one's attention. Indeed you are extremely good, but you must excuse me." And here Mrs Savage interposed desiring her daughter not to tease Miss Foster; and Mrs Strawdy seconded her friend's arguments, by a hint that supper would make its appearance in a few minutes.

Finally the maid announced that Miss Foster was fetched: and Maude shortening her adieus and turning a deaf ear to Annie's suggestion that their acquaintance should not terminate with the first meeting, returned home dissatisfied with her circumstances, her friends and herself.

III.

It was Christmas Eve. All day long Maude and her cousins were hard at work putting up holly and mistletoe in wreaths, festoons, or bunches, wherever the arrangement of the rooms admitted of such embellishment. The picture-frames were hidden behind foliage and bright berries; the bird-cages were stuck as full of green as though it had been Summer. A fine sprig of holly was set apart as a centre-bit for the pudding of next day: scratched hands and injured gowns were disregarded: hour after hour the noisy bustle raged:[50] until Mrs Foster, hunted from place to place by her young relatives, heard, with inward satisfaction, that the decorations were completed.

After tea Mary set the backgammon board in array and challenged her Aunt to their customary evening game: Maude, complaining of a headache, and promising either to wrap herself in a warm shawl or to go to bed, went to her room:[51] and Agnes, listening to the rattle of the dice, at last came to the conclusion that her presence was not needed down stairs, and resolved to visit the upper regions. Thinking that her cousin was lying down tired and might have fallen asleep, she forebore knocking; but opened the door softly and peeped in.

Maude was seated at a table, surrounded by the old chaos of stationery; before her lay the locking manuscript-book, into which she had just copied something. That day she had appeared more than usually animated: and now supporting her forehead upon her hand, her eyes cast down till the long lashes nearly rested upon her cheeks, she looked pale, languid, almost in pain. She did not move, but let her visitor come close to her without speaking: Agnes thought she was crying.

"Dear Maude, you have overtired yourself. Indeed, for all our sakes, you should be more careful:" here Agnes passed her arm affectionately round her friend's neck: "I hoped to find you fast asleep, and instead of this you have been writing in the cold. Still, I did not come to lecture; and am even ready to show my forgiving disposition by reading your new poem: may I?"

Maude glanced quickly up at her cousin's kind face; then answered: "Yes, if you like;" and Agnes read as follows:

> Vanity of vanities, the Preacher saith,
> All things are vanity. The eye and ear
> Cannot be filled with what they see and hear:
> > Like early dew; or like the sudden breath
> > Of wind, or like the grass that withereth
> Is man, tossed to and fro by hope and fear:
> So little joy hath he, so little cheer,
> > Till all things end in the long dust of death.
> Today is still the same as yesterday,
> > Tomorrow also even as one of them;
> And there is nothing new under the sun.
> Until the ancient race of time be run,
> > The old thorns shall grow out of the old stem,
> And morning shall be cold and twilight grey.—

This sonnet was followed by another, written like a postscript:

> I listen to the holy antheming
> That riseth in thy walls continually,
> What while the organ pealeth solemnly
> > And white-robed men and boys stand up to sing.
> I ask my heart with a sad questioning:
> "What lov'st thou here?" and my heart answers me:
> "Within the shadows of this sanctuary
> > To watch and pray is a most blessed thing."
> To watch and pray, false heart? it is not so:

>   Vanity enters with thee, and thy love
> Soars not to Heaven, but grovelleth below.
> Vanity keepeth guard, lest good should reach
>   Thy hardness; not the echoes from above
> Can rule thy stubborn feelings or can teach.—

"Was this composed after going to St. Andrew's?"

"No; I wrote it just now, but I was thinking of St. Andrew's. It is horrible to feel such a hypocrite as I do."

"Oh! Maude, I only wish I were as sensible of my faults as you are of yours. But a hypocrite you are not: don't you see that every line of these sonnets attests your sincerity?"

"You will stay to Communion tomorrow?" asked Maude after a short silence, and without replying to her cousin's speech; even these few words seemed to cost her an effort.

"Of course I shall; why, it is Christmas Day:—at least I trust to do so. Mary and I have been thinking how nice it will be for us all to receive together: so I want you to promise that you will pray for us at the Altar, as I shall for you. Will you?"

"I shall not receive tomorrow," answered Maude; then hurrying on as if to prevent the other from remonstrating: "No: at least I will not profane Holy Things; I will not add this to all the rest. I have gone over and over again, thinking I should come right in time, and I do not come right: I will go no more."

Agnes turned quite pale: "Stop," she said interrupting her cousin: "Stop; you cannot mean,—you do not know what you are saying. You will go no more? Only think, if the struggle is so hard now, what it will be when you reject all help."

"I do not struggle."

"You are ill tonight," rejoined Agnes very gently: "you are tired and overexcited. Take my advice, dear; say your prayers and get to bed. But do not be very long; if there is anything you miss and will tell me of, I will say it in your stead. Don't think me unfeeling: I was once on the very point of acting as you propose. I was perfectly wretched: harassed and discouraged on all sides. But then it struck me—you won't be angry?—that it was so ungrateful to follow my own fancies, instead of at least endeavouring to do God's Will: and so foolish too; for if your safety is not in obedience, where is it?"

Maude shook her head: "Your case is different. Whatever your faults may be, (not that I perceive any,) you are trying to correct them; your own conscience tells you that. But I am not trying. No one will say that I cannot avoid putting myself forward and displaying my verses. Agnes, you must admit so much."

Deep-rooted indeed was that vanity which made Maude take pleasure, on such an occasion, in proving the force of arguments directed against herself. Still Agnes would not yield; but resolutely did battle for the truth.

"If hitherto it has been so, let it be so no more. It is not too late: besides, think for one moment what will be the end of this. We must all die: what if you keep to your resolution, and do as you have said, and receive the Blessed Sacrament no more?"—Her eyes filled with tears.

Maude's answer came in a subdued tone: "I do not mean never to Communicate again. You remember Mr Paulson told us last Sunday that sickness and suffering are sent for our correction. I suffer very much. Perhaps a time will come when these will have done their work on me also; when I shall be purified indeed and weaned from the world. Who knows? the lost have been found, the dead quickened." She paused as if in thought; then continued: "You partake of the Blessed Sacrament in peace, Agnes, for you are good;[52] and Mary, for she is harmless[53]: but your conduct cannot serve to direct mine, because I am neither the one nor the other. Some day I may be fit again to approach the Holy Altar, but till then I will at least refrain from dishonouring it."

Agnes felt almost indignant: "Maude, how can you talk so? this is not reverence. You cannot mean that for the present you will indulge vanity and display; that you will court admiration and applause; that you will take your fill of pleasure until sickness, or it may be death, strips you of temptation and sin together. Forgive me; I am sure you never meant this: yet what else does a deliberate resolution to put off doing right come to?—and if you are determined at once to do your best, why deprive yourself of the appointed means of grace? Dear Maude, think better of it;" and Agnes knelt beside her cousin, and laid her head against her bosom.

But still Maude, with a sort of desperate wilfulness, kept saying: "It is of no use; I cannot go tomorrow; it is of no use." She hid her face, leaning upon the table and weeping bitterly; while Agnes, almost discouraged, quitted the room.

Maude, once more alone, sat for some time just as her cousin left her. Gradually the thick, low sobs became more rare; she was beginning to feel sleepy.[54] At last she roused herself with an effort and commenced undressing; then it struck her that her prayers had still to be said. The idea of beginning them frightened her, yet she could not settle to sleep without saying something. Strange prayers they must have been, offered with a divided heart and a reproachful conscience. Still they were said at length; and Maude lay down harassed, wretched, remorseful, everything but penitent. She was nearly asleep, nearly unconscious of her troubles, when the first stroke of midnight sounded. Immediately a party of Christmas waits and carollers burst forth with their glad music.[55] The first part was sung in full chorus:

"Thank God, thank God, we do believe;
Thank God that this is Christmas Eve.
Even as we kneel upon this day,
Even so the ancient legends say,
Nearly two thousand years ago
The stalled ox knelt, and even so
The ass knelt, full of praise, which they
Could not repress, while we can pray.
Thank God, thank God, for Christ was born
Ages ago, as on this morn.
In the snow-season undefiled
Christ came to earth a Little Child:
He put His ancient Glory by
To live for us and then to die."—

—Then half the voices sang the following stanza:

"How shall we thank God? how shall we
Thank Him and praise Him worthily?
What will He have Who loved us thus?
What presents will He take from us?—
Will He take gold? or precious heap
Of gems? or shall we rather steep
The air with incense? or bring myrrh?—
What man will be our messenger
To go to Him and ask His Will?
Which having learned, we will fulfil
Though He choose all we most prefer:
What man will be our messenger?"—

—This was answered by the other half:

"Thank God, thank God, the Man is found,
Sure-footed, knowing well the ground.
He knows the road, for this the way
He travelled once, as on this day.
He is our Messenger; beside,
He is our Door and Path and Guide;
He also is our Offering;
He is the Gift That we must bring."—

—Finally all the singers joined in the conclusion:

"Let us kneel down with one accord
And render thanks unto the Lord:

> For unto us a Child is born
> Upon this happy Christmas morn;
> For unto us a Son is given,
> Firstborn of God and Heir of Heaven."—

As the echoes died away, Maude fell asleep.

Part 3rd.

I.

Agnes Clifton to Maude Foster.

12th June, 18—.

My dear Maude,

Mamma has written to my Aunt that[56] Mary's marriage is fixed for the 4th of next month: but as I fear we cannot expect you both so many days before the time, I also write, hoping that you at least will come[57] without delay. At any rate I shall be at the Station tomorrow[58] afternoon with a chaise for your luggage; so pray take pity on my desolate condition, and avail yourself of the three o'clock train. As we are both bridesmaids elect, I thought it would be very nice for us to be dressed alike, so have procured double quantity of everything; thus you will perceive no pretence remains for your lingering in smoky London.

You will be amused when you see Mary: I have already lost my companion. Mr Herbert calls at least once a day, but sometimes oftener; so all day long Mary is on the alert. She takes much more interest in the roses over the porch than was formerly the case; the creepers outside the windows require continual training, not to say hourly care: I tell her the constitution of the garden must have become seriously weakened lately. One morning I caught her before the glass, trying the effect of seringa (the English orange-blossom, you know,) in her hair. She looked such a darling. I hinted how flattered Mr Herbert would feel when I told him; which provoked her to offer a few remarks on old maids. Was it not a shame?

Last Thursday Magdalen Ellis was finally[59] received into the Sisterhood of Mercy.[60] I wished much to be present, but could not, as the whole affair was conducted quite privately; only her parents were admitted of the world. However, I made interest for a lock of her beautiful hair, which I prize highly. It makes me sad to look at it: yet I know she has chosen well; and will, if she perseveres, receive hereafter an abundant recompense for all she has foregone here. Sometimes I think whether such a life can be suited to me; but then I could not bear to leave Mamma: indeed that is just what

Magdalen felt so much. I met her yesterday walking with some poor children. Her veil was down, nearly hiding her face; still I fancy she looked thoughtful, but very calm and happy. She says she always prays for me, and asked my prayers; so I begged her to remember you and Mary. Then she enquired how you are; desiring her kindest love to you, and assuring me she makes no doubt your name will be known at some future period: but checking herself almost immediately, she added that she could fancy you very different, as pale Sister Maude. This surprised me; I can fancy nothing of the sort. At last she mentioned the verses you gave her months ago, which she knows by heart and values extremely:—then, having nearly reached my home, we parted.

What a document I have composed; I who have not one minute to spare from Mary's trousseau. Will you give my love to my Aunt; and request her from me to permit your immediately coming to

Your affectionate cousin,
Agnes M. Clifton.—

P.S. Mary would doubtless send a message were she in the room; I conjecture her to be lurking about somewhere on the watch. Goodbye: or rather, Come.—

Maude handed the letter to her Mother: "Can you spare me, Mamma? I should like to go, but not if it is to inconvenience you."

"Certainly you shall go, my dear. It is a real pleasure to hear you express interest on some point, and you cannot be with any one I approve of more than Agnes. But you must make haste with the packing now: I will come and help you in a few minutes."

Still Maude lingered: "Did you see about Magdalen? I wonder what made her think of me as a Sister. It is very nice of her; but then she is so good she never can conceive what I am like. Mamma, should you mind my being a Nun?"

"Yes, my dear; it would make me miserable. But for the present take my advice and hurry a little, or the train will leave without you."

Thus urged, Maude proceeded to bundle various miscellaneous goods into a trunk; the only article on the safety of which she bestowed much thought, being the present destined for Mary; a sofa-pillow worked in glowing shades of wool and silk. This she wrapped carefully in a cloth, and laid at the bottom: then over it all else was heaped without much ceremony. Many were the delays occasioned by things mislaid, which must be looked for; ill-secured, which must be re-arranged; or remembered too late, which yet could not be dispensed with, and so must be crammed in somewhere. At length, however, the tardy preparations were completed; and Maude, enveloped in two[61] shawls, though it was the height of Summer, stepped into a cab; promising strict conformity to her Mother's injunction that both[62] windows should be kept closed.

Half an hour had not elapsed when another cab drove up to the door; and out of it Maude was lifted perfectly insensible. She had been overturned; and, though no limb was broken,[63] had neither stirred nor spoken since the accident.

II.

Maude Foster to Agnes Clifton.

2nd July, 18—.

My dear Agnes,

You have heard of my mishap? it keeps me not bedridden, but sofa ridden. My side is dreadfully hurt; I looked at it this morning for the first time, but hope never again to see so shocking a sight. The pain now and then is extreme, though not always so; sometimes, in fact, I am unconscious of any injury.

Will you convey my best love and wishes to Mary, and tell her how much I regret being away from her at such a time; especially as Mamma will not hear of leaving me. A day or two ago I tried to compose an Epithalamium[64] for our fair fiancée; which effort resulted in my present enclosure: not much to the purpose, we must admit. You may read it when no better employment offers. The first Nun no one can suspect of being myself, partly because my hair is far from yellow and I do not wear curls; partly because I never did anything half so good as profess. The second might be Mary, had she mistaken her vocation. The third is Magdalen, of course. But whatever you miss, pray read the mottoes. Put together they form a most exquisite little song which the Nuns sing in Italy. One can fancy Sister Magdalen repeating it with her whole heart.

The Surgeon comes twice a day to dress my wounds; still, all the burden of nursing falls on poor Mamma. How I wish you were here to help us both: we should find plenty to say.

But perhaps ere many months are passed I shall be up and about, when we may go together on a visit to Mary; a most delightful possibility. By the way, how I should love a baby of hers,[65] and what a pretty little creature it ought to be. Do you think Mr Herbert handsome? hitherto I have only heard a partial opinion.

Uh, my side! it gives an awful twinge now and then. You need not read my letter; but I must write it, for I am unable to do anything else. Did the pillow reach safely? It gave me so much pleasure to work it for Mary, who, I hope, likes it. At all events, if not to her taste, she may console herself with the reflection that it is unique; for the pattern was my own designing.

Here comes dinner; goodbye. When will anything so welcome as your kind face gladden the eyes of

Your affectionate
Maude Foster?—

P.S. I have turned tippler lately on port wine three times a day. "To keep you up," says my Doctor: while I obstinately refuse to be kept up, but insist on becoming weaker and weaker. Mind you write me a full history of your grand doings on a certain occasion: not omitting a detailed account of the lovely bride, her appearance, deportment and toilet. Goodbye once more: when shall I see you all again?—

THREE NUNS

1.

"Sospira questo core
E non sa dir perchè."[66]

Shadow, shadow on the wall
    Spread thy shelter over me;
Wrap me with a heavy pall,
    With the dark that none may see.
Fold thyself around me; come:
Shut out all the troublesome
Noise of life; I would be dumb.

Shadow thou hast reached my feet,
    Rise and cover up my head;
Be my stainless winding sheet,
    Buried before I am dead.
Lay thy cool upon my breast:
Once I thought that joy was best,
Now I only care for rest.

By the grating of my cell
    Sings a solitary bird;
Sweeter than the vesper bell,

Sweetest song was ever heard.*
Sing upon thy living tree:
Happy echoes answer thee,
Happy songster, sing to me.

When my yellow hair was curled
    Though men saw and called me fair,
I was weary in the world
    Full of vanity and care.
Gold was left behind, curls shorn
When I came here; that same morn
Made a bride no gems adorn.

Here wrapped in my spotless veil,
    Curtained from intruding eyes,
I whom prayers and fasts turn pale
    Wait the flush of Paradise.
But the vigil is so long
My heart sickens:—sing thy song,
Blithe bird that canst do no wrong.

Sing on, making me forget
    Present sorrow and past sin.
Sing a little longer yet:
    Soon the matins will begin;
And I must turn back again
To that aching worse than pain
I must bear and not complain.

Sing, that in thy song I may
    Dream myself once more a child
In the green woods far away
    Plucking clematis and wild
Hyacinths, till pleasure grew
Tired, yet so was pleasure too,
Resting with no work to do.

In the thickest of the wood,
    I remember, long ago
How a stately oak-tree stood,
    With a sluggish pool below
Almost shadowed out of sight.

---

*"Sweetest eyes were ever seen." E. B. Browning.[67]

On the waters dark as night,
Water-lilies lay like light.

There, while yet a child, I thought
    I could live as in a dream,
Secret, neither found nor sought:
    Till the lilies on the stream,
Pure as virgin purity,
Would seem scarce too pure for me:—
Ah, but that can never be.

2.

"Sospirerà d'amore,
Ma non lo dice a me."

I loved him, yes, where was the sin?
    I loved him with my heart and soul.
    But I pressed forward to no goal,
There was no prize I strove to win.
Show me my sin that I may see:—
Throw the first stone, thou Pharisee.

I loved him, but I never sought
    That he should know that I was fair.
    I prayed for him; was my sin prayer?
I sacrificed, he never bought.
He nothing gave, he nothing took;
We never bartered look for look.

My voice rose in the sacred choir,
    The choir of Nuns; do you condemn
    Even if, when kneeling among them,
Faith, zeal and love kindled a fire
And I prayed for his happiness
Who knew not? was my error this?

I only prayed that in the end
    His trust and hope may not be vain.
    I prayed not we may meet again:
I would not let our names ascend,
No, not to Heaven, in the same breath;
Nor will I join the two in death.

Oh sweet is death; for I am weak
    And weary, and it giveth rest.

The Crucifix lies on my breast,
And all night long it seems to speak
Of rest; I hear it through my sleep,
And the great comfort makes me weep.

Oh sweet is death that bindeth up
    The broke and the bleeding heart.
    The draught chilled, but a cordial part
Lurked at the bottom of the cup;
And for my patience will my Lord
Give an exceeding great reward.

Yea, the reward is almost won,
    A crown of glory and a palm.
    Soon I shall sing the unknown psalm;
Soon gaze on light, not on the sun;
And soon, with surer faith, shall pray
For him, and cease not night nor day.

My life is breaking like a cloud;
    God judgeth not as man doth judge—
    Nay, bear with me; you need not grudge
This peace; the vows that I have vowed
Have all been kept: Eternal Strength
Holds me, though mine own fails at length.

Bury me in the Convent ground
    Among the flowers that are so sweet;
    And lay a green turf at my feet,
Where thick trees cast a gloom around.
At my head let a Cross be, white
Through the long blackness of the night.

Now kneel and pray beside my bed
    That I may sleep being free from pain:
    And pray that I may wake again
After His Likeness, Who hath said
(Faithful is He Who promiseth,)
We shall be satisfied Therewith.

3.

"Rispondimi, cor mio,
    Perchè sospiri tu?

Risponde: Voglio Iddio,
    Sospiro per Gesù."

My heart is as a freeborn bird
    Caged in my cruel breast,
That flutters, flutters evermore,
    Nor sings, nor is at rest.
But beats against the prison bars,
    As knowing its own nest
Far off beyond the clouded West.

My soul is as a hidden fount
    Shut in by clammy clay,
That struggles with an upward moan;
    Striving to force its way
Up through the turf, over the grass,
    Up, up into the day,
Where twilight no more turneth grey.

Oh for the grapes of the True Vine
    Growing in Paradise,
Whose tendrils join the Tree of Life
    To that which maketh wise.
Growing beside the Living Well
    Whose sweetest waters rise
Where tears are wiped from tearful eyes.

Oh for the waters of that Well
    Round which the Angels stand.
Oh for the Shadow of the Rock
    On my heart's weary land.
Oh for the Voice to guide me when
    I turn to either hand,
Guiding me till I reach Heaven's strand.

Thou World from which I am come out,
    Keep all thy gems and gold;
Keep thy delights and precious things,
    Thou that art waxing old.
My heart shall beat with a new life,
    When thine is dead and cold:
When thou dost fear I shall be bold.

When Earth shall pass away with all
    Her pride and pomp of sin,

The City builded without hands
   Shall safely shut me in.
All the rest is but vanity
   Which others strive to win:
Where their hopes end my joys begin.

I will not look upon a rose
   Though it is fair to see:
The flowers planted in Paradise
   Are budding now for me.
Red roses like love visible
   Are blowing on their tree,
Or white like virgin purity.

I will not look unto the sun
   Which setteth night by night:
In the untrodden courts of Heaven
   My crown shall be more bright.
So, in the New Jerusalem
   Founded and built aright
My very feet shall tread on light.

With foolish riches of this World
   I have bought treasure, where
Naught perisheth: for this white veil
   I gave my golden hair;
I gave the beauty of my face
   For vigils, fasts and prayer;
I gave all for this Cross I bear.

My heart trembled when first I took
   The vows which must be kept;
At first it was a weariness
   To watch when once I slept.
The path was rough and sharp with thorns;
   My feet bled as I stepped;
The Cross was heavy and I wept.

While still the names rang in mine ears
   Of daughter, sister, wife;
The outside world still looked so fair
   To my weak eyes, and rife
With beauty; my heart almost failed;
   Then in the desperate strife
I prayed, as one who prays for life,

Until I grew to love what once
    Had been so burdensome.
So now when I am faint, because
    Hope deferred seems to numb
My heart, I yet can plead; and say
    Although my lips are dumb:
"The Spirit and the Bride say, Come."—

III.

Three weeks had passed away. A burning sun seemed baking the very dust in the streets, and sucking the last remnant of moisture from the straw spread in front of Mrs Foster's house, when the sound of a low muffled ring was heard in the sick-room; and Maude, now entirely confined to her bed, raising herself on one arm, looked eagerly towards the door; which opened to admit a servant with the welcome announcement that Agnes had arrived.

After tea Mrs Foster, almost worn out with fatigue, went to bed; leaving her daughter under the care of their guest. The first greetings between the cousins had passed sadly enough. Agnes perceived at a glance that Maude was, as her last letter hinted, in a most alarming state: while the sick girl, well aware of her condition, received her friend with an emotion[68] which showed she felt it might be for the last time. But soon her spirits rallied.

"I shall enjoy our evening together so much, Agnes;" said she, speaking now quite cheerfully: "You must tell me all the news. Have you heard from Mary since your last despatch to me?"

"Mamma received a letter this morning before I set off; and she sent it hoping to amuse you. Shall I read it aloud?"

"No, let me have it myself." Her eye travelled rapidly down the well-filled pages, comprehending at a glance all the tale of happiness. Mr and Mrs Herbert were at Scarborough; they would thence proceed to the Lakes; and thence, most probably, homewards, though a prolonged tour was mentioned as just possible. But both plans seemed alike pleasing to Mary; for she was full of her husband, and both were equally connected with him.

Maude smiled as paragraph after paragraph enlarged on the same topic. At last she said: "Agnes, if you could not be yourself, but must become one of us three: I don't mean as to goodness, of course, but merely as regards circumstances,—would you change with Sister Magdalen, with Mary, or with me?"

"Not with Mary, certainly. Neither should I have courage to change with you; I never should bear pain so well: nor yet with Sister Magdalen, for I want her fervour of devotion. So at present I fear you must even put up with me as I am. Will that do?"

There was a pause. A fresh wind had sprung up and the sun was setting.

At length Maude resumed: "Do you recollect last Christmas Eve when I was so wretched, what shocking things I said? How I rejoice that my next Communion was not indeed delayed till sickness had stripped me of temptation and sin together."

"Did I say that? It was very harsh."

"Not harsh: it was just and right as far as it went, only something more was required. But I never told you what altered me. The truth is, for a time I avoided as much as possible frequenting our parish Church, for fear of remarks. Mamma, knowing how I love S. Andrew's, let me go there very often by myself, because the walk is too long for her. I wanted resolution to do right; yet believe me I was very miserable: how I could say my prayers at that period is a mystery. So matters went on; till one day as I was returning from a shop, I met Mr Paulson. He enquired immediately whether I had been staying in the country? Of course I answered, No. Had I been ill? again, No. Then gradually the whole story came out. I never shall forget the shame of my admissions; each word seemed forced from me, yet at last all was told. I will not repeat[69] all we said then, and on a subsequent occasion when he saw me at Church: the end was that I partook of the Holy Communion on Easter Sunday. That was indeed a Feast. I felt as if I never could do wrong again, and yet—. Well, after my next impatient fit, I wrote this;" here she took a paper from the table: "Do you care to see it? I will rest a little, for talking is almost too much for me."

> I watched a rosebud very long
> > Brought on by dew and sun and shower,
> > Waiting to see the perfect flower:
> Then, when I thought it should be strong,
> > It opened at the matin hour
> > > And fell at evensong.
>
> I watched a nest from day to day,
> > A green nest, full of pleasant shade,
> > Wherein three little eggs were laid:
> But when they should have hatched in May,
> > The two old birds had grown afraid,
> > > Or tired, and flew away.
>
> Then in my wrath I broke the bough
> > That I had tended with such care,
> > Hoping its scent should fill the air:
> I crushed the eggs, not heeding how

Their ancient promise had been fair:—
I would have vengeance now.

But the dead branch spoke from the sod,
And the eggs answered me again:
Because we failed dost thou complain?
Is thy wrath just? And what if God,
Who waiteth for thy fruits in vain,
Should also take the rod?—

"You can keep it if you like;" continued Maude, when her cousin had finished reading: "Only don't let any one else know why it was written. And, Agnes, it would only pain Mamma to look over everything if I die; will you examine the verses, and destroy what I evidently never intended to be seen. They might all be thrown away together, only Mamma is so fond of them.— What will she do?"—and the poor girl hid her face in the pillows.

"But is there no hope, then?"

"Not the slightest, if you mean of recovery; and she does not know it. Don't go away when all's over, but do what you can to comfort her. I have been her misery from my birth, till now there is no time to do better. But you must leave me, please; for I feel completely exhausted. Or stay one moment: I saw Mr Paulson again this morning, and he promised to come tomorrow to administer the Blessed Sacrament to me; so I count on you and Mamma receiving with me, for the last time perhaps: will you?"

"Yes, dear Maude. But you are so young, don't give up hope. And now would you like me to remain here during the night? I can establish myself quite comfortably on your sofa."

"Thank you, but it could only make me restless. Goodnight, my own dear Agnes."

"Goodnight, dear Maude. I trust to rise early tomorrow, that I may be with you all the sooner." So they parted.

That morrow never dawned for Maude Foster.

———

Agnes proceeded to perform the task imposed upon her, with scrupulous anxiety to carry out her friend's wishes. The locked book she never opened: but had it placed in Maude's coffin, with all its records of folly, sin, vanity; and, she humbly trusted, of true penitence also. She next collected the scraps of paper found in her cousin's desk and portfolio, or lying loose upon the table; and proceeded to examine them. Many of these were mere fragments, many half-effaced pencil scrawls, some written on torn backs of letters, and some full of incomprehensible abbreviations. Agnes was astonished at the variety of Maude's compositions. Piece after piece she committed to the flames, fearful lest any should be preserved which were not intended for general perusal: but it cost her a pang to do so; and to see how small a number remained for Mrs Foster. Of three only she took copies for herself. The first was dated ten days after Maude's accident:

Sleep, let me sleep, for I am sick of care;
Sleep, let me sleep, for my pain wearies me.
Shut out the light; thicken the heavy air
With drowsy incense; let a distant stream
Of music lull me, languid as a dream,
Soft as the whisper of a Summer sea.

Pluck me no rose that groweth on a thorn,
No myrtle white and cold as snow in June,
Fit for a virgin on her marriage morn:
But bring me poppies brimmed with sleepy death,
And ivy choking what it garlandeth,
And primroses that open to the moon.

Listen, the music swells into a song,
A simple song I loved in days of yore;
The echoes take it up and up along
The hills, and the wind blows it back again:—
Peace, peace, there is a memory in that strain
Of happy days that shall return no more.

Oh peace, your music wakeneth old thought,
But not old hope that made my life so sweet,
Only the longing that must end in nought.
Have patience with me, friends, a little while:
For soon where you shall dance and sing and smile,
My quickened dust may blossom at your feet.

Sweet thought that I may yet live and grow green,
That leaves may yet spring from the withered root,
And buds and flowers and berries half unseen;
Then if you haply muse upon the past,
Say this: Poor child, she hath her wish at last;
Barren through life, but in death bearing fruit.—

The second, though written on the same paper, was evidently composed at a subsequent period:

Fade, tender lily,
    Fade, O crimson rose,
Fade every flower,
    Sweetest flower that blows.

Go, chilly Autumn,
    Come O Winter cold;
Let the green stalks die away
    Into common mould.

Birth follows hard on death,
    Life on withering.
Hasten, we shall come the sooner
    Back to pleasant Spring.—

The last was a sonnet, dated the morning before her death:

    What is it Jesus saith unto the soul?—
"Take up the Cross and come, and follow Me."
This word He saith to all; no man may be
    Without the Cross, wishing to win the goal.
    Then take it bravely up, setting thy whole
Body to bear; it will not weigh on thee
Beyond thy utmost strength: take it, for He
    Knoweth when thou art weak, and will control
The powers of darkness that thou needst not fear.
    He will be with thee, helping, strengthening,
    Until it is enough: for lo, the day
Cometh when He shall call thee: thou shalt hear
    His voice That says: "Winter is past, and Spring
    Is come; arise, My Love, and come away."—

Agnes cut one long tress from Maude's head; and on her return home laid it in the same paper with the lock of Magdalen's hair. These she treasured greatly: and, gazing on them, would long and pray for the hastening of that eternal morning, which shall reunite in God those who in Him, or for His Sake, have parted here.

Amen for us all.

The End.

From *Commonplace,*
and Other Short Stories (1870)

~~~~

Cᴏᴍᴍᴏɴᴘʟᴀᴄᴇ, *and Other Short Stories* (1870) is Christina's only major venture into publishing prose fiction. The mixed reviews may have discouraged her from attempting any more writing of this kind, though her brother Dante Gabriel had hardly affirmed her attempt. He had described *Commonplace* to Swinburne as "rather in the Miss Austen vein I judge, and quite worthy of its title, but very good and far from uninteresting" (*LDGR*, 2:818). He told Christina herself that "It certainly is not dangerously exciting to the nervous system, but it is far from being dull for all that, and I should think it likely to take." However, in a postscript he added, "Of course I think your proper business is to write poetry, and not Commonplaces" (*LDGR*, 2:826–27).

As Rossetti's "Prefatory Note" indicates, the earliest of the stories dates back to 1852. Six of them had been previously published, with "Vanna's Twins" and *Commonplace* being of most recent composition. Roberts Brothers, her American publisher in Boston, had considered publishing the first six of her stories, but when this possibility did not materialize she asked that they be returned to her (12 April 1869; Janet Camp Troxell, ed., *Three Rossettis: Unpublished Letters to and from Dante Gabriel, Christina, William* [Cambridge, Mass.: Harvard University Press, 1937], 155). The final two pieces were evidently written "to increase bulk," though she shrank from any further additions when Ellis broached this idea (29 March 1870; *RM*, 82).

Commonplace

Commonplace was completed in early March 1870, according to William Rossetti's diary (*RP*, 500). The volume for which it became the title piece was published on

7 May by F. S. Ellis. Her switch to Ellis from Macmillan is described by Packer (*RM*, p. 72). The more receptive reviewers of the collection single out *Commonplace* as having "permanent artistic value" (*Academy*, 9 July 1870, p. 252) and for its realism being "more absorbing in its interest than any sensational novel" (*Athenaeum*, 4 June 1870, p. 734).

The text here follows the first and only edition published in London by F. S. Ellis in 1870 (from the copy in the University of British Columbia Library).

Commonplace

Chapter 1.

Brompton-on-Sea—any name not in 'Bradshaw'[70] will do—Brompton-on-Sea in April.

The air keen and sunny; the sea blue and rippling, not rolling; everything green, in sight and out of sight, coming on merrily. Birds active over straws and fluff; a hardy butterfly abroad for a change; a second hardy butterfly dancing through mid-air, in and out, and round about the first. A row of houses all alike stands facing the sea—all alike so far as stucco fronts and symmetrical doors and windows could make them so: but one house in the monotonous row was worth looking at, for the sake of more numerous hyacinths and early roses in its slip of front garden, and on several of its window-sills. Judging by appearances, and for once judging rightly, this must be a private residence on an esplanade full of lodging-houses.

A pretty house inside too, snug in winter, fresh in summer; now in mid-spring sunny enough for an open window, and cool enough for a bright fire in the breakfast-room.

Three ladies sat at the breakfast-table, three maiden ladies, obviously sisters by strong family likeness, yet with individual differences strong also. The eldest, Catherine, Miss Charlmont, having entered her thirty-third year, had taken on all occasions to appearing in some sort of cap. She began the custom at thirty, when also she gave up dancing, and adopted lace over her neck and arms in evening dress. Her manner was formal and kindly, savouring of the provinces rather than of the capital; but of the provinces in their towns, not in their old county seats. Yet she was a well-bred gentlewoman in all essentials, tall and fair, a handsome member of a handsome family. She presided over the tea and coffee, and, despite modern usage, retained a tea-tray.

Opposite her sat Lucy, less striking in features and complexion, but with an expression of quicker sensibility. Rather pretty and very sweet-looking, not turned thirty as yet, and on some points treated by Catherine as still a young thing. She had charge of the loaf and ham, and, like her elder sister, never indulged in opening letters till every one at table had been served.

The third, Jane, free of meat-and-drink responsibilities, opened letters or turned over the newspaper as she pleased. She was youngest by many years, and came near to being very beautiful. Her profile was almost Grecian, her eyes were large, and her fair hair grew in wavy abundance. At first sight she threw Catherine and Lucy completely into the shade; afterwards, in spite of their additional years, they sometimes were preferred, for her face only of the three could be thought insipid. Pleasure and displeasure readily showed themselves in it, but the pleasure would be frivolous and the displeasure often unreasonable. A man might fall in love with Jane, but no one could make a friend of her; Catherine and Lucy were sure to have friends, however they might lack lovers.

On the morning when our story commences the elders were busied with their respective charges, whilst Jane already sipped her tea and glanced up and down the Births, Marriages, and Deaths, in the 'Times' Supplement. There she sat, with one elbow on the table and her long lashes showing to advantage over downcast eyes. Dress was with her a matter for deep study, and her pink-and-white breakfast suit looked as fresh and blooming as April's self. Her hair fell long and loose over her shoulders, in becoming freedom; and Catherine gazing at her felt a motherly pride in the pretty creature to whom, for years, she had performed a mother's duty; and Lucy felt how young and fresh Jane was, and remembered that she herself was turned twenty-nine: but if the thought implied regret it was untinctured by envy.

Jane read aloud: '"Halbert to Jane;" I wish I were Jane. And here, positively, are two more Janes, and not me. "Catherine"—that's a death. Lucy, I don't see you anywhere. Catherine was eighty-nine, and much respected. "Mrs. Anstruther of a son and heir." I wonder if those are the Anstruthers I met in Scotland: she was very ugly, and short. "Everilda Stella,"—how can anybody be Everilda?' Then, with a sudden accession of interest, 'Why, Lucy, Everilda Stella has actually married your Mr. Hartley!'

Lucy started, but no one noticed her. Catherine said, 'Don't say "your" Mr. Hartley, Jane: that is not a proper way of speaking about a married gentleman to an unmarried lady. Say "the Mr. Hartley you know," or, "the Mr. Hartley you have met in London." Besides, I am acquainted with him also; and very likely it is a different person. Hartley is not an uncommon name.'

'Oh, but it is that Mr. Hartley, sister,' retorted Jane, and she read:

'"On Monday the 13th, at the parish-church, Fenton, by the Rev. James Durham, uncle of the bride, Alan Hartley, Esq. of the Woodlands, Gloucestershire, to Everilda Stella, only child and presumptive heiress of George Durham, Esq. of Orpingham Place, in the same county."'

Chapter 2.

Forty years before the commencement of this story, William Charlmont, an Indian army-surgeon,[71] penniless, except for his pay, had come unexpectedly into some hundreds a-year, left him by a maiden great-aunt, who had seen him but once, and that when he was five years old, on which occasion she boxed his ears for misspelling 'elephant.' His stoicism under punishment, for he neither roared nor whined, may have won her heart; at any rate, from whatever motive, she, years afterwards, disappointed three nephews and a female first cousin by leaving every penny she was worth to him. This moderate accession of fortune justified him in consulting both health and inclination by exchanging regimental practice in India for general practice in England: and a combination of apparently trifling circumstances led him, soon after his return home, to settle at the then infant watering-place of Brompton-on-Sea, of which the reputation had just been made by a royal duke's visit; and the tide of fashion was setting to its shore.

The house in which our story opens then stood alone, and belonged to a clergyman's widow. As she possessed, besides, an only daughter, and but a small life annuity—nothing more—she sought for a lodger, and was glad to find one in the new medical practitioner. The widow, Mrs. Turner, was, and felt herself to be, no less a gentlewoman when she let lodgings than when with her husband and child she had occupied the same house alone; no less so when after breakfast she donned a holland apron and helped Martha, the maid, to make Mr. Charlmont's bed, than when in old days she had devoted her mornings to visiting and relieving her poorer neighbours.

Her daughter, Kate, felt their altered fortunes more painfully; and showed, sometimes by uncomfortable bashfulness, sometimes by anxious self-assertion, how much importance she attached to the verdict of Mrs. Grundy.[72] Her mother's holland apron was to her a daily humiliation, and single-handed Martha an irritating shortcoming. She chilled old friends by declining invitations, because her wardrobe lacked variety, and shunned new acquaintances lest they should call at some moment when herself or her mother might have to answer the door. A continual aim at false appearances made her constrained and affected; and persons who would never have dwelt upon the fact that Mrs. Turner let lodgings, were certain to have it recalled to mind by Miss Turner's uneasiness.

But Kate owned a pretty face, adorned by a pink-and-white complexion, most refreshing to eyes that had ached under an Indian sun. At first Mr. Charlmont set her down as merely affected and silly; then he began to dwell on the fact that, however silly and affected, she was indisputably pretty; next he reflected that reverses of fortune deserve pity and demand every gentleman's most courteous consideration. In himself such consideration at once took the form of books lent from his library; of flowers for the drawing-room, and fruit for dessert. Kate, to do her justice, was no flirt, and saw without seeing his attentions; but her more experienced mother seeing, pondered, and seized, or made, an opportunity for checking her lodger's intimacy. Mr. Charlmont, however, was not to be rebuffed; opposition made him earnest, whilst the necessity of expressing his feelings gave them definiteness: and not many months later Kate, with the house for her dowry, became Mrs. William Charlmont, the obnoxious lodger developed into an attached and dear husband, and Mrs. Turner retired on the life annuity to finish her days in independence.

A few years passed in hopes and disappointments. When hope had dwindled to despondency a little girl came—Catherine; after another few years a second girl, named Lucy in memory of her grandmother Turner, who had not lived to see her namesake. Then more years passed without a baby; and in due course the sisters were sent to Miss Drum's school as day-boarders, their mother having become ailing and indolent.

Time went on, and the girls grew wiser and prettier—Catherine very pretty. When she was nearly twelve years old, Mr. Charlmont said one evening to his wife, 'I have made my will, Kate, and left everything to you in the first instance, and between the children after you.' And she answered, blushing—she was still comely, and a blush became her:—'O William, but suppose another baby should come?' 'Well, I should make my will over again,' he replied: but he did not guess why his wife blushed and spoke eagerly; he had quite given up such hopes.

Mr. Charlmont was fond of boating, and one day, when the girls were at home for the Easter holidays, he offered to take them both for a row; but Catherine had a bad cold, and as Lucy was not a good sailor, he did not care to take charge of her without her sister. His wife never had liked boating. Thus it was that he went alone. The morning was dull and chilly; but there was no wind, and the sea was almost smooth. He took dinner and fishing tackle in the boat with him, and gave notice that he should not be at home till the evening.

No wind, no sun; the day grew duller and duller, dimmer and dimmer. A smoke-like fog, beginning on land, spread from the cliffs to the beach, from the beach over the water's edge; further and further it spread, beyond sight; it might be for miles over the sea. No wind blew to shift the dense fog which hid seamarks and landmarks alike. As day waned towards evening, and darkness deepened, all the fisher-folk gathered on the beach in pain and fear for those at sea. They lit a bonfire, they shouted, they fired off an old gun or two, such as they could get together, and still they watched, and feared, and hoped. Now one boat came in, now another; some guided by the glare, some by the sound of the firing: at last, by midnight, every boat had come in safe, except Mr. Charlmont's.

As concerned him, that night was only like all nights and all days afterwards; for neither man, nor boat, nor waif, nor stray from either, ever drifted ashore.

Mrs. Charlmont took the news of her husband's disappearance very quietly indeed. She did not cry or fret, or propose any measures for finding him; but she bade Catherine be sure to have tea ready when he came in. This she repeated every day, and often in the day; and would herself sit by a window looking out towards the sea, smiling and cheerful. If any one spoke to her she would answer at random, but quite cheerfully. She rose or went to bed when her old nurse called her, she ate and drank when food was set before her; but she originated nothing, and seemed indifferent to everything except the one anxiety, that tea should be ready for her husband on his return.

The holidays over, Lucy went back to Miss Drum's, trudging to and fro daily; but Catherine stayed at home to keep house and sit with her poor dazed mother.

A few months and the end came. One night nurse insisted with unusual determination on the girls going to bed early; but before daybreak Catherine was roused out of her sleep to see a new little sister and her dying mother.

Life was almost gone, and with the approach of death a sort of consciousness had returned. Mrs. Charlmont looked hard at Catherine, who was crying bitterly, and taking her hand said distinctly: 'Catherine, promise to stay here ready for your father when he comes on shore—promise some of you to stay here: don't let him come on shore and find me gone and no one—don't let the body come on shore and find us all gone and no one—promise me, Catherine!'

And Catherine promised.

———

Mr. Charlmont died a wealthy man. He had enjoyed a large lucrative practice, and had invested his savings profitably: by his will, and on their mother's death, an ample provision remained for his daughters. Strictly speaking, it remained for Catherine and Lucy: the baby, Jane, was unavoidably left dependent on her sisters; but on sisters who, in after-life, never felt that their own right to their father's property was more obvious or more valid than hers.

Mr. Charlmont had appointed but one trustee for his daughters—Mr. Drum, only brother of their schoolmistress, a thoroughly honest lawyer, practising and thriving in Brompton-on-Sea; a man somewhat younger than himself, who had speculated adroitly both with him and for him. On

Mrs. Charlmont's death, Mr. Drum proposed sending the two elder girls to a fashionable boarding-school near London, and letting nurse, with a wet-nurse under her, keep house in the old home with baby: but Catherine set her face against this plan, urging her promise to her dying mother as a reason for not going away; and so held to her point that Mr. Drum yielded, and agreed that the girls, who could not bear to be parted, should continue on the same terms as before at his sister's school. Miss Drum, an intimate friend of their mother's, engaged to take them into such suitable society as might offer until Catherine should come of age; and as she resided within two minutes' walk of their house, this presented no difficulty. At twenty-one, under their peculiar circumstances, Catherine was to be considered old enough to chaperone her sisters. Nurse, a respectable elderly woman, was to remain as housekeeper and personal attendant on the children; and a wet-nurse, to be succeeded by a nursery-girl, with two other maids, completed the household.

Catherine, though only in her thirteenth year, already looked grave, staid, and tall enough for a girl of sixteen, when these arrangements were entered into. The sense of responsibility waxed strong within her, and with the motherly position came something of the motherly instinct of self-postponement to her children.

Chapter 3.

The last chapter was parenthetical, this takes up the broken thread of the story.

Breakfast over, and her sisters gone their several ways, Lucy Charlmont seized the 'Times' Supplement and read the Hartley-Durham paragraph over to herself:—'On Monday the 13th, at the parish church, Fenton, by the Rev. James Durham, uncle of the bride, Alan Hartley, Esq., of the Woodlands, Gloucestershire, to Everilda Stella, only child and presumptive heiress of George Durham, Esq., of Orpingham Place, in the same county.'

There remained no lurking-place for doubt. Mr. Hartley,—'her' Mr. Hartley, as Jane dubbed him,—had married Everilda Stella, a presumptive heiress. Thus concluded Lucy's one romance.

Poor Lucy! the romance had been no fault of hers, perhaps not even a folly: it had arisen thus. When Miss Charlmont was twenty-one Lucy was eighteen, and had formally come out under her sister's wing; thenceforward going with her to balls and parties from time to time, and staying with her at friends' houses in town or country. This paying visits had entailed the necessity of Jane's having a governess. Miss Drum had by that time 'relinquished tuition,' as she herself phrased it, and retired on a comfortable competence earned by her own exertions; therefore, to Miss Drum's school

Jane could not go. Lucy, when the subject was started, declared, with affectionate impulsiveness, that she would not pay visits at all, or else that she and Catherine might pay them separately; but Catherine, who considered herself in the place of mother to both her sisters, and whose standard of justice to both alike was inflexible, answered, 'My dear'—when Miss Charlmont said 'my dear' it ended a discussion—'My dear, Jane must have a governess. She shall always be with us in the holidays, and shall leave the schoolroom for good when she is eighteen, and old enough to enter society; but at present I must think of you and your prospects.' So Jane had a fashionable governess, fresh from a titled family, and versed in accomplishments and the art of dress, whilst Catherine commenced her duties as chaperone. Lucy thought that her sister, handsomer than herself and not much older, might have prospects too, and tried hard to discover chances for her; but Catherine nursed no such fancies on her own account. Her promise to her dying mother, that some one of them should always be on the spot at Brompton-on-Sea, literally meant at the moment, she resolved as literally to fulfil, even whilst she felt that only by one not fully in her right mind could such a promise have been exacted. Grave and formal in manner, dignified in person, and in disposition reserved, though amiable, she never seemed to notice, or to return, attentions paid her by any man of her acquaintance; and if one of these ever committed himself so far as to hazard an offer, she kept his secret and her own.

Lucy, meanwhile, indulged on her own account the usual hopes and fears of a young woman. At first all parties and visits were delightful, one not much less so than another then a difference made itself felt between them; some parties turned out dull, and some visits tedious. The last year of Lucy's going everywhere with Catherine, before, that is, she began dividing engagements with Jane,—for until Lucy should be turned thirty, self-chaperoning was an inadmissible enormity in Miss Charlmont's eyes, in spite of what she had herself done; as she said, her own had been an exceptional case,—in that last year the two sisters had together spent a month with Dr. Tyke, whose wife had been before marriage another Lucy Charlmont, and a favourite cousin of their father's: concerning her, tradition even hinted that, in bygone years, she had refused the penniless army surgeon.

Be this as it may, at Mrs. Tyke's house in London, the sisters spent one certain June, and then and there Lucy 'met her fate,' as with a touch of sentiment, bordering on sentimentality, she recorded in her diary one momentous first meeting. Alan Hartley was a nephew of Dr. Tyke's—handsome, and clever on the surface, if not deep within. He had just succeeded his father at the Woodlands, had plenty of money, no profession, and no hindrance to idling away any amount of time with any pretty woman who was pleasant company. Such a woman was Lucy Charlmont. He harboured no present thoughts of marriage, but she did; he really did pay just as much attention to a dozen girls elsewhere, but she judged by his manner to herself, and drew from it a false conclusion. That delightful June came to an end, and he had not spoken; but two years later occurred a second visit, as pleasant and as full of misunderstanding as the first. Meanwhile, she had refused more than one offer. Poor Lucy Charlmont: her folly, even if it was folly, had not been very blameable.

The disenchantment came no less painfully than unexpectedly: and Lucy, ready to cry, but ashamed of crying for such a cause, thrust the Supplement out of sight, and sitting down, forced herself to face the inevitable future. One thing was certain, she could not meet Alan—in her thoughts he had long been Alan, and now it cost her an effort of recollection to stiffen him back into Mr. Hartley—she must not meet Mr. Hartley till she could reckon on seeing him and his wife with friendly composure. Oh! why—why—why had she all along misunderstood him, and he never understood her? Not to meet him, it would be necessary to decline the invitation from Mrs. Tyke, which she had looked forward to and longed for during weeks past, and which, in the impartial judgment of Miss Charlmont, it was her turn, not Jane's, to accept; which, moreover, might arrive by any post. Jane she knew would be ready enough to pay a visit out of turn, but Catherine would want a reason; and what reason could she give? On one point, however, she was determined, that, with or without her reasons being accepted as reasonable, go she would not. Then came the recollection of a cracker[73] she had pulled with him, and kept in her pocketbook ever since; and of a card he had left for her and her sister, or, as she had fondly fancied, mainly for herself, before the last return from Mrs. Tyke's to Brompton-on-Sea. Treasures no longer to be treasured, despoiled treasures,—she denied herself the luxury of a sigh, as she thrust them between the bars of the grate and watched them burn.

Chapter 4.

'Lucy, Jane,' said Miss Charlmont, some days afterwards, addressing her sisters, and holding up an open letter,—'Mrs. Tyke has sent a very kind invitation, asking me, with one of you, to stay a month at her house, and to fix the day. It is your turn, Lucy; so, if you have no objection, I shall write, naming next Thursday for our journey to London. Jane, I shall ask Miss Drum to stay with you during our absence; I think she will be all the better for a change, and there is no person more fit to have the charge of you. So don't be dull, dear, till we come back.'

But Jane pouted, and said in a cross tone, 'Really, sister, you need not settle everything now for me, as if I were a baby. I don't want Miss Drum, who is as old as the hills and as solemn. Can't you write to Mrs. Tyke and say, that I cannot be left alone here? What difference could it make in her large house?'

For once Catherine answered her favourite sister with severity, 'Jane, you know why it is impossible for us all to leave home together. This is the last year you will be called upon to remain behind, for after Lucy's next birthday it is agreed between us that she will take turns with me in chaperoning you. Do not make what may be our last excursion together unpleasant by your unkindness.'

Still Jane was not silenced. 'At any rate, it need not be Miss Drum. I will stay here alone, or I will have somebody more amusing than Miss Drum.'

Before Catherine could reply, Lucy with an effort struck into the dispute. 'Jane, don't speak like that to our sister; I should be ashamed to speak to her so. Still, Catherine,' she continued, without noticing a muttered retort from the other, 'after all, I am going to side with Jane on the main point, and ask you to take her to Notting Hill,[74] and leave me at home to keep house with dear old Miss Drum. This really was my own wish before Jane spoke, so pray let us not say another word on the subject.'

But Catherine saw how pale and languid she looked, and stood firm. 'No, Lucy, that would be unreasonable; Jane ought not to have made any difficulty. You have lost your colour lately and your appetite, and need a change more than either of us. I shall write to Mrs. Tyke, promising her and the doctor your company next Thursday; Jane will make up her mind like a good girl, and I am sure you, my dear, will oblige me by not withholding your assent.'

For the first time 'my dear' did not close the debate. 'Catherine,' said Lucy, earnestly, whilst, do what she would, tears gathered in her eyes, 'I am certain you will not press me further, when I assure you that I do not feel equal to paying this visit. I have felt weak lately,' she went on hurriedly, 'and I cannot tell you how much I long for the quiet of a month at home rather than in that perpetual bustle. Merely for my own sake, Jane must go.'

Catherine said no more just then; but later, alone with Lucy, resumed the subject so far as to ask whether she continued in the same mind, and answered her flurried 'yes' by no word of remonstrance, but by an affectionate kiss. This was all which passed between them; neither then nor afterwards did the younger sister feel certain whether Catherine had or had not guessed her secret.

Miss Drum was invited to stay with Lucy in her solitude, and gladly accepted the invitation. Lucy was her favourite, and when they were together, they petted[75] each other very tenderly.

Jane, having gained her point, recovered her good humour, and lost no time in exposing the deficiencies of her wardrobe. 'Sister', she said, smiling her prettiest and most coaxing smile, 'you can't think how poor I am, and how few clothes I've got.'

Catherine, trying to appear serenely unconscious of the drift of this speech, replied, 'Let us look over your wardrobe, dear, and we will bring it into order. Lucy will help, I know, and we can have Miss Smith to work here too, if necessary.'

'Oh dear, no!' cried Jane; 'there is no looking over what does not exist. If it comes to furbishing up old tags and rags, here I stay. Why, you're as rich as Jews, you and Lucy, and could give me five pounds a-piece without ever missing it; and not so much of a gift either, for I'm sure poor papa would never have left me such a beggar if he had known about me.'

This argument had been used more than once before. Catherine looked hurt. Lucy said, 'You should remember that you have exactly the same allowance for dress and pocket-money that we have ourselves, and we both make it do.'

'Of course,' retorted Jane, with latent spitefulness; 'and when I'm old and wise as you two, I may manage as well; but at present it is different. Besides, if I spend most on dress, you spend most on books and music, and dress is a great deal more amusing. And if I dressed like an old fright, I should like to know who'd look at me. You don't want me to be another old maid, I suppose.'

Lucy flushed up, and tried to keep her temper in silence: her sore point had been touched. Catherine, accustomed in such cases to protest first and yield afterwards, but half ashamed that Lucy's eye should mark the process from beginning to end, drew Jane out of the room, and with scarcely a word more wrote her a cheque for ten pounds, and dropped the subject of looking over her wardrobe.

An hour after the sisters had started for London, Miss Drum arrived to take their place.

Miss Drum was tall in figure, rather slim and well preserved, with pale complexion, hair, and eyes, and an unvarying tone of voice. She was mainly describable by negatives. She was neither unladylike, nor clever, nor deficient in education. She was old, but not very infirm; and neither an altogether obsolete nor a youthful dresser, though with some tendency towards the former style. Propriety was the most salient of her attributes, and was just too salient to be perfect. She was not at all amusing; in fact, rather tiresome, with an unflagging intention of being agreeable. From her Catherine acquired a somewhat old-fashioned formality; from her, also, high principles, and the instinct of self-denial. And because unselfishness, itself a negative, was Miss Drum's characteristic virtue, and because her sympathy, however prosy in expression, was sterling in quality, therefore Lucy, sore with unavowed heart-sorrow, could bear her companionship, and run down to welcome her at the door with affectionate cordiality.

Chapter 5.

London-Bridge Station, with its whirl of traffic, seems no bad emblem of London itself: vast, confused, busy, orderly, more or less dirty; implying enormous wealth in some quarter or other; providing luxuries for the rich, necessaries for the poor; thronged by rich and poor alike, idle and industrious, young and old, men and women.

London-Bridge Station at its cleanest is soiled by thousands of feet passing to and fro: on a drizzling day each foot deposits mud in its passage, takes and gives mud, leaves its impress in mud; on such a day the Station is not attractive to persons fresh from the unfailing cleanliness of sea coast and inland country; and on such a day, when, by the late afternoon, the drizzle had done, and the platform had suffered each its worst,—on such a day Miss Charlmont and her pretty sister, fresh and fastidious from sea salt and country sweetness, arrived at the Station.

Dr. Tyke's carriage was there to meet the train. Dr. Tyke's coachman, footman, and horses were fat, as befitted a fat master, whose circumstances and whose temperament might be defined as fat also; for ease, good-nature, and fat have an obvious affinity.

'Should the hood be up or down?' The rain had ceased, and Miss Charlmont, who always described London as stifling, answered, 'Up.' Jane, leaning back with an elegant ease, which nature had given and art perfected, felt secretly ashamed of Catherine, who sat bolt upright, according to her wont, and would no more have lolled in an open carriage than on the high-backed, scant-seated chair of her school-days.

The City looked at once dingy and glaring; dingy with unconsumed smoke, and glaring here and there with early-lighted gas. When Waterloo Bridge had been crossed matters brightened somewhat, and Oxford Street showed not amiss. Along the Edgware Road dirt and dinginess re-asserted their sway; but when the carriage finally turned into Notting Hill, and drove amongst the Crescents, Roads, and Gardens of that cleanly suburb, a winding-up shower, brisk and brief, not drizzly, cleared the way for the sun, and finished off the afternoon with a rainbow.

Dr. Tyke's abode was named Appletrees House, though the orchard whence the name was derived had disappeared before the memory of the oldest inhabitant. The carriage drew up, the door swung open: down the staircase came flying a little, slim woman, with outstretched hands and words of welcome; auburn-haired, though she had outlived the last of the fifties, and cheerful, though the want of children had not ceased to be felt as a hopeless disappointment: a pale-complexioned, high-voiced, little woman, all that remained of that fair cousin Lucy of bygone years and William Charlmont.

Behind her, and more deliberately, descended her husband, elastic of step, rotund of figure, bright-eyed, rosy, white-headed, not altogether unlike a robin redbreast that had been caught in the snow. Mrs. Tyke had a habit of running on with long-winded, perfectly harmless commonplaces; but notwithstanding her garrulity, she never uttered an ill-natured word or a false one. Dr. Tyke, burdened with an insatiable love of fun, and a ready, if not a witty, wit, was addicted to venting jokes, repartees, and so-called anecdotes; the last not always unimpeachably authentic.

Such were the hosts. The house was large and light, with a laboratory for the Doctor, who dabbled in chemistry, and an aviary for his wife, who doted on pets. The walls of the sitting-rooms were hung with engravings, not with family portraits, real or sham: in fact, no shame was admitted within doors, unless imaginary anecdotes and quotations must be stigmatized as shams; and as to these, when taxed with invention, the Doctor would only reply by his favourite Italian phrase: '*Se non è vero è ben trovato.*'[76]

'Jane,' said Mrs. Tyke, as the three ladies sat over a late breakfast, the Doctor having already retreated to the laboratory and his newspaper:—'Jane, I think you have made a conquest.'

Jane looked down in silence, with a conscious simper. Catherine spoke rather anxiously: 'Indeed, Cousin Lucy, I have noticed what you allude to, and I have spoken to Jane about not encouraging Mr. Durham. He is not at all a man she can really like, and she ought to be most careful not to let herself be misunderstood. Jane, you ought indeed.'

But Jane struck merrily in: 'Mr. Durham is old enough and—ahem!— handsome enough to take care of himself, sister. And, besides,' with a touch of mimicry, which recalled his pompous manner, 'Orpingham Place, my dear madam, Orpingham Place is a very fine place, a very fine place indeed. Our pineapples can really hardly be got rid of, and our prize pigs can't see out of their eyes; they can't indeed, my dear young lady, though it's not pretty talk for a pretty young lady to listen to.—Very well, if the pines and the pigs are smitten, why shouldn't I marry the pigs and the pines?'

'Why not?' cried Mrs. Tyke with a laugh; but Miss Charlmont, looking disturbed, rejoined: 'Why not, certainly, if you like Mr. Durham; but do you like Mr. Durham? And, whether or not, you ought not to laugh at him.'

Jane pouted: 'Really one would think I was a child still! As to Mr. Durham, when he knows his own mind and speaks, you may be quite sure

I shall know my own mind and give him his answer.—Orpingham Place, my dear Miss Catherine, the finest place in the county; the finest place in three counties, whatever my friend the Duke may say. A charming neighbourhood, Miss Catherine; her Grace the Duchess, the most affable woman you can imagine, and my lady the Marchioness, a fine woman—a very fine woman. But they can't raise such pines as my pines; they can't do it, you know; they haven't the means, you know.—Come now, sister, don't look cross; when I'm Mrs. Durham you shall have your slice off the pigs and the pines.'

Chapter 6.

Everilda Stella, poor Lucy's unconscious rival, had married out of the schoolroom. Pretty she was not, but with much piquancy of face and manner, and a talent for private theatricals. These advantages, gilded, perhaps, by her reputation as presumptive heiress, attracted to her a suitor, to whose twenty years' seniority she felt no objection. Mr. Hartley wooed and won her in the brief space of an Easter holiday; and bore her, nothing loth, to London, to enjoy the gaieties of the season. Somewhat to the bridegroom's annoyance, Mr. Durham accompanied the newly-married couple to town, and shared their pretty house at Kensington.

Alan Hartley, a favourite nephew of Dr. Tyke, had, as we know, been very intimate at his house in old days. Now he was proud to present his little wife of sixteen to his uncle and aunt, though somewhat mortified at having also to introduce his father-in-law, whose pompous manners, and habit of dragging titled personages into his discourse, put him to the blush. Alan had dropped Everilda, and called his wife simply Stella; her father dubbed her Pug; Everilda she was named, in accordance with the taste of her peerage-studious mother. This lady was accustomed to describe herself as of a north-country family—a Leigh of the Leazes; which conveyed an old-manorial notion to persons unacquainted with Newcastle-on-Tyne. But this by the way: Mrs. Durham had died before the opening of our tale.

At their first visit they were shown into the drawing-room by a smiling maid-servant, and requested to wait, as Dr. and Mrs. Tyke were expected home every moment. Stella looked very winning in her smart hat and feather and jaunty jacket, and Alan would have abandoned himself to all the genial glow of a bridegroom, but for Mr. Durham's behaviour. That gentleman began by placing his hat on the floor between his feet, and flicking his boots with a crimson silk pocket-handkerchief. This done, he commenced a survey of the apartment, accompanied by an apt running comment,—'Hem, no pictures—cheap engravings; a four-and-sixpenny Brussels carpet; a smallish mirror, wants regilding. Pug, my pet, that's a neat antimacassar[77]: see if you can't carry off the stitch in your eye. A piano—a harp; fiddlestick!'

When Dr. and Mrs. Tyke entered, they found the Hartleys looking uncomfortable, and Mr. Durham red and pompous after his wont; also, in opening the door, they caught the sound of 'fiddlestick!' All these symptoms, with the tact of kindness, they ignored. The bride was kissed, the father-in-law taken for granted, and Alan welcomed as if no one in the room had looked guilty.

'Come to lunch and take a hunch,' said the Doctor, offering his arm to Stella. 'Mother Bunch is rhyme, but not reason; you shall munch and I will scrunch—that's both. "Ah! you may well look surprised," as the foreign ambassador admitted when the ancient Britons noticed that he had no tail. But you won't mind when you know us better; I'm no worse than a barrel-organ.'

Yet with all Dr. Tyke's endeavour to be funny, and this time it cost him an effort, and with all his wife's facile commonplaces, two of the guests seemed ill at ease. Alan felt, as it were with every nerve, the impression his father-in-law must produce, while Stella, less sensitive for herself, was out of countenance for her husband's sake. Mr. Durham, indeed, was pompous and unabashed as ever; but whilst he answered commonplace remarks by remarks no less commonplace, he appeared to be, as in fact he was, occupied in scrutinizing, and mentally valuing, the plate and china.

'Charming weather,' said Mrs. Tyke, with an air of intelligent originality.

'Yes, ma'am; fine weather, indeed; billing and cooing weather; ha! ha!' with a glance across the table. 'Now I dare say your young ladies know what to do in this weather.'

'We have no children,' and Mrs. Tyke whispered, lest her husband should hear. Then, after a pause, 'I dare say Orpingham Place was just coming into beauty when you left.'

Mr. Durham thrust his thumbs into his waistcoat-pockets, and leaned back for conversation. 'Well, I don't know what to say to that,—I don't indeed; I don't know which the season is when Orpingham Place is *not* in beauty. Its conservatories were quite a local lion last winter—quite a local lion, as my friend the Duke remarked to me; and he said he must bring the Duchess over to see them, and he did bring her Grace over; and I gave them a luncheon in the largest conservatory, such as I don't suppose they sit down to every day. For the nobility have blood, if you please, and the literary beggars are welcome to all the brains they've got' (the Doctor smiled, Alan winced visibly); 'but you'll find it's us city men who've got backbone, and backbone's the best to wear, as I observed to the Duke that very day when I gave him such a glass of port as he hasn't got in his cellar. I said it to him, just as I say it to you, ma'am, and he didn't contradict me; in fact, you know, he couldn't.'

After this it might have been difficult to start conversation afresh, when, happily, Jane entered, late for luncheon, and with an apology for her sister, who was detained elsewhere. She went through the necessary introductions, and took her seat between Dr. Tyke and Mr. Durham, thus commanding an advantageous view of the bride, whom she mentally set down as nothing particular in any way.

Alan had never met Jane before. He asked her after Miss Charlmont and Lucy, after Lucy especially, who was 'a very charming old friend' of his, as he explained to Stella. For some minutes Mr. Durham sat silent, much impressed by Jane's beauty and grace; this gave people breathing-time for the recovery of ease and good humour; and it was not till Dr. Tyke had uttered three successive jokes, and every one, except Mr. Durham, had laughed at them, that the master of Orpingham Place could think of any remark worthy of his attractive neighbour; and then, with much originality, he too observed,—'Charming weather, Miss Jane.'

And Jane answered with a smile; for was not this the widower of Orpingham Place?

That Mr. Durham's conversation on subsequent occasions gained in range of subject, is clear from Jane's quotations in the last chapter. And that Mr. Durham was alive to Jane's fascinations appeared pretty evident, as he not only called frequently at Appletrees House, but made up parties, to which Dr. and Mrs. Tyke, and the Miss Charlmonts, were invariably asked.

Chapter 7.

Gaiety in London, sadness by the sea.

Lucy did her very best to entertain Miss Drum with the cheerfulness of former visits; in none of which had she shown herself more considerate of the old lady's tastes than now. She made breakfast half-an-hour earlier than usual; she culled for her interesting scraps from the newspaper; she gave her an arm up and down the Esplanade on sunny days; she reclaimed the most unpromising strayed stitches in her knitting; she sang her old-fashioned favourite ballads for an hour or so before tea-time, and after tea till bed-time played energetically at backgammon: yet Miss Drum was sensible of a change. All Lucy's efforts could not make her cheeks rosy and plump, and her laugh spontaneous; could not make her step elastic or her eyes bright.

It is easy to ridicule a woman nearly thirty years old for fancying herself beloved without a word said, and suffering deeply under disappointment: yet Lucy Charlmont was no contemptible person. However at one time deluded, she had never let a hint of her false hopes reach Mr. Hartley's observation; and however now disappointed, she fought bravely against a betrayal of her plight. Alone in her own room she might suffer visibly and keenly, but with any eye upon her she would not give way. Sometimes it felt as if the next moment the strain on her nerves might wax unendurable; but such a next moment never came, and she endured still. Only, who is there strong enough, day after day, to strain strength to the utmost, and yet give no sign?

'My dear,' said Miss Drum, contemplating Lucy over her spectacles and across the backgammon-board one evening when the eyes looked more sunken than ever, and the whole face more haggard, 'I am sure you do not take exercise enough. You really must do more than give me an arm on the Esplanade; all your bloom is gone, and you are much too thin. Promise me that you will take at least one long walk in the day whenever the weather is not unfavourable.'

Lucy stroked her old friend's hand fondly: 'I will take walks when my sisters are at home again; but I have not you here always.'

Miss Drum insisted: 'Do not say so, my dear, or I shall feel bound to go home again; and that I should not like at all, as we both know. Pray oblige me by promising.'

Thus urged, Lucy promised, and in secret rejoiced that for at least an hour or two of the day she should thenceforward be alone, relieved from the scrutiny of those dim, affectionate eyes. And truly she needed some relief. By day she could forbid her thoughts to shape themselves, even mentally, into words, although no effort could banish the vague, dull sorrow which was all that might now remain to her of remembrance. But by night, when sleep paralysed self-restraint, then her dreams were haunted by distorted spectres of the past; never alluring or endearing—for this she was thankful—but sometimes monstrous, and always impossible to escape from. Night after night she would awake from such dreams, struggling and sobbing, with less and less conscious strength to resume daily warfare.

Soon she allowed no weather to keep her indoors at the hour for walking, and Miss Drum, who was a hardy disciple of the old school, encouraged her activity. She always sought the sea, not the smooth, civilised esplanade, but the rough, irreclaimable shingle;—to stray to and fro till the last moment of her freedom; to and fro, to and fro, at once listless and unresting, with wide, absent eyes fixed on the monotonous waves, which they did not see. Gradually a morbid fancy grew upon her that one day she should behold her father's body washed ashore, and that she should know the face: from a waking fancy, this began to haunt her dreams with images unutterably loathsome. Then she walked no more on the shingle, but took to wandering along green lanes and country roads.

But no one struggling persistently against weakness fails to overcome: also, however prosaic the statement may sound, air and exercise *will* take effect on persons of sound constitution. Something of Lucy's lost colour showed itself, by fits and starts at first, next steadily; her appetite came back, however vexed she might feel at its return; at last fatigue brought sounder sleep, and the hollow eyes grew less sunken. This refreshing sleep was the turning-point in her case; it supplied strength for the day, whilst each day in its turn brought with it fewer and fewer demands upon her strength. Seven weeks after Miss Drum exacted the promise, Lucy, though graver of aspect, and at heart sadder than before Alan Hartley's wedding, had recovered in a measure her look of health and her interest in the details of daily life. She no longer greatly dreaded meeting her sisters when at length their much-prolonged absence should terminate; and in spite of some nervousness in the anticipation, felt confident that even a sight of Mr. and Mrs. Hartley would not upset the outward composure of her decorum.

Miss Drum triumphed in the success of her prescription, and brought forward parallel instances within her own experience. 'That is right,' she would say, 'my dear; take another slice of the mutton where it is not over-done. There is nothing like exercise for giving an appetite, only the mutton should not be overdone. You cannot remember Sarah Smith, who was with me before your dear mother entrusted you to my care; but I assure you three doctors had given her over as a confirmed invalid when I prescribed for her;' and the old lady laughed gently at her own wit. 'I made her take a walk every day, let the weather be what it might; and gave her nice, juicy mutton to eat, with a change to beef, or a chicken, now and then for variety; and very soon you would not have known her for the same girl; and Dr. Grey remarked, in his funny way, that I ought to be an M.D. myself.' Or, again: 'Lucy, my dear, you recollect my French assistant, Mademoiselle Leclerc, what a fine, strong young woman she was when you knew her. Now when she first came to me she was pale and peaking, afraid of wet feet or an open window; afraid of this, that, and the other, always tired, and with no appetite except for sweets. Mutton and exercise made her what you remember; and before she went home to France to marry an old admirer, she thanked me with tears in her eyes for having made her love mutton. She said "love" when she should have said "like;" but I was too proud and pleased to correct her English then, I only answered, "Ah, dear Mademoiselle, always love your husband and love your mutton."'

Lucy had a sweet, plaintive voice, to which her own secret sorrow now added a certain simple pathos; and when in the twilight she sang 'Alice Grey,' or 'She wore a wreath of roses,' or some other old favourite, good Miss Drum would sit and listen till the tears gathered behind her spectacles. Were tears in the singer's eyes also? She thought now with more tenderness than ever before of the suitors she had rejected in her hopeful, happy youth, especially of a certain Mr. Tresham, who had wished her all happiness as he turned to leave her in his dignified regret. She had always had a great liking for Mr. Tresham, and now she could feel for him.

Chapter 8.

On the 28th of June, four letters came to Lucy by the first delivery:—

I.

My dear Lucy,

Pray do not think me thoughtless if I once more ask whether you will sanction an extension of our holiday. Mrs. Tyke presses us to remain with her through July, and Dr. Tyke is no less urgent. When I hinted that their hospitality had already been trespassed upon, the Doctor quoted Hone[78] (as he said: I doubt if it is there):—

> 'In July
> No good-bye;
> In August
> Part we must.'

I then suggested that you may be feeling moped at home, and in want of change; but, of course, the Doctor had still an answer ready:—'Tell Lucy from me, that if she takes you away I shall take it very ill, as the homœopath said when his learned brother substituted cocoa-nibs for champagne.' And all the time Cousin Lucy was begging us to stay, and Jane was looking at me so earnestly: in short, dear Lucy, if 'No' must be said, pray will you say it; for I have been well-nigh talked over.

And, indeed, we must make allowances for Jane, if she seems a little selfish; for, to let you into a secret, I believe she means to accept Mr. Durham if he makes her the offer we all are expecting from him. At first I was much displeased at her giving him any encouragement, for it appeared to me impossible that she could view his attentions with serious approbation: but I have since become convinced that she knows her own mind, and is not trifling with him. How it is possible for her to contemplate union with one so unrefined and ostentatious I cannot conceive, but I have no power to restrain her; and when I endeavoured to exert my influence against him, she told me in the plainest terms that she preferred luxury with Mr. Durham to dependence without him. Oh, Lucy, Lucy! have we ever given her cause to resent her position so bitterly? Were she my own child, I do not think I could love her more or care for her more anxiously: but she has never understood me, never done me justice. I speak of myself only, not of you also, because I shall never marry, and all I have has been held simply in trust for her: with you it is, and ought to be, different.

But you must not suffer for Jane's wilfulness. If you are weary of our absence I really must leave her under Cousin Lucy's care—for she positively declines to accompany me home at present—and return to every-day duties. I am sick enough of pleasuring, I do assure you, as it is; though, were Mr. Durham a different man, I should only rejoice, as you may suppose.

Well, as to news, there is not much worth transmitting. Jane has been to the Opera three times, and to the English play once. Mr. Durham sends the boxes, and Dr. and Mrs. Tyke never tire of the theatre. The last time they went to the Opera they brought home with them to supper Mr. Tresham, whom you may recollect our meeting here more than once, and who has lately returned to England from the East. Through some misunderstanding he expected to see you instead of me, and looked out of countenance for a moment: then he asked after you, and begged me to remember him to you when I wrote. He appeared much interested in hearing our home news, and concerned when I mentioned that you have seemed less strong lately. Pray send compliments for him when next you write, in case we should see him again.

Mr. Hartley I always liked, and now I like his wife also: she is an engaging little thing, and gets us all to call her Stella. You, I am sure, will be fond of her when you know her. How I wish her father resembled her! She is as simple and as merry as a bird, and witnesses Mr. Durham's attentions to Jane with perfect equanimity. As to Mr. Hartley, he seems as much amused as if the bulk of his wife's enormous fortune were not at stake; yet any one must see the other man is in earnest. Stella is reckoned a clever actress, and private theatricals of some sort are impending. I say 'of some sort,' because Jane, who is indisputably the beauty of our circle, would prefer *tableaux vivants*[79]; and I know not which will carry her point.

My love to Miss Drum. Don't think me selfish for proposing to remain longer away from you; but, indeed, I am being drawn in two opposite directions by two dear sisters, of whom I only wish that one had as much good sense and good taste as the other.

Your affectionate sister,
Catherine Charlmont.

—⋇—

II.

My dear Lucy,

I know Catherine is writing, and will make the worst of everything, just as if I was cut out to be an old maid.

Surely at my age one may know one's own mind; and, though I'm not going to say before I am asked whether I like Mr. Durham, we are all very well aware, my dear Lucy, that I like money and comforts. It's one thing for Catherine and you, who have enough and to spare, to split hairs as to likes and dislikes; but it's quite another for me who have not a penny of my own, thanks to poor dear papa's blindness. Now do be a dear, and tell sister she is welcome to stay this one month more; for, to confess the truth, if I remain here alone I may find myself at my wit's end for a pound or two one of these days. Dress is so dear, and I had rather never go out again than be seen a dowdy; and if we are to have *tableaux* I shall want all sorts of things. I don't hold at all with charades and such nonsense, in which people are supposed to be witty; give me a piece in which one's arms are of some use; but of course, Stella, who has no more arm than a pump-handle, votes for theatricals.

The Hartleys are coming to-day, and, of course, Mr. Durham, to take us after luncheon to the Crystal Palace.[80] There is a grand concert coming off, and a flower-show, which would all be yawny enough but for the toilettes. I dare say I shall see something to set me raving; just as last time I was at the Botanic Gardens, I pointed out the loveliest suit of Brussels lace over white silk; but I might as well ask Catherine for wings to fly with.

Good-bye, my dear Lucy. Don't be cross this once, and when I have a house of my own, I'll do you a good turn.

Your affectionate sister,
Jane.

P.S. I enclose Mr. Durham's photograph, which he fished and fished to make me ask for, so at last I begged it to gratify the poor man. Don't you see all Orpingham Place in his speaking countenance?

III.

My dearest Lucy,

You owe me a kindness to balance my disappointment at missing your visit. So please let Catherine know that she and Jane may give us a month more. Dr. Tyke wishes it no less than I do, and Mr. Durham perhaps more than either of us; but a word to the wise.

Your affectionate cousin,
Lucy C. Tyke.

P.S. The Doctor won't send regards, because he means to write to you himself.

IV.

Dear Lucy,

If you agree with the snail, you find your house just the size for one; and lest bestial example should possess less force than human, I further remind you of what Realmah the Great affirms,—"I met two blockheads, but the one sage kept himself to himself." All which sets forth to you the charms of solitude, which, as you are such a proper young lady, is, of course, the only anybody you can be in love with, and of whose society I am bent on affording you prolonged enjoyment.

This can be effected, if your sisters stay here another month, and indeed you must not say us nay; for on your 'yes' hangs a tale which your 'no' may for ever forbid to wag. Miss Catherine looks glummish, but Jenny is all sparkle and roses, like this same month of June; and never is she more sparkling or rosier than when the master of Orpingham Place hails her with that ever fresh remark, 'Fine day, Miss Jane.' Don't nip the summer crops of Orpingham Place in the bud, or, rather, don't retard them by unseasonable frost; for I can't fancy my friend will be put off with anything less than a distinct 'no;' and when it comes to that, I think Miss Jane, in her trepidation, will say 'yes.' And if you are a good girl, and let the little one play out her play, when she come into the sugar and spice and all that's nice, you shall come to Notting Hill this very next May, and while the sun shines make your hay.

> *Your venerable cousin's husband*
> *(by which I merely mean),*
> *Your cousin's venerable husband,*
> *Francis Tyke, M.D.*

N.B. I append M.D. to remind you of my professional status, and so quell you by the weight of my advice.

Lucy examined the photograph of Mr. Durham with a double curiosity, for he was Mr. Hartley's father-in-law as well as Jane's presumptive suitor. She looked, and saw a face not badly featured, but vulgar in expression; a figure not amiss, but ill at ease in its studied attitude and superfine clothes. Assuredly it was not George Durham, but the master of Orpingham Place who possessed attractions for Jane; and Lucy felt, for a sister who could be thus attracted, the sting of a humiliation such as her own baseless hopes had never cost her.

Each of her correspondents was answered with judicious variation in the turn of the sentences. To Jane she wrote dryly, returning Mr. Durham's portrait wrapped in a ten-pound note; an arrangement which, in her eyes, showed a symbolic appropriateness, lost for the moment on her sister. Catherine she answered far more affectionately, begging her on no account to curtail a visit which might be of importance to Jane's prospects; and on the flap of the envelope, she added compliments to Mr. Tresham.

Chapter 9.

Mr. Tresham had loved Lucy Charlmont sincerely, and until she refused him had entertained a good hope of success. Even at the moment of refusal she avowed the liking for him which all through their acquaintance had been obvious; and then, and not till then, it dawned upon him that her indifference towards himself had its root in preference for another. But he was far too honourable a man either to betray or to aim at verifying his suspicion; and though he continued to visit at Dr. Tyke's, where Alan Hartley was so often to be seen idling away time under the comfortable conviction that he was doing no harm to himself or to any one else, it was neither at once, nor of set purpose, that Arthur Tresham penetrated Lucy's secret. Alan and himself had been College friends; he understood him thoroughly; his ready good-nature, which seemed to make every one a principal person in his regard; his open hand that liked spending; his want of deep or definite purpose; his unconcern as to possible consequences. Then Lucy,—in whom Mr. Tresham had been on one point woefully mistaken,—she was so composed and so cordial to all her friends; there was about her such womanly sweetness, such unpretentious, dignified reserve towards all: her face would light up so brightly when he, or any other, spoke what interested her, not seldom, certainly, when *he* spoke:—even after a sort of clue had come into his hands, it was some time before he felt sure of any difference between her manner to Alan and to others. When the conviction forced itself upon him, he grieved more for her than for himself; he knew his friend too intimately to mistake his pleasure in being amused for any anxiety to make himself beloved; he knew about Alan much that Lucy did not and could not guess, and from the beginning inferred the end.

In the middle of that London season Catherine and Lucy returned to Brompton-on-Sea; and before August had started the main stream of tourists from England to the continent, Mr. Tresham packed up his knapsack, and, staff in hand, set off on a solitary expedition, of undetermined length, to the East. He was neither a rich nor a poor man; had been called to the bar, but without pursuing his profession, and was not tied to any given spot; he went away to recruit his spirits, and, having recovered them, stayed on out of sheer enjoyment. Yet, when one morning his eye lighted on the Hartley-Durham marriage in the 'Times' Supplement, home feeling stirred within him; and he who, twenty-four hours earlier, knew not whether he might not end his days beside the blue Bosphorus, on the evening of that same day had started westward.

He felt curious, he would not own to himself that he felt specially interested, to know how Lucy fared; and he felt curious, in a minor degree, to inspect her successful rival. With himself Lucy had not yet had a rival; not yet, perhaps she might one day, he repeated to himself, only it had not happened yet. And then the sweet, dignified face rose before him kind and cheerful; cheerful still in his memory, though he guessed that now it must look saddened. He had never yet seen it with a settled expression of sadness, and he knew not how to picture it so.

Mr. Drum—or Mr. Gawkins Drum, as he scrupulously called himself, on account of a certain Mr. Drum, who lived somewhere and went nowhere, and was held by all outsiders to be in his dotage—Miss Drum's brother, Mr. Gawkins Drum, had for several years stood as a gay young bachelor of sixty. Not that, strictly speaking, any man (or, alas! any woman) can settle down at sixty and there remain; but at the last of a long series of avowed birthday parties, Mr. Drum had drunk his own health as being sixty that very day; this was now some years ago, and still, in neighbourly parlance, Mr. Drum was no more than sixty. At sixty-something-indefinite Gawkins brought home a bride, who confessed to sixty; and all Brompton-on-Sea indulged in a laugh at their expense, till it oozed out that the kindly old couple had gone through all the hopes and disappointments of a many years' engagement, been at a reasonable age for such matters, and now terminated only because the bedridden brother, to whom the bride had devoted herself during an ordinary lifetime, had at last ended his days in peace. Mr. and Mrs. Gawkins Drum forestalled their neighbours' laugh by their own, and soon the laugh against them died out, and every one accepted their house as amongst the pleasantest resorts in Brompton-on-Sea.

Miss Drum, however, felt less leniently towards her brother and sister-in-law, and deliberately regarded them from a shocked point of view. The wedding took place at Richmond, where the bride resided; and the honeymoon came to an end whilst Lucy entertained her old friend, during that long visit at Notting Hill, which promised to colour all Jane's future.

'My dear,' said Miss Drum to her deferential listener; 'My dear, Sarah,'—and Lucy felt that offending Sarah could only be the bride,—'Sarah shall not suffer for Gawkins' folly and her own. I will not fail to visit her in her new home, and to notice her on all proper occasions, but I cannot save her from being ridiculous. I did not wait till I was sixty to make up my mind against wedlock, though perhaps'—and the old lady bridled—'I also may have endured the preference of some infatuated man. Lucy, my dear, take an old woman's advice: marry, if you mean to marry, before you are sixty, or else remain like myself; otherwise, you make yourself simply ridiculous.'

And Lucy, smiling, assured her that she would either marry before sixty or not at all; and added, with some earnestness, that she did not think she should ever marry. To which Miss Drum answered with stateliness: 'Very well; do one thing or do the other, only do not become ridiculous.'

Yet the old lady softened that evening, when she found herself, as it were, within the radius of the contemned bride. Despite her sixty years, and in truth she looked less than her age, Mrs. Gawkins Drum was a personable little woman, with plump red cheeks, gentle eyes, and hair of which the soft brown was threaded, but not overpowered, by grey. There was no affectation of youthfulness in her gown, which was of slate-coloured silk; nor in her cap, which came well on her head; nor in her manner to her guests, which was cordial; nor in her manner to her husband, which was affectionate, with the undemonstrative affectionateness that might now have been appropriate had they married forty years earlier.

Her kiss of welcome was returned frostily by Miss Drum, warmly by Lucy. Mr. Drum at first looked a little sheepish under his sister's severe salutation. Soon all were seated at tea.

'Do you take cream and sugar?' asked the bride, looking at her new sister.

'No sugar, I thank you,' was the formal reply. 'And it will be better, Sarah, that you should call me Elizabeth. Though I am an old woman your years do not render it unsuitable, and I wish to be sisterly.'

'Thank you, dear Elizabeth,' answered Mrs. Gawkins, cheerily; 'I hope, indeed, we shall be sisterly. It would be sad times with me if I found I had brought coldness into my new home.'

But Miss Drum would not thaw yet. 'Yes, I have always maintained, and I maintain still, that there must be faults on both sides if a marriage, if any marriage whatever, introduces dissension into a family circle. And I will do my part, Sarah.'

'Yes, indeed;' but Sarah knew not what more to say.

Mr. Drum struck in,—'Lucy, my dear'—she had been a little girl perched on his knee when her father asked him years before to be trustee,—'Lucy, my dear, you're not in full bloom. Look at my old lady, and guess: what's a recipe for roses?'

'For shame, Gawkins!' cried both old ladies; one with a smile, the other with a frown.

Still, as the evening wore on, Miss Drum slowly thawed. Having, as it were once for all, placed her hosts in the position of culprits at the moral bar, having sat in judgment on them, and convicted them in the ears of all men (represented by Lucy), she admitted them to mercy, and dismissed them with a qualified pardon. What most softened her towards the offending couple was their unequivocal profession of rheumatism. When she unbendingly declined to remain seated at the supper-table one minute beyond half-past ten, she alleged rheumatism as her impelling motive; and Gawkins and Sarah immediately proclaimed their own rheumatic experience and sympathies. As Miss Drum observed to Lucy on their way home, 'Old people don't confess to rheumatism if they wish to appear young.'

Thus the feud subsided, though Miss Drum to the end of her life occasionally spoke of her sister-in-law as 'that poor silly thing,' and of her brother as of one who should have known better.

Whilst, on her side, Mrs. Gawkins Drum remarked to her husband, 'What a very old-looking woman that Miss Charlmont is, if she's not thirty, as you say. I never saw such an old, faded-looking woman of her age.'

Chapter 10.

Parties ran high at Kensington and Notting Hill. Stella stood up for charades, Jane for tableaux. Mr. Hartley naturally sided with his wife, Miss Charlmont held back from volunteering any opinion, Mrs. Tyke voted for the last speaker, Dr. Tyke ridiculed each alternative; at last Mr. Durham ingeniously threw his weight into both scales, and won for both parties a partial triumph. 'Why not,' asked he,—'why not let Pug speak, and Miss Jane be silent?'

This pacific suggestion once adopted, Dr. Tyke proposed that a charade word should be fixed upon, and performed by speech or spectacle, as might suit the rival stars; for instance, Love-apple.[81]

But who was to be Love?

Everybody agreed in rejecting little boys; and Jane, when directly appealed to, refused to represent the Mother of love and laughter; 'for,' as she truly observed, 'that would not be Love, after all.' Mr. Durham, looking laboriously gallant, aimed at saying something neat and pointed; he failed, yet Jane beamed a smile upon his failure. Then Dr. Tyke proposed a plaster Cupid; this, after some disputing, was adopted, with vague accessories of processional Greek girls, to be definitely worked out afterwards. For 'Apple'

Alan suggested Paris and the rival goddesses, volunteering himself as Paris: Jane should be Venus, and Catherine would make a capital Juno. Jane accepted her own part as a matter of course, but doubted about her sister. 'Yes,' put in Miss Charlmont, decisively, 'I will be Juno, or anything else which will help us forward a little.' So that was settled; but who should be Minerva? Stella declined to figure as the patroness of wisdom, and Jane drily observed, that they ought all to be tall, or all to be short, in her idea. At last a handsome, not too handsome, friend, Lady Everett, was thought of to take the part. The last scene Dr. Tyke protested he should settle himself with Stella, and not be worried any more about it. So those two went into committee together, and Alan edged in ere long for consultation; finally, Miss Charlmont was appealed to, and the matter was arranged amongst them without being divulged to the rest.

But all was peace and plenty, smiles and wax-candles, at Kensington, when at last the evening came for the performance. Mrs. Hartley's drawing-rooms being much more spacious than Mrs. Tyke's, had been chosen for convenience, and about two hundred guests assembled to hear Stella declaim and see Jane attitudinize, as either faction expressed it. Good-natured Mrs. Tyke played the hostess, whilst Mrs. Hartley remained occult in the green-room. Dr. Tyke was manager and prompter. Mr. Durham, vice Paris-Hartley, welcomed people in a cordial, fussy manner, apologising for the smallness of London rooms, and regretfully alluding to the vast scale of Orpingham Place, 'where a man can be civil to his friends without treading on their toes or their tails—ha! ha!'

But there is a limit to all things, even fussiness has an end. At last every one worth waiting for had arrived, been received, been refreshed. Orpingham Place died out of the conversation. People exchanged commonplaces, and took their seats; having taken their seats they exchanged more commonplaces. 'What's the word?'—'It's such a bore guessing: I never guess anything.'—'People ought to tell the word beforehand.'—'What a horrible man! Is that Mr. Hartley?'—'No, old Durham; backbone Durham.'—'Why backbone?'—'Don't know; hear him called so.'—'Isn't there a Beauty somewhere?'—'Don't know; there's the Beast,'—and the hackneyed joke received the tribute of a hackneyed laugh.

The manager's bell rang, the curtain drew up.

A plaster cast of Cupid, with fillet, bow, and quiver, on an upholstery pedestal, stood revealed. Music, commencing behind the scenes, approached; a file of English-Grecian maidens, singing and carrying garlands, passed across the stage towards a pasteboard temple, presumably their desired goal, although they glanced at their audience, and seemed very independent of Cupid on his pedestal. There were only six young ladies; but they moved slowly, with a tolerable space interposed between each and each, thus producing a processional effect. They sang, in time and in tune, words by Dr. Tyke; music (not in harmony, but in unison, to ensure correct execution) by Arthur Tresham:—

'Love hath a name of Death:
He gives a breath
And takes away.
Lo we, beneath his sway,
Grow like a flower;
To bloom an hour,
To droop a day,
And fade away.'

The first Anglo-Greek had been chosen for her straight nose, the last for her elegant foot; the intermediate four, possessing good voices, bore the burden of the singing. They all moved and sang with self-complacent ease, but without much dramatic sentiment, except the plainest of the six, who assumed an air of languishment.

Some one suggested 'cupid-ditty,' but without universal acceptance. Some one else, on no obvious grounds, hazarded 'Bore, Wild Boar:' a remark which stung Dr. Tyke, as playwright, into retorting, 'Boreas.'[82]

The second scene was dumb show. Alan Hartley as Paris, looking very handsome in a tunic and sandals, and flanked by the largest-sized, woolly toy lambs, sat, apple in hand, awaiting the rival goddesses. A flourish of trumpets announced the entrance of Miss Charlmont, a stately crowned Juno, robed in amber-coloured cashmere, and leading in a leash a peacock, with train displayed, and ingeniously mounted on noiseless wheels. She swept grandly in, and held out one arm, with a studied gesture, for the apple; which, doubtless, would have been handed to her then and there, had not warning notes on a harp ushered in Lady Everett: a modest, sensible-looking Minerva, robed and stockinged in blue, with a funny Athenian owl[83] perched on her shoulder, and a becoming helmet on her head. Paris hesitated visibly, and seemed debating whether or not to split the apple and the difference together, when a hubbub, as of birds singing, chirping, calling, cleverly imitated by Dr. Tyke and Stella on water-whistles, heralded the approach of Venus. In she came, beautiful Jane Charlmont, with a steady, gliding step, her eyes kindling with victory, both her small hands outstretched for the apple so indisputably hers, her lips parted in a triumphant smile. Her long, white robe flowed classically to the floor; two doves, seeming to nestle in her hair, billed and almost cooed; but her face eclipsed all beside it; and when Paris, on one knee, deposited the apple within her slim, white fingers, Juno forgot to look indignant and Minerva scornful.

After this the final scene fell dead and flat. In vain did Stella whisk about as the most coquettish of market-girls of an undefined epoch and country, balancing a fruit-basket on her head, and crying, 'Grapes, melons, peaches, love-apples,' with the most natural inflections. In vain did Arthur Tresham beat down the price of peaches, and Alan Hartley bid for love-apples:—Jane had attained one of her objects, and eclipsed her little friend for that evening.

The *corps dramatique* was to sit down to supper in costume; a point arranged ostensibly for convenience, secretly it may be for vanity's sake: only Stella laid her fruit-basket aside, and Miss Charlmont released her peacock. Lady Everett continued to wear the helmet, which did not conceal her magnificent black hair (she had been a Miss Moss before marriage, Clara Lyon Moss), and Jane retained her pair of doves.

But during the winding up of the charade, more of moment had occurred off the stage than upon it. Jane, her part over, left the other performers to their own devices, and quietly made her way into a conservatory which opened out of the room devoted for the evening to cloaks and hoods. If she expected to be followed she was not disappointed. A heavy step, and an embarrassed clearance of throat, announced Mr. Durham. He bustled up to her, where she sat fanning herself and showing white and brilliant against a background of flowers and leaves, whilst he looked at once sheepish and pompous, awkward and self-satisfied; not a lady's man assuredly.

'Hem—haw—Miss Jane, you surpassed yourself. I shall always think of you now as Venus; I shall, indeed.' Jane smiled benignantly. 'Poor Pug's nose is quite out of joint; it is, indeed. But the chit has got a husband, and can snap her fingers at all of us.' Jane surveyed him with grave interrogation, then cast down her lustrous eyes, and slightly turned her shoulder in his direction. Abashed, he resumed: 'But really, Miss Jane, now wasn't Venus a married lady too? and couldn't we——?' Jane interrupted him: 'Pray give me your arm, Mr. Durham;' she rose: 'let us go back to the company. I don't know what you are talking about, unless you mean to be rude and very unkind:' the voice broke, the large, clear eyes softened to tears; she drew back as he drew nearer. Then Mr. Durham, ill-bred, but neither scheming nor cold-hearted, pompous and fussy, but a not ungenerous man for all that,—then Mr. Durham spoke: 'Don't draw back from me, Miss Jane, but take my arm for once to lead you back to the company, and take my hand for good. For I love and admire you, Miss Jane; and if you will take an oldish man for your husband, you shall never want for money or for pleasure while my name is good in the City.'

Thus in one evening Jane Charlmont attained both her objects.

Supper was a very gay meal, as brilliant as lights, glass, and plate could make it. People were pleased with the night's entertainment, with themselves, and with each other. Mr. Durham, with an obtrusive air of festivity, sat down beside Jane, and begged his neighbours not to inconvenience themselves, as they did not mind squeezing. Jane coloured, but judged it too early to frown. Mr. Durham, being somewhat old-fashioned, proposed healths: the fair actresses were toasted, the Anglo-Greeks in a bevy, the distinguished stars one by one. Mr. Tresham returned thanks for the processional six; Dr. Dyke for Miss Charlmont, Sir James Everett and Mr. Hartley for their respective wives.

Then Jane's health was drunk: who would rise to return thanks? Mr. Durham rose: 'Hem—haw—' said he: 'haw—hem—ladies and gentlemen, allow me to return thanks for the Venus of the evening—I mean for the Venus altogether, whose health you have done me the honour to drink'— knowing smiles circled round the table. 'Done us, I should say: not that I unsay what I said; quite the contrary, and I'm not ashamed to have said it. I will only say one word more in thanking you for the honour you have done her and all of us: the champagne corks pop, and suggest popping; but after popping mum's the word. Ladies and gentlemen, my very good friends, I drink your very good health.'

And the master of Orpingham Place sat down.

Chapter 11.

Lucy received the news of Jane's engagement with genuine vexation, and then grew vexed with herself for feeling vexed. Conscience took alarm, and pronounced that envy and pride had a share in her vexation. Self retorted: It is not envy to see that Jane is mercenary, nor pride to dislike vulgarity. Conscience insisted: It is envy to be annoyed by Jane's getting married before you, and it is pride to brand Mr. Durham as vulgar, and then taboo him as beyond the pale. Self pleaded: No one likes growing old and being made to feel it; and who would not deprecate a connection who will put one out of countenance at every turn? But Conscience secured the last word: If you were younger than Jane, you would make more allowances for her; and if Mr. Durham were engaged to any one except your sister, you would think it fair not to condemn him as destitute of every virtue because he is underbred.

Thus did Conscience get the better of Self. And Lucy gulped down dignity and disappointment together when, in reply to Miss Drum's, 'My dear, I hope your sisters are well, and enjoying their little gaieties,' she said, cheerfully: 'Now, really, you should give me something for such wonderful news: Jane is engaged to be married.'

There was nothing Miss Drum relished more than a wedding 'between persons suited to each other, and not ridiculous on the score of age and appearance,' as she would have herself pointedly have defined it. Now Jane was obviously young enough and pretty enough to become a bride; so Miss Drum was delighted, and full of interest and of inquiries, which Lucy found it rather difficult to answer satisfactorily.

'And who is the favoured gentleman, my dear?'

'Mr. Durham, of Orpingham Place, in Gloucestershire. Very rich it seems, and a widower. His only daughter,' Lucy hurried on with an imperceptible effort, 'married that Mr. Hartley Catherine and I used to meet so often at Notting Hill. She was thought to be a great heiress; but I suppose this will make some difference.'

'Then he is rather old for Jane?'

'He is not yet fifty it seems, though of course that is full old. But what he says, Orpingham Place must be a very fine country-seat; and Jane appears cut out for wealth and pleasure, she has such a power of enjoying herself;' and Lucy paused.

Miss Drum, dropping the point of age, resumed: 'Now what Durham will this be, my dear? I used to know a Sir Marcus Durham—a gay, hunting Baronet: He was of a north-country family; but this may be a branch of the same stock. He married an Earl's daughter, Lady Mary; and she used to take precedence, let who would be in the room, which was not thought to be in very good taste when the dowager Lady Durham was present. Still an Earl's daughter to understand good breeding, and that was how she acted; I do not wish to express any opinion. Perhaps Mr. Durham may have a chance of the Baronetcy, for Sir Marcus left no children, but was succeeded by a bachelor brother; and then Jane will be "my lady" some day.'

'No,' replied Lucy; 'I don't think that likely. Mr. Durham is enormously wealthy, by what I hear; but not of a county family. He made his fortune in the City.'

Miss Drum persisted: 'The cadets[84] of even noble families have made money by commerce over and over again. It is no disgrace to make a fortune; and I see no reason why Mr. Durham should not be a baronet some day. Many a City man has been as fine a gentleman as any idler at court. Very likely Mr. Durham is an elegant man of talent, and well connected; if so, a fortune is no drawback, and the question of age may be left to the lady's decision.'

Lucy said no more: only she foresaw and shrank from that approaching day of undeceiving which should bring Mr. Durham to Brompton-on-Sea.

Once set off on the subject of family, there was no stopping Miss Drum, who, having had no proveable great-grandfather, was sensitive on the score of pedigree.

'You might not suppose it now, Lucy, but it is well known that our family name of Drum, though less euphonious than that of Durham, is in fact the same. I made the observation once to Sir Marcus, and he laughed with pleasure, and often afterwards addressed me as cousin. Lady Mary did not like the suggestion; but no one's fancies can alter a fact:' and the old lady looked stately, and as if the Drum-Durham theory had been adopted and emblazoned by the College of Heralds; whereas, in truth, no one besides herself, not even the easy-tempered Gawkins, held it.

Meanwhile, all went merrily and smoothly at Notting Hill. As Jane had said, she was old enough to know her own mind, and apparently she knew it. When Mr. Durham presented her with a set of fine diamonds, she dropped naturally into calling him George; and when he pressed her to name the day, she answered, with an assumption of girlishness, that he must talk over all those dreadful things with Catherine.

To Miss Charlmont he had already opened his mind on the subject of set-tlements: Jane should have everything handsome and ample, but Pug must not lose her fortune either. This Catherine, deeming it right and reasonable, undertook to explain to Jane. Jane sulked a little to her sister, but displayed only a smiling aspect to her lover, feeling in her secret heart that her own nest was being particularly well feathered: for not only were Mr. Durham's new marriage settlements most liberal, in spite of Stella's prospective twenty thousand pounds on coming of age, and twenty thousand at her father's demise; but Catherine, of her own accord, provided that at her death all her share of their father's property should descend to Jane, for her own separate use, and at her own absolute disposal. The younger sister, indeed, observed with safe generosity: 'Suppose you should marry, too, some day?' But Catherine, grateful for any gleam of unselfishness in her favourite sister, answered warmly and decisively: 'I never meant to marry, and I always meant what fortune I had to be yours at last: only, dear, do not again think hardly of our poor father's oversight.'

Mr. Durham was urgent to have the wedding-day fixed, and Jane reluc-tant merely and barely for form's sake. A day in August was named, and the honeymoon pre-devoted to Paris and Switzerland. Then Miss Charlmont pronounced it time to return home; and was resolute that the wedding should take place at Brompton-on-Sea, not at Notting Hill as the hospitable Tykes proposed.

Jane was now nothing loth to quit town; Mr. Durham unwilling to lose her, yet willing as recognising the step for an unavoidable preliminary. Nev-ertheless, he felt hurt at Jane's indifference to the short separation; whilst Jane, in her turn, felt worried at his expecting any show of sentiment from her, though, having once fathomed his feelings, she kept the worry to her-self and produced the sentiment. He looked genuinely concerned when they parted at London-Bridge Station; but Jane never in her life had experienced a greater relief than now, when the starting train left him behind on the platform. A few more days, and it would be too late to leave him behind: but she consoled herself by reflecting that without him she might despair of ever seeing Paris; Switzerland was secondary in her eyes.

Miss Drum had often set as a copy, 'Manners make the Man,' and explained to her deferential pupils how in that particular phrase 'Man' includes 'Woman.' Catherine in later life reflected that 'Morals make the Man' (including Woman) conveys a not inferior truth. Jane might have modified the sentence a trifle further, in employing it as an M copy, and have written, 'Money makes the Man.'

Chapter 12.

Lucy welcomed her sisters home, after an absence of unprecedented duration, with warm-hearted pleasure, but Jane went far to extinguish the feeling.

In the heyday of her blooming youth and satisfaction, she was not likely to acquire any tender tact lacking at other times; and an elder sister, mentally set down in her catalogue of old maids, was fair game.

'Why, Lucy,' she cried, as they sat together the first evening, herself the only idler of the three, 'you look as old as George, and about as lively: Miss Drum must be catching.'

'Do leave Miss Drum alone,' Lucy answered, speaking hastily from a double annoyance. 'And if,'—she forced a laugh,—'surely if my looks recall George to your mind they ought to please you.'

But Jane was incorrigible. 'My dear, George is Orpingham Place, and Orpingham Place is George; but your looks suggest some distinction between the two. Only think, he expected me to grow dismal at leaving him behind, and I did positively see his red pockethandkerchief fluttering in the breeze as we screamed out of the station. And he actually flattered himself I should not go out much till the wedding is over; catch me staying at home if I can help it! By-the-bye, did you mean a joke by wrapping his photograph up in the ten-pound note? it struck me afterwards as really neat in its way.'

'Oh, Jane!' put in Catherine, and more she might have added in reproof; but at that instant the door opened, and Mr. Ballantyne was announced.

Mr. Ballantyne was a solicitor, related to Mrs. Gawkins Drum, and taken into partnership by that lady's husband shortly before their marriage. Judging by looks, Mr. Ballantyne might have been own nephew to Miss Drum rather than to her sister-in-law, so neutral was he in aspect and manner; if ever any one liked him at first sight, it was because there was nothing on the surface to stir a contrary feeling; and if any one volunteered a confidence to him, it was justified by his habitual taciturnity, which suggested a mechanical aptitude at keeping a secret; yet, however appearances were against him, he was a shrewd man of business, and not deficient in determination of character.

He arrived by appointment to show Miss Charlmont the draft of her settlement on her sister, and take, if need be, further instructions. She was one to see with her own eyes rather than merely to hear with her own ears, and, therefore, retired with the papers to the solitude of her own room, leaving her sisters to entertain the visitor.

Thus left, Mr. Ballantyne took a respectful look at Jane, whose good luck in securing the master of Orpingham Place he considered rare indeed. Looking at her he arrived at the conclusion that Mr. Durham also had been lucky. Jane just glanced at Mr. Ballantyne, mentally appraising him as a nonentity; but in that glance she saw his admiration; admiration always propitiated[85] her, and she deigned to be gracious.

Various maiden ladies in Brompton-on-Sea would have been gracious to Mr. Ballantyne from a different motive. Though still a youngish man he was a widower, already in easy circumstances, and with a prospect of growing rich. His regard for his late wife's memory was most decorous, but not such as to keep him inconsolable; and his only child, Frank, being no more than five years old and healthy, need scarcely be viewed as a domestic drawback; indeed, certain spinsters treated the boy with a somewhat demonstrative affection, but these ladies were obviously not in their teens.

Mr. Ballantyne meanwhile, though mildly courteous to all, had not singled out any one for avowed preference. Possibly he liked Miss Edith Sims, a doctor's daughter, a bold equestrian, a first-rate croquet player; she hoped so sincerely, for she had unbecoming carroty hair and freckles; possibly he liked Lucy Charlmont, but she had never given the chance a thought. Of Miss Charlmont, whom he had seen twice, and both times exclusively on business, he stood in perceptible awe.

Catherine, finding nothing to object to in the draft, returned it to Mr. Ballantyne with her full assent. Then tea was brought in, and Mr. Ballantyne was asked to stay. His aptitude for carrying cups and plates, recognised and admired in other circles, here remained in abeyance; Miss Charlmont adhering to the old fashion of people sitting round the tea-table at tea no less formally than round the dining-table at dinner.

A plan for a picnic having been set on foot by the Gawkins Drums, Lucy had been invited, and had accepted before Jane's engagement was announced. So now Mr. Ballantyne mentioned the picnic, taking for granted that Lucy would join, and empowered by the projectors to ask her sisters also; Jane brightened at the proposal, being secretly charmed at a prospect of appearing amongst her familiar associates as mistress elect of Orpingham Place; but Catherine demurred,—

'Thank you, Mr. Ballantyne; I will call myself and thank Mrs. Drum, but Mr. Durham might object, and I will stay at home with my sister. No doubt we shall find future opportunities of all meeting.'

'Dear me!' cried Jane; 'Mr. Durham isn't Bluebeard;[86] or, if he is, I had better get a little fun first. My compliments, please, and I shall be too glad to come.'

'Oh, Jane!' remonstrated Miss Charlmont; but it was a hopeless remonstrance. Jane, once bent on amusement, was not to be deterred by doubtful questions of propriety; and the elder sister, mortified, but more anxious for the offender's credit than for her own dignity, changed her mind perforce, and, with a sigh, accepted the invitation. If Jane was determined to go, she had better go under a middle-aged sister's eye; but the party promised to be a large one, including various strange gentlemen, and Catherine honestly judged it objectionable.

Jane, however, was overflowing with glee, and questioned Mr. Ballantyne energetically as to who were coming. When he was gone she held forth to her sisters,—

'That hideous Edith Sims, of course she will ride over on Brunette, to show her figure and her bridle hand. I shall wear pink, and sit next her to bring out her freckles. I've not forgotten her telling people I had no fortune. Don't you see she's trying to hook Mr. Ballantyne? you heard him say she has been consulting him about something or other. Let's drive Mr. Ballantyne over in our carriage, and the baby can perch on the box.'

Lucy said, 'Nonsense, Jane; Mr. Ballantyne has his own dog-cart,[87] and he is tiresome enough without keeping him all to ourselves.'

And Catherine added, this time peremptorily, 'My dear, that is not to be thought of; I could not justify it to Mr. Durham. Either you will drive over with Lucy and me, and any other person I may select, or you must find a carriage for yourself, as I shall not go to the picnic.'

Chapter 13.

The environs of Brompton-on-Sea were rich in spots adapted to picnics, and the Gawkins Drums had chosen the very prettiest of these eligible spots. Rocky Drumble,[88] a green glen of the floweriest, but with fragments of rock showing here and there, possessed an echo point and a dripping well: it was, moreover, accredited by popular tradition with a love-legend, and, on the same authority, with a ghost for moonlight nights. Rocky Drumble was threaded from end to end by a stream which nourished watercresses; at one season its banks produced wild strawberries, at another nuts, sometimes mushrooms. All the year round the glen was frequented by song-birds; not seldom a squirrel would scamper up a tree, or a rabbit sit upright on the turf, winking his nose. Rocky Drumble on a sunny summer-day was a bower of cool shade, and of a silence heightened, not broken, by sounds of birds and of water, the stream at hand, the sea not far off; a bower of sun-chequered shade, breaths of wind every moment shifting the shadows, and the sun making its way in, now here, now there, with an endless, monotonous changeableness.

On such a day the Charlmonts drove to their rendezvous in Rocky Drumble. The carriage held four inside; Miss Drum and Catherine sitting forward, with Lucy and Jane opposite. On the box beside the driver perched little Frank Ballantyne, very chatty and merry at first; but to be taken inside and let fall asleep when, as was foreseen, he should grow tired. The child had set his heart on going to the picnic, and good Miss Drum had promised to take care of him—Miss Drum nominally, Lucy by secret understanding, for the relief of her old friend.

Miss Drum wore a drawn silk bonnet, which had much in common with the awning of a bathing-machine. Catherine surmounted her inevitable cap by a broad-brimmed brown straw hat. Lucy wore a similar hat without any cap under it, but looked, in fact, the elder of the two. Jane, who never sacrificed complexion to fashion, also appeared in a shady hat, dove-coloured, trimmed with green leaves, under which she produced a sort of apple-blossom effect, in a cloud of pink muslin over white, and white *appliqué* again over the pink. Catherine had wished her to dress soberly, but Jane had no notion of obscuring her beauties. She had bargained with Mr. Durham that he was not to come down to Brompton-on-Sea till the afternoon before the wedding; and when he looked hurt at her urgency, had assumed an air at once affectionate and reserved, assuring him that this course seemed to her due to the delicacy of their mutual relations. Five days were still wanting to the wedding-day, George was not yet inalienably at her elbow, and no moment could appear more favourable for enjoyment. Surely if a skeleton promised to preside at the next banquet, this present feast was all the more to be relished: for though, according to Jane's definition, George was Orpingham Place, she would certainly have entered upon Orpingham Place with added zest had it not entailed George.

Miss Charlmont had delayed starting till the very last moment, not wishing to make more of the picnic than could be helped; and when she with her party reached the Drumble, they found their friends already on the spot. The last-comers were welcomed with a good deal of friendly bustle, and half-a-dozen gentlemen, in scarcely more than as many minutes, were presented to Jane by genial little Mrs. Drum, who had never seen her before, and was charmed at first sight. Jane, happily for Catherine's peace of mind, assumed an air of dignity in unison with her distinguished prospects: she was gracious rather than coquettish—gracious to all, but flattering to none; a change from former days, when her manner used to savour of coaxing. Edith Sims had ridden over on Brunette, and Jane, keeping her word as to sitting next her, produced the desired effect.

The Charlmonts coming late, every one was ready for luncheon on their arrival, and no strolling was permitted before the meal. As to the luncheon, it included everything usual and nothing unusual, and most of the company consuming it displayed fine, healthy appetites. Great attention was paid to Jane, who was beyond all comparison the best-looking woman present; whilst two or three individuals made mistakes between Catherine and Lucy, as to which was Miss Charlmont.

Poor Lucy! she had seldom felt more heavy-hearted than now, as she sat talking and laughing. She felt herself getting more and more worn-looking as she talked and laughed on, getting visibly older and more faded. How she wished that Frank, who had fallen asleep on a plaid after stuffing unknown sweets into his system—how she wished that Frank would wake and become troublesome, to give her some occupation less intolerable than 'grinning and bearing!'

Luncheon over, the party broke up, splitting into twos and threes, and scattering themselves here and there through the Drumble. Miss Charlmont attaching herself doggedly to Jane, found herself clambering up and down banks and stony excrescences in company with a very young Viscount and his tutor: as she clambered exasperation waxed within her at the futility of the young men's conversation and the complacency of Jane's rejoinders; certainly, had any one been studying Catherine's face (which nobody was), he would have beheld an unwonted aspect at a picnic.

Miss Drum, ostentatiously aged because in company with her brother and her bride, had chosen before luncheon was well over to wrap herself up very warmly, and ensconce herself for an avowed nap inside one of the flys. 'You can call me for tea,' she observed to Lucy; 'and when Frank tires you, you can leave him in the carriage with me.' But Frank was Lucy's one resource: minding him served as an excuse for not joining Mr. Drum, who joked, or Mr. Ballantyne, who covertly stared at her, or Edith Sims, who lingering near Mr. Ballantyne talked of horses, or any other person whose conversation was more tedious than silence.

When Frank woke, he recollected that nurse had told him strawberries grew in the Drumble; a fact grasped by him without the drawback of any particular season. Off he started in quest of strawberries, and Lucy zealously started in his wake, not deeming it necessary to undeceive him. The little fellow wandered and peered about diligently awhile after imaginary strawberries; failing these, he suddenly clamoured for a game at hide-and-seek: he would hide, and Lucy must not look.

They were now among the main fragments of rock found in the Drumble, out of sight of their companions. Lucy had scarcely shut her eyes as desired, when a shout of delight made her open them still more quickly, in time to see Frank scampering, as fast as his short legs would carry him, after a scampering rabbit. He was running—she recollected it in an instant—headlong towards the stream, and was already some yards from her. She called after him, but he did not turn, only cried out some unintelligible answer in his babyish treble. Fear lent her speed; she bounded after him, clearing huge stones and brushwood with instinctive accuracy. She caught at his frock—missed it—caught at it again—barely grasped it—and fell, throwing him also down in her fall. She fell on stones and brambles, bruising and scratching herself severely: but the child was safe, and she knew it, before she fainted away, whilst even in fainting her hand remained tightly clenched on his frock.

Frank's frightened cries soon brought friends to their assistance. Lucy, still insensible, was lifted on to smooth turf, and then sprinkled with water till she came to herself. In few words, for she felt giddy and hysterical but was resolute not to give way, she accounted for the accident, blaming herself for having carelessly let the child run into danger. It was impossible for any carriage to drive so far along the Drumble, so she had to take some one's arm to steady her in walking to meet the fly. Mr. Ballantyne, as pale as a sheet, offered his arm; but she preferred Mr. Drum's, and leaned heavily on it for support.

Lucy was soon safe in the fly by Miss Drum's side, whose nap was brought to a sudden end, and who, waking scared and fidgety, was disposed to lay blame on every one impartially, beginning with herself, and ending, in a tempered form, with Lucy. The sufferer thus disposed of, and packed for transmission home, the remaining picnickers, influenced by Mrs. Drum's obvious bias, declined to linger for rustic tea or other pleasures, and elected then and there to return to their several destinations. The party mustered round the carriages ready to take their seats: but where were Catherine and Jane, Viscount and tutor? Shouting was tried, whistling was tried, 'Cooee' was tried by amateur Australians for the nonce:[89] all in vain. At last Dr. Sims stepped into the fly with Lucy, promising to see her safe home; Miss Drum, smelling-bottle in hand, sat sternly beside her; Frank, after undergoing a paternal box on the ear, was degraded from the coachman's box to the back seat, opposite the old lady, who turned towards him the aspect as of an ogress: and thus the first carriage started, with Edith reining in Brunette beside it. The others followed without much delay, one carriage being left for the truants; and its driver charged to explain, if possible without alarming the sisters, what had happened to cut short the picnic.

Chapter 14.

The day before the wedding Lucy announced that she still felt too much bruised and shaken to make one of the party, either at church or at breakfast. Neither sister contradicted her: Catherine, because she thought the excuse valid; Jane, because Lucy, not having yet lost the traces of her accident, must have made but a sorry bridesmaid: and, as Jane truly observed, there were enough without her, for her defection still left a bevy of eight bridesmaids in capital working order.

Brompton-on-Sea possessed only one hotel of any pretensions,—'The Duke's Head,' so designated in memory of that solitary Royal Duke who had once made brief sojourn beneath its roof. He found it a simple inn, bearing the name and sign of 'The Three Mermaids;' the mermaids appearing in paint as young persons, with yellow hair and combs, and faces of a type which failed to account for their uninterrupted self-ogling in hand-mirrors; tails were shadowily indicated beneath waves of deepest blue. After the august visit this signboard was superseded by one representing the Duke as a gentleman of inane aspect, pointing towards nothing discoverable; and this work of art, in its turn, gave place to a simple inscription, 'The Duke's Head Hotel.'

Call it by what name you would, it was as snug a house of entertainment as rational man or reasonable beast need desire, with odd little rooms opening out of larger rooms and off staircases; the only trace now visible of the Royal Duke's sojourn (beyond the bare inscription of his title) being Royal Sentries in coloured pasteboard effigy, the size of life, posted on certain landings and at certain entrances. All the windowsills bore green boxes of flowering plants, whence a sweet smell, mostly of mignonette, made its way within doors. The best apartments looked into a square courtyard, turfed along three sides, and frequented by pigeons; and the pigeon-house, standing in a turfy corner, was topped by a bright silvered ball.

The landlord of the 'Duke's Head,' a thin, tallowy-complexioned man, with a manner which might also be described as unpleasantly oily or tallowy, was in a bustle that same day, and all his household was bustling around him: for not merely had the 'Duke's Head' undertaken to furnish the Durham-Charlmont wedding-breakfast with richness and elegance, but the bridegroom elect, whom report endowed with a pocketful of plums, the great Mr. Durham himself, with sundry fashionable friends, was coming down to Brompton-on-Sea by the 5.30 train, and would put up for one night at the 'Duke's Head.' The waiters donned their whitest neckcloths, the waitresses their pinkest caps; the landlady, in crimson gown and gold chain, loomed like a local Mayor; the landlord shone, as it were, snuffed and trimmed: never, since the era of that actual Royal Duke, had the 'Duke's Head' smiled such a welcome.

Mr. Durham, stepping out of the carriage on to the railway platform, and followed by Alan Hartley, Stella, and Arthur Tresham, indulged hopes that Jane might be there to meet him, and was disappointed. Not that the matter had undergone no discussion. Miss Charlmont, that unavoidable drive home from the picnic with a young Viscount and a tutor for *vis-à-*

vis[90] still rankling in her mind, had said, 'My dear, there would be no impropriety in our meeting George at the Station, and he would certainly be gratified.' But Jane had answered, 'Dear me, sister! George will keep, and I've not a moment to spare; only don't stay at home for me.'

So no one met Mr. Durham. But when he presented himself at the private house on the Esplanade, Jane showed herself all smiling welcome, and made him quite happy by her pretty ways. True, she insisted on his not spending the evening with her; but she hinted so tenderly at such restrictions vanishing on the morrow, and so modestly at remarks people might make if he did stay, that he was compelled to yield the point and depart in great admiration of her reserve, though he could not help recollecting that his first wooing had progressed and prospered without any such amazing proprieties. But then the mother of Everilda Stella had seen the light in a second-floor back room at Gateshead, and had married out of a circle where polite forms were not in the ascendant; whereas Jane Charlmont looked like a Duchess, or an Angel, or Queen Venus herself, and was altogether a different person. So Mr. Durham, discomfited, but acquiescent, retreated to the 'Duke's Head,' and there consoled himself with more turtle-soup and crusty old port than Dr. Tyke would have sanctioned. Unfortunately Dr. and Mrs. Tyke were not coming down till the latest train that night from London, so Mr. Durham gorged unrebuked. He had seen Lucy, and taken rather a fancy to her, in spite of her blemished face, and had pressed her to visit Orpingham Place as soon as ever he and Jane should have returned from the Continent. He preferred Lucy to Catherine, with whom he never felt quite at ease; she was so decided and self-possessed, and so much better bred than himself. Not that Backbone Durham admitted this last point of superiority; he did not acknowledge, but he winced under it. Lucy on her side had found him better than his photograph; and that was something.

After tea she was lying alone on the drawingroom sofa in the pleasant summer twilight; alone, because her sisters were busy over Jane's matters upstairs; alone with her own thoughts. She was thinking of very old days, and of days not so old and much more full of interest. She tried to think of Jane and her prospects; but against her will Alan Hartley's image intruded itself on her reverie, and she could not banish it. She knew from Mr. Durham that he had come down for the wedding; she foresaw that they must meet, and shrank from the ordeal, even whilst she wondered how he would behave and how she herself should behave. Alone, and in the half darkness, she burned with shamefaced dread of her own possible weakness, and mortified self-love wrung tears from her eyes as she inwardly prayed for help.

The door opened, the maid announced Mr. and Mrs. Hartley.

Lucy, startled, would have risen to receive them, but Stella was too quick for her, and seizing both her hands, pressed her gently backwards on the sofa. 'Dear Miss Charlmont, you must not make a stranger of me, and my husband is an old friend. Mayn't I call you Lucy?'

So this was Alan's wife, this little, winning woman, still almost a child; this winning woman, who had won the only man Lucy ever cared for. It cost Lucy an effort to answer, and to make her welcome by her name of Stella.

Then Alan came forward and shook hands, looking cordial and handsome, with that kind tone of voice and tenderness of manner which had deceived poor Lucy once, but must never deceive her again. He began talking of their pleasant acquaintanceship in days of yore, of amusements they had shared, of things done together, and things spoken and not forgotten; it required the proof positive of Stella seated there smiling in her hat and scarlet feather, and with the wedding-ring on her small hand, to show even now that Alan only meant friendliness, when he might seem to mean so much more.

Lucy revolted under the fascination of his manner; feeling angry with herself that he still could wield power over her fancy, and angry a little with him for having made himself so much to her and no more. She insisted on leaving the sofa, rang the bell for a second edition of tea, and sent up the visitors' names to her sisters. When they came down she turned as much shoulder as good breeding tolerated towards Alan, and devoted all the attention she could command to Stella. Soon the two were laughing together over some feminine little bit of fun; then Lucy brought out an intricate piece of tatting, which, when completed, was to find its way to Notting Hill—the antimacassar of Mr. Durham's first visit there being, in fact, her handiwork; and, lastly, Lucy, once more for the moment with pretty pink cheeks and brightened eyes, convoyed her new friend upstairs to inspect Jane's bridal dress, white satin, under Honiton lace.[91]

When the visit was over, and Lucy safe in the privacy of her own room, a sigh of relief escaped her, followed by a sentiment of deep thankfulness; she had met Alan again, and he had disappointed her. Yes, the spectre which had haunted her for weeks past had, at length, been brought face to face and had vanished. Perhaps surprise at his marriage had magnified her apparent disappointment, perhaps dread of continuing to love another woman's husband had imparted a morbid and unreal sensitiveness to her feelings; be this as it might, she had now seen Alan again, and had felt irritated by the very manner that used to charm. In the revulsion of her feelings she was almost ready to deem herself fortunate and Stella pitiable.

She felt excited, exalted, triumphant rather than happy; a little pained, and, withal, very glad. Life seemed to glow within her, her blood to course faster and fuller, her heart to throb, lightened of a load. Recollections which she had not dared face alone, Mr. Hartley, by recalling, had stripped of their dangerous charm; had stripped of the tenderness she had dreaded, and the sting under which she had writhed; for he was the same, yet not the same. Now, for the first time, she suspected him not indeed of hollowness, but of shallowness.

She threw open her window to the glorious August moon and stars, and, leaning out, drank deep of the cool night air. She ceased to think of persons, of events, of feelings; her whole heart swelled, and became uplifted with a thankfulness altogether new to her, profound, transporting. When at length she slept, it was with moist eyes and smiling lips.

Chapter 15.

The wedding was over. Jane might have looked still prettier but for an un-mistakable expression of gratified vanity; Mr. Durham might have borne himself still more pompously but for a deep-seated wordless conviction, that his bride and her family looked down upon him. Months of scheming and weeks of fuss had ended in a marriage, to which the one party brought nei-ther refinement nor tact, and the other neither respect nor affection.

Wedding guests, however, do not assemble to witness exhibitions of re-spect or affection, and may well dispense with tact and refinement when del-icacies not in season are provided; therefore, the party on the Esplanade waxed gay as befitted the occasion, and expressed itself in toasts of highly improbable import.

The going off was, perhaps, the least successful point of the show. Catherine viewed flinging shoes as superstitious, Jane as vulgar; therefore no shoes were to be flung. Mr. Durham might have made head against 'super-stitious,' but dared not brave 'vulgar;' so he kept to himself the fact that he should hardly feel thoroughly married without a tributary shoe, and meanly echoed Jane's scorn. But Stella, who knew her father's genuine sentiment, chose to ignore 'superstition' and 'vulgarity' alike; so, at the last moment, she snatched off her own slipper, and dexterously hurled it over the carriage, to Jane's disgust (no love was lost between the two young ladies), and to Mr. Durham's inward satisfaction.

Lucy had not joined the wedding party, not caring overmuch to see Jane marry the man who served her as a butt; but she peeped wistfully at the going off, with forebodings in the heart, which turned naturally into prayers, for the ill-matched couple. In the evening, however, when many of the party had returned to London, the few real friends and familiar acquaintances who reassembled as Miss Charlmont's guests found Lucy in the drawing-room, wrapped up in something gauzily becoming to indicate that she had been ill, and looking thin under her wraps.

In Miss Charlmont's idea a wedding-party should be at once mirthful and grave, neither dull nor frivolous. Dancing and cards were frivolous, conver-sation might prove full; games were all frivolous except chess, which, being exclusive, favoured general dulness. These points she had impressed several times on Lucy, who was suspected of an inopportune hankering after bagatelle; and who now sat in the snuggest corner of the sofa, feeling shy, and at a loss what topic to start that should appear neither dull nor frivolous.

Dr. Tyke relieved her by turning her embarrassment into a fresh channel: what had she been doing to make herself 'look like a turnip-ghost before its candle is lighted?'

'My dear Lucy!' cried Mrs. Tyke, loud enough for everybody to hear her, 'you really do look dreadful, as if you were moped to death. You had much better come with the Doctor and me to the Lakes. Now I beg you to say yes, and come.'

Alan heard with good-natured concern; Arthur Tresham heard as if he heard not. But the first greeting had been very cordial between him and Lucy, and he had not seemed to remark her faded face.

'Yes,' resumed Dr. Tyke. 'Now that's settled. You pack up to-night and start with us to-morrow, and you shall be doctored with the cream of drugs for nothing.'

But Lucy said the plan was preposterous, and she felt old and lazy.

Mrs. Tyke caught her up: 'Old? my dear child! and I feeling young to this day!'

And the Doctor added: 'Why not be preposterous and happy? "*Quel che piace giova*,"[92] as our sunny neighbours say. Besides, your excuses are incredible: "Not at home," as the snail answered to the woodpecker's rap.'

Lucy laughed, but stood firm; Catherine protesting that she should please herself. At last a compromise was struck: Lucy, on her cousins' return from their tour, should go to Notting Hill, and winter there if the change did her good. 'If not,' said she, wearily, 'I shall come home again, to be nursed by Catherine.'

'If not,' said Dr. Tyke, gravely for once, 'we may think about our all seeing Naples together.'[93]

Edith Sims, her hair and complexion toned down by candlelight, sat wishing Mr. Ballantyne would come and talk to her; and Mr. Ballantyne, unmindful of Edith at the other end of the room, sat making up his mind. Before the accident in the Drumble he had thought of Lucy with a certain distinction, since that accident he had felt uncomfortably in her debt, and now he sat reflecting that, once gone for the winter, she might be gone for good so far as himself was concerned. She was nice-looking and amiable; she was tender towards little motherless Frank; her fortune stood above rather than below what he had proposed to himself in a second wife:—if Edith could have read his thoughts, she would have smiled less complacently when at last he crossed over to talk to her of Brunette and investments, and when later still he handed her in to supper. As it was, candlelight and content became her, and she looked her best.

Mrs. Gawkins Drum, beaming with good will, and harmonious in silver-grey moire[94] under old point lace, contrasted favourably with her angular sister-in-law, whose strict truthfulness forbade her looking congratulatory: for now that she had seen the 'elegant man of talent' of her previsions, she could not but think that Jane had married his money-bags rather than himself: therefore Miss Drum looked severe, and when viewed in the light of a wedding guest, ominous.

Catherine, no less conscientious than her old friend, took an opposite line, and laboured her very utmost to hide mortification and misgivings, and to show forth that cheerful hospitality which befitted the occasion when contemplated from an ideal point of view; but ease was not amongst her natural gifts, and she failed to acquire it on the spur of an uneasy moment. 'Manners make the Man,' 'Morals make the Man,' kept running obstinately in her head, and she could not fit Mr. Durham to either sentence. In all Brompton-on-Sea there was no heavier heart that night than Catherine Charlmont's.

Chapter 16.

November had come, the Tykes were settled at home again, and Lucy Charlmont sat in a railway-carriage on her way from Brompton-on-Sea to Notting Hill. Wrapped up in furs, and with a novel open on her lap, she looked very snug in her corner; she looked, moreover, plumper and brighter than at Jane's wedding-party. But her expression of unmistakable amusement was not derived from the novel lying unread in her lap: it had its source in recollections of Mr. Ballantyne, who had made her an offer the day before, and who had obviously been taken aback when she rejected his suit. All her proneness to bring herself in the wrong could not make her fear that she had even for one moment said or done, looked or thought, what ought to have misled him: therefore conscience felt at ease, and the comic side of his demeanour remained to amuse her, despite a decorous wish to feel sorry for him. He had looked so particularly unimpulsive in the act of proposing, and then had appeared so much more disconcerted than grieved at her positive 'No,' and had hinted so broadly that he hoped she would not talk about his offer, that she could not imagine the matter very serious to him: and if not to him assuredly to nobody else. 'I dare say it will be Edith Sims at last,' mused she, and wished them both well.

A year earlier his offer might have been a matter of mere indifference to her, but not now; for her birthday was just over, and it was gratifying to find herself not obsolete even at thirty. This birthday had loomed before her threateningly for months past, but now it was over; and it became a sensible relief to feel and look at thirty very much as she had felt and looked at twenty-nine. Her mirror bore witness to no glaring accession of age having come upon her in a single night. 'After all,' she mused, 'life isn't over at thirty.' Her thoughts flew before her to Notting Hill; if they dwelt on any one in especial, it was not on Alan Hartley.

Not on Alan Hartley, though she foresaw that they must meet frequently for he and Stella were at Kensington again, planning to stay there over Christmas. Stella she rather liked than disliked; and as she no longer deemed her lot enviable, to see more of her would be no grievance. Mr. Tresham also was in London, and likely to remain there; for since his return from the East he had taken himself to task for idleness, and had joined a band of good men in an effort to visit and relieve the East-end poor in their squalid homes. His hobby happened to be emigration, but he did not ride his hobby rough-shod over his destitute neighbours. He was in London hard at work, and by no means faring sumptuously every day; but glad sometimes to get a mouthful of pure night air and of something more substantial at Notting Hill. He and Lucy had not merely renewed acquaintance at the wedding-party, but had met more than once afterwards during a week's holiday he gave himself at the seaside; had met on the beach, or in country lanes, or down in some of the many drumbles.[95] They had botanised in company; and one day had captured a cuttle-fish[96] together, which Lucy insisted on putting safe back into the sea before they turned homewards. They had talked of what grew at their feet or lay before their eyes; but neither of them had alluded to those old days when first they had known and liked each other, though they obviously liked each other still.

Lucy, her thoughts running on some one who was not Alan, would have made a very pretty picture. A sort of latent smile pervaded her features without deranging them, and her eyes, gazing out at the dreary autumn branches, looked absent and soft; soft, tender, and pleased, though with a wistful expression through all.

The short, winter-like day had darkened by the time London bridge was reached. Lucy stepped on to the platform in hopes of being claimed by Dr. Tyke's man; but no such functionary appeared, neither was the fat coachman discernible along the line of vehicles awaiting occupants. It was the first time Lucy had arrived in London without being either accompanied or met at the Station, and the novel position made her feel shy and a little nervous; so she was glad to stand unobtrusively against a wall, whilst more enterprising individuals found or missed their luggage. She preferred waiting, and she had to wait whilst passengers craned their necks, elbowed their neighbours, blundered, bawled, worried the Company's servants, and found everything correct after all. At last the huge mass of luggage dwindled to three boxes, one carpet-bag, and one hamper, which were Lucy's own; and which, with herself, a porter consigned to a cab. Thus ended her anxieties.

From London Bridge to Notting Hill the cabman of course knew his way, but in the mazes of Notting Hill he appealed to his fare for guidance. Lucy informed him that Appletrees House stood in its own large garden, and was sure to be well lighted up; and that it lay somewhere to the left, up a steep-ish hill. A few wrong turnings first made and next retrieved, a few lucky guesses, brought them to a garden-wall, which a passing postman told them belonged to Dr. Tyke's premises. Lucy thrust her head out, and thought it all looked very like, except that the house itself stood enveloped in grim dark-ness; she had never noticed it look so dark before: could it be that she had been forgotten and every one had gone out?

They drove round the little sweep and knocked; waited, and knocked again. It was not till the grumbling cabman had knocked loud and long a third time that the door was opened by a crying maid-servant, who admitted Lucy into the unlighted hall with the explanation: O Miss, Miss, master has had a fit, and mistress is taking on so you can hear her all over the place. At the same instant a peal of screaming, hysterical laughter rang through the house.

Without waiting for a candle, Lucy ran stumbling up the broad staircase, guided at once by her familiarity with the house and by her cousin's screams. On the second-floor landing one door stood open revealing light at last, and Lucy ran straight in amongst the lights and the people. For a moment she was dazzled, and distinguished nothing clearly: in another moment she saw and understood all. Arthur Tresham and a strange gentleman were standing pale and silent at the fireplace, an old servant, stooping over the pillows, was busied in some noiseless way, and Mrs. Tyke had flung herself face down-wards on the bed beside her husband.

Her husband? No, not her husband any longer, for she was a widow.

Chapter 17.

A week of darkened windows, of condolence-cards and hushed inquiries, of voices and faces saddened, of footsteps treading softly on one landing. A week of many tears and quiet sorrow; of many words, for in some persons grief speaks; and of half-silent sympathy, for in some even sympathy is silent. A week wherein to weigh this world and find it wanting, wherein also to re-alise the far more exceeding weight of the other. A week begun with the hope whose blossom goes up as dust, and ending with the sure and certain hope of the resurrection.

In goods and chattels, Mrs. Tyke remained none the poorer for her husband's death. He had left almost everything to her and absolutely at her disposal, well knowing that their old faithful servants were no less dear to her than to himself, and having on his side no poor relations to provide for. His nephew Alan Hartley, and Mr. Tresham, were appointed his executors. Alan the good-natured, addicted to shirking trouble in general, consistently shirked this official trouble in particular. Arthur Tresham did what little work there was to do, and did it in such a way as veiled his friend's shortcomings. Mrs. Tyke, with a life-long habit of leaning on some one, came, as a matter of course, to lean on him, and appealed to him as to all sorts of details, without once considering whether the time he devoted to her service was reclaimed out of his work, or leisure, or rest; he best knew, and the knowledge remained with him. Alan, though sincerely sorry for his uncle's death, cut private jokes with Stella about his co-executor's frequent visits to Appletrees House, and ignored the shortcomings which entailed their necessity.

Mrs. Tyke, in her bereavement, clung to Lucy, and was thoroughly amiable and helpless. She would sit for hours over the fire, talking and crying her eyes and her nose red, whilst Lucy wrote her letters, or grappled with her bills. Then they would both grow sleepy, and doze off in opposite chimney-corners. So the maid might find them when she brought up tea, or so Arthur when he dropped in on business, or possibly on pleasure. Mrs. Tyke would sometimes merely open sleepy eyes, shake hands, and doze off again; but Lucy would sit up wide awake in a moment, ready to listen to all his long stories about his poor people. Soon he took to making things for them, which he carried away in his pocket, or, when too bulky for his pocket, in a parcel under his arm. At last it happened, that they began talking of old days, before he went to the East, and then each found that the other remembered a great deal about those old days. So gradually it came to pass that, from looking back together, they took also to looking forward together.

Lucy's courtship was most prosaic. Old women's flannel and old men's rheumatism alternated with some more usual details of love-making, and the exchange of rings was avowedly an exchange of old rings. Arthur presented Lucy with his mother's wedding-guard; but Lucy gave him a fine diamond solitaire which had been her father's, and the romantic corner of her heart was gratified by the inequality of the gifts. She would have preferred a little more romance certainly on his side; if not less sense, at least more sentiment; something reasonable enough to be relied upon, yet unreasonable enough to be flattering. 'But one cannot have everything,' she reflected, meekly remembering her own thirty years; and she felt what a deep resting place she had found in Arthur's trusty heart, and how shallow a grace had been the flattering charm of Alan's manner. Till, weighing her second love against her first, tears, at once proud and humble, filled her eyes, and 'one cannot have everything' was forgotten in 'I can never give him back half enough.'

After the exchange of rings, she announced her engagement to Catherine and Mrs. Tyke; to Jane also and Mr. Durham in few words; and as all business connected with Dr. Tyke's will was already satisfactorily settled, and Appletrees House about to pass into fresh hands, she prepared to return home. Mrs. Tyke, too purposeless to be abandoned to her own resources, begged an invitation to Brompton-on-Sea, and received a cordial welcome down from both sisters. Arthur was to remain at work in London till after Easter; and then to join his friends at the seaside, claim his bride, and take her away to spend their honeymoon beside that beautiful blue Bosphorus[97] which had not made him forget her.

If there was a romantic moment in their courtship, it was the moment of parting at the noisy, dirty, crowded railway-station, when Arthur terrified Lucy, to her great delight, by standing on the carriage-step, and holding her hand locked fast in his own, an instant after the train had started.

Chapter 18.

A short chapter makes fitting close to a short story.

In mid May, on a morning which set forth the perfection either of sunny spring warmth or of breezy summer freshness, Arthur Tresham and Lucy Charlmont took each other for better for worse, till death should them part. Mr. Gawkins Drum gave away the bride; Miss Drum appeared auspicious as a rainbow; Catherine glowed and expanded with unselfish happiness; Mrs. Gawkins Drum pronounced the bride graceful, elegant, but old-looking; Mr. Durham contributed a costly wedding present, accompanied by a speech both ostentatious and affectionate; Jane displayed herself a little disdainful, a little cross, and supremely handsome; Alan and Stella—there was a young Alan now, a comical little fright, more like mother than father—Alan and Stella seemed to enjoy their friend's wedding as light-heartedly as they had enjoyed their own. No tears were shed, no stereotyped hypocrisies uttered, no shoes flung; this time a true man and a true woman who loved and honoured each other, and whom no man should put asunder, were joined together; and thus the case did not lend itself to any tribute of lies, miscalled white.

Four months after their marriage Mr. Tresham was hard at work again in London among his East-end poor; while Lucy, taking a day's holiday at Brompton-on-Sea, sat in the old familiar drawing-room, Catherine's exclusively now. She had returned from the East blooming, vigorous, full of gentle fun and kindly happiness: so happy, that she would not have exchanged her present lot for aught except her own future; so happy, that it saddened her to believe Catherine less happy than herself.

The two sisters sat at the open window, alike yet unlike: the elder handsome, resolute, composed; the younger with the old wistful expression in her tender beautiful eyes. They had talked of Jane, who, though not dissatisfied with her lot, too obviously despised her husband; once lately, she had written of him as the 'habitation-tax' paid for Orpingham Place: of Jane, who was too worldly either to keep right in the spirit, or go wrong in the letter. They had talked, and they had fallen silent; for Catherine, who loved no one on earth as she loved her frivolous sister, could best bear in silence the sting of shame and grief for her sake.

Full in view of the drawing-room windows spread the sea, beautiful, strong, resistless, murmuring; the sea which had cast a burden on Catherine's life, and from which she now never meant to absent herself; the sea from which Lucy had fled in the paroxysm of her nervous misery.

At last Lucy spoke again very earnestly,—'Oh, Catherine, I cannot bear to be so happy when I think of you! If only you, too, had a future.'

Catherine leaned over her happy sister and gave her one kiss, a rare sign with her of affectionate emotion. Then she turned to face the open sky and sea.—'My dear,' she answered, whilst her eyes gazed beyond clouds and waves, and rested on one narrow streak of sunlight which glowed at the horizon,—'My dear, my future seems further off than yours; but I certainly have a future, and I can wait.'

The Lost Titian

First published in the American magazine *The Crayon* in 1856, this story is regarded as perhaps Rossetti's most successful, for it so well evokes artistic rivalries in Renaissance Italy; it is "a brilliant sketch of artist life in Venice," wrote the reviewer in the *London Quarterly Review* (36 [April 1871]: 259). The story appears as the second selection in *Commonplace, and Other Short Stories*. The enigmatic epigraph from Scott is elusive; but the common source is in Shakespeare, *As You Like It*, 5.4.94 ff. Titian (ca. 1490–1576), the celebrated Venetian painter, greatly influenced subsequent artists by his use of color.

The Lost Titian

"A lie with a circumstance."
—Walter Scott

The last touch was laid on. The great painter stood opposite the masterpiece of the period; the masterpiece of his life.

Nothing remained to be added. The orange drapery was perfect in its fruit-like intensity of hue; each vine-leaf was curved, each tendril twisted, as if fanned by the soft south wind; the sunshine brooded drowsily upon every dell and swelling upland: but a tenfold drowsiness slept in the cedar shadows. Look a moment, and those cymbals must clash, that panther bound forward; draw nearer, and the songs of those ripe, winy lips must become audible.

The achievement of his life glowed upon the easel, and Titian was satisfied.

Beside him, witnesses of his triumph, stood his two friends—Gianni the successful, and Giannuccione the universal disappointment.

Gianni ranked second in Venice; second in most things, but in nothing first. His *colorito*[98] paled only before that of his illustrious rival, whose supremacy, however, he ostentatiously asserted. So in other matters. Only the renowned Messer Cecchino was a more sonorous singer; only fire-eating Prince Barbuto a better swordsman; only Arrigo il Biondo a finer dancer or more sculpturesque beauty; even Caterina Suprema, in that contest of gallantry which has been celebrated by so many pens and pencils, though she awarded the role of honour to Matteo Grande, the wit, yet plucked off a leaf for the all but victor Gianni.

A step behind him lounged Giannuccione, who had promised everything and fulfilled nothing. At the appearance of his first picture—"Venus whipping Cupid with feathers plucked from his own wing"—Venice rang with his praises, and Titian foreboded a rival: but when, year after year, his works appeared still lazily imperfect, though always all but perfect, Venice subsided into apathetic silence, and Titian felt that no successor to his throne had as yet achieved the purple.

So these two stood with the great master in the hour of his triumph: Gianni loud, and Giannuccione hearty, in his applauses.

Only these two stood with him: as yet Venice at large knew not what her favourite had produced. It was, indeed, rumoured, that Titian had long been at work on a painting which he himself accounted his masterpiece, but its subject was a secret; and while some spoke of it as an undoubted *Vintage of red grapes,* others maintained it to be a *Dance of wood-nymphs;* while one old gossip whispered that, whatever else the painting might contain, she knew whose sunset-coloured tresses and white brow would figure in the foreground. But the general ignorance mattered little; for, though words might have named the theme, no words could have described a picture which combined the softness of a dove's breast with the intensity of an October sunset: a picture of which the light almost warmed, and the fruit actually bloomed and tempted.

Titian gazed upon his work, and was satisfied: Giannuccione gazed upon his friend's work, and was satisfied: only Gianni gazed upon his friend and upon his work, and was enviously dissatisfied.

'To-morrow,' said Titian,—'to-morrow Venice shall behold what she has long honoured by her curiosity. To-morrow, with music and festivity, the unknown shall be unveiled; and you, my friends, shall withdraw the curtain.'

The two friends assented.

'To-morrow,' he continued, half amused, half thoughtful, 'I know whose white brows will be knit, and whose red lips will pout. Well, they shall have their turn: but blue eyes are not always in season; hazel eyes, like hazel nuts, have their season also.'

'True,' chimed the chorus.

'But to-night,' he pursued, 'let us devote the hours to sacred friendship. Let us with songs and bumpers rehearse to-morrow's festivities, and let your congratulations forestall its triumphs.'

'Yes, *evviva!*' returned the chorus, briskly; and again '*evviva!*'[99]

So, with smiles and embraces, they parted. So they met again at the welcome coming of Argus-eyed night.[100]

The studio was elegant with clusters of flowers, sumptuous with crimson, gold-bordered hangings, and luxurious with cushions and perfumes. From the walls peeped pictured fruit and fruit-like faces, between the curtains and in the corners gleamed moonlight-tinted statues; whilst on the easel reposed the beauty of the evening, overhung by budding boughs, and illuminated by an alabaster lamp burning scented oil. Strewn about the apartment lay musical instruments and packs of cards. On the table were silver dishes, filled with leaves and choice fruits; wonderful vessels of Venetian glass, containing rare wines and iced waters; and footless goblets, which allowed the guest no choice but to drain his bumper.

That night the bumpers brimmed. Toast after toast was quaffed to the success of to-morrow, the exaltation of the unveiled beauty, the triumph of its author.

At last Giannuccione, flushed and sparkling, rose: 'Let us drink,' he cried, 'to our host's success to-morrow: may it be greater than the past, and less than the future!'

'Not so,' answered Titian, suddenly; 'not so: I feel my star culminate.'

He said it gravely, pushing back his seat, and rising from table. His spirits seemed in a moment to flag, and he looked pale in the moonlight. It was as though the blight of the evil eye had fallen upon him.

Gianni saw his disquiet, and laboured to remove it. He took a lute from the floor, and tuning it, exerted his skill in music. He wrung from the strings cries of passion, desolate sobs, a wail as of one abandoned, plaintive, most tender tones as of the *solitario passero*.[101] The charm worked: vague uneasiness was melting into delicious melancholy. He redoubled his efforts; he drew out tinkling notes joyful as the feet of dancers; he struck notes like fire, and, uniting his voice to the instrument, sang the glories of Venice and of

Titian. His voice, full, mellow, exultant, vibrated through the room; and, when it ceased, the bravos of his friends rang out an enthusiastic chorus.

Then, more stirring than the snap of castanets on dexterous fingers; more fascinating, more ominous, than a snake's rattle, sounded the music of the dice-box.

The stakes were high, waxing higher, and higher; the tide of fortune set steadily towards Titian. Giannuccione laughed and played, played and laughed with reckless good-nature, doubling and redoubling his bets apparently quite at random. At length, however, he paused, yawned, laid down the dice observing that it would cost him a good six months' toil to pay off his losses—a remark which elicited a peculiar smile of intelligence from his companions—and, lounging back upon the cushions, fell fast asleep.

Gianni also had been a loser: Gianni the imperturbable, who won and lost alike with steady hand and unvarying colour. Rumour stated that one evening he lost, won back, lost once more, and finally regained his whole property unmoved: at last only relinquishing the game, which fascinated, but could not excite him, for lack of an adversary.

In like manner he now threw his possessions, as coolly as if they been another's, piecemeal into the gulph. First his money went, then his collection of choice sketches; his gondola followed, his plate, his jewelry. These gone, for the first time he laughed.

'Come,' he said, '*amico mio,*[102] let us throw the crowning cast. I stake thereon myself; if you win, you may sell me to the Moor to-morrow, with the remnant of my patrimony; to wit, one house, containing various articles of furniture and apparel; yea, if aught else remains to me, that also do I stake: against these set you your newborn beauty, and let us throw for the last time; lest it be said cogged dice are used in Venice, and I be taunted with the true proverb,—"*Save me from my friends, and I will take care of my enemies.*"'

'So be it,' mused Titian, 'even so. If I gain, my friend shall not suffer; if I lose, I can but buy back my treasure with this night's winnings. His whole fortune will stand Gianni in more stead than my picture; moreover, luck favours me. Besides, it can only be that my friend jests, and would try my confidence.'

So argued Titian, heated by success, by wine and play. But for these, he would freely have restored his adversary's fortune, though it had been multiplied tenfold, and again tenfold, rather than have risked his life's labour on the hazard of the dice.

They threw.

Luck had turned, and Gianni was successful.

Titian, nothing doubting, laughed as he looked up from the table into his companion's face; but no shadow of jesting lingered there. Their eyes met, and read each other's heart at a glance.

One, discerned the gnawing envy of a life satiated: a thousand mortifications, a thousand inferiorities, compensated in a moment.

The other, read an indignation that even yet scarcely realised the treachery which kindled it; a noble indignation, that more upbraided the false friend than the destroyer of a life's hope.

It was a nine-days' wonder in Venice what had become of Titian's masterpiece; who had spirited it away,—why, when, and where. Some explained the mystery by hinting that Clementina Beneplacida, having gained secret access to the great master's studio, had there, by dint of scissors, avenged her slighted beauty, and in effigy defaced her nut-brown rival. Others said that Giannuccione, paying tipsy homage to his friend's performance, had marred its yet moist surface. Others again averred, that in a moment of impatience, Titian's own sponge flung against the canvas, had irremediably blurred the principal figure. None knew, none guessed the truth. Wonder fulfilled its little day, and then, subsiding, was forgotten: having, it may be, after all, as truly amused Venice the volatile as any work of art could have done, though it had robbed sunset of its glow, its glory, and its fire.

But why was the infamy of that night kept secret?

By Titian, because in blazoning abroad his companion's treachery, he would subject himself to the pity of those from whom he scarcely accepted homage; and, in branding Gianni as a traitor, he would expose himself as a dupe.

By Gianni, because had the truth got wind, his iniquitous prize might have been wrested from him, and his malice frustrated in the moment of triumph; not to mention that vengeance had a subtler relish when it kept back a successful rival from the pinnacle of fame, than when it merely exposed a friend to humiliation. As artists, they might possibly have been accounted rivals; as astute men of the world, never.

Giannuccione had not witnessed all the transactions of that night. Thanks to his drunken sleep, he knew little; and what he guessed, Titian's urgency induced him to suppress. It was, indeed, noticed how, from that time forward, two of the three inseparables appeared in a measure, estranged from the third; yet all outward observances of courtesy were continued, and, if embraces had ceased, bows and doffings never failed.

For weeks, even for months, Gianni restrained his love for play, and, painting diligently, laboured to rebuild his shattered fortune. All prospered in his hands. His sketches sold with unprecedented readiness, his epigrams charmed the noblest dinner-givers, his verses and piquant little airs won him admission into the most exclusive circles. Withal, he seemed to be steadying. His name no more pointed stories of drunken frolics in the purlieus of the city, of mad wagers in the meanest company, of reckless duels with nameless adversaries. If now he committed follies, they were committed in the best society; if he sinned, it was, at any rate, in a patrician *casa;* and, though his morals might not yet be flawless, his taste was unimpeachable. His boon companions grumbled, yet could not afford to dispense with him; his warmest friends revived hopes which long ago had died away into despair. It was the heyday of his life: fortune and Venice alike courted him; he had but to sun himself in their smiles, and accept their favours.

So, nothing loth, he did, and for a while prospered. But, as the extraordinary stimulus flagged, the extraordinary energy flagged with it. Leisure returned, and with leisure the allurements of old pursuits. In proportion as his expenditure increased, his gains lessened; and, just when all his property, in fact, belonged to his creditors, he put the finishing stroke to his obvious ruin, by staking and losing at the gambling-table what was no longer his own.

That night beheld Gianni grave, dignified, imperturbable, and a beggar. Next day, his creditors, princely and plebeian, would be upon him: everything must go; not a scrap, not a fragment, could be held back. Even Titian's masterpiece would be claimed; that prize for which he had played away his soul, by which, it may be, he had hoped to acquire a worldwide fame, when its mighty author should be silenced for ever in the dust.

Yet to-morrow, not to-night, would be the day of reckoning; to-night, therefore, was his own. With a cool head he conceived, with a steady hand he executed, his purpose. Taking coarse pigments, such as, when he pleased, might easily be removed, he daubed over those figures which seemed to live, and that wonderful background, which not Titian himself could reproduce; then, on the blank surface, he painted a dragon, flaming, clawed, preposterous. One day he would recover his dragon, recover his Titian under the dragon, and the world should see.

Next morning the crisis came.

After all, Gianni's effects were worth more than had been supposed. They included Giannuccione's *Venus whipping Cupid*—how obtained, who knows?—a curiously wrought cup, by a Florentine goldsmith, just then rising into notice; within the hollow of the foot was engraved *Benvenuto Cellini,*[103] surmounted by an outstretched hand, symbolic of welcome, and quaintly allusive to the name; a dab by Giorgione, a scribble of the brush by Titian, and two feet square of genuine Tintoret.[104] The creditors brightened; there was not enough for honesty, but there was ample for the production of a most decorous bankrupt.

His wardrobe was a study of colour; his trinkets, few but choice, were of priceless good taste. Moreover, his demeanour was unimpeachable and his delinquencies came to light with the best grace imaginable. Some called him a defaulter, but all admitted he was a thorough gentleman.

Foremost in the hostile ranks stood Titian; Titian, who now, for the first time since that fatal evening, crossed his rival's threshold. His eye searched eagerly among the heap of nameless canvasses for one unforgotten beauty, who had occasioned him such sore heartache; but he sought in vain; only in the forefront sprawled a dragon, flaming, clawed, preposterous; grinned, twinkled, erected his tail, and flouted him.

'Yes,' said Gianni, answering his looks, not words, yet seeming to address the whole circle, '*Signori miei,* these compose all my gallery. An immortal sketch, by Messer Tiziano'—here a complimentary bow—'a veritable Giorgione; your own work, Messer Robusti, which needs no comment of mine to fix its value. A few productions by feebler hands, yet not devoid of merit. These are all. The most precious part of my collection was destroyed (I need not state, accidentally), three days ago by fire. That dragon, yet moist, was designed for mine host, Bevilacqua Mangiaruva;[105] but this morning, I hear, with deep concern, of his sudden demise.'

Here Lupo Vorace of the *Orco decapitato*[106] stepped forward. He, as he explained at length, was a man of few words (this, doubtless, in theory); but to make a long story short, so charmed was he by the scaly monster that he would change his sign, accept the ownerless dragon, and thereby wipe out a voluminous score which stood against his debtor. Gianni, with courteous thanks, explained that the dragon, still moist, was unfit for immediate transport; that it should remain in the studio for a short time longer; and that, as soon as its safety permitted, he would himself convey it to the inn of his liberal creditor. But on this point Lupo was inflexible. In diffuse but unvarying terms he claimed instant possession of Gianni's masterstroke. He seized it, reared it face upwards on to his head, and by his exit broke up the conclave of creditors.

What remains can be briefly told.

Titian, his last hope in this direction wrecked, returned to achieve, indeed, fresh greatnesses: but not the less returned to the tedium of straining after an ideal once achieved, but now lost for ever. Giannuccione, half amused, half mortified, at the slighting mention made of his performances, revenged himself in an epigram, of which the following is a free translation:—

> 'Gianni my friend and I both strove to excel,
> But, missing better, settled down in well.
> Both fail, indeed; but not alike we fail—
> My forte being Venus' face, and his a dragon's tail.'

Gianni, in his ruin, took refuge with a former friend; and there, treated almost on the footing of a friend, employed his superabundant leisure in concocting a dragon superior in all points to its predecessor; but, when this was almost completed, this which was to ransom his unsuspected treasure from the clutches of Lupo, the more relentless clutches of death fastened upon himself.

His secret died with him.

An oral tradition of a somewhere extant lost Titian having survived all historical accuracy, and so descended to another age, misled the learned Dr. Landau into purchasing a spurious work for the Gallery of Lunenberg; and even more recently induced Dr. Dreieck to expend a large sum on a nominal Titian, which he afterwards bequeathed to the National Museum of Saxe Eulenstein. The subject of this latter painting is a *Vintage of red grapes,* full of life and vigour, exhibiting marked talent, but clearly assignable to the commencement of a later century.

There remains, however, a hope that some happy accident may yet restore to the world the masterpiece of one of her most brilliant sons.

Reader, should you chance to discern over wayside inn or metropolitan hotel a dragon pendant, or should you find such an effigy amid the lumber of a broker's shop, whether it be red, green, or piebald, demand it importunately, pay for it liberally, and in the privacy of home scrub it. It *may* be that from behind the dragon will emerge a fair one, fairer than Andromeda, and that to you will appertain the honour of yet further exalting Titian's greatness in the eyes of a world.

Nick

Probably the first of Rossetti's stories following *Maude,* "Nick" was likely written in 1852 (William Rossetti told Mackenzie Bell this in a letter of 4 April 1895; Janet Camp Troxell Collection, Princeton University Library). Published initially in the *National Magazine* (1857), this violent cautionary tale concerns the dangers of fantasy and ingratitude.

Nick

There dwelt in a small village, not a thousand miles from Fairyland, a poor man, who had no family to labour for or friend to assist. When I call him poor, you must not suppose he was a homeless wanderer, trusting to charity for a night's lodging; on the contrary, his stone house, with its green veran-dah and flower-garden, was the prettiest and snuggest in all the place, the doctor's only excepted. Neither was his store of provisions running low: his farm supplied him with milk, eggs, mutton, butter, poultry, and cheese in abundance; his fields with hops and barley for beer, and wheat for bread; his orchard with fruit and cider; and his kitchen-garden with vegetables and wholesome herbs. He had, moreover, health, an appetite to enjoy all these good things, and strength to walk about his possessions. No, I call him poor because, with all these, he was discontented and envious. It was in vain that his apples were the largest for miles around, if his neighbour's vines were the most productive by a single bunch; it was in vain that his lambs were fat and thriving, if some one else's sheep bore twins: so, instead of enjoying his own prosperity, and being glad when his neighbours prospered too, he would sit grumbling and bemoaning himself as if every other man's riches were his poverty. And thus it was that one day our friend Nick leaned over Giles Hodge's gate, counting his cherries.

'Yes,' he muttered, 'I wish I were sparrows to eat them up, or a blight to kill your fine trees altogether.'

The words were scarcely uttered when he felt a tap on his shoulder, and looking round, perceived a little rosy woman, no bigger than a butterfly, who held her tiny fist clenched in a menacing attitude. She looked scorn-fully at him, and said: 'Now listen, you churl, you! henceforward you shall straightway become everything you wish; only mind, you must remain under one form for at least an hour.' Then she gave him a slap in the face, which made his cheek tingle as if a bee had stung him, and disappeared with just so much sound as a dewdrop makes in falling.

Nick rubbed his cheek in a pet,[107] pulling wry faces and showing his teeth. He was boiling over with vexation, but dared not vent it in words lest some unlucky wish should escape him. Just then the sun seemed to shine brighter than ever, the wind blew spicy from the south; all Giles's roses looked redder and larger than before, while his cherries seemed to multiply, swell, ripen. He could refrain no longer, but, heedless of the fairy-gift he had just received, exclaimed, 'I wish I were sparrows eating—' No sooner said than done: in a moment he found himself a whole flight of hungry birds, pecking, devouring, and bidding fair to devastate the envied cherry-trees. But honest Giles was on the watch hard by; for that very morning it had struck him he must make nets for the protection of his fine fruit. Forthwith he ran home, and speedily returned with a revolver furnished with quite a marvellous array of barrels. Pop, bang—pop, bang! he made short work of the sparrows, and soon reduced the enemy to one crestfallen biped with bro-ken leg and wing, who limped to hide himself under a holly-bush. But though the fun was over, the hour was not; so Nick must needs sit out his allotted time. Next a pelting shower came down, which soaked him through his torn, ruffled feathers; and then, exactly as the last drops fell and the sun came out with a beautiful rainbow, a tabby cat pounced upon him. Giving himself up for lost, he chirped in desperation, 'O, I wish I were a dog to worry you!' Instantly—for the hour was just passed—in the grip of his horrified adversary, he turned at bay, a savage bull-dog. A shake, a deep bite, and poor puss was out of her pain. Nick, with immense satisfaction, tore her fur to bits, wishing he could in like manner exterminate all her progeny. At last, glutted with vengeance, he lay down beside his victim, relaxed his ears and tail, and fell asleep.

Now that tabby-cat was the property and special pet of no less a personage than the doctor's lady; so when dinner-time came, and not the cat, a general consternation pervaded the household. The kitchens were searched, the cellars, the attics; every apartment was ransacked; even the watch-dog's kennel was visited. Next the stable was rummaged, then the hay-loft; lastly, the bereaved lady wandered disconsolately through her own private garden into the shrubbery, calling 'Puss, puss,' and looking so intently up the trees as not to perceive what lay close before her feet. Thus it was that, unawares, she stumbled over Nick, and trod upon his tail.

Up jumped our hero, snarling, biting, and rushing at her with such blind fury as to miss his aim. She ran, he ran. Gathering up his strength, he took a flying-leap after his victim; her foot caught in the spreading root of an oak-tree, she fell, and he went over her head, clear over, into a bed of stinging-nettles. Then she found breath to raise that fatal cry, 'Mad dog!' Nick's blood curdled in his veins; he would have slunk away if he could; but already a stout labouring-man, to whom he had done many an ill turn in the time of his humanity, had spied him, and, bludgeon in hand, was preparing to give chase. However, Nick had the start of him, and used it too; while the lady, far behind, went on vociferating, 'Mad dog, mad dog!' inciting doctor, servants, and vagabonds to the pursuit. Finally, the whole village came pouring out to swell the hue and cry.

The dog kept ahead gallantly, distancing more and more the asthmatic doctor, fat Giles, and, in fact, all his pursuers except the bludgeon-bearing labourer, who was just near enough to persecute his tail. Nick knew the magic hour must be almost over, and so kept forming wish after wish as he ran,—that he were a viper only to get trodden on, a thorn to run into some one's foot, a man-trap in the path, even the detested bludgeon to miss its aim and break. This wish crossed his mind at the propitious moment; the bull-dog vanished, and the labourer, overreaching himself, fell flat on his face, while his weapon struck deep into the earth, and snapped.

A strict search was instituted after the missing dog, but without success. During two whole days the village children were exhorted to keep indoors and beware of dogs; on the third an inoffensive bull pup was hanged, and the panic subsided.

Meanwhile the labourer, with his shattered stick, walked home in silent wonder, pondering on the mysterious disappearance. But the puzzle was beyond his solution; so he only made up his mind not to tell his wife the whole story till after tea. He found her preparing for that meal, the bread and cheese set out, and the kettle singing softly on the fire. 'Here's something to make the kettle boil, mother,' said he, thrusting our hero between the bars and seating himself; 'for I'm mortal tired and thirsty.'

Nick crackled and blazed away cheerfully, throwing out bright sparks, and lighting up every corner of the little room. He toasted the cheese to a nicety, made the kettle boil without spilling a drop, set the cat purring with comfort, and illuminated the pots and pans into splendour. It was provocation enough to be burned; but to contribute by his misfortune to the well-being of his tormentors was still more aggravating. He heard, too, all their remarks and wonderment about the supposed mad-dog, and saw the doctor's lady's own maid bring the labourer five shillings as a reward for his exertions. Then followed a discussion as to what should be purchased with the gift, till at last it was resolved to have their best window glazed with real glass. The prospect of their grandeur put the finishing-stroke to Nick's indignation. Sending up a sudden flare, he wished with all his might that he were fire to burn the cottage.

Forthwith the flame leaped higher than ever flame leaped before. It played for a moment about a ham, and smoked it to a nicety; then, fastening on the woodwork about the chimney-corner, flashed full into a blaze. The labourer ran for help, while his wife, a timid woman, with three small children, overturned two pails of water on the floor, and set the beer-tap running. This done, she hurried, wringing her hands, to the door, and threw it wide open. The sudden draught of air did more mischief than all Nick's malice, and fanned him into quite a conflagration. He danced upon the rafters, melted a pewter-pot and a pat of butter, licked up the beer, and was just making his way towards the bedroom, when through the thatch and down the chimney came a rush of water. This arrested his progress for the moment; and before he could recover himself, a second and a third discharge from the enemy completed his discomfiture. Reduced ere long to one blue flame, and entirely surrounded by a wall of wet ashes, Nick sat and smouldered; while the good-natured neighbours did their best to remedy the mishap,—saved a small remnant of beer, assured the labourer that his landlord was certain to do the repairs, and observed that the ham would eat 'beautiful.'

Our hero now had leisure for reflection. His situation precluded all hope of doing further mischief; and the disagreeable conviction kept forcing itself upon his mind that, after all, he had caused more injury to himself than to any of his neighbours. Remembering, too, how contemptuously the fairy woman had looked and spoken, he began to wonder how he could ever have expected to enjoy her gift. Then it occurred to him, that if he merely studied his own advantage without trying to annoy other people, perhaps his persecutor might be propitiated; so he fell to thinking over all his acquaintances, their fortunes and misfortunes; and, having weighed well their several claims on his preference, ended by wishing himself the rich old man who lived in a handsome house just beyond the turnpike.[108] In this wish he burned out.

The last glimmer had scarcely died away, when Nick found himself in a bed hung round with faded curtains, and occupying the centre of a large room. A night-lamp, burning on the chimney-piece, just enabled him to discern a few shabby old articles of furniture, a scanty carpet, and some writing materials on a table. These objects looked somewhat dreary; but for his comfort he felt an inward consciousness of a goodly money-chest stowed away under his bed, and of sundry precious documents hidden in a secret cupboard in the wall.

So he lay very cosily, and listened to the clock ticking, the mice squeaking, and the house-dog barking down below. This was, however, but a drowsy occupation; and he soon bore witness to its somniferous influence by sinking into a fantastic dream about his money-chest. First, it was broken open, then shipwrecked, then burned; lastly, some men in masks, whom he knew instinctively to be his own servants, began dragging it away. Nick started up, clutched hold of something in the dark, found his last dream true, and the next moment was stretched on the floor—lifeless, yet not insensible—by a heavy blow from a crowbar.

The men now proceeded to secure their booty, leaving our hero where he fell. They carried off the chest, broke open and ransacked the secret closet, overturned the furniture, to make sure that no hiding-place of treasure escaped them, and at length, whispering together, left the room. Nick felt quite discouraged by his ill success, and now entertained only one wish— that he were himself again. Yet even this wish gave him some anxiety; for he feared that if the servants returned and found him in his original shape they might take him for a spy, and murder him in downright earnest. While he lay thus cogitating two of the men reappeared, bearing a shutter and some tools. They lifted him up, laid him on the shutter, and carried him out of the room, down the back-stairs, through a long vaulted passage, into the open air. No word was spoken; but Nick knew they were going to bury him.

An utter horror seized him, while, at the same time, he felt a strange consciousness that his hair would not stand on end because he was dead. The men set him down, and began in silence to dig his grave. It was soon ready to receive him; they threw the body roughly in, and cast upon it the first shovelful of earth.

But the moment of deliverance had arrived. His wish suddenly found vent in a prolonged unearthly yell. Damp with night dew, pale as death, and shivering from head to foot, he sat bolt upright, with starting, staring eyes and chattering teeth. The murderers, in mortal fear, cast down their tools, plunged deep into a wood hard by, and were never heard of more.

Under cover of night Nick made the best of his way home, silent and pondering. Next morning he gave Giles Hodge a rare tulip-root, with full directions for rearing it; he sent the doctor's wife a Persian cat twice the size of her lost pet; the labourer's cottage was repaired, his window glazed, and his beer-barrel replaced by unknown agency; and when a vague rumour reached the village that the miser was dead, that his ghost had been heard bemoaning itself, and that all his treasures had been carried off, our hero was one of the few persons who did not say, 'And served him right, too.'

Finally, Nick was never again heard to utter a wish.

Pros and Cons

Under the original title of "Some Pros and Cons about Pews," and together with "The Waves of this Troublesome World" and "A Safe Investment," this didactic story was first published in the *Churchman's Shilling Magazine* 1 (1867):496–500. The "special subject" (Rossetti's phrase in her preface to the 1870 volume) is the rent parishioners customarily paid for church pews. As Lona Mosk Packer notes in her biography (p. 270), in the mid-1860s the Reverend Burrows of Christ Church, Albany Street (Rossetti's parish), was trying to overcome congregational opposition to the abolition of pew rents. The issues presented in the story were therefore very likely a central part of Christina's experience at this time. Kathleen Jones (p. 18) even suggests that the Rossetti family had left their previous parish (Trinity Church, Marylebone Road) because Mrs. Rossetti "had been bullied by the rector about her pew rent."

Pros and Cons

'But, my dear doctor,' cried Mrs. Plume, 'you never can seriously mean it.'

The scene was the Rectory drawing-room—tea-time; some dozen parishioners drinking tea with their Rector and his wife. Mrs. Goodman looked down; her husband, the Rector, looked up.

'I really did mean it,' said he, courteously; 'and, with your permission, I mean it still. Let us consider the matter calmly, my dear Mrs. Plume, calmly and fairly; and to start us fairly I will restate my proposal, which is that we should all combine to do our best towards bringing about the abolition of pews from our parish church.'

'Then I,' returned Mrs. Plume, shaking her head airily, 'must really re-state my protest. You never seriously can mean it.'

'Nay,' resumed the Rector, 'don't think that I am unmindful of your feel-ings on this point;' and he glanced round the circle. 'If I spoke hastily I ask your pardon and patience; but this matter of pews and pew-rents is on my conscience, and *that* I must lighten at all costs; even, Mr. Sale,'—for Mr. Sale frowned—'at the cost of my income. However, why should we conclude ourselves to be at variance before we have ventilated the matter in hand? I for one will never take for granted that any good Christian is against the ac-knowledgment of our absolute equality before God.'

'Sir,' interposed Mr. Blackman, 'we are equals, whatever may be our colour of our country. But whilst the Zenana counts its victims by thou-sands, whilst the Japanese make boast of their happy despatch, whilst the Bushman, dwindling before our face, lives and dies as the beasts that perish, shall we divert our attention from such matters of life and death to fix it on a petty question of appearance?[109] Pardon me if tears for our benighted brethren blind me to such a matter as this.'

'Our benighted brethren,' said the Rector, gravely, 'have my pity, have my prayers, have my money in some measure. Of your larger gifts in these sev-eral kinds I will not ask you to divert one throb,[110] or one word, or one penny in favour of our poor fellow-parishioners. No, dear friend, help us by your good example to enlarge our field of charitable labour; to stretch full handed towards remote spots; but not meanwhile to fail in breaking up our own fallow ground at home. We all know that if at this moment either our foreign or our native ragged brother were to present himself in church, how-ever open our hearts may be to him, our pew-doors would infallibly be shut against him, and he would find himself looked down upon both literally and figuratively. This, I own to you, were I he, would discomfit me, and put a stumbling-block in my way as a worshipper.'

'Pooh! pooh!' broke in Mr. Wood, testily: 'My dear fellow, I really thought you a wiser man. What hardship is it for a flunky or a clodhopper[111] to sit in a seat without a door?'

'Ah!' rejoined the Rector quietly, 'for a servant, as you say, or for a mere sower of our fields, or (why not?) for a carpenter's son either? But allow me to name two points which strike me forcibly,—two very solemn points;' and Dr. Goodman spoke with solemnity, and bowed his head. 'First, that if our adorable Lord were now walking this world as once He walked it, and if He had gone into our parish church last Sunday, as long ago He used to frequent the synagogue of Nazareth, He would certainly not have waited long to be ushered into a pew, but would, at least as willingly, have sat down amongst His own "blessed" poor; and, secondly, that we should all have left Him to do so unmolested; for I cannot suppose that His were the gold ring and goodly apparel which would have challenged attention.'

There was a pause, broken by Mrs. Plume, who, turning to her hostess, observed: 'Ah, dear Mrs. Goodman, we know and revere the zeal of our dear good apostle. But you and I are old housekeepers, old birds not to be caught with chaff;' and she shook a fascinating finger at her pastor; 'and we know that the poor are not nice neighbours; quite infectious, in fact. They do very well together all in a clump, but one really couldn't risk sitting amongst them, on various grounds, you know.'

'Well,' resumed the Rector, 'I plead guilty to being but a tough man, thick-skinned, and lacking certain subtler members, entitled nerves. But what will you? You must make allowances for me, and even put up with me as I am. With docility, and all the imagination of which I am master, I throw myself into your position, and shudder with you at these repulsively infectious poor. I even seek to deepen my first impression of horror by questioning myself in detail, and I dwell on the word "infectious." This brings before me small-pox, typhus fever, and other dreadful ailments; and I hasten (in spirit) to slam to, if only I could to bolt and bar, my pew-door. Safely ensconced within, I peer over my necessary barrier, and, relieved from the pressure of instant peril, gaze with pity on the crowd without, all alike typhus-stricken, all alike redolent of small-pox. A new terror thrills me. Are "all alike" infectious? or have we grouped together sound and unsound, sick and healthy? Ah, you hint, that amount of risk cannot be helped if they are to come to church at all. I am corrected, and carrying out the lesson of my Teacher I echo: That amount of risk cannot be helped if we are to come to church at all.'

'These men! these men!' cried Mrs. Plume, gaily. And Miss Crabb observed, from behind her blue spectacles, 'Well, I suppose a woman of my age may allude to anything she pleases; so I make bold to tell you, Dr. Goodman, that small-pox may be all nonsense; but that nobody would like to sit amongst smells, and cheek-by-jowl with more heads than one in a bonnet.'

'Smells,' rejoined the Rector, 'I do strongly object to; including scents, my dear Mrs. Plume; but that is a matter of taste. The other detail, which I know not how to express more pointedly than in the striking words of Miss Crabb, is yet more to be deprecated: but let us consider whether pews fairly meet the difficulty. Fairly? I ask; and then unhesitatingly answer, No. For all the poor, both clean and dirty, occupy our free seats together; and surely to sit next a dirty neighbour is, at the least, as great a hardship on the cleanly poor as it would be on the rich, who are so far better able to have their clothes cleansed, or even, in case of need, to discard them. If, indeed, all dirty individuals would have the good feeling to compact themselves into one body it might be reassuring to their fellows, but this it were invidious to propose; and besides, we are at present mooting pews or no pews, not any third possible—or shall we say impossible?—alternative. I confess to you,' he resumed, very seriously, 'when I remember the little stress laid by Christ on clean hands, and the paramount importance in His eyes of a clean heart; when I reflect on the dirt of all kinds which must have touched Him in the crowds He taught and healed; when I realise that every one of my parishioners, poor as well as rich, will confront me at His judgment-bar, I tremble lest any should be deterred from coming to Him because I am too fine a gentlemen to go out into the highways and hedges, and compel to come in those actual poor—foul of body, it may be, as well as of soul—whom yet He has numbered to me as my flock.'

Silence ensued—an uncomfortable silence; broken by Mrs. Goodman's nervous proffer of tea to Mr. Sale, who declined it.

Mr. Home resumed the attack. 'Doctor,' observed he, 'all other objections to open seats might perhaps be overruled; but consider the sacredness of family affection, and do not ask us to scatter ourselves forlornly through the church, here a husband, there a wife;' and he interchanged a smile with Mrs. Home; 'there, again, a practical orphan. I for one could not possibly say my prayers without my little woman at my elbow.'

'Here,' cried the Rector, 'I joyfully meet you halfway. The division of the sexes in distinct aisles is a question by itself, and one which I am not now discussing. Only go betimes to church'—at this a glance of intelligence passed round the circle, whilst Mrs. Home coloured,—'and I stake my credit that you will hardly ever fail to find six contiguous seats for your party.'

Then Mr. Stone spoke up—Mr. Stone, the warmest man in the parish. He spoke with his fat hands in his fat pockets.

'Dr. Goodman, sir,'—the courteous Rector bowed,—'my attachment to the church and my respect for your cloth must not prevent my doing my duty by my fellow-parishioners, whose mouthpiece on the present occasion I claim to be.' A general movement of relief accepted him as the lay champion. 'We acknowledge, sir, and appreciate your zeal amongst us, but we protest against your innovations. We have borne with chants, with a surpliced choir, with daily services, but we will not bear to see all our rights trampled under foot, and all our time-hallowed usages set at nought.[112] The tendency of the day is to level social distinctions and to elevate unduly the lower orders. In this parish at least let us combine to keep up wise barriers between class and class, and to maintain that fundamental principle practically bowed to all over our happy England, that what you can pay for you can purchase. This, sir, has been our first dissension'—a statement not quite correct,—'let it be our last; and in token that we are at one again, here is my hand.'

Dr. Goodman grasped the proffered hand, looking rather pale as he did so.

'Let this betoken,' rejoined he, 'that whatever is discarded amongst us, it shall not be Christian charity. And now it grows late. I must not selfishly prolong our discussion; yet, as your pastor, with a sacred duty to discharge towards all my flock, suffer me to add one word. What Mr. Stone has alleged may be the system of worldly England; though many a man professing far less than we do would repudiate so monstrous a principle; but as Churchmen we can have nothing to do with it. God's gifts are bought without money and without price: "Ho, every one," cries His invitation. I, therefore, as His most unworthy ambassador, protest that in His house I will no longer buy and sell as in a market. I confess myself in fault that I have so long tolerated this monstrous abuse; and I avow that you, my brethren, have this evening furnished me with the only plausible argument in favour of pews which has ever been suggested to me, for it *is* hard upon our open-hearted poor that they should be compelled to sit by persons who, instead of viewing them as brethren beloved, despise the poor.'

Speaking Likenesses (1874)

P ublished in 1874, with illustrations by Arthur Hughes, these "3 short stories in a common framework" (*RM*, 98) were deliberately written by
Rossetti in the "*Alice* style with an eye to the market" (*FL*, 44) and to capitalize on Lewis Carroll's popularity. The narrator's tone is cautious, corrective, even
at times stern, and the quarrelsome, rude children in parts of the narrative help create a picture of childhood that is far from idealized. The book was not enthusiastically received, the reviewer in *The Academy* (5 December 1874), for example,
remarking that "this will probably be one of the most popular children's books this
winter. We wish we could understand it. . . . [B]ut we have an uncomfortable feeling that a great deal more is meant than appears on the surface, and that every part
of it ought to mean something if we only knew what it was." In the past decade, indeed, a number of readings have disclosed the subversive tenor and complex symmetries of Rossetti's "antifantasy," for instance, Nina Auerbach and U. C.
Knoepflmacher, eds., *Forbidden Journeys: Fairy Tales and Fantasies by Victorian Women
Writers* (Chicago: University of Chicago Press, 1992), 319; and see 317–23 for perceptive introductory comments; Roderick McGillis, "Simple Surfaces: Christina
Rossetti's Work for Children," in Kent, 224–29, and Marsh, 418–25, give acute
analyses. Knoepflmacher's "Avenging Alice: Christina Rossetti and Lewis Carroll"
examines *Speaking Likenesses* within the wider context of Rossetti's friendship with
Charles Dodgson. Pamela K. Gilbert, "'A Horrid Game': Woman as Social Entity in
Christina Rossetti's Prose," (*English* 41 [Spring 1992]: 1–23), compares the tales of
Speaking Likenesses with *Maude* which she sees as stories illustrative of Rossetti's
sense of "self-postponement" and ambivalence toward her world.

The text and illustrations are based on a personal copy of the first and only
edition.

Speaking Likenesses

Come sit round me, my dear little girls, and I will tell you a story. Each of
you bring her sewing, and let Ella take pencils and colour-box, and try to
finish some one drawing of the many she has begun. What Maude! pouting
over that nice clean white stocking because it wants a darn? Put away your
pout and pull out your needle, my dear; for pouts make a sad beginning to
my story. And yet not an inappropriate beginning, as some of you may notice as I go on. Silence! Attention! All eyes on occupations, not on me lest I
should feel shy! Now I start my knitting and my story together.

Whoever saw Flora on her birthday morning, at half-past seven o'clock on
that morning, saw a very pretty sight. Eight years old to a minute, and not
awake yet. Her cheeks were plump and pink, her light hair was all tumbled,
her little red lips were held together as if to kiss some one; her eyes also, if
you could have seen them, were blue and merry, but for the moment they
had gone fast asleep and out of sight under fat little eyelids. Wagga the dog
was up and about, Muff the cat was up and about, chirping birds were up
and about; or if they were mere nestlings and so could not go about (supposing, that is, that there were still a few nestlings so far on in summer), at
least they sat together wide awake in the nest, with wide open eyes and most
of them with wide open beaks, which was all they could do: only sleepy
Flora slept on, and dreamed on, and never stirred.

Her mother stooping over the child's soft bed woke her with a kiss.
"Good morning, my darling, I wish you many and many happy returns of
the day," said the kind, dear mother: and Flora woke up to a sense of sunshine, and of pleasure full of hope. To be eight years old when last night one
was merely seven, this is pleasure: to hope for birthday presents without any
doubt of receiving some, this also is pleasure. And doubtless you now think
so, my children, and it is quite right that so you should think: yet I tell you,
from the sad knowledge of my older experience, that to every one of you a
day will most likely come when sunshine, hope, presents and pleasure will
be worth nothing to you in comparison with the unattainable gift of your
mother's kiss.

On the breakfast table lay presents for Flora: a story-book full of pictures
from her father, a writing-case from her mother, a gilt pincushion like a
hedgehog from nurse, a box of sugar-plums and a doll from Alfred her
brother and Susan her sister; the most tempting of sugar-plums, the most
beautiful of curly-pated dolls, they appeared in her eyes.

"Her mother stooping over the child's soft bed woke her with a kiss."

A further treat was in store. "Flora," said her mother, when admiration was at last silent and breakfast over: "Flora, I have asked Richard, George, Anne and Emily to spend the day with you and with Susan and Alfred. You are to be queen of the feast, because it is your birthday; and I trust you will all be very good and happy together."

Flora loved her brother and sister, her friend Emily, and her cousins Richard, George and Anne: indeed I think that with all their faults these children did really love each other. They had often played together before; and now if ever, surely on this so special occasion they would play pleasantly together. Well, we shall see.

Anne with her brothers arrived first: and Emily having sent to ask permission, made her appearance soon after accompanied by a young friend, who was spending the holidays with her, and whom she introduced as Serena.

[What an odd name, Aunt!—Yes, Clara, it is not a common name, but I knew a Serena once; though she was not at all like this Serena, I am happy to say.]

Emily brought Flora a sweet-smelling nosegay; and Serena protested that Flora was the most charming girl she had ever met, except of course dearest Emily.

"Love me," said Serena, throwing her arms round her small hostess and giving her a clinging kiss: "I will love you so much if you will only let me love you."

The house was a most elegant house, the lawn was a perfect park, the elder brother and sister frightened her by their cleverness: so exclaimed Serena: and for the moment silly little Flora felt quite tall and superior, and allowed herself to be loved very graciously.

After the arrivals and the settling down, there remained half-an-hour before dinner, during which to cultivate acquaintance and exhibit presents. Flora displayed her doll and handed round her sugar-plum box. "You took more than I did and it isn't fair," grumbled George at Richard: but Richard retorted, "Why, I saw you picking out the big ones." "Oh," whined Anne, "I'm sure there were no big ones left when they came to me." And Emily put in with a smile of superiority: "Stuff, Anne: you got the box before Serena and I did, and *we* don't complain." "But there wasn't one," persisted Anne. "But there were dozens and dozens," mimicked George, "only you're such a greedy little baby." "Not one," whimpered Anne. Then Serena remarked soothingly: "The sugar-plums were most delicious, and now let us admire the lovely doll. Why, Flora, she must have cost pounds and pounds."

Flora, who had begun to look rueful, brightened up: "I don't know what she cost, but her name is Flora, and she has red boots with soles. Look at me opening and shutting her eyes, and I can make her say Mamma. Is she not a beauty?" "I never saw half such a beauty," replied smooth Serena. Then the party sat down to dinner.

Was it fact? Was it fancy? Each dish in turn was only fit to be found fault with. Meat underdone, potatoes overdone, beans splashy, jam tart not sweet enough, fruit all stone; covers clattering, glasses reeling, a fork or two dropping on the floor. Were these things really so? or would even finest strawberries and richest cream have been found fault with, thanks to the children's mood that day?

[Were the dishes all wrong, Aunt?—I fancy not, Ella; at least, not more so than things often are in this world without upsetting every one's patience. But hear what followed.]

Sad to say, what followed was a wrangle. An hour after dinner blindman's buff in the garden began well and promised well: why could it not go on well? Ah, why indeed? for surely before now in that game toes have been trodden on, hair pulled, and small children overthrown. Flora fell down and accused Alfred of tripping her up, Richard bawled out that George broke away when fairly caught, Anne when held tight muttered that Susan could see in spite of bandaged eyes. Susan let go, Alfred picked up his little sister, George volunteered to play blindman in Susan's stead: but still pouting and grumbling showed their ugly faces, and tossed the apple of discord to and fro as if it had been a pretty plaything.

[What apple, Aunt?—The Apple of Discord,[113] Clara, which is a famous apple your brothers would know all about, and you may ask them some day. Now I go on.]

Would you like, any of you, a game at hide-and-seek in a garden, where there are plenty of capital hiding-places and all sorts of gay flowers to glance at while one goes seeking? I should have liked such a game, I assure you, forty years ago. But these children on this particular day could not find it in their hearts to like it. Oh dear no. Serena affected to be afraid of searching along the dusky yew alley unless Alfred went with her; and at the very same moment Flora was bent on having him lift her up to look down into a hollow tree in which it was quite obvious Susan could not possibly have hidden. "It's my birthday," cried Flora; "it's my birthday." George and Richard pushed each other roughly about till one slipped on the gravel walk and grazed his hands, when both turned cross and left off playing. At last in sheer despair Susan stepped out of her hiding-place behind the summer-house: but even then she did her best to please everybody, for she brought in her hand a basket full of ripe mulberries which she had picked up off the grass as she stood in hiding.

Then they all set to running races across the smooth sloping lawn: till Anne tumbled down and cried, though she was not a bit hurt; and Flora, who was winning the race against Anne, thought herself ill-used and so sat

"The Apple of Discord"

and sulked. Then Emily smiled, but not good-naturedly, George and Richard thrust each a finger into one eye and made faces at the two cross girls, Serena fanned herself, and Alfred looked at Susan, and Susan at Alfred, fairly at their wits' end.

An hour yet before tea-time: would another hour ever be over? Two little girls looking sullen, two boys looking provoking: the sight was not at all an encouraging one. At last Susan took pouting Flora and tearful Anne by the hand, and set off with them for a walk perforce about the grounds; whilst Alfred fairly dragged Richard and George after the girls, and Emily arm-in-arm with Serena strolled beside them.

The afternoon was sunny, shady, breezy, warm, all at once. Bees were humming and harvesting as any bee of sense must have done amongst so many blossoms: leafy boughs danced with their dancing shadows; bell flowers rang without clappers:—

[Could they, Aunt?—Well, not exactly, Maude: but you're coming to much more wonderful matters!]

Now and then a pigeon cooed its soft water-bottle note; and a long way off sheep stood bleating.

Susan let go the little hot hands she held, and began as she walked telling a story to which all her companions soon paid attention—all except Flora.

Poor little Flora: was this the end of her birthday? was she eight years old at last only for this? Her sugar-plums almost all gone and not cared for, her chosen tart not a nice one, herself so cross and miserable: is it really worth while to be eight years old and have a birthday, if this is what comes of it?

"—So the frog did not know how to boil the kettle; but he only replied: I can't bear hot water," went on Susan telling her story. But Flora had no heart to listen, or to care about the frog. She lagged and dropped behind not noticed by any one, but creeping along slowly and sadly by herself.

Down the yew alley she turned, and it looked dark and very gloomy as she passed out of the sunshine into the shadow. There were twenty yew trees on each side of the path, as she had counted over and over again a great many years ago when she was learning to count; but now at her right hand there stood twenty-one: and if the last tree was really a yew tree at all, it was at least a very odd one, for a lamp grew on its topmost branch. Never before either had the yew walk led to a door: but now at its further end stood a door with bell and knocker, and "Ring also" printed in black letters on a brass plate; all as plain as possible in the lamplight.

Flora stretched up her hand, and knocked and rang also.

She was surprised to feel the knocker shake hands with her, and to see the bell handle twist round and open the door. "Dear me," thought she, "why could not the door open itself instead of troubling the bell?" But she only said, "Thank you," and walked in.

The knocker shakes hands with Flora.

The door opened into a large and lofty apartment, very handsomely furnished. All the chairs were stuffed arm-chairs, and moved their arms and shifted their shoulders to accommodate sitters. All the sofas arranged and re-arranged their pillows as convenience dictated. Footstools glided about, and rose or sank to meet every length of leg. Tables were no less obliging, but ran on noiseless castors here or there when wanted. Tea-trays ready set out, saucers of strawberries, jugs of cream, and plates of cake, floated in, settled down, and floated out again empty, with considerable tact and good taste: they came and went through a square hole high up in one wall, beyond which I presume lay the kitchen. Two harmoniums, an accordion, a pair of kettledrums and a peal of bells played concerted pieces behind a screen, but kept silence during conversation. Photographs and pictures made the tour of the apartment, standing still when glanced at and going on when done with. In case of need the furniture flattened itself against the wall, and cleared the floor for a game, or I dare say for a dance. Of these remarkable details some struck Flora in the first few minutes after her arrival, some came to light as time went on. The only uncomfortable point in the room, that is, as to furniture, was that both ceiling and walls were lined throughout with looking-glasses: but at first this did not strike Flora as any disadvantage; indeed she thought it quite delightful, and took a long look at her little self full length.

[Jane and Laura, don't *quite* forget the pocket-handkerchiefs you sat down to hem. See how hard Ella works at her fern leaves, and what pains she is taking to paint them nicely. Yes, Maude, that darn will do: now your task is ended, but if I were you I would help Clara with hers.]

The room was full of boys and girls, older and younger, big and little. They all sat drinking tea at a great number of different tables; here half a dozen children sitting together, here more or fewer; here one child would preside all alone at a table just the size for one comfortably. I should tell you that the tables were like telescope tables; only they expanded and contracted of themselves without extra pieces, and seemed to study everybody's convenience.

Every single boy and every single girl stared hard at Flora and went on staring: but not one of them offered her a chair, or a cup of tea, or anything else whatever. She grew very red and uncomfortable under so many staring pairs of eyes: when a chair did what it could to relieve her embarrassment by pressing gently against her till she sat down. It then bulged out its own back comfortably into hers, and drew in its arms to suit her small size. A footstool grew somewhat taller beneath her feet. A table ran up with tea for one; a cream-jug toppled over upon a saucerful of strawberries, and then righted itself again; the due quantity of sifted sugar sprinkled itself over the whole.

A chair pressed gently against Flora till she sat down.

[How could it sprinkle itself?—Well, Jane, let us suppose it sprang up in its china basin like a fountain; and overflowed on one side only, but that of course the right side, whether it was right or left.]

Flora could not help thinking everyone very rude and ill-natured to go on staring without speaking, and she felt shy at having to eat with so many eyes upon her: still she was hot and thirsty, and the feast looked most tempting. She took up in a spoon one large, very large strawberry with plenty of cream; and was just putting it into her mouth when a voice called out crossly: "You shan't, they're mine." The spoon dropped from her startled hand, but without any clatter: and Flora looked round to see the speaker.

[Who was it? Was it a boy or a girl?—Listen, and you shall hear, Laura.]

The speaker was a girl enthroned in an extra high armchair; with a stool as high as an ottoman under her feet, and a table as high as a chest of drawers in front of her. I suppose as she had it so she liked it so, for I am sure all the furniture laid itself out to be obliging. Perched upon her hair she wore a coronet made of tinsel; her face was a red face with a scowl: sometimes perhaps she looked nice and pretty, this time she looked ugly. "You shan't, they're mine," she repeated in a cross grumbling voice: "it's my birthday, and everything is mine."

Flora was too honest a little girl to eat strawberries that were not given her: nor could she, after this, take even a cup of tea without leave. Not to tantalize her, I suppose, the table glided away with its delicious untasted load; whilst the armchair gave her a very gentle hug as if to console her.

If she could only have discovered the door Flora would have fled through it back into the gloomy yew-tree walk, and there have moped in solitude, rather than remain where she was not made welcome: but either the door was gone, or else it was shut to and lost amongst the multitude of mirrors. The birthday Queen, reflected over and over again in five hundred mirrors, looked frightful, I do assure you: and for one minute I am sorry to say that Flora's fifty million-fold face appeared flushed and angry too; but she soon tried to smile good-humouredly and succeeded, though she could not manage to feel very merry.

[But, Aunt, how came she to have fifty million faces? I don't understand.—Because in such a number of mirrors there were not merely simple reflections, but reflections of reflections, and reflections of reflections of reflections, and so on and on and on, over and over again, Maude: don't you see?]

The meal was ended at last: most of the children had eaten and stuffed quite greedily; poor Flora alone had not tasted a morsel. Then with a word and I think a kick from the Queen, her high footstool scudded away into a corner: and all the furniture taking the hint arranged itself as flat as possible round the room, close up against the walls.

The cross fairy deprives Flora of her strawberry feast.

[And across the door?—Why, yes, I suppose it may have done so, Jane: such active and willing furniture could never be in the way anywhere.—And was there a chimney corner?—No, I think not: that afternoon was warm we know, and there may have been a different apartment for winter. At any rate, as this is all make-believe, I say No. Attention!]

All the children now clustered together in the middle of the empty floor; elbowing and jostling each other, and disputing about what game should first be played at. Flora, elbowed and jostled in their midst, noticed points of appearance that quite surprised her. Was it themselves, or was it their clothes? (only who indeed would wear such clothes, so long as there was another suit in the world to put on?) One boy bristled with prickly quills like a porcupine, and raised or depressed them at pleasure; but he usually kept them pointed outwards. Another instead of being rounded like most people was facetted at very sharp angles. A third caught in everything he came near, for he was hung round with hooks like fishhooks. One girl exuded a sticky fluid and came off on the fingers; another, rather smaller, was slimy and slipped through the hands. Such exceptional features could not but prove inconvenient, yet patience and forbearance might still have done something towards keeping matters smooth: but these unhappy children seemed not to know what forbearance was; and as to patience, they might have answered me nearly in the words of a celebrated man—"Madam, I never saw patience."

[Who was the celebrated man, Aunt?—Oh, Clara, you an English girl and not know Lord Nelson! But I go on.]

"Tell us some new game," growled Hooks threateningly, catching Flora's hair and tugging to get loose.

Flora did not at all like being spoken to in such a tone, and the hook hurt her very much. Still, though she could not think of anything new, she tried to do her best, and in a timid voice suggested "Les Grâces."[114]

"That's a girl's game," said Hooks contemptuously.

"It's as good any day as a boy's game," retorted Sticky.

"I wouldn't give *that* for your girl's games," snarled Hooks, endeavouring to snap his fingers, but entangling two hooks and stamping.

"Poor dear fellow!" drawled Slime, affecting sympathy.

"It's quite as good," harped on Sticky: "It's as good or better."

Angles caught and would have shaken Slime, but she slipped through his fingers demurely.

"Think of something else, and let it be new," yawned Quills, with quills laid for a wonder.

"I really don't know anything new," answered Flora half crying: and she was going to add, "But I will play with you at any game you like, if you will teach me;" when they all burst forth into a yell of "Cry, baby, cry!—

Flora and the children in the enchanted room.

Cry, baby, cry!"—They shouted it, screamed it, sang it: they pointed fingers, made grimaces, nodded heads at her. The wonder was she did not cry outright.

At length the Queen interfered: "Let her alone;—who's she? It's *my* birthday, and we'll play at Hunt the Pincushion."

So Hunt the Pincushion it was. This game is simple and demands only a moderate amount of skill. Select the smallest and weakest player (if possible let her be fat: a hump is best of all), chase her round and round the room, overtaking her at short intervals, and sticking pins into her here or there as it happens: repeat, till you choose to catch and swing her; which concludes the game. Short cuts, yells, and sudden leaps give spirit to the hunt.

[Oh, Aunt, what a horrid game! surely there cannot be such a game?— Certainly not, Ella: yet I have seen before now very rough cruel play, if it can be termed play.—And did they get a poor little girl with a hump?—No, Laura, not this time: for]

The Pincushion was poor little Flora. How she strained and ducked and swerved to this side or that, in the vain effort to escape her tormentors! Quills with every quill erect tilted against her, and needed not a pin: but Angles whose corners almost cut her, Hooks who caught and slit her frock, slime who slid against and passed her, Sticky who rubbed off on her neck and plump bare arms, the scowling Queen, and the whole laughing scolding pushing troop, all wielded longest sharpest pins, and all by turns overtook her. Finally the Queen caught her, swung her violently round, let go suddenly,—and Flora losing her balance dropped upon the floor. But at least that game was over.

Do you fancy the fall jarred her? Not at all: for the carpet grew to such a depth of velvet pile below her, that she fell quite lightly.

Indeed I am inclined to believe that even in that dreadful sport of Hunt the Pincushion, Flora was still better off than her stickers: who in the thick of the throng exasperated each other and fairly maddened themselves by a free use of cutting corners, pricking quills, catching hooks, glue, slime, and I know not what else. Slime, perhaps, would seem not so much amiss for its owner: but then if a slimy person cannot be held, neither can she hold fast. As to Hooks and Sticky they often in wrenching themselves loose got worse damage than they inflicted: Angles many times cut his own fingers with his edges: and I don't envy the individual whose sharp quills are flexible enough to be bent point inwards in a crush or a scuffle. The Queen must perhaps be reckoned exempt from particular personal pangs: but then, you see, it was her birthday! And she must still have suffered a good deal from the eccentricities of her subjects.

The next game called for was Self Help. In this no adventitious aids were tolerated, but each boy depended exclusively on his own resources. Thus pins were forbidden: but every natural advantage, as a quill or fishhook, might be utilized to the utmost.

[Don't look shocked, dear Ella, at my choice of words; but remember that my birthday party is being held in the Land of Nowhere.[115] Yet who knows whether something not altogether unlike it has not ere now taken place in the Land of Somewhere? Look at home, children.]

The boys were players, the girls were played (if I may be allowed such a phrase): all except the Queen who, being Queen, looked on, and merely administered a slap or box on the ear now and then to some one coming handy. Hooks, as a Heavy Porter, shone in this sport; and dragged about with him a load of attached captives, all vainly struggling to unhook themselves. Angles, as an Ironer, goffered or fluted[116] several children by sustained pressure. Quills, an Engraver, could do little more than prick and scratch with some permanence of result. Flora falling to the share of Angles had her torn frock pressed and plaited after quite a novel fashion: but this was at any rate preferable to her experience as Pincushion, and she bore it like a philosopher.

Yet not to speak of the girls, even the boys did not as a body extract unmixed pleasure from Self Help; but much wrangling and some blows allayed their exuberant enjoyment. The Queen as befitted her lofty lot did, perhaps, taste of mirth unalloyed; but if so, she stood alone in satisfaction as in dignity. In any case, pleasure palls in the long run.

The Queen yawned a very wide loud yawn: and as everyone yawned in sympathy the game died out.

A supper table now advanced from the wall to the middle of the floor, and armchairs enough gathered round it to seat the whole party. Through the square hole,—not, alas! through the door of poor Flora's recollection,—floated in the requisite number of plates, glasses, knives, forks, and spoons; and so many dishes and decanters filled with nice things as I certainly never saw in all my lifetime, and I don't imagine any of you ever did.

[How many children were there at supper?—Well, I have not the least idea, Laura, but they made quite a large party: suppose we say a hundred thousand.]

This time Flora would not take so much as a fork without leave: wherefore as the Queen paid not the slightest attention to her, she was reduced to look hungrily on while the rest of the company feasted, and while successive dainties placed themselves before her and retired untasted. Cold turkey, lobster salad, stewed mushrooms, raspberry tart, cream cheese, a bumper of champagne, a méringue, a strawberry ice, sugared pine apple, some greengages: it may have been quite as well for her that she did not feel at liberty to eat such a mixture: yet it was none the less tantalizing to watch so many good things come and go without taking even one taste, and to see all her companions stuffing without limit. Several of the boys seemed to think nothing of a whole turkey at a time: and the Queen consumed with her own mouth and of sweets alone one quart of strawberry ice, three pine apples, two melons, a score of méringues, and about four dozen sticks of angelica, as Flora counted.

After supper there was no need for the furniture to withdraw: for the whole birthday party trooped out through a door (but still not through Flora's door) into a spacious playground. What they may usually have played at I cannot tell you; but on this occasion a great number of bricks happened to be lying about on all sides mixed up with many neat piles of stones, so the children began building houses: only instead of building from without as most bricklayers do, they built from within, taking care to have at hand plenty of bricks as well as good heaps of stones, and inclosing both themselves and the heaps as they built; one child with one heap of stones inside each house.

[Had they window panes at hand as well?—No, Jane, and you will soon see why none were wanted.]

I called the building material bricks: but strictly speaking there were no bricks at all in the playground, only brick-shaped pieces of glass instead. Each of these had the sides brilliantly polished; whilst the edges, which were meant to touch and join, were ground, and thus appeared to acquire a certain tenacity. There were bricks (so to call them) of all colours and many different shapes and sizes. Some were fancy bricks wrought in open work, some were engraved in running patterns, others were cut into facets or blown into bubbles. A single house might have its blocks all uniform, or of twenty different fashions.

Yet, despite this amount of variety, every house built bore a marked resemblance to its neighbour: colours varied, architecture agreed. Four walls, no roof, no upper floor; such was each house: and it needed neither window nor staircase.

All this building occupied a long long time, and by little and little a very gay effect indeed was produced. Not merely were the glass blocks of beautiful tints; so that whilst some houses glowed like masses of ruby, and others shone like enormous chrysolites or sapphires, others again showed the milkiness and fiery spark of a hundred opals, or glimmered like moonstone: but the playground was lighted up, high, low, and on all sides, with coloured lamps. Picture to yourselves golden twinkling lamps like stars high overhead, bluish twinkling lamps like glowworms down almost on the ground; lamps like illuminated peaches, apples, apricots, plums, hung about with the profusion of a most fruitful orchard. Should we not all have liked to be there with Flora, even if supper was the forfeit?

Ah no, not with Flora: for to her utter dismay she found that she was being built in with the Queen. She was not called upon to build: but gradually the walls rose and rose around her, till they towered clear above her head; and being all slippery with smoothness, left no hope of her ever being able to clamber over them back into the road home, if indeed there was any longer such a road anywhere outside. Her heart sank within her, and she could scarcely hold up her head. To crown all, a glass house which contained no vestige even of a cupboard did clearly not contain a larder: and Flora began to feel sick with hunger and thirst, and to look forward in despair to no breakfast to-morrow.

Acoustics must have been most accurately studied,—

[But, Aunt, what are acoustics?—The science of sounds, Maude: pray now exercise your acoustical faculty.]

As I say, they must have been most accurately studied, and to practical purpose, in the laying out of this particular playground; if, that is, to hear distinctly everywhere whatever might be uttered anywhere within its limits, was the object aimed at. At any rate, such was the result.

Their residences at length erected, and their toils over, the youthful architects found leisure to gaze around them and bandy compliments.

First: "Look," cried Angles, pointing exultantly: "just look at Quills, as red as fire. Red doesn't become Quills. Quills's house would look a deal better without Quills."

"Talk of becomingness," laughed Quills, angrily, "you're just the colour of a sour gooseberry, Angles, and a greater fright than we've seen you yet. Look at him, Sticky, look whilst you have the chance:" for Angles was turning his green back on the speaker.

But Sticky—no wonder, the blocks *she* had fingered stuck together!— Sticky was far too busy to glance around; she was engrossed in making faces at Slime, whilst Slime returned grimace for grimace. Sticky's house was blue, and turned her livid: Slime's house—a very shaky one, ready to fall to pieces at any moment, and without one moment's warning:—Slime's house, I say, was amber-hued, and gave her the jaundice. These advantages were not lost on the belligerents, who stood working each other up into a state of frenzy, and having got long past variety, now did nothing but screech over and over again: Slime: "You're a sweet beauty,"—and Sticky (incautious Sticky!): "You're another!"

Quarrels raged throughout the playground. The only silent tongue was Flora's.

Suddenly, Hooks, who had built an engraved house opposite the Queen's bubbled palace (both edifices were pale amethyst coloured, and trying to the complexion), caught sight of his fair neighbour, and, clapping his hands, burst out into an insulting laugh.

"You're another!" shrieked the Queen (the girls all alike seemed well-nigh destitute of invention). Her words were weak, but as she spoke she stooped: and clutched—shook—hurled—the first stone.

"Oh don't, don't, don't," sobbed Flora, clinging in a paroxysm of terror, and with all her weight, to the royal arm.

That first stone was, as it were, the first hailstone of the storm: and soon stones flew in every direction and at every elevation. The very atmosphere seemed petrified. Stones clattered, glass shivered, moans and groans resounded on every side. It was as a battle of giants: who would excel each emulous peer, and be champion among giants?

The Queen. All that had hitherto whistled through mid-air were mere pebbles and chips compared with one massive slab which she now heaved up—poised—prepared to launch—

"Oh don't, don't, don't," cried out Flora again, almost choking with sobs. But it was useless. The ponderous stone spun on, widening an outlet through the palace wall on its way to crush Hooks. Half mad with fear, Flora flung herself after it through the breach—

And in one moment the scene was changed. Silence from human voices and a pleasant coolness of approaching twilight surrounded her. High overhead a fleet of rosy grey clouds went sailing away from the west, and outstripping these, rooks on flapping black wings flew home to their nests in the lofty elm trees, and cawed as they flew. A few heat-drops pattered down on a laurel hedge hard by, and a sudden gust of wind ran rustling through the laurel leaves. Such dear familiar sights and sounds told Flora that she was sitting safe within the home precincts: yes, in the very yew-tree alley, with its forty trees in all, not one more, and with no mysterious door leading out of it into a hall of misery.

She hastened indoors. Her parents, with Alfred, Susan, and the five visitors, were just sitting down round the tea-table, and nurse was leaving the drawing-room in some apparent perturbation.

Wagga wagged his tail, Muff came forward purring, and a laugh greeted Flora. "Do you know," cried George, "that you have been fast asleep ever so long in the yew walk, for I found you there? And now nurse was on her way to fetch you in, if you hadn't turned up."

Flora said not a word in answer, but sat down just as she was, with tumbled frock and hair, and a conscious look in her little face that made it very sweet and winning. Before tea was over, she had nestled close up to Anne, and whispered how sorry she was to have been so cross.

And I think if she lives to be nine years old and give another birthday party, she is likely on that occasion to be even less like the birthday Queen of her troubled dream than was the Flora of eight years old: who, with dear friends and playmates and pretty presents, yet scarcely knew how to bear a few trifling disappointments, or how to be obliging and good-humoured under slight annoyances.

"Aunt, Aunt!"

"What, girls?"

"Aunt, do tell us the story of the frog who couldn't boil the kettle."

"But I was not there to hear Susan tell the story."

"Oh, but you know it, Aunt."

"No, indeed I do not. I can imagine reasons why a frog would not and should not boil a kettle, but I never heard any such stated."

"Oh, but try. You know, Aunt, you are always telling *us* to try."

"Fairly put, Jane, and I will try, on condition that you all help me with my sewing."

"But we got through our work yesterday."

"Very well, Maude, as you like: only no help no story. I have too many poor friends ever to get through *my* work. However, as I see thimbles coming out, I conclude you choose story and labour. Look, these breadths must be run together, three and three. Ella, if you like to go to your music, don't stay listening out of ceremony: still, if you stay, here are plenty of button-holes to overcast. Now are we all seated and settled? Then listen. The frog and his peers will have to talk, of course; but that seems a marvel scarcely worth mentioning after Flora's experience."

Edith and a teakettle were spending one warm afternoon together in a wood. Before proceeding with my story, let me introduce each personage to you more particularly.

The wood should perhaps be called a grove rather than a wood, but in Edith's eyes it looked no less than a forest. About a hundred fine old beech-trees stood together, with here and there an elegant silver birch drooping in their midst. Besides these there was one vine which, by some freak, had been planted near the centre of the group, and which, year after year, trailing its long graceful branches over at least a dozen neighbours, dangled bunches of pale purple grapes among its leaves and twisted tendrils. The kettle was of brilliant copper, fitted up with a yellow glass handle: it was also on occasion a pleasing singer. Edith was a little girl who thought herself by no means such a very little girl, and at any rate as wise as her elder brother, sister, and nurse. I should be afraid to assert that she did not reckon herself as wise as her parents: but we much hope not, for her own sake.

The loving mother had planned a treat for her family that afternoon. A party of friends and relations were to assemble in the beech-wood, and partake of a gipsy tea: some catch-singing might be managed, cold supper should be laid indoors, and if the evening proved very delightful, the open-air entertainment might be prolonged till full-moonrise.

Preparations were intrusted to nurse's care, others of the household working under her, and she promising to go down to the beeches at least half an hour before the time fixed for the party, to see that all was ready. An early dinner throughout the house and no lessons in the schoolroom set the afternoon free for the gipsy feast.

After dinner Edith dressed her doll in its best clothes, tied on its broadbrimmed hat and veil, and hooked a miniature parasol into its waistband. Her sister was busy arranging flowers for the supper-table, her brother was out taking a walk, nurse was deep in jams, sandwiches, and delicacies in general; for nurse, though going by her old name, and still doing all sorts of things for her old baby, was now in fact housekeeper.

None of these could bestow much attention on Edith, who, doll in arm, strolled along into the kitchen, and there paused to watch cook rolling puff paste at her utmost speed. Six dozen patty-pans stood in waiting, and yawned as they waited.

Edith set down her doll on the window-seat and began to talk, whilst cook, with a goodnatured red face, made her an occasional random answer, right or wrong as it happened.

"What are we to have besides sandwiches and tarts?"

"Cold fowls, and a syllabub, and champagne, and tea and coffee, and potato-rolls, and lunns,[117] and tongue, and I can't say what besides."

"Where are the fowls, cook?"

"In the larder, where they ought to be, Miss Edith, not lying about in a hot kitchen."

"Do you like making tarts?"

"I like tarts, but not often."

"Cook, you're not attending to what I say."

"No, the attendance is just what I should not have liked."

Edith looked about till a bright copper kettle on a shelf caught her eye. "Is that the kettle for tea?"

"Yes, miss."

The doll gazing out of window was forgotten, while, mounting on a stool, Edith reached down the kettle.

"I will carry the kettle out ready."

"The fire will have to be lighted first," answered cook, as she hurried her tarts into the oven, and ran out to fetch curled parsley from the kitchen-garden.

"I can light the fire," called out Edith after her, though not very anxious to make herself heard: and thus it happened that cook heard nothing beyond the child's voice saying something or other of no consequence.

So Edith found a box of lucifers, and sallied forth kettle in hand. Striking on the burnished copper, the sun's rays transformed that also into a resplendent portable sun of dazzling aspect. The beautiful sunshine bathed garden, orchard, field, lane and wood; bathed flower, bush and tree; bathed bird, beast and butterfly. Frisk, the Newfoundland dog, and

Edith, with her dog Frisk, her cat Cosy, and Crest the cockatoo.

Cosy, the Persian cat, meeting their young mistress, turned round, to give her their company. Crest, the cockatoo, taking a constitutional on the lawn, fluttered up to her shoulder and perched there. The four went on together, Frisk carrying the kettle in his mouth, and Crest pecking at the match-box. Several lucifers dropped out, and not more than six reached their destination.

Edith knew that the gipsy party was to be held just where the vine grew, and thither she directed her steps. A pool, the only pool in the wood, gleamed close at hand, and mirrored in its still depths the lights, shadows, and many greens of beech-tree, birch-tree, and vine. How she longed for a cluster of those purple grapes which, hanging high above her head, swung to and fro with every breath of wind; now straining a tendril, now displacing a leaf, now dipping towards her but never within reach. Still, as Edith was such a very wise girl, we must not suppose she would stand long agape after unattainable grapes: nor did she. Her business just then was to boil a kettle, and to this she bent her mind.

Three sticks and a hook dependent therefrom suggested a tripod erected for the kettle: and so it was.

[Why a tripod, Aunt?—I have been wondering at the no remarks, but here comes one at last. Three sticks, Maude, are the fewest that can stand up firmly by themselves; two would tumble down, and four are not wanted. The reel? here it is: and then pass it to Clara.]

Within the legs of the tripod lay a fagot,[118] supported on some loose bricks. The fagot had been untied, but otherwise very little disturbed.

By standing on the fagot, Edith made herself more than tall enough to hang the kettle on its hook: then jumping down she struck her first match. A flash followed; and in one instant the match went out, as might have been expected in the open air and with no shelter for the flame. She struck a second lucifer, with the like result: a third, a fourth, with no better success. After this it was high time to ponder well before sacrificing a fifth match; for two only remained in the broken box.

Edith sat down to reflect, and stayed quiet so long, with her cheek leaning on her hand and her eyes fixed on a lucifer, that the aborigines of the wood grew bold and gathered round her.

[Who were the aborigines, Aunt?—The natives of the wood, Laura; the creatures born and bred there generation after generation.]

A squirrel scampered down three boughs lower on the loftiest beech-tree, and cracked his beech-mast audibly. A pair of wood pigeons advanced making polite bows. A mole popped a fleshy nose and a little human hand out of his burrow—popped them in, and popped them out again. A toad gazed deliberately round him with his eye like a jewel. Two hedgehogs came along and seated themselves near the toad. A frog—

Edith thinking how she shall light the fire and boil her kettle in the wood.

[*The* frog, Aunt?—Yes, Laura,]

—*the* frog hopped at a leisurely pace up the pond bank, and squatted among the long grasses at its edge.

The wonder is that Frisk, Cosy, and Crest, let this small fry come and go at pleasure and unmolested; but, whatever their motive may have been, they did so. They sat with great gravity right and left of their mistress, and kept themselves to themselves.

Edith's situation had now become, as it seems to me, neither pleasant nor dignified. She had volunteered to boil a kettle, and could not succeed even in lighting a fire. Her relations, friends, and other natural enemies would be arriving, and would triumph over her: for if her fire would not light, her kettle would certainly never boil. She took up the fifth lucifer and prepared to strike—paused—laid it back in the box: for it was her last but one. She sat on thinking what to do, yet could think of nothing to the purpose: of nothing better, that is, than of striking the match and running the risk. What should she do?

She had not even so much as half an eye to spare for the creatures around her, whilst they on their side concentrated their utmost attention on her. The pigeons left off bowing: the squirrel did not fetch a second beechmast.

"Oh dear!" exclaimed Edith at last; "what shall I do?"

Two voices, like two gurgling bottles, answered, "Couldn't you fly away, dear?" and the two pigeons bowed like one pigeon.

Edith was so thoroughly preoccupied by her troubles as to have very little room left in her mind for surprise: still, she did just glance at the pigeons before answering, "I wish you'd advise something sensible, instead of telling me to fly without wings."

"If you can only get so much as one twig to light," called out the squirrel hopefully, "I'll fan the flame with my tail."

"Ah," retorted Edith, "but that's just it: how am I to light the first twig with lucifers that do nothing but go out?"

A pause. "What should you say," suggested the mole, rubbing his hands together, "to my rearranging the sticks?"

"Very well," answered Edith, "do what you please." But she looked as if she did not expect much good to result from the mole's co-operation.

However, the mole clambered up one of the bricks, and then by pushing and pulling with his handy little hands, really did arrange the sticks in a loose heap full of hollows and tunnels for admitting currents of air; and so far matters looked promising.

The two hedgehogs sat silent and staring; why they came and why they stayed never appeared from first to last; but the frog hopped past them, and enquired, with a sudden appearance of interest, "Does not the kettle want filling?" No one noticed what he said, so he added under his breath, "Perhaps it is full already."

[Was it full, Aunt?—No, Maude, there was not a drop in it: so after all it was fortunate that it hung above black sticks instead of over a blazing fire, or it would soon have been spoilt. Remember, girls, never put an empty kettle on the fire, or you and it will rue the consequence.]

The toad peered with his bright eye in among the sticks. "I should vote," said he mildly, "that the next lucifer be held and struck inside the heap, to protect the spark from draughts."

[How came the toad to be so much cleverer than his neighbours, Aunt?—Well, Jane, I suppose such a bright thought may have occurred to him rather than to the rest, because toads so often live inside stones: at least, so people have said. And suppose his father, grandfather and great-grandfather all inhabited stones, the idea of doing everything inside something may well have come naturally to him.]

The toad's suggestion roused Edith from despondency to action. She knelt down by the tripod, although just there the ground was sprinkled with brickdust and sawdust; thrust both hands in amongst the wood, struck a match, saw it flash,—and die out. "Try again," whispered the toad; and as she could devise no better plan she tried again.

The sixth and last venture was crowned with success. One twig caught fire, as a slight crackling followed by a puff of smoke attested. The squirrel took his seat on a brick and whisked his tail to and fro. The hedgehogs turning their backs on the smoke, sniffed in the opposite direction; waiting as I suppose for the event, though they showed not the least vestige of interest in it.

"Now," cried the frog hopping up and down in his excitement and curiosity, "Now to boil the kettle."

But that first spark of success was followed by a dim, smoky, fitful smouldering which gave merely the vaguest promise of a coming blaze. A pair of bellows would have answered far better than the squirrel's tail: and though, with a wish to oblige, the two wood-pigeons fluttered round and round the tripod, they did not the slightest good.

Just then a fox bustled up, and glanced askance at Frisk: but receiving a reassuring and friendly nod, joined the party under the shady vine-branches. This fox was a tidy person, and like most foxes always carried about a brush with him: so without more ado he went straight up to Edith, and gave her dusty frock a thorough brushing all round. Next he wrapped his fore paws about the vine, and shook it with all his force; but as no grapes fell, though several bunches bobbed up and down and seemed ready to drop into his mouth, he gave one leap upwards off all four feet at once towards the lowest cluster he could spy; this also failing he shook his head, turned up his nose, shrugged his shoulders, muttered, "They must be sour" (and this once

I suspect the fox was right), trotted away, and was soon lost to view among the beech-trees.

"Now," cried the frog once more, "now for the kettle."

"Boil it yourself," retorted Edith.

So the frog did not know how to boil the kettle, but he only replied, "I can't bear hot water." This you may remark was a startling change of tone in the frog: but I suppose he was anxious to save his credit. Now if he had only taken time to look at what was under his very eyes he might have saved his credit without belying his principles: for

The fire had gone out!

And here my story finishes: except that I will just add how

As Edith in despair sat down to cry,

As the pigeons withdrew bowing and silent,

As the squirrel scudded[119] up his beech-tree again,

As the mole vanished underground,

As the toad hid himself behind a toadstool,

As the two hedgehogs yawned and went away yawning,

As the frog dived,

As Frisk wagged, Cosy purred, and Crest murmured, "Pretty Cockatoo," to console their weeping mistress,

Nurse arrived on the ground with a box of lucifers in one hand, two fire-wheels in the other, and half-a-dozen newspapers under her arm, and exclaimed, "Oh, my dear child, run indoors as fast as you can: for your mother, father, brother and sister are hunting up and down all over the house looking for you; and cook is half out of her wits because she cannot find the kettle."

"My dear children, what is all this mysterious whispering about?"

"It's Jane, Aunt."

"Oh, Maude, I'm sure it's you quite as much."

"Well then, Jane and Maude, what is it?"

"We were only saying that both your stories are summer stories, and we want you to tell us a winter story some day. That's all, Aunty dear."

"Very well, Maudy dear; but don't say 'only,' as if I were finding fault with you. If Jane and you wish for a winter story, my next shall freeze hard. What! now? You really do allow me very little time for invention!"

"And please, Aunt, be wonderful."

"Well, Laura, I will try to be wonderful; but I cannot promise first-rate wonders on such extremely short notice. Ella, you sitting down too? Here is my work for you all, the same as yesterday, and here comes my story."

Old Dame Margaret kept the village fancy shop. Her window was always filled with novelties and attractions, but about Christmastide, it put forth extra splendours, and as it were blossomed gorgeously. Flora's doll, her sugar-plum box and hedgehog pincushion, came I should say from this very window; and though her hoops and sticks for *les grâces* can scarcely have looked smart enough for a place of honour, they emerged probably from somewhere behind the counter.

[Did Edith's doll come out of the window too?—Yes, Clara, if Flora's did I have no doubt Edith's did; for as they say in the Arabian Nights, "each was more beautiful than the other."]

In spite of her gay shop, Dame Margaret was no fine lady, but a nice simple old woman who wore plain clothes, and made them last a long time: and thus it was that over and over again she found money to give or lend among her needy neighbours. If a widow's cow died, or a labourer's cottage was burnt down, or if half-a-dozen poor children were left orphans, Dame Margaret's purse would be the first to open, and the last to shut; though she was very cautious as to helping idlers who refused to help themselves, or drunkards who would only do more harm with more money.

I dare say her plain clothes and her plain table (for she kept a plain table too) were what enabled her, amongst other good deeds, to take home little Maggie, her orphan granddaughter, when the child was left almost without kith or kin to care for her. These two were quite alone in the world: each was the other's only living relation, and they loved each other very dearly.

Hour after hour on Christmas Eve, business raged in Dame Margaret's shop. I shrink from picturing to myself the run on burnt almonds, chocolate, and "sweeties" of every flavour, all done up in elegant fancy boxes; the run on wax dolls, wooden dolls, speaking dolls, squeaking dolls; the run on woolly lambs and canaries with removable heads; the run on everything in general. Dame Margaret and Maggie at her elbow had a busy time behind their counter, I do assure you.

[Did Maggie serve too?—Yes, Jane; and it was her delight to run up steps and reach down goods from high shelves.]

About three o'clock, the shop happened for a moment to be empty of customers, and Dame Margaret was glancing complacently round upon her diminished stock, when her eye lighted on some parcels which had been laid on a chair and forgotten. "Oh dear, Maggie," exclaimed she, "the doctor's young ladies have left behind them all the tapers for their Christmas tree, and I don't know what besides." Now that doctor resided with his family in a large house some distance out of the village, and the road to it lay through the outskirts of an oak forest.

"Let me take them, Granny," cried Maggie eagerly: "and perhaps I may get a glimpse of the Christmas tree."

"But it will soon be dark."

"Oh, Granny, I will make haste: do, please, let me go."

So kind Dame Margaret answered, "Yes; only be sure to' make great haste:" and then she packed up the forgotten parcels very carefully in a basket. Not merely the red tapers, but a pound of vanilla chocolate, a beautiful bouncing ball, and two dozen crackers, had all been left behind.

Basket on arm, Maggie started for the doctor's house: and as she stepped out into the cold open air it nipped her fingers and ears, and little pugnose. Cold? indeed it was cold, for the thermometer marked *half-a-dozen* degrees of frost; every pond and puddle far and near was coated with thick sheet ice, or turned to block ice from top to bottom; every branch of every bare oak shivered in a keen east wind. How the poor little birds kept warm, or whether in fact any did keep warm on the leafless boughs, I cannot tell: I only know that many a thrush and sparrow died of cold that winter, whilst robin redbreast begged crumbs at cottage windows. His snug scarlet waistcoat could scarcely keep hungry robin's heart warm; and I am afraid to think about his poor little pretty head with its bright eye.

Maggie set off on her journey with a jump and a run, and very soon got a fall: for without any suspicion of what awaited her she set her foot on a loose lump of ice, and down she went, giving the back of her head a sounding thump. She was up again directly, and ran on as if nothing had happened; but whether her brain got damaged by the blow, or how else it may have been, I know not; I only know that the thwack seemed in one moment to fill the atmosphere around her with sparks, flames and flashes of lightning; and that from this identical point of time commenced her marvellous adventures.

Were the clouds at play? they went racing across the sky so rapidly! Were the oaks at play? they tossed their boughs up and down in such rattling confusion! Maggie on her travels began to think that she too should dearly like a game of play, when an opening in the forest disclosed to her a green glade, in which a party of children were sporting together in the very freest and easiest manner possible.

Such a game! Such children! If they had not been children they must inevitably have been grasshoppers. They leaped over oaks, wrestled in mid-air, bounded past a dozen trees at once; two and two they spun round like whirlwinds; they darted straight up like balloons; they tossed each other about like balls. A score of dogs barking and gambolling in their midst were evidently quite unable to keep up with them.

[Didn't they all get very hot, Aunt?—Very hot indeed, Maude, I should think.]

The children's cheeks were flushed, their hair streamed right out like comets' tails; you might have heard and seen their hearts beat, and yet no one appeared in the least out of breath. Positively they had plenty of breath amongst them to time their game by singing.

"One, two, three," they sang,—

"One, two, three," they sang,—

"One, two, three," they sang, "and away,"—as they all came clustering like a swarm of wasps round astonished Maggie.

How she longed for a game with them! She had never in her life seen anything half so funny, or so sociable, or so warming on a cold day. And we must bear in mind that Maggie had no play-fellows at home, and that cold winter was just then at its very coldest. "Yes," she answered eagerly; "yes, yes; what shall we play at?"

A glutinous-looking[120] girl in pink cotton velvet proposed: "Hunt the pincushion."

"No, Self Help," bawled a boy clothed in something like porcupine skin.

[Oh, Aunt, are these those monstrous children over again?—Yes, Ella, you really can't expect me not to utilize such a brilliant idea twice.]

"No, running races," cried a second girl, wriggling forward through the press like an eel.

"No, this,"—"No, that,"—"No, the other," shouted every one in general, bounding here, spinning there, jumping up, clapping hands, kicking heels, in a tempest of excitement.

"Anything you please," panted Maggie, twirling and leaping in emulation, and ready to challenge the whole field to a race; when suddenly her promise to make haste crossed her mind—her fatal promise, as it seemed to her; though you and I, who have as it were peeped behind the scenes, may well believe that it kept her out of no very delightful treat.

She ceased jumping, she steadied her swinging basket on her arm, and spoke resolutely though sadly: "Thank you all, but I mustn't stop to play with you, because I promised Granny to make haste. Good-bye;"—and off she started, not venturing to risk her decision by pausing or looking back; but feeling the bouncing ball bounce in her basket as if it too longed for a game, and hearing with tingling ears a shout of mocking laughter which followed her retreat.

The longest peal of laughter comes to an end. Very likely, as soon as Maggie vanished from view among the oak-trees the boisterous troop ceased laughing at her discomfiture; at any rate, they did not pursue her; and she soon got beyond the sound of their mirth, whilst one by one the last echoes left off laughing and hooting at her. Half glad that she had persisted in keeping her word, yet half sorry to have missed so rare a chance, Maggie trudged on solitary and sober. A pair of wood-pigeons alighting almost at her feet pecked about in the frozen path, but could not find even one mouthful for their little empty beaks: then, hopeless and silent, they fluttered up and perched on a twig above her head. The sight of these hungry creatures made Maggie hungry from sympathy; yet it was rather for their sakes than for her own that she lifted the cover of her basket and peered underneath it, to see whether by any chance kind Granny had popped in a hunch[121] or so of cake,—alas! not a crumb. Only there lay the chocolate, sweet and tempting, looking most delicious through a hole in its gilt paper.

Would birds eat chocolate, wondered Maggie,—

[Would they, Aunt?—Really, I hardly know myself, Laura: but I should suppose some might, if it came in their way.]

—and she was almost ready to break off the least little corner and try, when a sound of rapid footsteps coming along startled her; and hastily shutting her basket, she turned to see who was approaching.

A boy: and close at his heels marched a fat tabby cat, carrying in her mouth a tabby kitten. Or was it a real boy? He had indeed arms, legs, a head, like ordinary people: but his face exhibited only one feature, and that was a wide mouth. He had no eyes; so how he came to know that Maggie and a basket were standing in his way I cannot say: but he did seem somehow aware of the fact; for the mouth, which could doubtless eat as well as speak, grinned, whined, and accosted her: "Give a morsel to a poor starving beggar."

"I am very sorry," replied Maggie, civilly; and she tried not to stare, because she knew it would be rude to do so, though none the less amazed was she at his aspect; "I am very sorry, but I have nothing I can give you."

"*Nothing*, with all that chocolate!"

"The chocolate is not mine, and I cannot give it you," answered Maggie bravely: yet she felt frightened; for the two stood all alone together in the forest, and the wide mouth was full of teeth and tusks, and began to grind them.

"Give it me, I say. I tell you I'm starving:" and he snatched at the basket.

"I don't believe you are starving," cried Maggie, indignantly, for he looked a great deal stouter and sleeker than she herself did; and she started aside, hugging her basket close as the beggar darted out a lumpish-looking hand to seize it. "I'm hungry enough myself, but I wouldn't be a thief!" she shouted back to her tormentor, whilst at full speed she fled away from him, wondering secretly why he did not give chase, for he looked big enough and strong enough to run her down in a minute: but after all, when she spoke so resolutely and seemed altogether so determined, it was he that hung his head, shut his mouth, and turned to go away again faster and faster, till he fairly scudded out of sight among the lengthening shadows.

Had this forest road always been so long? Never before certainly had it appeared so extremely long to Maggie. Hungry and tired, she lost all spirit, and plodded laggingly forward, longing for her journey's end, but without energy enough to walk fast. The sky had turned leaden, the wind blew bleaker than ever, the bare boughs creaked and rattled drearily. Poor desolate

The boy with the great mouth full of teeth grins at Maggie.

Maggie! drowsiness was creeping over her, and she began to wish above all things that she might just sit down where she stood and go fast asleep: never mind food, or fire, or bed; only let her sleep.

[Do you know, children, what would most likely have happened to Maggie if she had yielded to drowsiness and slept out there in the cold?—What, Aunt?—Most likely she would never have woke again. And then there would have been an abrupt end to my story.]

Yet she recollected her promise to make haste, and went toiling on and on and on, step after tired step. At length she had so nearly passed through the forest that five minutes more would bring her out into the by-road which led straight to the doctor's door, when she came suddenly upon a party of some dozen persons sitting toasting themselves around a glowing gipsy fire, and all yawning in nightcaps or dropping asleep.

They opened their eyes half-way, looked at her, and shut them again. They all nodded. They all snored. Whoever woke up yawned; whoever slept snored. Merely to see them and hear them was enough to send one to sleep.

A score or so of birds grew bold, hopped towards the kindly fire, and perched on neighbouring shoulder, hand, or nose. No one was disturbed, no one took any notice.

If Maggie felt drowsy before, she felt ready to drop now: but remembering her promise, and rousing herself by one last desperate effort, she shot past the tempting group. Not a finger stirred to detain her, not a voice proffered a word, not a foot moved, not an eye winked.

At length the cold long walk was ended, and Maggie stood ringing the doctor's door-bell, wide awake and on tiptoe with enchanting expectation: for surely now there was a good prospect of her being asked indoors, warmed by a fire, regaled with something nice, and indulged with a glimpse of the Christmas tree bending under its crop of wonderful fruit.

Alas, no! The door opened, the parcel was taken in with a brief "Thank you," and Maggie remained shut out on the sanded doorstep.

Chilled to the bone, famished, cross, and almost fit to cry with disappointment, Maggie set off to retrace her weary steps. Evening had closed in, the wind had lulled, a few snowflakes floated about in the still air and seemed too light to settle down. If it looked dim on the open road, it looked dimmer still in the forest: dim, and solitary, and comfortless.

Were all the sleepers gone clean away since Maggie passed scarcely a quarter of an hour before? Surely, yes: and moreover not a trace of their glowing fire remained, not one spark, not one ember. Only something whitish lay on the ground where they had been sitting: could it be a nightcap? Maggie stooped to look, and picked up, not a nightcap, but a wood-pigeon with ruffled feathers and closed eyes, which lay motionless and half frozen in her hand. She snuggled it tenderly to her, and kissed its poor little beak and drooping head before she laid it to get warm within the bosom of her frock. Lying there, it seemed to draw anger and discontent out of her heart: and soon she left off grumbling to herself, and stepped forward with renewed energy, because the sooner the pigeon could be taken safe indoors out of the cold, the better.

Mew, mew, mew: such a feeble pitiful squeak of a mew! Just about where the Mouth had met her a mew struck upon Maggie's ear, and wide she opened both ears and eyes to spy after the mewer. Huddled close up against the gnarled root of an oak, crouched a small tabby kitten all alone, which mewed and mewed and seemed to beg for aid. Maggie caught up the helpless creature, popped it into her empty basket, and hurried forward.

But not far, before she paused afresh: for suddenly, just in that green glade where the grasshopper children in general and one glutinous girl in particular had stood hooting her that very afternoon, her foot struck against some soft lump, which lay right in her path and made no effort to move out of harm's way. What could it be? She stooped, felt it, turned it over, and it was a short-haired smooth puppy, which put one paw confidingly into her hand, and took the tip of her little finger between its teeth with the utmost friendliness. Who could leave such a puppy all abroad on such a night? Not Maggie, for one. She added the puppy to her basketful,—and a basketful it was then!—and ran along singing quite merrily under her burden.

And when, the forest shades left behind her, she went tripping along through the pale clear moonlight, in one moment the sky before her flashed with glittering gold, and flushed from horizon to zenith with rosy glow; for the northern lights came out, and lit up each cloud as if it held lightning, and each hill as if it smouldered ready to burst into a volcano. Every oak-tree seemed turned to coral, and the road itself to a pavement of dusky carnelian.[122]

Then at last she once more mounted a door-step and rang a door-bell, but this time they were the familiar step and bell of home. So now when the door opened she was received, not with mere "Thank you," but with a loving welcoming hug; and not only what she carried, but she herself also found plenty of light and warmth awaiting all arrivals, in a curtained parlour set out for tea. And whilst Maggie thawed, and drank tea, and ate buttered toast in Granny's company, the pigeon thawed too, and cooed and pecked up crumbs until it perched on the rail of a chair, turned its head contentedly under its wing, and dropped fast asleep; and the kitten thawed too, and lapped away at a saucerful of milk, till it fell asleep on the rug; and the puppy—well, I cannot say the puppy thawed too, because he was warm and cordial when Maggie met him; but he wagged his stumpy tail, stood bolt upright and begged, munched tit-bits, barked, rolled over, and at last settled down under the table to sleep: after all which, Dame Margaret and Maggie followed the good example set them, and went to bed and to sleep.

Maggie drinks tea and eats buttered toast with Granny.

True in the Main:
Two Sketches

(from *The Dawn of Day*, 1882)

The first of these "sketches" of suffering and redemption was published 1 May 1882, the second on 1 June 1882, in the S.P.C.K. magazine *The Dawn of Day*—"an illustrated monthly for Sunday school and parish use" (Marsh, 587). William Michael Rossetti's diary describes these "little sketches" as "narrating facts regarding two poor families of her acquaintance, the Meaders and Bakers" (*FL*, 212). Christina's short narratives describe the good works of the compassionate "Miss M." (her sister, Maria) whose charity leads several individuals into full communion with the Church.

The Society of All Saints, the first Anglican sisterhood, began in the London parish of Christ Church (where the Rossettis attended) in 1845. Maria was affiliated with the order by 1860, became a novice in 1873, and was fully professed in 1875.

True in the Main. Two Sketches.

1.

John Meads, in a drunken fury, turned his wife out of their one room, and locked the door.

Poor woman, she was not far from her seventh confinement, and felt none the brighter or the brisker for that circumstance. She had nothing on but her night-dress, and being torn out of her bed and almost thrown on to the outside landing, there she sat huddled up, shivering and crying. Three of her five living children were locked in with their drunken father, and could not get at her to comfort her or help her in any way. So she could only shiver and cry, till at last from sheer exhaustion she dropped off to sleep.

Next morning her husband, no longer furious, but sullen, slouched and stumbled down stairs to his day's work, without vouchsafing her a word or a look. Then she crept back into bed again; and Jack, her third son, aged eight, made and brought her a cup of very poor tea. The tea was poor, but the love with which he brought it sweetened it to her taste, and after they had cried together, they both felt better.

John Meads was a bricklayer, and now he had undertaken a long job of work some miles out of London, and did not mean to return home for several weeks to come. But of this his wife was not informed. Had she known it, it might have distressed her one way, and consoled her another. It was not easy to get on without his wages, but it was a perfect luxury to get on without himself: not even a good wife, and this poor woman was an excellent wife, can take pleasure in the company of a husband who growls and swears and sometimes kicks her, who brings home pence when he ought to bring shillings, who knocks the children about or smashes crockery in drunken rage, and who in drunken jealousy tosses clothes just washed into the coals-cuttle. So poor Mrs. Meads, having merely a choice of discomforts, did not much care which lot befel her; and saw him or did not see him return, with a contented mind.

At length, however, the last day's washing was finished off, and the last washing money paid her, at any rate for some time to come: for in her one room and scanty bed she lay in of a wailing skinny little boy.

Jack, aged eight, was now the acting head of the house: for his elder brothers were out in the world, and the two below himself (not reckoning the new baby) were over young to be helpful. Jack could and did light the fire, make gruel,[123] and look up a good natured woman to lend a hand occasionally to his mother. But who, at least till charing[124] or laundry work could be resumed—who was to earn money and make both ends meet? There appeared no one except himself, so clearly himself it must be. His mind was soon made up, and his plan matured. The good natured woman lent him a stump of a broom at a charge of a penny a-day, to be paid out of his earnings; "no earnings, no pay," was the wary agreement; and engaged even the first day to keep his secret even from his mother. So the very next morning after the baby's birth, Jack marched out to seek his fortune as crossing sweeper in a square.

He worked with a will, eking out a defective broom by energetic brushing. He did not beg of passers by; but his diligence and efficiency pleaded for him, and brought him pence and halfpence in a slender stream. Perhaps his appearance also pleaded for him, for he looked even younger than his years, being short and rosy and childish of aspect, as befitted a twin whose fellow-twin was dead. Such was Jack. And at night when he went home with sevenpence net after paying for the broom, and handed his earnings and told his secret to his mother, and when she blessed him and hugged him, and said she should not know which way to turn but for him, I do not suppose there were many happier boys in London than tired, hungry, muddy, honest Jack.

Day after day Jack returned to his crossing, and evening after evening he carried home halfpence, sometimes more, sometimes fewer, to his mother. An exceptional evening occurred on Saturdays, when Jack made a great bustle and slop, and washed up everything that came handy, including his juniors, in a leaky tub, and the floor, without much soap.

Now in that square where Jack swept lived a lady full of Christian love and good works. Several weeks before our hero's start in life she had noticed certain idle boys who played with brooms and begged in the neighbourhood, and she had done her utmost to induce them to attend school, promising to pay their school fees: but no, their idleness baffled her energetic good-will, and to school they would not go with any approach to regularity. But Jack had heard of that good chance wasted, and longed to secure for himself the lost opening and the discouraged friend. So touching his cap, and looking shy and pleasant, he one day accosted kind Miss M., who had already given him many a penny at his post, and asked her whether she could tell him of a night school into which he might gain admittance? "After his day's work," said he stoutly, ready to forego even coveted book-learning if incompatible with duty.

Miss M. stood still to listen. Yes, she knew of a night school not very far off, kept by certain Sisters who devoted their lives to praying, teaching, and other holy pursuits. She would speak for him to the head Sister, would pay his weekly fee, and provide for him such books as became necessary. What would be required on his part was regularity, painstaking, and strict obedience to rules. All this Jack promised. And thus occurred the turning-point of his life.

At the Sisters' School he learnt to read, write, and cipher. Without being unusually clever, he read attentively, and took pains to recollect what he read. Thus he learnt many good and useful things. Best of all, he learnt the truths and duties of religion; and putting in practice what he was taught, he became even a better and still more affectionate son than heretofore to his much-tried mother: who was deserted sometimes by her husband, or else at other times was driven by his brutality to keep out of his way if any how she could escape him. Jack remained under the good Sisters' eye till, after careful preparation, he was confirmed and admitted to Holy Communion.

But I will not attempt to follow step by step his prosperous career. As time went on the younger children began to earn something: and then their mother by washing and charing managed, all put together, to get on tolerably. Miss M. continued to help Jack in various ways and on many occasions; and not least when, the head Sister having found a place for him as a photographer's errand boy, money was wanted for his decent outfit. After serving the photographer faithfully, Jack met with an opening to transfer his service at advanced wages to a Medical Practitioner: so he did, and again throve and acquired friends.

Meanwhile even John Meads, the selfish drunken father, came (we may trust) to repentance. Mortal disease, as so often happens to drunkards, laid hold upon him before he was an old man; and then he grew desirous of home and home comforts, and a wife's kind nursing. His wife, poor woman, forgave and forgot; took him home, nursed him, and had the happiness of seeing him leave her for the great last time in a better mind.

When Jack was about twenty, his staunch friend Miss M. died; and knowing how truly she had loved and cared for him, I let him know of her death. Ere long he called upon me, by the act rather than by words expressing his respect and sympathy. He was now under butler, well dressed and prosperous looking, no longer rosy, but still short, doing well, and likely I trust to continue doing well until the final day of account, when "every man shall have praise of God,"[125] and when benefactors and benefactresses shall shine forth surrounded by those they have succoured as by a crown of rejoicing.

Surely we cannot doubt that Jack Meads is inheriting the blessing which rests on all who keep the fifth Commandment, that "first commandment with promise."[126]

2.

Mrs. Bates was a far happier woman than poor Mrs. Meads, though I daresay the latter would not have exchanged her excellent Jack for the other's comforts.

Not that everything went smoothly with Mrs. Bates either. Her husband while still in the prime of life fell into almost desperate ill health, tottered on the brink of the grave, and all but tottered in. But they loved each other as married couples should do: and Mrs. Bates would no more have suffered him to end his days in the workhouse, than she would have crept into that unattractive refuge herself. Wherefore this valiant woman, who could neither read nor write, but who could and would work, strained every nerve to keep a roof over her dear William's head; bent upon letting him live, and (if so it must be) letting him die, in his own bed and in the midst of his beloved children. She washed, she chared, she took in needlework, though no great hand at her needle; she made a shilling go as far as ever shilling went in London, and habitually owed not one penny to any single person.

Before William Bates quite lost his health, his wife lay in of twin girls: and these twins brought about an acquaintance which in the long run proved of essential service to the Bateses. A kind hearted old lady, who loved souls in general and babies in particular, heard of the duplicate baby Bates; and sent a beautiful bundle of baby clothes of her own making to help the mother. One thing grew out of another. Miss M. (the old lady's niece) conceived a warm friendship for the Bateses; and used her affectionate influence over them with such good effect, that in time she led both husband and wife, after earnest preparation, to be confirmed, and to become devout and habitual communicants. Thenceforward they in their turn became messengers of good within their own circle: and (please God) at the Day of Resurrection some will rise with them who owe to them, under God, eternal gratitude.

Now by this time at which I am writing, the worst of their troubles I hope are over. William Bates, beyond all probability, has so far recovered health and strength as to be able to undertake and carry on (though not without assistance) the duties of organ blower in his district church. Mrs. Bates fulfils a regular engagement as cleaner in another church, where the pew-opener is her helpful friend; and besides this she washes, and more especially irons, for a small connection of paying customers. Her elder daughter, aged nineteen, was married last Easter to a steady young man in constant work: while Bessie, the younger daughter (one of the twins, and rapidly growing up), is willing and competent in some measure to take her elder sister's place by becoming their good mother's right hand and assistant. These few persons, four in all, or, reckoning the son-in-law, five, now make up the entire Bates family: and Bessie having been confirmed this year, all five enjoyed the privilege of receiving Holy Communion together on a recent Sunday.

Yet when I began to write about this exemplary family, I was thinking more especially of two children who died a dozen years or so ago,—Bill, and little twin Rose. Bill was an admirable and endearing boy: his uncommonly pretty face seemed aptly to express his beautiful soul. He lived to be about ten years old; and then died of scarlet fever, wringing his mother's heart, and nevermore to be forgotten by her. Besides my general knowledge of his being good and dear, I recollect in particular how in the house where at that time the Bateses lodged, he has been known voluntarily and out of his own proper turn, to undertake the weekly cleaning of the common entrance or staircase, in order to spare a fellow-lodger who was an old woman, and who must otherwise have toiled through the work in question.

Very soon after Bill's death, which took place in an Infirmary, little Rose, still scarcely more than a baby, sickened of the same dreadful fever: and she grew so afraid of being sent away from all she loved, that she lay quiet and uncomplaining in hopes of not calling attention to her suffering plight; and only when she thought herself unobserved would she stretch out her poor little fevered hand to reach a mouthful of drink. And thus she did at least contrive to die in her own home.

Keen as is the grief of bereaved parents, I trust both father and mother are ready from the depths of their heart to bless God for these dear children.

"Is it well with the child? . . . It is well."[127]

Part 2

Miscellaneous Prose

Selections from the
Imperial Dictionary
of Universal Biography (1857–63)

A nswering a letter in February 1885, Rossetti made the following remarks: "Perhaps it is not worth adding that my name appears amongst the writers of the 'Imperial Dictionary of Universal Biography' to which work I contributed some articles on Italian literary men" (Troxell, 175). According to William Michael Rossetti (who also contributed articles), the dictionary was "brought out by subscription in Glasgow from 1857 to 1863, and edited by Dr. Waller" (*Reminiscences*, 2:301). Christina and William had been recruited as contributors by Mrs. Mary Howitt (Marsh, 189). In addition to the articles on Leopardi and Petrarch (vol. 3, 183–84 and 542–44) reprinted here, Christina wrote thirty-three other biographical articles ranging in length from forty or fifty to several hundred words.

The selections reprinted here are from the 3 volume edition, ed. John Francis Waller (London: W. Mackenzie, 1863).

LEOPARDI, Giacomo, Count, poet, philologist, philosopher, born at Recanati in the March of Ancona, 29th June, 1798; died at Capodimonte, Naples, 14th June, 1837. He was the eldest son of Count Monaldo Leopardi and the Marchioness Adelaide Antici, his family on both sides being reckoned amongst the noblest of his native place. Their fortune would appear not to have corresponded with their rank, if we may judge by the very straitened means of Giacomo. Other facts, however, seem to indicate that his father, a zealous Catholic, may merely have endeavoured by scanty supplies to keep his son out of harm's way. In early childhood Giacomo's education was conducted by two priests; but after his fourteenth year he was emancipated from tutelage. At the age of eight he commenced unaided the study of Greek; and speedily rejecting the Paduan grammar as inadequate, launched out at random amongst the Greek volumes of his father's library; these he subsequently perused methodically. At sixteen, besides being versed in all the ancient classics, he had read many of the later Greek and Latin authors, and a portion of the writings of the fathers; he had mastered the delicacies of his native tongue, as well as learned the English, French, Spanish, German, and Hebrew languages. In 1814 he prepared a Life of Plotinus, which furnished matter for the Addenda et Corrigenda of Creuzer's subsequent edition of that author. He translated copiously from the works of Homer, Hesiod, Virgil, and others; and speaking of certain translators amongst his fellow-countrymen made memorable by their great originals, he exclaims, "It is a goodly destiny, not to die except it be in company with an immortal." In 1816–17 he contributed articles to the *Spettatore* of Milan; and in the latter year published two anacreontic odes and a hymn to Neptune, composed indeed by himself, but purporting to be genuine Greek originals, and as such generally accepted. In 1822 he went to Rome, and became acquainted with Niebuhr, then Prussian minister at the pontifical court, who recognized with astonishment in a shy, insignificant young man, the erudite author of an admired work. Leopardi loathed his life at Recanati, and through Niebuhr he was now offered a chair of philosophy in Berlin; this he declined on the score of ill health. The same friend then endeavoured to interest Cardinal Gonsalvi in his favour, but preferment in that quarter was hindered by a refusal on his part to take orders. Most justly did he refuse; for apparently even before this sojourn in Rome he had exchanged his early pious impressions for total incredulity concerning all religion, whether revealed or natural. His intimate friend, Giordani, reported to have been a Benedictine seceded from the rule of his order, probably in this regard exercised a baneful influence on his mind, as their intercourse was tenderly affectionate. This infidelity, tainting Leopardi's finest works, was, however, united with pure morals, a loving heart, and an exalted intellect. He was a true poet. For beauty, note amongst his Canzoni the one on "Primo Amore," and those grand opening lines commencing "O patria mia;" for satiric humour read the exquisitely comic passage from his "Paralipomeni della Batrachomyomachia," where a distinction is laid down between "king of mice" and "king of mousedom." In the "Bruto Minore" he appears to have embodied many of his own sentiments; in the "Operette Morali," first published complete in Milan in 1827, there is an epitaph which may probably sum up under a feigned name his estimate of his own career. His death at the house of his faithful friend Ranieri was but the natural conclusion of his life of incurable sickness and suffering, resulting probably from original malformation. Gioberti, in the prefatory remarks to his Gesuito Moderna, informs us that at the last a priest was called in and blessed the dying Leopardi; but that the story of his having confessed to a Jesuit, and avowed some bias towards joining the followers of S. Ignatius, is false.

PETRARCA, *Francesco,* one of the four most renowned poets of Italy, born at Arezzo in Tuscany, 20th July, 1304; was found dead either of apoplexy or epilepsy, seated with his head resting on a book in his library at Arquà, 19th July, 1374. (The date of both birth and death differ slightly in various records, and the circumstances of the death are diversely narrated.) In 1302, the year when Dante and many of the Bianchi faction were banished from Florence, Pietro (commonly called Petracco or Petraccolo) da Parengo, an adherent of the same party, went into exile; and with his wife Eletta (called elsewhere Brigida) Canigiani, took up his abode at Arezzo, where their son Francesco di Petracco or Petrarca was born. After various vicissitudes, the exile's hope of return died out; and about 1312 he and his family removed to Avignon, where, under Clement V., the papal court held its state, and formed a centre of attraction to strangers from every quarter. Here and in the neighbouring town of Carpentras Francesco cultivated grammar, dialectics, and rhetoric. His father subsequently sent him to Montpellier, and finally to the Bolognese university to study law as his profession; but the born poet pored far more willingly over Latin classics than over legal documents; and appears to have loathed a calling in which, as he deemed, he might secure success at the cost of conscience, but could scarcely hope to do so with clean hands. Petracco's death put an end to the conflict between filial deference and strong inclination. Francesco abandoned the career selected for him; but, perhaps, made no wiser choice when, at the age of twenty-two, he, with his younger brother Gherardo, assumed the clerical habit, and found it constituted a passport into the corrupt gaieties of the court of Pope John XXII. His studies, however, were not superseded by frivolous pleasure, and he formed various solid friendships; those with Cardinal Giovanni Colonna and his brother Giacomo, bishop of Lombes, proved both tenderly intimate and enduring, whilst for their father Stefano he conceived the reverent affection which he evinces in some of his verses, as in the sonnet beginning—

"Gloriosa Colonna, in cui s'appoggia."
(Glorious Colonna, *i.e.,* Column, on which leans.)

In 1327 occurred that event which may be represented as the turning-point of Petrarca's life, which inspired so much of his Italian *Canzoniere,* and of which the traces are discernible more or less openly in his correspondence and in other of his compositions, yet which is shrouded with a veil of mystery, and of which the accounts irreconcilably differ. To follow one of the most popular narratives:—On Good Friday, 6th April, in the church of St. Clara, in Avignon, Petrarca first beheld that incomparable golden-haired Laura, who for precisely twenty-one years swayed, living, the current of his life; whose eyes and voice, habitual reserve and exceptional piety, inspired poem after poem; and from whose thrall not even the lady's death availed to release him. Her bare hand and dainty glove, her sweet speech and sweet laugh, her tears, her paleness, her salutation, are noted with untiring minuteness; he records how he watched with rapture a young girl washing the veil of Laura; and on another occasion how he beheld a group of ladies with Laura in the midst, like the sun girt by twelve stars. To read these elegant Tuscan strains, one might imagine that this veritable slave of love had few cares or interests or occupations, but what sprang from the master passion; that Avignon and Vaucluse, Rome and Naples, busy court life and solitary retirement, took their colour alike from the presence or absence of Laura; but the historic facts of Petrarca's life bear a different witness. Between 1330 and 1334, in the endeavour, as some say, to alleviate his disastrous passion, Petrarca took sundry short journeys, which at any rate served to augment his love of Italy; and the accession in 1334 of Benedict XII. to the pontificate, was followed by the first of those appeals, poetic and epistolary, which Petrarca addressed to popes and to temporal powers, urging the restitution of the papal court to Rome, and the deliverance of Italy. In 1335 Azzo da Correggio appeared at Avignon to solicit, in opposition to Marsiglio Rossi, the pontifical confirmation of the house of La Scala in the lordship of Parma; and formed an acquaintance with Petrarca, which gave rise to so great a mutual affection that for this dear friend's sake Francesco waived his rooted antipathy to the legal profession, pleaded Azzo's cause before Pope Benedict XII., and triumphed over the rival claimant. Late in 1336 Petrarca quitted Avignon, and early in the following year reached Rome, where he met with a warm reception from the Colonna family, and explored the antique monuments of the Eternal City; nor did he return to Avignon until the summer, soon again quitting it for the comparative solitude of Vaucluse, where he purchased a small house and estate, and found leisure to compose many of his works, both in prose and in verse, and to commence that Latin poem "Africa," on the exploits of Scipio in the second Punic war, which procured for him the laurel crown, but which has been handed down to us in an imperfect form, probably the result of intentional mutilation. In August, 1340, Petrarca received from the senate an invitation to Rome, there to be crowned poet-laureate; and on the self-same day a letter reached him from the chancellor of the university of Paris, proffering him the like honour in that capital. His own inclination and the advice of his friends made him prefer the former offer; and early in March, 1341, he arrived at the court of Robert, king of Naples and Jerusalem, to make before that most learned monarch of the period a solemn exhibition of his powers. For three days he discoursed publicly of poetry and science; after which the king formally certified his worthiness of the laurel, and deputed the poet Giovanni Barrili, one of his own courtiers, to represent the majesty of Naples at the ensuing ceremonial. On the following 8th of April, being Easter-day, Petrarca at the capitol delivered an oration, long and flowery, in honour of the muses; after which Orso degli Orsini, count of Anguillara, a senator, pronounced a discourse in praise of the poet-aspirant, and crowned him with the laurel wreath, in presence of an approving concourse of the Roman people and of many dignified personages. Boccaccio avers that the capitol had not witnessed a similar function since the coronation of Statius, under Domitian. From Rome Petrarca removed to Parma, and spent some months with the Correggi lords of that city, especially with his friend Azzo. In 1342 he was one of the ambassadors sent into France by the Roman senate and people to congratulate Pope Clement VI. on his assumption of the triple crown; and joined with him in this embassy was Niccola Gabrino, better known by his historic name of Cola di Rienzi. About this time Petrarca's brother Gherardo abandoned the world for a monastic life; being moved thereto, it is said, by the death of a woman whom he loved, and whose loss is commemorated by Francesco in the sonnet commencing—

"La bella donna che cotanto amavi."
(The beautiful lady whom thou lovedst so much.)

In 1343 Pope Clement VI. sent Petrarca on a mission to Queen Giovanna, who had mounted the Neapolitan throne on the death of her uncle King Robert, and under whose youthful sway the court presented a widely altered aspect. The great Roman revolution effected by Rienzi in 1347 was hailed by Petrarca as the new birth of Italian liberty; and his letters and his verses were not spared to incite the tribune to further deeds. Notice the canzone beginning—

"Spirto gentil che quelle membra reggi"—
(Choice spirit who rulest those members)—

which is very generally explained as addressed to Rienzi, though by some appropriated to Stefano Colonna. In 1348 a fearful pestilence ravaged Europe, and amongst its victims was Laura—to other eyes less beautiful than when, twenty-one years before, precisely to the month, day, and hour, she had captivated the heart of her Tuscan lover; but ever regarded by him as invested with the pristine charm. A note in his own handwriting records his bitter sorrow at her death, of which the news reached him in Verona; and for some days afterwards he is described as scarcely breaking silence, or eating except at the importunity of friends. The second part of the Canzoniere, concluding with six short poems called "I Trionfi" (The Triumphs), from which Titian is said to have painted four well-known pictures, was composed after her death. In the following July Cardinal Giovanni Colonna died; having outlived by some years his brother Giacomo, bishop of Lombes. In 1350 Petrarca addressed a remarkable letter to the Emperor Charles IV., exhorting him to come and succour Italy; and this being the great year of jubilee, towards the close of summer, after the manner of pious pilgrims Francesco repaired to Rome, taking Florence in his way; and thus for the first time beholding his mother city. In 1351 Florence, ashamed of the long alienation of this her celebrated son whom other states delighted to honour, appropriated a sum of money to redeem his confiscated property; and charged his friend and fellow-citizen, Giovanni Boccaccio, with a letter to Petrarca, then resident in Padua, informing him of what had been done, and urging him to honour by his presence the infant Florentine university—a request finally not complied with. In this same year Petrarca directed a highly complimentary epistle to Andrea Dandolo, doge of Venice, exhorting him to make peace with Genoa; and received in answer a letter which lauded his eloquence and learning, but declined to adopt his counsel. A corresponding document subsequently addressed by the poet to the doge of Genoa, proved equally without result. In 1354 Petrarca, sent by Visconti of Milan to Venice, once more treated of peace; but though honourably received, was again unsuccessful. The long list of Petrarca's friends, patrons, and admirers includes popes and princes, warriors and men of letters; and various were the missions, diplomatic or otherwise honourable, which he undertook, visiting divers foreign countries and courts, and possibly the English shores; at home amongst great men, but ever affable towards those of lower degree. At the marriage of Violante Visconti with Prince Lionel of England, Petrarca sat at table with the august bride and bridegroom and their most distinguished guests. In 1370 he retired to Arquà, a village in the Luganean hills, where alone of all his numerous residences the house he occupied is shown to the curious; and here occurred that colloquy with certain disciples of Averroes which led to their stigmatizing Petrarca as a worthy man but illiterate; and to his confessing his own ignorance, but maintaining theirs, in his book "De sui ipsius et multorum aliorum Ignorantia." His last public appearance occurred in 1373, when in the suite of Francesco Novello da Carrara he harangued the Venetian senate. On the first day, awed by his august auditory, and oppressed by old age and fatigue, he stood silent; but on the next performed his assigned part with great applause. Petrarca left an illegitimate daughter, Francesca, elsewhere called Tullia, married to Francesco da Brossano of Milan. To this couple he bequeathed his property, after leaving legacies to various friends and domestics; and a gift of books which he had made to Venice in 1362 formed the nucleus of the world-renowned library of St. Mark. Boccaccio, a warm admirer of Petrarca, describes him as tall and handsome, round-faced, grave and mild of aspect, with eyes at once gladsome and penetrating, and a merry but not undignified laugh; placid and joyous of speech, though seldom speaking except in answer, and then weightily; in dress conformable to custom; in music a lover not merely of the human voice and instrumentation, but also of the song of birds; patient, or if angered beyond reason, soon recollecting himself; truthful, very faithful; in religion eminently Christian, though harassed (as Petrarca himself confesses) by temptations of the flesh. Elsewhere we read of his systematic fasts, his masses put up for the soul of Laura, his social habits, contempt of riches, and pious practices. His funeral was attended by Francesco da Carrara, with the bishop and chapter of Parma, and a throng of nobles and clergy, doctors and students; the body, laid on a bier covered with cloth of gold and overshadowed by a golden canopy lined with ermine, was carried to the church of Arquà, and there deposited in a ladye chapel built by Petrarca; and Francesco da Brossano raised to his memory a monument, supported by four columns, and approached by two steps, all alike of red marble. Besides the works already particularized in the course of this article, Petrarca has left many others, including several on biographical, political, philosophical, or religious themes; a Syrian Itinerary, composed, as has been suggested, for the use of Giovanni di Mandello, sometime podestà of Piacenza; Epistles, both in prose and in verse; and certain Latin Eclogues or Bucolics, avowedly allegorical. The question remains—Who was Laura? and is answered by the Abbé de Sade: She was the daughter of Audebert de Noves, syndic of Avignon, and the wife of Hugh, son of Paul de Sade; and was, in fact, my own ancestress, as family documents prove. This assertion has been endorsed by common opinion. Yet various writers, both prior and posterior to the abbé, have voted for some different Laura; and, of course, have found reasons to allege in their own favour. Amongst these recusants is Lord Woodhouselee, in his Historical and Critical Essay on the Life and Character of Petrarque, Edinburgh, 1812. Modern students have observed with astonishment that the elder biographers of Petrarca give no adequate account of this lady, whom he himself depicts as altering the tenor of his life. Boccaccio, indeed, the contemporary of Petrarca, in one place where he mentions Laura, explains her as a symbol of the laurel crown. Even in Petrarca's own record of his connection with her, apparent irreconcilable discrepancies have been noted, and special stress has been laid on the fact that in the year 1327 the 6th of April was indeed Monday in Holy Week; but certainly not Good

Friday, in spite of Petrarca's distinct statement that so it was. To those who still prefer a flesh and blood Laura to a mysterious impersonation, it may be interesting to know that a pamphlet published in 1821 tells how in the Casa Peruzzi at Florence was preserved the alleged veritable effigy of Laura, sculptured by the painter Simone Memmi, and carried from place to place by the poet-lover in his frequent wanderings. On the back of the marble is inscribed the following quatrain attributed to Petrarca:—

> "Splendida luce in cui chiaro si vede
> Quel bel che può mostrar nel mondo Amore,
> O vero exemplo del Sopran Valore
> E d'ogni meraviglia intiera fede."
> ["Splendid light in which we can see
> what beauty Love can show in the world,
> Oh true example of the Supreme Worth
> and complete faith of every marvel." (ed.)]

"Dante, An English Classic"

(from *The Churchman's Shilling Magazine,* 1867)

"Onorate l'altissimo poeta."[1]

Published in *The Churchman's Shilling Magazine and Family Treasury* 2 (October 1867): 200–5, this "commendatory article" defends the translation of the *Divina Commedia* done by Christina's close friend, Charles Bagot Cayley, after a review in *Blackwood's* (cited in her notes) ranked it lower than a translation by J. Dayman. Although the reviewer did describe the "system of rhyme" in Cayley as "more frequently grotesque than imperfect" (743), he praised it as a "spirited and able version" and placed it above four other translations (742). Many years later, William Michael Rossetti still doubted whether Cayley's translation "has ever been excelled, or even equalled" (*Reminiscences,* 1:173). Kamilla Denman and Sarah Smith suggest that Christina planned to publish a second edition of Cayley's translation (in "Christina Rossetti's Copy of C. B. Cayley's Divine Comedy," *Victorian Poetry* 32.3–4 [Autumn-Winter 1994]: 315–38, esp. 321–22).

Footnotes throughout this section are Rossetti's own.

Dante, An English Classic

Viewing the matter of nationality exclusively as one of literary interest, now in this nineteenth century when it is impossible to be born an ancient Greek, a wise man might choose not unwisely to be born an Italian, thus securing Dante as his elder brother, and the "Divina Commedia" as his birthright. But no man has his choice on this point, neither can every man be of the privileged few; and we at least in nineteenth century England, happier in so far than our forefathers, owe (let us hope, pay) the unburdensome debt of gratitude to more than one admirable translator who has felt that to reanimate the venerable father of modern poetry as a fellow-citizen amongst sometime aliens is a nobler achievement than to bring before the world a new and lesser man. To reproduce Dante in all fulness and subtlety of beauty would demand Dante's self, and must be abandoned as hopeless: indeed, a question may be raised whether, as no two things can be absolutely the same as each other, and thus apparently one must exceed, one fall short, he is not the consummate translator who sits nearest, yet below not above, his original; invested with all communicable glory, not shining with independent lustre; though, as most rules admit of some exception, an occasional added grace may be condoned to the ideal translator as some balance against frequent inevitable shortcomings.

It seems to us that, valuable to the Dantesque student as every example of translation is when first-rate of its kind, the only adequate form into which to render the "Divina Commedia" is terza rima. Had such an English version not hitherto been produced, the task might appear hopeless of achievement; but more than one poet has proved that our language also is rich enough to lend itself even to the sustained sonorous music of this most august metre; and now we feel that to strip Dante to prose, or chasten him into blank verse, or deform him by couplets or any other unauthorized vehicle, is as indefensible (when, that is, the writer's aim is to add the "Divina Commedia" to English literature; not merely to secure some one special feature, best perhaps attained by the special means adopted) as it would be to deprive organ music of its majestic swelling and sinking continuity of sound, substituting for this the disconnectedness of pianoforte notes, or the monotonous jog of a drum.

As to the comparative merits of each translator, we have no wish to obtrude any personal predilection of our own on the reader. Of the terza rima versions several deserve high praise, and can well afford to dispense with ours; indeed, as their authors are persons to be looked up to, not down upon, by us, we feel in no position either to endorse their work by our approval or annihilate it by our blame. Our humbler ambition is to introduce some English readers hitherto less fortunate than ourselves to one noble reproduction of the great poet's supreme poem.

Many desultory readers entertain, we suspect, no adequate idea of the plan and working out of the "Divina Commedia" as a whole, and have not even grasped its plot in the baldest outline; how Dante, ensnared by earth, yet cared for by heaven, can only be disenthralled from the past and renewed for the future by exploring the world of desperate ruin, the world of hope, and lastly, that world which eye hath not seen, nor ear heard, neither hath entered into the heart of man to conceive;[2] how the lost love of earth is found again as one higher, lovelier, and better loved in paradise; and how even this sainted and exalting passion pales at last, and is, as it were, no more accounted of before the supreme revelation of the love of God.

No reader ought, of course, to stop at so bare an understanding of what may be termed the surface-plot as this. Without touching upon the allegorical significations which meet us with more or less of salience in page after page, without approaching that more abstruse anagogical system of interpretation which, as may be inferred from the "Convito," Dante himself suggests as applicable to the "Divina Commedia," the entire poem is alive with classical and historical allusions, for lack of familiarity with which numberless passages can only remain as keyless puzzles. We are perhaps no less indebted to Mr. Cayley for the volume of copious notes, at once learned,* interesting, and most elegant, which he has appended to his translation, than for that admirable translation itself; notes which remain of high value to the student, let him adopt whatever version of the "Commedia" he will.

When Mr. Cayley's "Inferno" appeared in 1851, the metrical form of his work seems to have given it in some eyes the air of a *tour de force;* thus one reviewer, in comparing him with Mr. Pollok, suggested that Mr. Cayley had encumbered himself with an extra length of chain before dancing his hornpipe. Whether or not this critic approached his grave subject with due graciousness of gravity need not here be discussed; certainly any critic who may have treated the translation then under review merely as a *tour de force,* and not much rather as a permanent contribution to our English classics, fell into momentous error. Before Mr. Cayley, Dante's niche in England stood

---

*A recent critic ("Dante in English Terza Rima," *Blackwood's Edinburgh Magazine,* June, 1867), quoting Mr. Cayley's superb triplet,—

"As saints, upon the latest heralding,
Shall rise up, each from his obscure sojourn,
With new-flesht voices halleluiahing"

("Purgatory," xxx., 10–12),

observes:—"His last line is a very displeasing one in itself, and, as there is nothing said of 'halleluiahing' in the Italian, urgently requires removal." This gentleman has, perhaps, not noticed that there are two received readings of the Italian text: one gives,—

"La rivestita carne alleviando;"—

the other,—

"La rivestita voce allelujando."

empty;** other men have followed worthily in his footsteps, whilst the structure of their versions, grown more familiar, and now even naturalized in our literature, has ceased to excite ridicule; but they followed only to find the niche already occupied by Dante living and speaking amongst us.†

Vain as it must be for those to whose ears Dante's tongue is but an unknown tongue, and his music but an unintelligible musical sound, to hope ever fully to appreciate his master poem, yet the beauty of the best translations goes far towards suggesting the surpassing beauty of their original; whilst passages of which vigour is one main characteristic appear less difficult to render into vigorous English. Pathos, again, is common to all hearts and languages, and reasonings deep and high are no way dependent on idiom. We appeal to our readers whether the quotations with which we ask leave to close our commendatory article do not show us Mr. Cayley in his translation as a master of vigour and beauty, of pathos and philosophy.

> A Rebuking Angel Fords the Styx.
> "Hell," canto ix., v. 64–81.

> "And now there came along the turbid river
>   The crashing of an uproar full of dread,
> That made on either side the margins quiver;
>   Not otherwise than like a wind that sped
> By the confronting heats impetuously
> Shall strike the forests, and by nothing stayed,
> Break branches down, and carry flowers from tree,
>   And onward proudly sweeping, dust enrolled,
> Makes both the cattle and the herdsmen flee.
>   Then said he, loosing from mine eyes his hold,
> 'Thy seeing nerve adown this ancient scum
>   Direct, this way that bitterest fumes enfold.'
> As frogs that see the hostile serpent come,
>   Disperse along the waters to their holes,
> Till in the ground they nestle all and some;
>   I saw above a thousand blasted souls
> Fly thus before the face of one, who passed
>   Over the Styx at ford with unwet soles."

**Mr. Cary's translation, not being in terza rima, seems to us necessarily defective as a standard work; and so of various others.

†We say this advisedly, although aware that Mr. Dayman's "Inferno" was published before Mr. Cayley's; for, on the other hand, Mr Cayley's entire "Divina Commedia" preceded by several years Mr. Dayman's.

The Descent of Beatrice.
"Purgatory," canto xxx., v. 7–30.

"And one thereof, as heaven's legate should,
    Come, 'bride, from Lebanon,' began to sing
Three times, then joined him all the multitude.
    As saints, upon the latest heralding
Shall rise up, each from his obscure sojourn,
    With new-flesht voices halleluiahing;
So did I on the heavenly wain discern
    Fivescore to rise, ad vocem tanti senis,
Vassals and harbingers of life eterne.
    They shouted all, 'Benedictus qui venis,'
And scattering flowers around them and between,
    'Manibus, O date lilia plenis.'
I have upon approach of morning seen
    The eastern part of heaven with rosy hue,
And all the rest adorned with blue serene,
    And the sun's face arising umbered through
The vapours, by whose mitigating powers
    The eye a longer time sustained his view;
So in the midmost of a cloud of flowers,
    That sallied upwards from the angel's aim,
And inwards and around fell down in showers,
    In veil of white, with olive bordered, came
A lady, that beneath her mantle green
    Was clad in colour like the living flame."

[The essay concludes with further illustrative translations from "Paradise," xiv., v.37–66 and xxiv., v.64–108.]

"Dante: The Poet Illustrated Out of the Poem"

(from *The Century Magazine,* 1884)

Rossetti was invited by Edmund Gosse to submit an article on Dante to *The Century Magazine* in New York. It was written in 1883 and published in February 1884 (27:566–73); she received 20 guineas (see Troxell, 173). At the outset she requested permission through Gosse to use Cayley's translation of *The Divine Comedy* rather than Longfellow's. Mary Arseneau discusses Christina and the "Rossetti family obsession" with Dante in "'May my great love avail me': Christina Rossetti and Dante" in *New Essays on Christina Rossetti,* eds. Mary Arseneau, Lorraine Janzen Kooistra, and Antony H. Harrison (forthcoming from Ohio University Press). For Dante's influence on Rossetti, see chap. 5 in Harrison, *Christina Rossetti in Context.* For further commentary on this article, see Marsh, 508–9.

Footnotes throughout this section are Rossetti's own.

⁓✦⁓

Dante: The Poet Illustrated Out of the Poem

It is a grave if not a formidable undertaking to treat of that soldier, states-man, philosopher, above all poet, whom successive generations reverence under the musical name of Dante Alighieri. Fifty-six years sufficed him to live his life and work his work: centuries have not sufficed to exhaust the rich and abstruse intellectual treasure which the world inherits from him. Still, acute thinkers abide at variance as to his ultimate meaning; and still able writers record the impressions of wonder, sympathy, awe, admiration, which—however wide and manifold his recondite meanings may be—he leaves even on simple hearts so long as these can respond to what is lovely or is terrible. "*Quanti dolci pensier, quanto desio*" ("How many sweet thoughts, how much desire"), has he not bequeathed to us!

If formidable for others, it is not least formidable for one of my name, for *me,* to enter the Dantesque field and say my little say on the Man and on the Poem; for others of my name have been before me in the same field, and have wrought permanent and worthy work in attestation of their diligence. My father, Gabriele Rossetti, in his "Comento Analitico sull' Inferno di Dante" ("Analytical Commentary upon Dante's Hell"), has left to tyros[3] a clew and to fellow-experts a theory. My sister, Maria Francesca Rossetti, has in her "Shadow of Dante" eloquently expounded the Divina Commedia as a discourse of most elevated Christian faith and morals. My brother Dante has translated with a rare felicity the "Vita Nuova" ("New Life") and other minor (poetical) works of his great name-sake. My brother William has, with a strenuous endeavor to achieve close verbal accuracy, rendered the Inferno into English blank verse.[4] I, who cannot lay claim to their learning, must approach my subject under cover of "*Mi valga . . . il grande amore*" ("May my great love avail me"), leaving to them the more confident plea, "*Mi valga il lungo studio*" ("May my long study avail me").

It is not out of disrespect to Mr. Longfellow's blank-verse translation of the Divina Commedia,[5] a translation too secure of public favor to need my commendation, that I propose to make my extracts (of any importance) not from his version, but from Mr. Cayley's. The latter, by adhering to the *terza rima* (ternary rhyme) of the original poem, has gone far toward satisfying an ear rendered fastidious by Dante's own harmony of words; with a master hand he conveys to us the sense amid echoes of the familiar sound. My first quotation (Paradise, canto 1), consisting of an invocation of the Spirit of Poetry, befits both Dante and his translator, while, as it were, striking one dominant note of our study:

> "O good Apollo, for this last emprise
>   Render me such a vessel of thy might
> As to the longed-for laurel may suffice.
> Till now hath sped me one Parnassian height,
>   But on my last arena now, beneath
> The double safeguard, I must needs alight.
> Do thou into my bosom come, and breathe,
>   As when thou drewest Marsyas of old
> Out of his body's perishable sheath."

Dante or Durante Alighieri, Allighieri, or Aldighieri—for in all these forms the names are recorded—was born a noble citizen of Florence on the 8th of May, 1265, the sun being then in the sign of Gemini, an auspicious sign according to popular opinion of that day. And a meaning has been found for "Alighieri" apposite to him who so eminently bore the name: it has been turned (by a process I attempt not to analyze) into Aligero (winged), when at once we recognize how suitable it is to be the master spirit that fathomed Hell and ascended through Purgatory to the heights of Heaven. Nor need "Dante, Durante," remain without an appropriate gloss. Dante (giving) befits one who has enriched the after ages; Durante (enduring) suits no less that much-enduring man who (writing after the event) puts an apparent prophecy of his own banishment into the mouth of one of the personages of his poem (Paradise, 17):

> "Thou shalt leave all things, which thou long ago
>   Hast loved most dearly, and I've herein said
> What dart is soonest shot from exile's bow.
> Thou shalt experience how another's bread
>   Is salt upon our palate, and what bale
> 'Tis up and down another's stairs to tread."

Boccaccio in his "Life of Dante" traces back his hero's family to a certain Eliseo of the noble Roman house of Frangipani, who, toward the date of the rebuilding of Florence by the Emperor Charlemagne, settled in that city. In course of time the descendants of Eliseo, dropping their original cognomen, renamed themselves as Elisei. Prominent among them in the days of the Emperor Conrad III arose Cacciaguida, knight and crusader, who married a lady of the Aldighieri of Ferrara, or perhaps of Parma; her birthplace seems uncertain. This lady bestowed her patronymic on one of her sons, Dante's ancestor in the direct line; and he becoming a man of note, his descendants adopted his name as their own surname; thus permanently distinguishing as Alighieri their branch of the house of the Elisei.

On his pilgrimage through Paradise, Dante encounters in the fifth heaven, that of the planet Mars, the spirit of his venerable forefather Cacciaguida, who discourses with him at considerable length, and after describing the happy thrift and simplicity of Florence in his own day—in Dante's day become a hotbed of luxury and extravagance—briefly narrates some circumstances of his birth and after life (Paradise, 15):

> "To a civic life thou seest how goodly, how
>   Reposeful, fellow-citizens how leal,
> How sweet a homestead Mary, with loud vow

> Solicited, gave me, and of Christ the seal
> > I took within your ancient Baptistere,
> As Cacciaguida for His Commonweal.
> . . . .
>
> > The camp of Emperor Conrad then I sought,
> > And by him was I girded for his knight,
> So well I pleased him, for I bravely wrought.
> I followed him, yon wicked faith to fight,
> > Whose votaries by your Shepherd's fault despoil
> Your jurisdiction of its native right.
> By this unholy people from the coil
> > Of the false world obtained I my release
> (Ah, World, whose love doth many a spirit soil),
> And entered out of Martyrdom this Peace."

If, as we have seen, mutation of name and residence characterizes that dignified stock from which Dante sprang, no less conspicuously did mutability of faction and fortune, and a bandying of names, now one in the ascendant and now another, characterize that beautiful Florence which called him son. Her citizens were divided into Guelphs and Ghibellines: these names, in their primitive form, having been the battle-cries on a far-off field where, more than a century before Dante's birth, a crown was lost and won between two contending princes. The crown in dispute was the imperial crown of the Holy Roman Empire: the aristocratic party of Imperialists attached to the victorious Conrad of Hohenstaufen became known as Ghibellines, the overthrown opposition as Guelphs. And as the standing opponent of the Empire was the Popedom, the Papalist party in Italy, equally definable as National or as Democratic, was styled Guelph.

Here already were sufficient grounds for strife. Yet, as if insufficient, private rancor heaped fuel and explosives on the public flame. First, a feud between the Florentine families of Buondelmonte and Amideo widened and confirmed the political breach; secondly, a brawl among the children of one Florentine citizen by two successive wives split the Guelph party into subdivisions distinguished respectively as Black and White.

Nor were words and names, orations and counter orations, the chief political weapons of those days. Sword and fire, confiscation and banishment, made and left their mark on either side, in accordance with the ever-shifting preponderance of this or that faction. The elder Alighieri, a lawyer by profession, a Guelph by party, was long with his party living in exile at the time of his son Dante's birth; but in the year 1267 the Guelphs returned to Florence, and the banished man rejoined his family.

Let us with that absence and that reunion connect such thoughts of home-longing and (in a figure) of home contentment as breathe in the following lines (Purgatory, 8; Paradise, 23):

> "It was that hour which thaws the heart and sends
>   The voyagers' affection home, when they
> Since morn have said Adieu to darling friends;
> And smites the new-made pilgrim on his way
>   With love, if he a distant bell should hear,
> That seems a-mourning for the dying day."
> . . . .
> "As when the bird among the boughs beloved,
>   Keeping beside her darlings' nest her seat,
> By night, when things are from the view removed,
> That sooner she the dear ones' looks may meet,
>   And that by which she feeds them to purvey,
> Counting for them her anxious labor sweet,
> Forestalls the hours upon the unsheltered spray,
>   And waits the sun with burning eagerness,
> Poring with fixed eye for the peep of day."

Not long did the elder Alighieri survive this renewal of happiness. Yet our hopes follow him out of sight into the veiled and better land, there to behold him awaiting the restitution of all things, even as Dante, in his Divine Comedy, represents a congregation of elect souls as yearning after the resurrection of the body (Paradise, 14).

Despite so irreparable a loss, the young Dante received, under his widowed mother's protection, a refined and liberal education. His taste was for study rather than for amusement, and to such a taste, allied to perseverance and wedded to a preëminent intellect, the treasures of knowledge lay open and accessible. His mother's circumstances, though not opulent, were easy. Thus she was able to intrust her son's education to Brunetto Latini, a notary by profession, by occasional office an ambassador of the Florentine Republic, an attractive man of the world; moreover, a scholar and a poet. Between him and his pupil a tender affection grew up, as Dante himself assures us (Hell, 15) when he encounters his master's shade.

Dante also studied at the universities of Padua and Bologna, and in mature life augmented his stores of knowledge in learned and polite Paris. According to an uncertain tradition, he visited England, and in particular Oxford.

In a period of broils, heart-burnings, rivalries, Dante was not the man to observe a tepid neutrality. He bore arms on the field of Campaldino and at the siege of Caprona, and on one or both occasions with credit to himself and to his cause. The battle of Campaldino was followed by a storm—the stirring up of which storm is attributed to diabolical agency by the shade of Buonconte, a noble Ghibelline who fell on the losing side, and who accosts Dante in the Ante-Purgatory (Purgatory, 5).

Yet, though a soldier, Dante was not primarily a soldier; rather, it may be, a statesman, a ruler, a legislator.

From the highest civil dignity, however, that of the Priorato, or chief magistracy of Florence, Dante found himself excluded by a circumstance which at once dignified his social position and threatened to impede his public career. Giano della Bella, Prior of Florence in 1292, had ordained that such families as counted a cavaliere (knight) among their ancestry should be reckoned noble, while for that very reason they should lose certain civic privileges. Thus Cacciaguida the Crusader, by ennobling his descendants, cut them off from sundry more substantial honors. To rehabilitate him, as we may suppose, for public office, Dante's name is found inscribed among the *Medici e Speziali* (Leeches and Druggists), their "art" standing sixth in the list of principal arts; and documents still extant in the archives of Florence show that he did actually take part in the councils of several years, commencing with the year 1295.

On June 15th, 1300, Dante, supported by five less noted colleagues, was created Prior. The Black and White broils were at this time raging with such virulence that the Papal Legate, Cardinal Matteo d'Acquasparta, sent to Florence for purposes of pacification, failed in his mission, finally (though at a period considerably later) laying the rebellious city under an interdict. In such troublous times Dante assumed the command; nor was he one to rule with a tremulous hand. By him and his colleagues was enacted a law which banished chiefs and adherents of both parties into separate exile; to Corso Donati, Dante's brother-in-law, with his "Blacks," a spot in the Tuscan mountains was assigned for residence; the Whites, among whom was Dante's dearest friend, Guido Cavalcanti, were dispatched into the baneful Maremma.

They went, but they returned; and divided as they went, so they returned, the Blacks keen for vengeance. This faction now denounced the Whites as Ghibellines, anti-papalists, foes of France; and, invoking foreign aid, induced Charles of Valois, then on his road to Rome, to countenance their machinations. Dante, his tenure of office as Prior being expired, was hereupon sent by his successors, as one of four ambassadors, on a counter embassy to the Roman court. Like the turbulent factions he had helped to banish, he also went; but, unlike them, he returned no more.

Charles of Valois occupied the oltr' Arno (beyond the river Arno). Corso Donati raised the Black standard, and, by the help of the French prince, gained a crushing victory. Fire and sword devastated Florence; one Podestà (magistrate or mayor) was expelled, another appointed; a multitude of Whites were exiled and doomed to beggary. Well might Dante choose Fortune for his theme (Hell, 7):

> "This Fortune whom thou namest: What is she?
> . . . .
> He, whose high wisdom all beside transcends,
> Has made the spheres, appointing one that might
> Rule over them, whence every part extends
> To each, in tenor uniform, its light;
> So to the glories of the world He did
> One common regent and conductress plight,*
> Who might from time to time, from seed to seed,
> And place to place, their empty riches shake,
> Beyond forestalling by your wit and heed.
> She doth one people raise, and one doth make
> To languish, by the allotment of her hand,
> Which is concealed, as by the sward the snake.
> Your wisdom can against her make no stand;
> She judges and foresees, and aye pursues
> Her sway, like every god in his command.
> Her revolutions have no pause nor truce;
> Her swiftness from necessity is wrung;
> So many be they who for change have use.
> And she it is who should on cross be hung,
> As many tell, who blame her much amiss,
> Where they should praise, with foul and wicked tongue.
> But she is happy, hearing naught of this,
> Among the glad first-born of God attending
> To turn her sphere about, and bide in bliss."

Dante was fined, was banished for two years from Tuscany, was permanently excluded from office. This in January, 1302. In the following March he was condemned to fagot and stake should he ever again set foot in Florence. Yet in 1316 this sentence was conditionally reversed. The state of Florence published an amnesty, whereby, on payment of a fine and performance of public penance, Dante, among others, would be free to return. Such an alternative, however, only served to double-bar the gates of his city forever

---

*I have ventured to replace a rhyme.

against him. Hearken to the thunder of his indignation at the humiliating overture:**

"Is this, then, the glorious fashion of Dante Alighieri's recall to his country, after suffering exile for well-nigh three lusters?[6] Is this the due recompense of his innocence manifest to all? This the fruit of his abundant sweat and toil endured in study? Far from the man of philosophy's household this baseness proper to a heart of mire, that he . . . should endure, as a prisoner, to be put to ransom! Far from the proclaimer of justice that he, offended and insulted, to his offenders, as to those who have deserved well of him, should pay tribute! This, father, is not the way to return to my country; but if, by you or by another, there can be found another way that shall not derogate from Dante's fame and honor, readily will I thereto betake myself. But, if by no honorable way can entrance be found into Florence, there will I never enter. What? Can I not from any corner of the earth behold the sun and the stars? Can I not, under every climate of heaven, meditate the all-sweet truths, except I first make myself a man of no glory, but rather of ignominy, in the face of the people and city of Florence?"

That Florence which could neither break nor bend the spirit of her mighty son had, meanwhile, wrought in him a far different transformation. Under sentence of banishment, confiscation of goods, contingent death, Dante the Guelph had changed into Dante the Ghibelline: the Papal temporal power became the object of his outspoken abhorrence, the Imperial sway, of his devoted advocacy. A passage (abridged) from Dante's prose treatise, "De Monarchiâ," sets before us his theory of world-government:

"Only Man among beings holds mid place between things corruptible and things incorruptible. Therefore that unspeakable Providence proposed to man two ends: the one the beatitude of this life, which consists in the operations of his own virtue; the other the beatitude of eternal life, which consists in the fruition of the Divine Countenance. To these two beatitudes by divers means must we come. Wherefore by man was needed a double directive according to the double end; that is, of the Supreme Pontiff, who, according to Revelation, should lead mankind to eternal life; and of the Emperor, who, according to philosophic teachings, should direct mankind to temporal felicity. And whereas to this port none or few, and those with overmuch difficulty, could attain, unless mankind, the waves of enticing cupidity being quieted, should

---

**I need not even wish to excel my sister's translation of this passage, which I extract, word for word, from "A Shadow of Dante" [p. 29]. The original occurs in a private letter from Dante to a religious.

repose free in the tranquillity of peace; this is the aim to be mainly kept in view by the Guardian of the Globe, who is named Roman Prince, to wit, that in the garden-plot of mortals freely with peace men may live."[†]

The Whites, exiled while Guelphs, sought to regain their citizenship under Ghibelline auspices. In 1304 they attempted to reenter Florence by force of arms, and failed. Years later their hopes revived under the Emperor Henry of Luxemburg, but received in his sudden death their own death-blow.

In fact, though not at once in appearance, Dante's efficient public life was well-nigh ended when Florence cast him out. Yet not so, if we look beyond his active services and the brief span of his mortal day. For, taught by bitter experience in what scales to weigh this world and the things of this world, he bequeathed to future generations the undying voice of his wisdom,—a wisdom distilled in eloquence, modulated to music, sublimed by imagination, or rather subliming that imagination which is its congruous vehicle and companion.

Disowned by his mother city, Dante thenceforward found a precarious refuge here or there, chiefly in the petty courts of Ghibelline potentates. Thus he sojourned with Count Guido Salvatico in the Casentino, with Uguccione della Faggiuola in the mountains of Urbino; afterward under the protection of Moroello della Spina in the Lunigiana, to whom the Purgatory is said to have been dedicated, and to whose hereditary and personal hospitality the following lines, addressed to the shade of his father Conrad, refer (Purgatory, 8):

> "The fame, which nobly of your house doth tell,
>   Proclaimeth hamlet, and proclaimeth peer,
> That those who have not been there note her well.
> And as I would arrive aloft, I swear,
>   Your honorable house the adorning prize
> Of arms or largess doth not cease to bear.
> A privilege in their kind or custom lies."

As foremost among Dante's friendly hosts may perhaps be reckoned Can Grande della Scala, Lord of Verona. Yet from Can Grande's court he was driven (as the story goes) by an insult from a privileged buffoon. Nevertheless, we find the praises of this eminent noble, preceded by those of an elder head

---

[†]Maria F. Rossetti. [The reference is to *SD*, 38–39.]

of the same house, put into the mouth of Cacciaguida, and thereby perpetuated (Paradise, 17).

Ravenna became the exiled poet's final refuge, Guido da Polenta his last and generous earthly protector. For him Dante undertook a mission to Venice; and this failing, he seems to have lost heart. His homeward journey lay through the malarious lagoons: no marvel is it that he contracted a fever, and at length found a sure resting-place in Ravenna, where he died on the 14th of September, 1321, and where he was buried.

Looking back for a moment to that crisis in Dante's life as a patriot, when from a Guelph he became a Ghibelline,—that is (as at the first glance might appear), when, from having been champion of an Italian Italy, free and sole mother and mistress of her own free children, he became, whether from personal disgust or sheer despair or from whatever other motive, as ardent a champion of that Imperial power which aspired to rule over her,—we may feel disposed to wonder at the transformation, perhaps to condemn the citizen. Not so, I would plead, until we have studied in his writings and have pondered over his own lofty view and exposition of a world-wide political theory; until we have striven to realize how the Italy before his eyes had in part become a field of mutual destruction, and therefore of self-destruction; until by virtue of reverent, compassionate sympathy we have hungered with him on the bitter bread of exile, and have trodden the wearisome, dusty roads of his wandering banishment. At its best our judgment may be erroneous; only let us not suffer it to settle down into stagnant and contented shallowness. By the mouth of St. Thomas Aquinas, Dante himself cautions us against rash judgment, and elsewhere, by one multitudinous, harmonious utterance of unnumbered glorified souls combined into the semblance of an eagle, sets forth the impartiality of God's final, irreversible sentence (Paradise, 13–19):

> "And let not folk in judging trust their wit
>   Too fast, as one who counteth up the corn
> In 's field before the sun has ripened it;
> For I have all through winter seen a thorn
>   Appearing poisonless and obdurate,
> Which then the rose upon the sprig hath borne:
> And I have seen a ship, that swift and straight
>   Has run upon the mid-sea all her race,
> And perished, entering at the harbor gate.
> . . . .
>   . . . As the stork in circles flies
>   Above that nest wherein she feeds her young,
> And as those fed attend her with their eyes,
> So moved (and so mine eyes upon him clung)

> That figure blest, whose movement of each plume
> Was on such numbers of free counsels hung.
> Circling he chanted, 'As to thee, by whom
>   They are not understood, my notes be, so
> To mortals is God's everlasting doom.'
> Then went on one and every flaming glow
>   Of God's own spirit, in that sign enmailed,
> Which made to Roman arms the World bend low.
> 'This kingdom,' he began, 'was never scaled
>   By mortal that had not believed in Christ,
> Before, or after, He on Cross was nailed.
> But look, there's many calleth Christ, O Christ,
>   That shall, for meeting Him in judgment, want
> Much more than such a one as knew not Christ.
> The Æthiop shall judge, and cry, Avaunt
>   Such Christians, when those congregations two
> Part, one for Wealth eterne, and one for Want.'"

Hitherto we have contemplated Dante mounted, as it were, on a public pedestal. We have recalled his career mainly according to that aspect under which it forms a portion of the history of his age and nation. The man among men, the leader or the victim of his fellow-countrymen, has engrossed our attention.

But thus we have beheld only half a Dante. We have not looked, or even attempted to look, into that heart of fire which burned first and last for one beloved object. For, whatever view we take of Beatrice, unless indeed we are prepared wholly to set aside the poet's own evidence concerning himself, either she literally, or else that occult something which her name was employed at once to express and to veil, must apparently have gone far to mold her lover; to make him what he was, to withhold him from becoming such as he became not.

On Dante's own showing (in his "Vita Nuova" and elsewhere), this object, fruitlessly beloved on earth, but to be attained to and enjoyed in the heavenly communion of saints, was Beatrice, daughter of Folco Portinari, beautiful, gracious, replete with virtue, courteous, and humble. Not, it may be, that when first they met she shone, even in farthest-seeing poetic eyes, with her full luster; for at that first meeting they were both but children of nine years old, he somewhat the elder. She at her father's house, he brought thither by his own father on a holiday occasion—thus they met whom love was to unite by an indissoluble, because by a spiritual, bond. For no courtship, as it would seem, ensued. Not a hint remains that Beatrice even guessed her boy-friend's secret. He sought her company, and felt the ennobling influence of her presence—so noble an influence that love (he avers) ruled him not contrary to the dictates of reason. With equal emphasis Boccaccio dwells on the intact purity of both lover and beloved in this absorbing passion; for absorbing it was on Dante's side, whether or not it was returned.

And we may well hope that it was neither returned nor so much as surmised by its object; for, at the age of twenty, Beatrice Portinari became the wife of Simon de' Bardi. Of Dante's consequent grief we find no distinct mention, although one passage in the "Vita Nuova" may refer to it. Of his bitter grief when, in the year 1290, at the still youthful age of twenty-four, she died, he has left us an ample record.

It is narrated, but I know not whether on trustworthy authority, that, in this period of bereavement, Dante donned the Franciscan habit as a novice in the monastery of San Benedetto in Alpe among the Apennines, and some writers of the same order have laid claim to him as wearing their affiliating cord and dying in their habit. However this may have been, tonsure and cowl were not for him, as an early day declared.

Boccaccio thus describes Dante in his desolation:

> "He was, indeed, through tear-shed, and through the affliction felt within his heart, and through his neglect of all outward personal care, become well-nigh a savage creature to behold: lean, bearded, and almost wholly transformed from his previous self, insomuch that his aspect, not in his friends only, but no less in such others as beheld him, by its own virtue wrought compassion; he withal, this tearful life subsisting, seldom suffering himself to be seen by any but friends. This compassion, and apprehension of worse to come, set his kindred on the alert for his solace. They, marking the tears abated and the consuming sighs according some truce to the wearied bosom, with long-lost consolations set themselves to reconsole the unconsoled one, who, although up to that hour he had obstinately stopped his ears against every one, began not merely somewhat to open them, but willingly to entertain comforting suggestions. Which thing his kindred beholding, to the end that they might not only altogether withdraw him from anguish, but might lead him into joy, they proposed among themselves to bestow upon him a wife; that, even as the lost lady had caused his grief, so the newly acquired one might become to him source of gladness. And, having found a maiden of creditable condition, with such reasons as appeared to them most influential, they declared to him their intention. Whereupon, after long conflict, without further waste of time, to words succeeded effects, and he was married."

This marriage, contracted about a year after the death of Beatrice, proved more or less unhappy; so we deem on indirect evidence. Gemma Donati, sister of that Corso Donati who subsequently, at the head of the Black faction, overran Florence with fire and sword,—Gemma Donati was the chosen bride, the accepted wife. Seven children she bore to her husband, surely a dear and binding link between them; yet, from the moment of his exile, he and she met no more. When, he being already and, as the event proved, finally absent, his Florentine house was burnt, she saved his manuscripts, which were afterward restored to his own keeping. This suggests, though it does not prove, affection on her side. But while some, if not all, of his children rejoined him after a time, his wife never. Perhaps no living woman of mere flesh and blood could have sufficed to supersede that Beatrice whom Dante terms "this youngest angel" long before death had (as we trust) exalted her to the society of all her blessed fellows, whether elect angels or beatified spirits. If so, Gemma is truly to be pitied in her comparatively thankless and loveless lot; nevertheless, such hope remained to her as, of old, Leah may have cherished when altogether eclipsed by Rachel,—such hope as removes from earth to heaven. Nor could Dante himself have denied her that hope, for thus he writes (Purgatory, 27):

> . . ."Sleep over me
> Came, even sleep, which oftentimes doth know
> The tidings of events before they be.
> . . . .
> My dreams did, young and beautiful, present
>   A lady to me, that by lawny lands
> Was gathering flowers, and singing as she went:
> 'Now know ye, whosoe'er my name demands,
>   That I am Leah, that about me ply,
> To make myself a chaplet, my fair hands;
> That I may in the mirror please mine eye
>   I deck me; but my sister Rachel, she
> Is ne'er uncharmed, and sits all day thereby.
> She hath as lief her goodly eyes to see,
>   As I have with my hands to deck me here;
> So study pleaseth her, and labor me.'"

Yet it seems hard to accept as full and final such an explanation, because Dante, on his own showing, lapsed from pure, unbroken faith to his first love into unworthy pleasure. Hear how, even amid the peace and bliss of the Terrestrial Paradise, Beatrice, with veiled countenance and stinging words, addresses him, "*Guardami ben; ben son, ben son Beatrice*" ("Look on me well; yes, I am Beatrice"), and, despite his overwhelming shame, resumes the thread of her discourse by speaking no longer *to*, but *at* him (Purgatory, 30):

> "Some while at heart my presence kept him sound;
>   My girlish eyes to his observance lending,

I led him with me on the right way bound.
When, of my second age the steps ascending,
  I bore my life into another sphere,
Then stole he from me, after others bending.
When I arose from flesh to spirit clear,
  When beauty, worthiness upon me grew,
I was to him less pleasing and less dear.
He set his feet upon a path untrue,
  Chasing fallacious images of weal,
Whose promise never doth result pursue.
It helpt me nought, to make him my appeal
  In sleep, through inspirations that I won,
Or otherwise; so little did he feel.
So far he fell adown, that now not one
  Device for his redemption could bestead,
Except by showing him the souls undone."

It is of course possible that the one woman whom Dante could not—or, rather, would not—love was that only woman who had an indefeasible claim upon his heart. Whatever the explanation may be, it remains for the present hidden. Time has not shown; eternity, if not time, will show it. Meanwhile let us, by good wishes, commend him, after the prolonged disappointment of life, to that satisfying peace whereunto he consigns Boethius—a philosopher whose writings had aforetime cheered him under depression, and whose spirit he places in the sun among the lovers of true wisdom, where his fellow-sage, St. Thomas Aquinas, thus sums up his history (Paradise, 10):

"Now, if the eye-beam of thy mind proceed
  From light to light, the follower of my praise,
To know the eighth already thou wilt need.
There, blessed from beholding all good, stays
  That soul untarnished who the treacherous lease,
If well perused, of worldly joys displays.
That body, whence her violent decease
  She made, Cieldauro covers, and she ran
From pangs and exile into th' endless peace."

If the master Boethius was wise, wise also must we account Dante the disciple. Some students speak of hidden lore underlying the letter of our poet's writings: in Beatrice they think to discern an impersonation rather than a woman, in the Divine Comedy a meaning political rather than dogmatic,—or, if in any sense dogmatic, yet not such as appears on the surface. So obscure a field of investigation is not for me or for my readers; at least, not for them through any help of mine: to me it is and it must remain dim and unexplored, even as that "*selva oscura*" (dark wood) with which the Cantica of the Hell opens.

What then, according to the obvious signification, is in few words the subject or plot of the Divine Comedy?

Dante, astray in a gloomy wood and beset by wild beasts, is rescued by the shade of Virgil, who, at the request of Beatrice, already an inhabitant of heaven, has left his proper abode in a painless region of hell, for the purpose of guiding Dante first of all through the nether-world of lost souls, that, by their irremediable ruin, he may learn to flee from evil as from the face of a serpent, retrieving his errors and amending his ways. Over Hell gate an awful inscription is placed (Hell, 3):

> "Through me you pass into the city of woe;
> Through me you pass eternal woes to prove;
> Through me among the blasted race you go.
> 'Twas Justice did my most high Author move,
>   And I have been the work of Power divine,
> Of supreme Wisdom, and of primal Love.
> No creature has an elder date than mine,
>   Unless eternal, and I have no end.
> O you that enter me, all hope resign."

Immediately beyond this gate swarms a throng of despicable souls, refuse even in hell, mere self-seekers; the "spued-out, lukewarm" ones, so to say. These left behind, and the river Styx passed over, a painless, hopeless region is entered,—the permanent home of Virgil, with all other virtuous heathens who lived and died before our Lord Christ was born: painless, because their lives were good; hopeless, because they lacked faith. Beyond this point of our pilgrims' journey peace, even hopeless peace, finds no place. A furious, whirling storm is the first torment they encounter. Thenceforward, from agony to agony they plunge deeper and deeper into the abyss of Hell, meeting sinner after sinner whose ghastly story is told at more or less length, until they reach the visible, abhorrent presence of Lucifer, who from "perfect in beauty" has by rebellion become absolute in hideous horror.

Mid-Lucifer occupies the earth's center of gravity. Virgil, with Dante clinging to him, clambers down the upper half of Lucifer and climbs up the lower half, whereby the twain find themselves emerging from the depth of Hell upon the Mountain of Purgatory.

This Purgatory is the domain of pain and hope,—finite pain, assured hope. Again a number of episodes charm us while we track the pilgrims along the steep ascent, until, on the summit, they reach the Terrestrial

Paradise; and here, the shade of Beatrice assuming in her own person the guidance of her lover, Virgil vanishes.

Under the guardianship of Beatrice, Dante mounts through eight successive Heavens to that ninth which includes within itself all blessedness. In each of them he encounters jubilant souls grown loquacious by impulse of charity, delighting to share with him their edifying experiences, to resolve his doubts, to lighten his darkness. All culminates in an unutterable revelation of God made Man and the All-Holy Trinity in Unity.

Chief among Dante's works, and in itself complete, the Divine Comedy yet requires an introduction if we would fully understand its starting-point. Our poet's earlier work, the "Vita Nuova," composed of alternate prose and verse, supplies that introduction. There we read an elaborate continuous exposition of his love for Beatrice, interspersed with ever-renewed tribute of praise from his lowliness to her loftiness; interspersed, too, with curiosities of structure and perhaps of style which some may deem pedantic. In the following passage Dante relates how, by means of a dream, he experienced beforehand what anguish should befall him on the death of Beatrice ("Vita Nuova"):

> . . . "In myself I said, with sick recoil:
> 'Yea, to my lady too this Death must come.'
> . . . .
> Then saw I many broken hinted sights
>   In the uncertain state I stepp'd into.
>   Meseem'd to be I know not in what place,
> Where ladies through the street, like mournful lights,
>   Ran with loose hair, and eyes that frighten'd you
> By their own terror, and a pale amaze:
> The while, little by little, as I thought,
> The sun ceased, and the stars began to gather,
>   And each wept at the other;
>   And birds dropp'd in mid-flight out of the sky;
>   And earth shook suddenly;
>   And I was 'ware of one, hoarse and tired out,
> Who ask'd of me: 'Hast thou not heard it said? . . .
> Thy lady, she that was so fair, is dead.'
>
> "Then lifting up mine eyes, as the tears came,
>   I saw the angels, like a rain of manna,
> In a long flight flying back heavenward;
> Having a little cloud in front of them,
>   After the which they went and said, 'Hosanna';
>   And if they had said more, you should have heard.
>   Then Love said, 'Now shall all things be made clear:
> Come and behold our lady where she lies.'

> "These 'wildering phantasies
> Then carried me to see my lady dead.
>   Even as I there was led,
> Her ladies with a veil were covering her;
> And with her was such very humbleness
> That she appeared to say, 'I am at peace.'"
>   (D. G. Rossetti.)[7]

Such readers as would fully enter into the mind of Dante—as fully, that is, as ordinary intelligences can hope to explore the extraordinary—must not limit themselves to the Divine Comedy and "Vita Nuova," but must study also the "Convito" (Banquet), a philosophical work, besides minor poems, epistles, and Latin compositions. On the threshold of such studies, I bid them good-bye in our great author's own words:

> "Se Dio ti lasci, lettor, prender frutto
> Di tua lezione."
> (May God vouchsafe thee, reader, to cull fruit
> From this thy reading.)

"The House of Dante Gabriel Rossetti" (1892)

Published in *Literary Opinion* 2 (1892): 127–29, this brief but affectionate memoir leaps back in time over the difficult later years of Dante Gabriel's life and is offered as a corrective to those who characterized him as eccentric or melancholy. An elegiac piece—in a kind of composition of place—Christina's thoughts wander through the grounds of Tudor House and end with happy recollections of her charismatic brother among family and friends.

The House of Dante Gabriel Rossetti

To anyone who recollects Tudor House (16, Cheyne Walk), during my brother Dante Gabriel Rossetti's long tenancy, a black and white sketch may more aptly represent it than a coloured one now taken could do. For, in his time, it exhibited no front of unbroken red colour, but natural-looking, uncoloured brick, without, at the earliest period, even so much as a Roman-cement centre.[8] Cement was added for safety's sake as time went on. The flat roof was not then crowned by a poised Mercury; but in its seemly unadornedness, was attainable from within up a ladder-stair and through a trap-door, afforded a walk to inmates and privileged guests, and commanded a pleasing view. Once, from the street below, a policeman felt it his duty to call attention to the presence of persons on the roof!

The construction of the Chelsea Embankment was not unmixed gain to No. 16; it may have retrenched low-water marginal mud, but it also interfered with certain well-grown trees which fronted the gate.

That gate led into a little partly-paved entrance-court, the house with its small front and large back garden presenting somewhat the figure of a gigantic portly bottle. The house formed (so to say) the internal cork, the little front court the protruding portion of the cork, the narrow back strip of ground between contiguous premises, the neck; until having passed beyond the precincts of Nos. 15 and 17, the bottle broadened its shoulders, and expanded right and left into quite a large London garden, never, perhaps, in thoroughly good order, yet, at the worst, more or less a wilderness of verdure and flowers. Back or front there grew fig trees, mulberry trees, a peach and a plum, a morella cherry, jessamine, roses, marigolds, and, in especial Solomon's seal and a hyacinth which was, or which resembled, the inimitably graceful wild blue hyacinth. Particularly good rhubarb flourished amongst other plants, until extirpated by its nonappreciative owner, and at one time a small mushroom bed was laid out. Alas! little, if anything, now stretches backward beyond the "neck of the bottle," the bulk of the garden ground having been divided amongst neighbouring houses.

There were, as has often been stated, various creatures, quaint or beautiful, about the house and grounds, some of them at liberty. I particularly recall Bobby—a little owl with a very large face and a beak of a sort of egg-shell green; a woodchuck, a deer, and a wombat, nameless, or of name unknown to me.[9] Gabriel (his family never called him Dante, Gabriel being indeed his first Christian name), was amused by some lines I wrote on that wombat:—

> O Uommibatto
>   Agil, giocondo,
> Che ti sei fatto
>   Liscio e rotondo!
> Deh non fuggire
>   Qual vagabondo,
> Non disparire
>   Forando il mondo:
> Pesa davero
>   D'un emisfero
> Non lieve il pondo.

But far from "liscio" the wombat turned out rough, and I altered l. 4 to:— "Irsuto e tondo."[10]

With such inhabitants, Tudor House and its grounds became a sort of wonderland; and once the author of "Wonderland" photographed us in the garden.[11] It was our aim to appear in the full family group of five: but whilst various others succeeded, that particular negative was spoilt by a shower, and I possess a solitary print taken from it in which we appear as if splashed by ink.

Allowing for long lapse of years and consequent possible defects of memory, such as these are my recollections of happy days when family or friendly parties used to assemble at Tudor House there to meet with an unfailing affectionate welcome. Gloom and eccentricity such as have been alleged were at any rate not the sole characteristics of Dante Gabriel Rossetti: when he chose he became the sunshine of his circle, and he frequently chose so to be. His ready wit and fun amused us; his good nature and kindness of heart endeared him to us.

Part 3

Devotional Prose

From *Annus Domini: A Prayer for Each Day of the Year, Founded on a Text of Holy Scripture* (1874)

T he first of Christina Rossetti's nonfictional devotional works, and written after a long illness from which she was still recovering, *Annus Domini* is a kind of thank offering, filled with joy and resolution. James Parker and Company published it in the spring of 1874 as one in its shilling series that included such notable seventeenth-century divines as Lancelot Andrewes, John Cosin, Jeremy Taylor, and Thomas Ken. Parker had already published its scholarly "Library of Anglo-Catholic Theology" in more than 80 volumes, which aimed to recover and celebrate these and other Caroline divines. Rossetti's little book thus enjoyed an honorable association from its beginning.

The book contains 366 collects, one for each day of the year. Each collect begins with a scriptural text, opening with Genesis 3.15, and continuing in sequence from the Old to the New Testament, and ending with a final collect based on Revelation 23.16. Rossetti favored texts of a prophetic nature, which may account for the fact that forty of the collects are based on texts from Isaiah, with forty-two on the Apocalypse. Also much favored are the Psalms, with sixty-four collects, the Gospels (with thirty-two from John), and the Epistles, especially Hebrews. The scriptural text becomes the occasion of the opening of the collect, with an invocation always to Christ, followed by a meditation on a word or idea suggested by the text, often leading inward toward personal reflection. In general, Rossetti tries to give prayers that will help herself and others to compose their thoughts around the mystery of the Incarnation, the Word made flesh.

The calendar to which Rossetti refers in her brief prefatory note arranges the collects around Advent, Christmas, Epiphany, Septuagesima, Lent, Passiontide, Holy Week, Easter, Ascension, Whitsuntide, Holy Trinity, Saints' Days, Feasts of the Blessed Virgin, St. Michael and All Angels, Ember Weeks, and the Rogation Days. Not all 366 collects are numbered in this calendar; but, perhaps not surprisingly, more than half of the approximately one hundred appearing in this list are assigned to the penitential seasons of Advent and Lent. The small format of the book (printed in foolscap 8o), which measures 9 x 12 cm., with marginal rules on every page and an ornamental cross at each corner of the rule, neatly bound in limp, morocco buckram, is declaring itself a suitable devotional supplement to set next to the *Book of Common Prayer*. Perhaps the Reverend H. W. Burrows, Christina Rossetti's old friend and incumbent of her parish of Christ Church, Albany Street, may be gently warning readers of the book's limitations in his slightly qualified commendation. Yet *Annus Domini* is a compilation of prayers inspired by the Tractarian Movement and a worthy addition to its literature.

Rossetti means to meditate on different scriptural passages that appeal to her through a kind of intimate conversation with the personal Jesus; and these passages remind her of yet more biblical locations so that the whole work is nearly a conflation of scriptural texts. From Genesis to Revelation, Christina selects verses on which to base her intercessory prayers, frequently referring to specific concerns, and we have wished to display these in our selections.

In one prayer (141), Rossetti invokes the "Lord Jesus Christ, Who was numbered with the transgressors," and who recorded his descent through Tamar, Rahab and Bathsheba. Show mercy, she prays, on all fallen women; "and give to them and to those who have sinned with them, repentance and amendment of life and salvation." Here Rossetti strikes a theme common in these prayers, that of "fallen women." We are reminded of her association through her sister Maria with St. Mary Magdalene's, Highgate, in the 1860s, with its mission for the reclamation of impoverished and cast off women, and also reminded of her poetry of "fallenness," such as "From Sunset to Star Rise" (*Poems*, 1979–90, 1:191–92). In another prayer (234), Rossetti addresses the sea of contemporary doubt, also a familiar concern in her prose and poetry. She begins as usual by invoking Christ, "whose Name is called Wonderful. . . . Suffer us not to be seduced from the faith

by miscalled reason, or apparent facts of science, or wit and learning of misbelievers, or subtilties of Satan."

The text given here is from a copy of the very rare first (and only) edition, in
the Colbeck Collection, University of British Columbia Library. The notes record
a number of further scriptural allusions and Prayer Book references that help to
demonstrate the inventive way in which Rossetti blends texts and ideas.

Annus Domini

I have had great pleasure in looking over these Prayers as they passed
through the Press, for they seem to me valuable in themselves from their fervour, reverence, and overflowing charity, and also because they are suggestive of the use which should be made of Holy Scripture in our devotions.
Each little Prayer may be considered as the result of a meditation, and as an
example of the way in which that exercise should issue in worship.

It will be observed that all the prayers are addressed to the Second Person
in the Blessed Trinity, and are therefore intended only to be used as supplementary to other devotions.

H. W. Burrows.

I have planned my little Book to supply a Text and Collect for each day of
the year; and a short Calendar assigns certain Prayers to certain seasons, if
such a classification is wished for. In quoting from the Psalms, I have made
use sometimes of the Authorized Version, and sometimes of that found in
the Book of Common Prayer.

C. G. R.

1.

Gen. 3.15.

**I will put enmity between thee and the woman, and between thy seed
and her Seed; It shall bruise thy head, and thou shalt bruise His heel.**

O Lord Jesus Christ, Seed of the woman, Thou Who hast bruised the serpent's head, destroy in us, I entreat Thee, the power of that old serpent the
devil. Give us courage to resist him, strength to overcome him; deliver the
prey from between his teeth, bid his captives go free; for his kingdom, set up

Thy kingdom; and for the death he brought in, bring Thou in life everlasting. Amen.

4.

Gen. 28.13.

I am the Lord God of Abraham thy father, and the God of Isaac.

O Lord Jesus Christ, God of Isaac, grant, I entreat Thee, that as at Thy Word he willingly gave himself up to die, so we may after his example offer to Thee a willing obedience, eating and drinking and doing all things to Thy Glory: and that, having lived unto Thee, we may die unto Thee. Amen.

7.

Exod. 3.14.

I AM THAT I AM.

O Lord Jesus Christ, the I AM, cast down, I beseech Thee, before the unapproachable Majesty of Thy Being, all man's haughtiness of will and pride of intellect. Make the wise and prudent of this world as babes, that they may desire the sincere milk of Thy Word: let them not wrest Thy good gifts to their own destruction; but with great abilities and great responsibilities bestow, O Lord our Wisdom, greater grace. Amen.

11.

Exod. 33.19.

I will make all My Goodness pass before thee, and I will proclaim the Name of the Lord before thee; and will be gracious to whom I will be gracious, and will shew mercy on whom I will shew mercy.

O Lord Jesus Christ, Who wilt shew mercy on whom Thou wilt shew mercy, all mankind groaneth unto Thee in helplessness, sin, and misery.[1] Thou Who wouldest that all men should be saved and come to the knowledge of the Truth, oh, shew mercy on whom Thou wilt shew mercy. Amen.

16.

Deut. 4.24.

The Lord thy God is a consuming Fire, even a Jealous God.

O Lord Jesus Christ, Who art a Consuming Fire, even a Jealous God, make us, I implore Thee, so to love Thee that Thou mayest be to us a Fire of Love, purifying and not destroying. As Thou in Love art Jealous over us, so make us also in love jealous over ourselves lest we dishonour Thee: jealous of our thoughts lest they stray from Thee, jealous of our hearts lest they do homage to any King but Thee.—Alas, O Lord, alas for me, I have wandered from Thee, I have loved others instead of Thee, I have done Thee despite: but for Thine own sake Who didst die for us, I entreat Thee, recall me and all sinners into Thine obedience; cast out the idol from every heart, reconcile all men to Thee in love. Amen.

21.

Deut. 32.31.

Their rock is not as our Rock, even our enemies themselves being judges.

O Lord Jesus Christ, our Rock, give us wisdom, I beseech Thee, to build our house upon The Rock and not upon the sand: that so when floods of temptation, rain of affliction, winds of persecution, beat upon that house it may not fall, because it is founded upon a Rock. Amen.

24.

1 Sam. 15.29.

**The Strength of Israel will not lie nor repent: for
He is not a man, that He should repent.**

O Lord Jesus Christ, Strength of Israel, keep, I entreat Thee, Thy holy Church militant from backslidings and errors, from laxity and superstition, from coldness and lukewarmness, from dead faith and dead works, from the gates of hell and from the bottomless pit.[2] Amen.

26.

2 Kings 2.14.

He took the mantle of Elijah that fell from him, and smote the waters, and said, Where is the Lord God of Elijah? and when he also had smitten the waters, they parted hither and thither: and Elisha went over.

O Lord Jesus Christ, Lord God of Elijah, as Thou didst put a word in his mouth which a king could neither gainsay nor resist, so now, I beseech Thee, endue Thy priests and preachers with power to convince the world of sin, and to set forth righteousness.[3] Give them grace to wait on their preaching with earnest prayer, devout study, humble painstaking:

strengthen them to plant and water, and do Thou, O Lord, give the increase. Amen.

27.

2 Chron. 30.9.

**The Lord your God is Gracious and Merciful, and will not
turn away His face from you, if ye return unto Him.**

O Lord Jesus Christ, God Gracious and Merciful, give us, I entreat Thee, a humble trust in Thy mercy, and suffer not our heart to fail us. Though our sins be seven, though our sins be seventy times seven,[4] though our sins be more in number than the hairs of our head, yet give us grace in loving penitence to cast ourselves down into the depth of Thy compassion. Let us fall into the Hand of the Lord. Amen.

30.

Job 12.16.

**With Him is strength and wisdom: the
deceived and the deceiver are His.**

O Lord Jesus Christ, with Whom are Strength and Wisdom, put forth Thy Strength, I implore Thee, for Thine own sake and for our sakes, and stand up to help us. Deliver us from Satan's assaults and wiles, from his fury and his smooth words: for we are deceivable and weak persons, frail and brief, unstable and afraid, unless Thou put the Might of Thy Holy Spirit within us. Amen, O Lord, Amen.

46.

Ps. 38.18.

**They prevented me in the day of my calamity:
but the Lord was my Stay.**

O Lord Jesus Christ, the Lord our Stay, support us, I entreat Thee, under every temptation. Against frailty of the flesh, be Thou our Stay; against pressure of the world, be Thou our Stay; against goadings of the devil, be Thou our Stay. When the enemy cometh in as a flood, O God, lift up a standard against him.[5] Amen.

56.

Ps. 31.12.

I am forgotten as a dead man out of mind: I am like a broken vessel.

O Lord Jesus Christ, Who wast forgotten as a dead man out of mind, shew forth Thy loving kindness, I entreat Thee, to all persons who in this world feel themselves neglected, or little loved, or forgotten. Be Thou their beloved Companion, and let communion with Thee be to them more dear than tenderest earthly intercourse. Teach them to seek Thee in prayer, and to find Thee in Thy Blessed Sacrament; teach them to discern Thee in all with whom they come in contact, and to love and serve Thee in them. On earth grant them comfort by the repentance of any who have wronged them, and in Heaven comfort in the communion of all Saints with each other and with Thee. Amen.

58.

Ps. 33.11.

The Counsel of the Lord standeth for ever,
the Thoughts of His Heart to all generations.

O Lord Jesus Christ, Whose Counsel standeth for ever, let not dust and ashes, a worm, a puff of wind, creatures of a day, let us not, O Lord, ever set our will against Thy Will, or despise our birthright with Esau, or harden our hearts with Pharaoh. But to-day before the night cometh, to-day in the day of grace, grant us repentance unto amendment of life; that in the last great Day of account Thou sweep us not away with the besom of destruction.[6] Amen.

59.

Ps. 33.18.

Behold, the Eye of the Lord is upon them that fear Him,
upon them that hope in His Mercy.

O Lord Jesus Christ, Whose Eye is upon them that fear Thee and hope in Thy Mercy, put far from us, I pray Thee, slavish fear and presumptuous hope. While we stay our hearts on Thee give us grace to remember that Thou art a Jealous God Who will by no means spare the guilty; while we fear Thee, to remember that Thou art our infinitely merciful Saviour. Amen.

68.

Ps. 45.3.

**Thou art fairer than the children of men: full of Grace are
Thy Lips, because God hath blessed Thee for ever.**

O Lord Jesus Christ, Fairer than the children of men, give us grace, I entreat
Thee, to love Thee above every creature, and to offer up ourselves a living
sacrifice unto Thee. Help us to live after Thy Pattern of devotion, to die after
Thine Example of loving resignation, and to rise again after Thy Likeness,
that we may see Thee as Thou art. Amen.

74.

Ps. 47.7.

God is the King of all the earth: sing ye praises with understanding.

O Lord Jesus Christ, King of all the earth, Thy Kingdom come. Give, I pray
Thee, to all who are called Christians, the graces of continual repentance and
final perseverance. Give to those who as yet know Thee not, zeal to press into
Thy fold and therein steadfastly to abide. Give to us all such love of Thee and
of one another, that our lips and our lives may praise Thee.[7] Amen.

76.

Ps. 48.14.

**This God is our God for ever and ever:
He will be our Guide even unto death.**

O Lord Jesus Christ, our Guide even unto death, grant us, I pray Thee, grace
to follow Thee whithersoever Thou goest. In little daily duties to which
Thou callest us, bow down our wills to simple obedience, patience under
pain or provocation, strict truthfulness of word and manner, humility, kindness: in great acts of duty or perfection if Thou shouldest call us to them,
uplift us to self-sacrifice, heroic courage, laying down of life for thy Truth's
sake or for a brother. Amen.

91.

Ps. 104.2.

**Thou deckest Thyself with light as it were with
a garment: and spreadest out the heavens like a curtain.**

O Lord Jesus Christ, Who spreadest out the heavens like a curtain, give us,
I pray Thee, faithful wills and loving hearts that in Thy works we may ever

discern Thee, and may never be misled by false science from holding fast those truths which Thou hast revealed.[8] O Lord, I humbly bless Thee for what Thou givest, and for what Thou withholdest; for the knowledge Thou bestowest, and for the knowledge Thou keepest back. Amen.

102.

Song of Sol. 2.3.

As the Apple Tree among the trees of the wood,
so is my Beloved among the sons.

O Lord Jesus Christ, Who art as the Apple Tree among the trees of the wood, give us to taste of Thy Sweetness, that eating we may yet be hungry, and drinking we may yet be thirsty. Infuse of Thy Sweetness, I pray Thee, into Thy servants, that cleaving to Thee they may attract others also to Thee: until as the hart desireth the water brooks, all souls may long after Thee, O God.[9] Amen.

103.

Song of Sol. 2.3; Isa. 25.4.

I sat down under His Shadow with great delight.

O Lord Jesus Christ, our Shadow from the heat when the blast of the terrible ones is as a storm against the wall, save us, I implore Thee, under all stress of terrible temptation. Deliver us from rebellion of passion, seduction of the flesh, allurements of the world, provocations of the devil: deliver us from siege and from surprise, from our foes and from ourselves, O Lord. Amen.

111.

Isa. 4.2.

In that day shall the Branch of the Lord be Beautiful and Glorious,
and the fruit of the earth shall be excellent and comely for them
that are escaped of Israel.

O Lord Jesus Christ, Branch of the Lord Beautiful and Glorious, I beseech Thee so to sustain us by Thy Life, and so to possess us with adoring love of Thy Glorious Beauty, that in our eyes sin may appear vile, hideous, and without allurement. Help us to abhor it as poison, to cast it from us as filth, to flee from it as death. Give us grace to return thanks for all Thou givest, and for all Thou deniest: give us grace having food and raiment therewith to be content; yea, though we lack and suffer hunger, be Thine every Word bread to us. Amen.

112.

Isa. 5.16.

The Lord of hosts shall be exalted in judgment, and God
That is Holy shall be sanctified in righteousness.

O Lord Jesus Christ, Holy God, I beseech Thee help us, that when we make our petitions before Thy Mercy-Seat we may take heed to lift up holy hands unto Thee; lest our prayer be turned into sin, lest when we cry to Thee Thou hear us not, lest we bring a curse upon us and not a blessing. Amen.

113.

Isa. 6.1.

I saw also the Lord sitting upon a Throne, high and
lifted up, and His Train filled the Temple.

O Lord Jesus Christ, Whose Train filled the Temple, fill, I entreat Thee, with Thy Life-giving Presence Thy living Temple the Church; her length, breadth, depth, height, her courts and outer courts. Make her every member a willing Temple of the Holy Ghost.[10] Bid her enlarge the place of her tent, that the fulness of the Gentiles may press in. Clothe her with Thy Righteousness, adorn her with Thy Graces, support her by Thy Love of her and her love of Thee, crown her with Thy Glory. Amen.

141.

Isa. 53.12.

He was numbered with the transgressors; and He bare the sin of many,
and made intercession for the transgressors.

O Lord Jesus Christ, Who wast numbered with the transgressors, and hast vouchsafed to place on record Thy human descent through Tamar, Rahab and Bathsheba, shew mercy, I beseech Thee, on all fallen women; and give to them and to those who have sinned with them, repentance and amendment of life unto salvation.[11] Amen.

147.

Isa. 57.15.

I dwell in the High and Holy Place, with him also that is of a contrite and humble spirit, to revive the spirit of the humble, and to revive the heart of the contrite ones.

O Lord Jesus Christ, Who dwellest in the High and Holy Place, with him also that is of a contrite and humble spirit, revive, I entreat Thee, the spirit of the humble, and the heart of the contrite. Here give us humility and contrition, hereafter exaltation and perfection. Amen.

152.

Jer. 17.13.

O Lord, the Hope of Israel, all that forsake Thee shall
be ashamed, and they that depart from Me shall be written
in the earth, because they have forsaken the Lord,
the Fountain of Living Waters.

O Lord Jesus Christ, Fountain of Living Waters, preserve us, I implore Thee, from that second death which separateth from Thee. We thirst: bring us to the Waters, let us take the Water of Life freely. If Thou come not to judgment in our mortal lifetime, let our death be sleep in Thee, and our awakening be after Thy Likeness.[12] In the Day of Thy most awful Judgment, Good Lord deliver us. Amen.

153.

Jer. 32.19; Isa. 9.6.

Great in Counsel, and Mighty in Work: for Thine Eyes are open
upon all the ways of the sons of men: to give every one according
to his ways, and according to the fruit of his doings.

O Lord Jesus Christ, Whose Name is called Counsellor, give us grace, I beseech Thee, always to hear and obey Thy Voice which saith to every one of us, "This is the way, walk ye in it." Nevertheless, let us not hear It behind us saying, This is the way; but rather before us saying, Follow Me.[13] When Thou puttest us forth, go before us; when the way is too great for us, carry us; in the darkness of death, comfort us; in the day of resurrection, satisfy us. Amen.

159.

Hos. 14.9.

**The Ways of the Lord are right, and the just shall walk in them:
but the transgressors shall fall therein.**

O Lord Jesus Christ, the Lord Whose Ways are right, keep us in Thy mercy
from lip-service and empty forms; from having a name that we live, but
being dead. Help us to worship Thee by righteous deeds and lives of holiness; that our prayer also may be set forth in Thy sight as the incense, and
the lifting up of our hands be as an evening sacrifice.[14] Amen.

163.

Hab. 1.13.

**Thou art of purer Eyes than to behold evil,
and canst not look on iniquity.**

O Lord Jesus Christ, Who art of purer Eyes than to behold evil, make us, I
pray Thee, abhor ourselves for all our defilements of flesh and spirit. Give us
grace to dread and avoid occasions of sin; to restrain our eyes, our thoughts,
our affections: and do Thou of Thy mercy forgive and cleanse us, O our
most merciful Lord, Thou Who badest the woman that was a sinner go in
peace.[15] Amen.

165.

Hag. 2.7.

I will shake all nations, and the Desire of all nations shall come.

O Lord Jesus Christ, Desire of all nations, Who seest that all hearts are
empty except Thou fill them, and all desires balked except they crave after
Thee; give us light and grace to seek and find Thee, that we may be Thine
and Thou mayest be ours for ever. Amen.

166.

Zech. 6.12.

**Behold the Man Whose Name is The Branch; and He shall grow up out
of His place, and He shall build the Temple of the Lord.**

O Lord Jesus Christ, the Branch, unite us wholly unto Thyself, I entreat
Thee, and make us lovely branches to Thy praise. Quicken us to bear fruit,

and prune us that we may bring forth more fruit. By Thy Life nourish us, by Thine Overshadowing shelter us,[16] by Thy Love ripen us, by Thy Likeness perfect us. Amen.

170.

St. Matt. 1.21; Isa. 9.6.

She shall bring forth a Son, and thou shalt call His Name Jesus: for He shall save His people from their sins.

O Lord Jesus Christ, the Son given unto us, Root of our life, Flower of our stock, its Fruit all perfect, and its Sweetness beyond all sweetness, teach us, I beseech Thee, to worship and adore, to love and delight in Thee. As the Father hath given Thee unto us, grant us grace to give back to Him through Thee all we are and all we have. Be Thou formed in every heart: that in each one of us the Almighty Father may behold Thee, and be well pleased. Amen.

174.

St. Matt. 11.19.

A Friend of Publicans and sinners.

O Lord Jesus Christ, Friend of sinners, save, I implore Thee, perishing sinners. From mistrust of Thy mercy, presumption on Thy mercy, abuse of Thy mercy, contempt of Thy mercy, O most merciful Lord, deliver us. Amen.

176.

St. Matt. 11.30.

My Yoke is easy, and My Burden is light.

O Lord Jesus Christ, Whose Yoke is easy, grant, I pray Thee, to all Christian children, grace and wisdom to bow down their necks and bear Thy yoke. Fill their minds with Thine awful reverence, cover and turn away their eyes lest they behold vanity, stop their ears lest so they conceive iniquity; pre-occupy their hearts, O Lord of infinite Love, that no idol may ever reign therein. Amen.

197.

St. John 1.14.

The Word was made Flesh, and dwelt among us, full of Grace and Truth.

O Lord Jesus Christ, the Word, I pray Thee give us hearing ears, that in every circumstance and choice of our lives we may recognise Thy Voice, saying, Follow Me: and grant us grace hearing to hearken, and hearkening to persevere unto the end; that so of Thine infinite mercy we may at last hear from Thee that other word, Come, ye blessed of My Father, inherit the kingdom prepared for you from the foundation of the world.[17] Amen.

199.

St. John 1.17.

The law was given by Moses, but Grace and Truth came by Jesus Christ.

O Lord Jesus Christ, by Whom came Grace and Truth, with Thy truth send forth Thy grace, I entreat Thee, throughout all the world, and hasten that day when the earth shall be full of the knowledge of the Lord, as the waters cover the sea.[18] Impart true wisdom to those who as yet know Thee not, that they may behold, accept, love and cleave to Thee their only Saviour; and preserve in the way of Thy Truth such as now walk therein. Amen.

205.

St. John 5.21; 1 Cor. 15.45.

**As the Father raiseth up the dead, and quickeneth them;
even so the Son quickeneth whom He will.**

O Lord Jesus Christ, made a Quickening Spirit, quicken, I entreat Thee, with the Life that is in Thee, the true Life, the deathless Life, those who have a name to live, but are dead. Call back hypocrites into the simplicity of Thy Truth; to those who use them, fill forms and ceremonies with Thy Spirit; bid sleepers awake; bid them that sit in darkness arise, draw near, see and believe unto life eternal.[19] Amen.

215.

St. John 12.35.

Jesus said unto them, Yet a little while is the Light with you. Walk while ye have the Light, lest darkness come upon you: for he that walketh in darkness knoweth not whither he goeth.

O Lord Jesus Christ, Light with us, be Light, I entreat Thee, unto every man born into the world. Give us grace to work while it is day, fulfilling diligently and patiently whatever duty Thou appointest us; doing small things in the day of small things, and great labours if Thou summon us to any: rising and working, sitting still and suffering, according to Thy Word. Go with me, and I will go; but if Thou go not with me, send me not: go before me, if Thou put me forth; let me hear Thy Voice when I follow. Amen.

224.

St. John 18.37; Rev. 3.14.

To this end was I born, and for this cause came I into the world, that I should bear witness unto the Truth.

O Lord Jesus Christ, the Faithful and True Witness, I beseech Thee, where-insoever we have offended in faith or practice, grant us now repentance unto amendment, that Thou mayest blot out the handwriting that is against us: lest when Thou judgest, no tears of ours be in Thy bottle, but only our sins be noted in Thy book.[20] Amen.

234.

Rom. 11.33; Isa. 9.6.

O the depth of the riches both of the Wisdom and Knowledge of God! how unsearchable are His Judgments, and His Ways past finding out!

O Lord Jesus Christ, Whose Name is called Wonderful, give us grace, I beseech Thee, with all prostration of heart and intellect to adore Thee, Who art with the Father and the Holy Ghost One only Lord God. Suffer us not to be seduced from the faith by miscalled reason, or apparent facts of science, or wit and learning of misbelievers, or subtilties of Satan. Have compassion on those who err; and give us all faith to discern Thee, hope to reach after Thee, love to cleave unto Thee the Truth: Who with the Father and the Holy Ghost livest and reignest one God Blessed for ever. Amen.

245.

2 Cor. 11.2.

I am jealous over you with godly jealousy: for I have espoused you to one Husband, that I may present you as a chaste virgin to Christ.

O Lord Jesus Christ, to Whom we are espoused, keep us ever, I entreat Thee, with virgin souls, faithful in Thy love. Suffer no earthly affection to intrude between Thee and us; but be Thou our Beloved in all whom we love, and teach us to love all in Thee. Amen.

248.

Eph. 2.14.

He is our Peace, Who hath made both one, and hath broken down the middle wall of partition between us.

O Lord Jesus Christ, our Peace, restore, I entreat Thee, unity to Thy Church, weakened, crippled and brought into contempt by her divisions. Convert heretics, reconcile schismatics, convince infidels, perfect the faithful. Pour forth on Thy Church the Spirit of love and zeal, bless and multiply her missions, and endue with such power Thy Word in her mouth that no man may be able to gainsay or resist it. Amen.

268.

Heb. 2.10.

It became Him, for Whom are all things, and by Whom are all things, in bringing many sons unto glory, to make the Captain of their Salvation perfect through sufferings.

O Lord Jesus Christ, Captain of our Salvation, help us, I pray Thee, always to bear in mind our vows, and to fight manfully under the banner of Thy Cross against the world, the flesh and the devil.[21] By Thy Sufferings sanctify our sufferings; in Thy Strength make us stronger than our enemies; by virtue of Thy Victory give us victory. Amen.

275.

Heb. 5.8.

Though He were a Son, yet learned He obedience by the things which He suffered.

O Lord Jesus Christ, Who though a Son didst learn obedience by things suffered, teach us, I pray Thee, though by suffering, the lesson of unquestioning obedience. By Thy pang of sorrow when Thy friends forsook Thee and fled, support us under loneliness; by Thy stripes and mocking, nerve us to endure insult and provocation; by Thy thirst upon the Cross, give us patience in any extremity of bodily anguish. Conform our will to Thy Will:

make us hate what Thou hatest, choose what Thou choosest, reject what Thou rejectest. Amen.

282.

Heb. 7.25.

He is able also to save them to the uttermost that come unto God by Him, seeing He ever liveth to make intercession for them.

O Lord Jesus Christ, Who ever livest to make intercession for us, plead for us, I implore Thee, plead for us all with Thy prevailing Advocacy before the Throne of God the Father. And because being compassed with infirmities we oftentimes sin and ask pardon, help us to forgive as we would be forgiven; neither mentioning old offences committed against us, nor dwelling upon them in thought, nor being influenced by them in heart: but loving our brother freely as Thou freely lovest us, and shewing mercy that we may obtain mercy. Amen.

292.

Heb. 12.6.

Whom the Lord loveth He chasteneth, and scourgeth every son whom He receiveth.

O Lord Jesus Christ, Who chastenest whom Thou lovest, grant us grace, I pray Thee, to discern Thy Love in whatever suffering Thou sendest us. Support us in patient thankfulness under pain, anxiety, or loss; move us with pity and tenderness for our afflicted neighbour; give each of us that good gift which Thou designest for us by Thy chastening. Before I was troubled I went wrong, but now will I keep Thy law. Amen.

297.

St. James 2.1.

My brethren, have not the faith of our Lord Jesus Christ, the Lord of Glory, with respect of persons.

O Lord Jesus Christ, Lord of Glory, Who didst empty Thyself of Glory for our sakes, give us grace, I beseech Thee, with willing hearts to offer ourselves to Thee, all we are and all we have. Raise up according to Thy Will and for Thy Glory, saintly priests, heroic missionaries, self-denying rich and poor, men and women devoted to Thy service, virgins espoused to Thee, married persons loving Thee above all and each other as Thy precious and cherished gift. Guide us by That Wisdom which is pure, peaceable, gentle, easily intreated, merciful, fruitful, without partiality or hypocrisy. And prosper, O Lord, Thy work in our hands. Amen.

305.

1 St. Peter 2.24.

Who His own Self bare our sins in His own Body on the Tree, that we, being dead to sins, should live unto righteousness.

O Lord Jesus Christ, Who didst bear our sins in Thine own Body on the Tree, preserve, I pray Thee, in blessed innocence, all baptized children. But I, woe is me, I have sinned, have deeply sinned, have sinned wilfully and carelessly, have sinned against mercies and against judgments, have sinned without excuse: by penitence, I beseech Thee, bring me and all others who have sinned back to purity. And on the heathen, and on all who have never known Thee, shew mercy, O Lord, shew the fulness of Thy limitless mercy: cleanse them in Thy Blood, renew them by Thy Spirit, perfect them by Thy Grace. Amen.

313.

2 St. Peter 3.9.

The Lord is not slack concerning His Promise, as some men count slackness; but is longsuffering to us-ward, not willing that any should perish, but that all should come to repentance.

O Lord Jesus Christ, Who art not slack concerning Thy Promise, but longsuffering to us-ward, I plead with Thee for every human soul: O Lord help us, bring us to repentance, give us grace and peace, grant us glory and joy in the day of Thy promised coming. Help those who know Thee not, to know and love Thee; those who know Thee, to love Thee and live after Thy Pattern. Help us all, I entreat Thee, up the steep hill of salvation into the heavenly garden of Thy planting. Amen.

314.

1 St. John 1.1.

That Which was from the beginning, Which we have heard, Which we have seen with our eyes, Which we have looked upon, and our hands have handled, of the Word of Life.

O Lord Jesus Christ, Word of life, speak peace unto Thy people; speak peace to those who are far off, and to those who are near. Fill us with reverence, I pray Thee, for Thy most holy written Word: give us grace to study and meditate in it, with prayer and firm adoring faith; not questioning its authority, but obeying its precepts, and becoming imbued by its spirit. Teach us to prostrate our understandings before its mysteries; to live by its law, and abide by its promises. Amen.

318.

1 St. John 2.2.

He is the Propitiation for our sins: and not for ours only, but also for the sins of the whole world.

O Lord Jesus Christ, the Propitiation for the sins of the whole world, be Thou, in the overflow of Thine exceeding mercy, Propitiation for all sinners, for each sinner, for me a sinner. Thou Who comfortest as no mother comforteth, comfort us: Thou who rememberest as no mother remembereth, remember us. Break, I implore Thee, proud wills, bend stiff necks, wring hard hearts: convert sinners into saints, and let all Thy saints praise Thee. Amen.

319.

1 St. John 2.20.

Ye have an Unction from the Holy One, and ye know all things.

O Lord Jesus Christ, the Holy One, make us, I pray Thee, ashamed in Thy Presence, because we are of depraved understanding, unclean heart and impure will. My soul is a corrupt fountain, mine eyes behold vanity, out of my mouth cometh that which defileth: O Lord, on me a sinner, on all sinners, have mercy. Wash us in Thy most precious Blood, cleanse us continually by the spotless Food of Thy Blessed Sacrament; teach and sanctify us by Thy Most Holy Spirit, the Spirit of Purity. Amen.

324.

St. Jude 25.

To the only Wise God our Saviour, be Glory and Majesty, Dominion and Power, both now and ever. Amen.

O Lord Jesus Christ, the only Wise God our Saviour, hold us fast, I beseech Thee, lest we fall. We are short of sight and narrow of understanding; the flesh craves, the devil sets traps, the world dazzles us: O Lord, let it be Thy good pleasure to deliver us. Open our eyes and purge our hearts, that we may see as Thou seest and judge as Thou judgest. Keep our feet: be Thou before and behind us, on our right hand and on our left. Be Thy Word our Law, Thy Wisdom our Instructor, Thy Love our Safeguard: so in that Day may we stand blameless and with exceeding joy, giving thanks in the Presence of Thy Glory. Amen.

338.

Rev. 3.20.

Behold, I stand at the door, and knock: if any man hear My Voice, and open the door, I will come in to him, and will sup with him, and he with Me.

O Lord Jesus Christ, Who standest at the door and knockest, give us wisdom, I entreat Thee, to open our hearts wide unto Thee, that Thou mayest enter in to abide and sup with us. Grant us grace to discern and love Thee in Thy poor: and according as Thou shalt call us, to feed Thee in the hungry, refresh Thee in the thirsty, clothe Thee in the naked, visit Thee in the sick, comfort Thee in the prisoner, receive Thee in the stranger, bury that which is made after Thine Image in the dead. Amen.

362.

Rev. 22.1; Rev. 2.21.

He shewed me a pure River of Water of Life, clear as crystal, proceeding out of the Throne of God and of the Lamb.

O Lord Jesus Christ, Who overcamest and art set down with Thy Father in His Throne, by virtue of Thy victory give us also, I entreat Thee, victory. Let Thy pierced Heart win us to love Thee, Thy torn Hands incite us to every good work, Thy wounded Feet urge us on errands of mercy, Thy crown of thorns prick us out of sloth, Thy thirst draw us to thirst after the Living Water Thou givest:[22] let Thy life be our pattern while we live, and Thy death our triumph over death when we come to die. Amen.

366.

Rev. 22.16.

I am the Root and the Offspring of David, and the Bright and Morning Star.

O Lord Jesus Christ, the Bright and Morning Star, as once by a star Thou didst lead the Wise Men unto the sure mercies of David, so now by Thine Illuminating Spirit guide us, I pray Thee, to Thyself: that we with them, and by the Grace of the Same Most Holy Spirit, may offer unto Thee gold of love, frankincense of adoration, and myrrh of self-sacrifice. Amen.

From *Seek and Find:*
A Double Series of Short Studies of the Benedicite (1879)

—✦—

The "Benedicite, Omnia Opera," that is, "all you works [of the Lord], bless the Lord," is the canticle provided in the *Book of Common Prayer* as an alternative to the "Te Deum Laudamus": "We praise thee, O God," appointed to be said or sung after the first lesson in the office of morning prayer. It is known also as the "Song of the Three Children," Ananiah, Azariah, and Mishael, whom Nebuchadnezzar threw into the fiery furnace because they had refused to bow down and worship before his golden statue. This canticle, an apocryphal (Greek) addition to the Book of Daniel (inserted between 3.23 and 3.24), is a long poetic litany of exaltation and blessing of God's works in thirty-two sections—the heavens, the waters, the sun and moon, dews and frosts, whales, fowl and beasts, "children of men," and so on. In composing her "double series" of studies, Rossetti sets out all the separate objects of praise in a first series that she considers in terms of "creation," drawing together many relevant scriptural references. Then, in the second series of studies on the "redemption," she gathers other scriptural texts around the same subjects as before. The result is a kind of "harmony" of the Benedicite, with its thirty-two "Praise-Givers" each being elucidated by "God's Creatures" and texts from the Old Testament that frequently prefigure the New Testament texts of "Christ's Servants" that follow. The work opens with a table in three columns, the first providing the sections of the Benedicite, the second and third columns relating texts expressing the praise of "Creatures" (anticipating the first half, or "series," of the book on Creation), and "Servants" (the second half, or "series," on Redemption). The opening page appears:

The Praise Givers Are	*God's Creatures,*	*Christ's Servants.*
O all ye Works of the Lord, bless ye the Lord: praise Him, and magnify Him for ever.	God saw every thing that He had made, and, behold, it was very good. (Gen. 1.31).	The Word was God. All things were made by Him; and without Him was not anything made that was made (John 1.1, 3).
O ye Angels of the Lord, &c.	Who maketh His angels spirits; His ministers a flaming fire (Ps. 104.4).	When he bringeth in the First-begotten into the world, He saith, And let all the angels of God worship Him (Heb. 1.6).
O ye Heavens, &c.	Thou, even Thou, art Lord alone; Thou hast made heaven, the heaven of all heavens with all their host (Neh. 9.6).	He that descended is the same also that ascended up far above all heavens, that He might fill all things (Eph. 4.10).
O ye Waters that be above the Firmament, &c.	God divided the waters which were under the firmament from the waters which were above the firmament: and it was so (Gen. 1.7).	They which came out of great tribulation, and have washed their robes, and made them white in the blood of the Lamb. The Lamb which is in the midst of the Throne shall feed them, and shall lead them unto living fountains of waters (Rev. 7.14, 17).
O all ye Powers of the Lord, &c.	Whether they be thrones, or dominions, or principalities, or powers: all things were created by Him, and for Him (Col. 1.16).	Jesus Christ: Who is gone into heaven, and is on the right hand of God; angels and authorities and powers being made subject unto Him (1 Pet. 3.21, 22).
O ye Sun, and Moon, &c.	O give thanks unto the Lord; for He is good. To Him that made great lights: the sun to rule the day: the moon to rule by night: for His mercy endureth for ever (Ps. 136.1–9).	The light of the moon shall be as the light of the sun, and the light of the sun shall be sevenfold, as the light of seven days, in the day that the Lord bindeth up the breach of His people (Isa. 30.26).

The "series" thus continues for a further five pages.

Rossetti had previously written a similarly systematic study of St. Paul's fa-mous chapter on charity, the verses appearing in column 1, with corroborative scriptural passages in a second column called "Our Lord," and a third column on "His School." She took up this work as an "exercise" during the Lent of 1878, and published it as "A Harmony on First Corinthians XIII," in an obscure "parochial magazine," *New and Old* 7 (January 1879): 34–39, which was recently edited by Mary Arseneau and Jan Marsh. Rossetti would have seen other "harmonies," es-pecially by the Reverend Isaac Williams, whom she acknowledges in her prefatory note, and certainly G. C. Child Chaplin, whose *Benedicite; or, The Song of the Three Children*, 2 vols. (London: John Murray, 1866) largely prefigures *Seek and Find*. Rossetti's poem on the creation, "All Thy Works Praise Thee, O Lord," perhaps composed at about the same time as *Seek and Find*—possibly being intended for this book—is a further expression of praise. Another "Benedicite," this also re-veals the author's delight in seeing the connectedness of earth and heaven, where all creatures express emblematically the divine order (*Poems*, 1979–90, 2:129).

An autograph manuscript of this work survives, called by its original title "Treasure-Trove," in the Fitzwilliam Museum, Cambridge, MS FMK 25320 32X. As Palazzo suggests (p. 91, n. 61), this title seems to have been derived from the quotation that heads the chapter on "Winds" in the first series: "He bringeth the wind out of His treasuries" (Ps. 134.7), and Rossetti's opening statement, "What God brings out of His treasury cannot but be a treasure: our treasure if He blesses it to us" (p. 43). The manuscript differs from the printed text in many respects, principally in accidentals, where roman numer-als appear in the manuscript and arabic in the printed version, capitalization is less frequent, and punctuation somewhat lighter. Such variants might or might not reflect an authorial change of mind, for these are mostly minor editorial changes. But verbal differences are also numerous and often of such a charac-ter that one must assume authorial intervention and revision. The manuscript appears to have been compared with the printed text, for there are indications of which sections are italicized, or alterations that were made, or where pagi-nation occurred. There is a note that accompanies the manuscript, also in Ros-setti's hand, written from her home at 30 Torrington Square, and dated 21 August 1879, and addressed "Dear Sir": "My brother William tells me that you have expressed a wish to acquire the M.S. of a little book of mine which is on the eve of publication, & I have great pleasure in forwarding it to the ad-dress he indicates to me: but (tho' I dare say such a precaution is needless) I wish first to inform you that the copyright is already disposed." Across the title page, Rossetti has written "To be retained by Author." The book appeared in the autumn of 1879, published by SPCK, and one supposes that Rossetti introduced most of the verbal, if not the accidental, changes at the proof stage.

The minutes of the General Literature Committee of the SPCK show that Rossetti first presented "Treasure-Trove" to them on 14 March 1879, but they declined the manuscript (see W. K. Lowther Clark, *A History of the SPCK*, London, 1985, 148). Yet later in the same year, Rossetti sold *Seek and Find* to the SPCK for £40, and, according to one of her biographers (Packer 329 and 430, n. 8), before the volume was published, she sold Charles Fairfax Murray the printer's copy for £10, the receipt of which, dated 23 August 1879, is in the Murray Collection at the University of Texas. If the Fitzwilliam manuscript is Murray's copy, then Rossetti must have made many revisions while the book was in page proofs.

While the present selections follow the text of this first printed edition, we have given in the notes the substantive variants of the Fitzwilliam manuscript, for they clearly reveal Rossetti's careful attention to the details of composition and revision, and we note as well those substantive variants, or corrections that appear in the text but not in the manuscript. We have followed the accidentals of the text except in the presentation of scriptural references where citations are given in arabic numerals (as in the manuscript) and in the preservation of Rossetti's distinctive capitalization. We have preserved all of the scriptural references that Rossetti provides within her text. While very numerous, these citations nevertheless make up an important part of the discourse and often form narrative links within it.

Seek and Find: A Double Series of Short Studies of the Benedicite

Prefatory Note.

In writing the following pages, when I have consulted a Harmony it has been that of the late Rev. Isaac Williams.[23]

Any textual elucidations, as I know neither Hebrew nor Greek, are simply based upon some translation; many valuable alternative readings being found in the Margin[24] of an ordinary Reference Bible.

C. G. R.

THE FIRST SERIES: CREATION.

All Works.

"Whence then cometh wisdom? and where is the place of understanding? Seeing it is hid from the eyes of all living. God understandeth the way thereof, and He knoweth the place thereof. And unto man He said, Behold, the fear of the Lord, that is wisdom; and to depart from evil is understanding."

Job 28.20–28.

Not to fathom the origin of evil, but to depart from evil, is man's understanding. Its origin is inscrutable by us: but depart from it we can. And if at the very outset we lack wisdom, St. James (1.5) prescribes for us a remedy: "If any of you lack wisdom, let him ask of God, that giveth to all men liberally, and upbraideth not; and it shall be given him." Amen, through Jesus Christ our Lord. He helping us, let us bring love and faith to our study of the Benedicite.

"God saw every thing that He had made, and, behold, it was very good" (Gen. 1.31). A work is less noble than its maker: he who makes a good thing is himself better than it: God excels the most excellent of His creatures. Matters of everyday occurrence illustrate our point: an artist may paint a lifelike picture, but he cannot endow it with life like his own[25]; he may carve an admirable statue, but can never compound a breathing fellow-man. Wise were those ancients who felt[26] that all forms of beauty could be[27] but partial expressions of Beauty's very self:[28] and who by clue of what they saw groped after Him they saw not. Beauty Essential is the archetype of imparted beauty;[29] Life essential, of imparted life; Goodness essential, of imparted goodness:[30] but such objects, good, living, beautiful, as we now behold, are not that Very Goodness, Life, Beauty, which (please God) we shall one day contemplate in Beatific Vision. Then shall fully come to pass that saying: "They that eat me shall yet be hungry, and they that drink me shall yet be thirsty" (Ecclus. 24.21); only with a hunger and thirst which shall abide at once satisfied and insatiable. Then, not now: now let us turn to a spiritual signification[31] the prayer of Agur: "Remove far from me vanity and lies: give me neither poverty nor riches; feed me with food convenient for me" (Prov. 30.8). If even St. Paul might have been exalted above measure through abundance of revelation (2 Cor. 12.7), let us thank God that we in our present frailty know not any more than His Wisdom[32] reveals[33] to us: not that man's safety resides in ignorance any more than in knowledge, but in conformity[34] of the human to the Divine Will. See the Parable of the Talents, St. Luke 19.12–26; where the sentence[35] depends on the fidelity[36] of the servants, rather than[37] on the amount of the trust.[38]

The Divine Bounty and Mercy are good: the Divine Justice and chastisements are good also. The decree being good, that creature which fully and simply executes the decree is also good. Wherefore every obedient creature, whatever its particular act of obedience whether in judgment or in mercy, may by and for that act render praise to God.

As regards our own impressions, we often make mistakes between mercies and judgments, putting bitter for sweet and sweet for bitter (Isa. 5.20). Saints and sinners alike are liable to fall into such errors. Jacob said, "All these things are against me" (Gen. 42.36), at the very moment when step by step his reunion with Joseph was drawing nigh. Balaam carried his point (Num. 22.34,35), but what a death he died and what an end was his! (Num. 23.10; 31.7,8).

Waters above the Firmament.
"The heavens declare the glory of God; and the firmament
sheweth His handywork." *Ps. 19.1.*

Since many of the "Waters that be above the Firmament" are named one by one further on in the Canticle, let us for the moment dwell on the firmament itself, "the sky, which is strong, and as a molten looking glass" (Job 37.18).

To our eyes it appears blue, sometimes deepening towards purple, sometimes passing into pale green; purple, an earthly hue of mourning, and green our tint of hope. One[39] colour seems to prophesy of that day when the Sign of the Son of Man shall appear in heaven, and all the tribes of the earth shall mourn (St. Matt. 24.30): one,[40] to symbolize that Veil of separation beyond which faith and love discern our ascended Lord, and whereinto hope as an anchor of the soul sure and stedfast entereth (Heb. 6. 19,20). Remote from either extreme stretches the prevalent blue, pure and absolute: thus the sky and its azure become so at one in our associations, that all fair blue objects within our reach,[41] stone or flower, sapphire or harebell, act as terrene mirrors, conveying to us an image of that which is above themselves, as "earthly pictures with heavenly meanings." And although the atmosphere is in reality full of currents and commotions, yet to our senses the sky appears to stand aloof[42] as the very type of stability; overarching and embosoming not earth and sea only, but clouds and meteors, planets and stars. Beneath it and within it all moves, waxes, wanes, while itself changes not: setting before us as by a parable the little-loftiness of the loftiest things of time;[43] "there be higher than they" (see Eccles. 5.8). Yet has the unchanging sky no final stability, but at its appointed hour it shall be rolled up as a scroll and shall pass away (Isa. 34.4; Rev. 6.14).

Thus while all the good creatures of God teach us some lesson concerning the unapproached Perfections of their Creator, that which they display is a glimpse, that which they cannot display is infinite. "They shall perish, but Thou shalt endure" (Ps. 102.26).

Powers.

"Do all to the glory of God." *1 Cor. 10.31.*

One order of elect Spirits we designate Powers, but these have virtually been considered under the head of "Angels of the Lord." Perhaps under the head of "Powers" may not improperly be classed what are termed Forces.

And I think it will even answer our purpose if we here go no further than to recal [sic] a few familiar facts and agents which bring home unmistakably to our consciousness the existence of powers at work all around us, however these may oftentimes elude our senses: of powers which working in harmony bear witness to that "great First Cause" Who ordained and Who rules them. "Lo, He goeth by me, and I see Him not: He passeth on also, but I perceive Him not" (Job 9.11).

Electricity: the dangerous element of the storm, announcing its awful passage by lightning flash and thunder-clap, yet in speed outstripping both light and sound: electricity, of strength to rend trees, shatter rocks, and destroy life, has nevertheless become man's servant; available in the physician's hands for treatment of disease, and in the telegraph and telephone for communication of intelligence. "Thou madest[44] him to have dominion over the works of Thy hands" (Ps. 8.6).[45]

Steam, that is, water: water, the very symbol of instability. "Unstable as water, thou shalt not excel" (Gen. 49.4), said dying Jacob, moved by the Spirit of prophecy: or if we study an alternative rendering of his words, "Bubbling up as water," we may still perhaps trace the same idea of instability, inasmuch as what is easily excited does very commonly as easily subside. Yet as man's servant, and in the form of steam, water acquires power not merely to upheave, but to wield and to apply with the Utmost delicacy of touch, masses of enormous weight; and puts forth a sustained swiftness outspeeding the horse and his rider, though not the eagle or the carrier pigeon.

Light and Heat, to our apprehension the great vivifiers of the material world, are in like manner brought into subjection by man: under whose regulations one effects a permanent record of beauties which themselves consume away like a moth (Ps. 39.11); while the other enables us to transfer[46] tropical vegetation to temperate zones, and to make fruits ripen,[47] and animals exist and even propagate in alien climates.

Or, to lift our thoughts above the sphere of man's dominion,—Gravitation, Attraction, Repulsion: whereby the earth we dwell on and the celestial luminaries her companions occupy their assigned abodes and fulfil their prefixed courses: whereby the tide flows and ebbs in accordance with the moon's phases; whereby alone the planets escape not from their prescribed circuits[48] and the apple falls.

Wonderful and awful are those forces[49] which launch, arrest, guide, compact, dissolve, the members of the material universe. Yet more wonderful, more awful, are those intellectual faculties which shrined within mortal man, gauge height and depth, deduce cause from effect, and track out the invisible by clue of the visible: thus a certain master-mind by the aberration of one celestial body from the line of its independent orbit, argued the influential neighbourhood of a second luminary till then undiscerned.

In a more or less degree every one of us inherits this awful birthright of intellectual power. With Esau we may despise and squander our birthright (Gen. 25.29–34), with Reuben disgrace and forfeit it (1 Chron. 5.1); but ours it is: and so far as the tremendous responsibility originally[50] involved in its possession is concerned, ours it must remain, though shorn of every privilege and bringing on us a curse and not a blessing.

Let each of us take heed that it bring on our own self a blessing and not a curse: for be our past what it may, by God's grace we may yet be trained in the nurture and admonition of the Lord. And then shall this intellectual power entrusted to us become verily and indeed a "Power of the Lord." Not all knowledge is good: as Isaiah declares to "delicate" Chaldea, "Thy wisdom and thy knowledge, it hath perverted thee" (Isa. 47.1,10). Ignorantly with Eve we may learn shame (Gen. 3.6,7; 1 Tim. 2.14); or deliberately with Solomon study wisdom, madness, and folly; but to increase knowledge which is not true wisdom, increaseth sorrow (Eccles. 1.17,18). Let us to-day be content to remain ignorant of many things while we seek first the Kingdom of God and His righteousness: to-morrow, if not to-day, knowledge and all other good things shall be added unto us (St. Matt. 6.33; 1 Tim. 4.7,8; 1 Cor. 13.12). Let us not exercise ourselves in matters[51] beyond our present powers of estimate, lest amid the shallows (not the depths) of science we make shipwreck of our faith. To-day is the day of small things (see Zech. 4.10): let us to-day be content with the small things of to-day, knowing assuredly that all they[52] who are Christ's are made one with Him Who is the Heir of all things (St. John 17.21–23; Heb. i.2). Thus shall our path be as the shining light, that shineth more and more unto the perfect day (Prov. 4.18), while we go from strength to strength until every one of us appear before God in Zion (Ps. 84.7).

Stars.

"Behold the height of the stars, how high they are!" *Job 22.12.*

There is something awe-striking, overwhelming, in contemplation of the stars. Their number, magnitudes, distances, orbits, we know not: any multitude our unaided eyes discern is but an instalment of that vaster multitude which the telescope reveals; and of this the heightened and yet again heightened power bringing to light more and more stars, opens before us a vista unmeasured, incalculable. Knowledge runs apace: and our globe which once seemed large is now but a small planet among planets, while not one of our group of planets is large as compared with its central sun; and the sun itself may be no more than a sub-centre, it and all its system coursing but as satellites and sub-satellites around a general centre; and this again,—what of this? Is even this remote centre truly central, or is it no more than yet another sub-centre revolving around some point of overruling attraction, and swaying with it the harmonious encircling dance of its attendant worlds? Thus while knowledge runs apace, ignorance keeps ahead of knowledge: and all which the deepest students know proves to themselves, yet[53] more convincingly than to others,[54] that much more exists[55] which still they know not. As saints in relation to spiritual wisdom, so sages in relation to intellectual wisdom, eating they yet hunger and drinking they yet thirst (Ecclus. 24.21).

Deep only can call to deep: still, we who occupy comparative shallows of intelligence are not wholly debarred from the admiration and delights of noble contemplations. We can marvel over the many tints of the heavenly bodies, ruddy, empurpled, golden, or by contrast pale; we can understand the conclusion, though we cannot follow the process by which analysis of a ray certifies various component elements as existing in the orb which emits it; we can realise mentally how galaxies, which by reason of remoteness present to our eyes a mere modification of sky-colour, are truly a host of distinct luminaries; we can long to know more of belts and atmospheres; we can ponder reverently over interstellar spaces so vast as to exhaust the attractive force of suns and more than suns.

And we can make of what we know and of what we know not stepping-stones towards heaven, adoring our Creator for all that He is and that His creatures are not; adoring Him also for what many of our fellows already are, and for what we ourselves are and may become. We shall not run to waste in idle curiosity if we bear in mind that "knowledge puffeth up, but charity edifieth" (1 Cor. 8.1), and that whoso understood all mysteries and all knowledge, not having charity would be nothing (13.2). The innumerable number of the stars will profit us while we bear in mind that, though we know not, God telleth[56] their number and "calleth them all by their names" (Ps. 147.4). Their material light will become to us light spiritual, if, because "they that turn many to righteousness" shall shine "as the stars for ever and ever" (Dan. 12.3), zeal burn within us not for our own righteousness only, but for our neighbour's also. The awful familiar heavens now by fixed laws exhibiting motions, influences, aspects, phenomena (now, but not for ever after this present temporal fashion), are even now night by night instructing pious souls who watch and pray and wait for their beloved Lord.

"Seek Him that maketh the seven stars and Orion" (Amos 5.8).

Winter and Summer.
"Lo, the winter is past." *Song of Solomon 2.11.*
"The summer is ended." *Jer. 8.20.*

Winter and summer are unlike at a thousand points. Winter has bareness, cold, the aspects and circumstances which produce and result from these: Summer has exuberance, heat, and all their delightful train. In one thing they are alike: both "pass," both "end." Their likeness is absolute, their unlikeness is a matter of degree merely. For the bareness of Winter is yet not without many a leaf, and its coldness is warmed and brightened by many a sunbeam: the exuberance of Summer brings not forth the treasures of other seasons, nor does its heat preclude the blast of chilly winds. Both pass, both end. Winter by comparison lifeless, leads up to Spring, the birthday of visible nature: Summer, instinct with vitality, ripens to the harvest and decay of Autumn. Winter at its bitterest will pass: Summer at its sweetest must end. It is emphatically "while the earth remaineth" that Summer and Winter shall not cease (Gen. 8.22): in the better world which is to come we find no trace of either; not of cold, and expressly not of heat (Rev. 7.16); and though leaves and fruit appear (22.2), no mention is made of flowers, so characteristic of the Summer we love. Just because we love it and revel in it, Summer is steeped for us in sadness: at the longest its days shorten, at the fairest its flowers fade; next after Summer comes Autumn, and Autumn means decay. Winter even while we shrink from it abounds in hope; or ever its short days are at the coldest they lengthen and wax more sunny. Winter is the threshold of Spring, and Spring resuscitates and reawakens the world. Winter which nips can also brace: Summer which fosters may also enervate. There is a time for all things (Eccles. 3.1), all things are double against each other (Ecclus. 42.24), and God hath made all things good (Gen. 1.31), for all are His servants (Ps. 119.91).

The seasons of the waxing and waning year have an obvious parallel in the periods of our mortal life; a parallel so obvious that it need not be drawn out in detail, for to speak of one series is to describe the other. Also the privilege and, so to say, the duty of both are the same: "all are His servants." Alas, with which of us has it fully been so, or even now is it so to the full, be it the Spring or Summer, the Autumn or Winter of our course?

"If it bear fruit, well" (St. Luke 13.9).

Ice and Snow.
"Hast thou entered into the treasures of the snow?
or hast thou seen the treasures of the hail?" *Job 38.22.*

The beauty of Snow needs no proof. Perfect in whiteness, feathery in lightness, it often floats down with hesitation as if it belonged to air rather than to earth: yet once resting on that ground it seemed loath to touch, it silently and surely accomplishes its allotted task; it fills up chasms, levels inequalities, cloaks imperfections, arrests the evaporation of heat, nurses vegetation; it prepares floods for arid water-courses, and abundant moisture for roots and seeds. Snow, as we are familiar with it, is uncertain in its arrival and brief in its stay; having done its work it vanishes utterly, becoming as though it had never been. Not so in northern regions and on mountain-ranges where it occupies a permanent habitation: there it wraps itself in mist or overlooks the clouds, and thence not in silence but in thunder it rushes down upon the valleys. The beauties of snow are not exhausted when we have watched it afloat in air, or heaped in dazzling whiteness on the earth, or even when we have beheld it on mountain-heights flushed with pure rosiness at the fall of day: the microscope is required to reveal to us the exquisite symmetry of its crystals, starry, foliated, mimicking with minute perfection features of the firmament and of the flower-bed.

In symbolic analogies we find snow suggestive both of guilt and of cleansing. The whiteness of leprosy, that loathsome type of more loathsome sin, is "as snow" (Exod. 4.6; Num. 12.10; 2 Kings 5.27): while in the other sense Psalmist and Prophet bring forward material snow as a[57] standard of spiritual purification; David saying, "Wash me, and I shall be whiter than snow" (Ps. 51.7), and Isaiah, "Though your sins be as scarlet, they shall be as white as snow" (Isa. 1.18). Job also in one of his passionate appeals cries out from instinctive feeling if not from close reasoning, "If I wash myself with snow water, and make my hands never so clean. . . ." (Job 9.30); thus attributing to "*snow* water" an exceptional purifying virtue.[58]

Ice, viewed as hail, seems exclusively, or almost exclusively, in the Inspired Text,[59] to be or to represent a weapon of God's wrath and righteous vengeance; and this is its aspect[60] whether we study prophets or historians, the Old Testament or the New. Following a[61] scheme of chronology which makes Job a contemporary of Moses, we hear about thirty years before the Exodus this purpose of the hail indicated to Job by Almighty God Himself: "Hast thou seen the treasures of the hail, which I have reserved against the time of trouble, against the day of battle and war?" (Job 38.22,23); and the earliest hailstorm recorded in Holy Scripture is that[62] which scourged Egypt with its seventh plague, "The Lord rained hail upon the land of Egypt" (Exod. 9.23), and to which passages in the Psalms refer (78.47,48; 105.32,33). So also in the wars of Joshua the hail fought on God's side, and slew more of the army of the Amorites than did the sword of the children of Israel (Josh. 10.11). David, again, celebrating his deliverance from his enemies, and especially from Saul, describes his troubles under figure of a flood ready to engulph him, and his rescue as achieved by a manifestation of the Divine Presence, amid mighty convulsions of nature, "hail stones and coals of fire" (Ps. 18.4–17). Isaiah (28.2,17; 30.30; and presumably 32.19), and Ezekiel (13.10–14; 38.22), name hail in their prophecies of vengeance: Haggai mentions it among the agents of an unavailing Divine discipline (Hag. 2.17): St. John thrice beholds it in awful vision (Rev. 8.7; 11.19; 16.21).

If the weapon be mighty, mightier is He Who wields it: nevertheless, if it be good to tremble before God's judgments, it is yet better to confide in His mercy and love. Let us, not neglecting the performance of either duty, add to both humility; and carry our heads as it were low, in memory of that wheat and rye which not being grown up escaped unscathed, while the forwarder flax and barley were smitten.[63]

"Enter into the rock, and hide thee in the dust, for fear of the Lord, and for the glory of His Majesty. The lofty looks of man shall be humbled, and the haughtiness of men shall be bowed down, and the Lord alone shall be exalted in that day" (Isa. 2.10,11).

Seas and Floods.
"When that which is perfect is come, then that which is in part shall be done away." *1 Cor. 13.10.*

These words in which St. Paul treats of[64] partial knowledge, incomplete revelation, imperfect sight, childhood (1 Cor. 13.9–12), though each of those is good and not evil in its allotted sphere and during its assigned period,— seem in some sort applicable to the sea also,[65] according to St. John's vision of the final consummation of all things: "I saw a new heaven and a new earth: for the first heaven and the first earth were passed away; and there was no more sea" (Rev. 21.1). Equally, the Sun and Moon appear then to be, if not obliterated,[66] at the least superseded: "The city had no need of the sun, neither of the moon, to shine in it: for the Glory of God did lighten it, and the Lamb is the light thereof" (v.23).

At first reading "there was no more sea," our heart sinks at foresight of[67] the familiar sea expunged from earth and heaven; that sea to us so long and so inexhaustibly a field of wonder and delight. "Was Thy wrath against the sea . . . ? The overflowing of the water passed by: the deep uttered his voice, and lifted up his hands on high" (Hab. 3.8,10).

Whatever mystery may attach to this subject, various plain points are, I think, open to our consideration. The Inspired Volume seems written rather for our instruction as regards ourselves, and consequently as regards the visible creation in reference to ourselves, than from a more general purpose of enlarging our knowledge touching matters wholly extraneous; and many a subject too wide or too deep for our grasp may yet teach us an unmistakable lesson.

"No more sea" does not exclude from the Presence of the Throne "a sea of glass like unto crystal" (Rev. 4.6); or, be it the same sea or not, "as it were a sea of glass mingled with fire" whereon the victorious redeemed take their stand (15.2). Thus we shall not lose the translucent purity of ocean, nor yet a glory as of its myriad waves tipped by sunshine; no, nor even the volume of its voice, when all God's servants uplift their praises "as the voice of many waters" (19.5,6). What shall we lose? Not our friends, for the sea shall give up its dead (20.13), when earth also shall no more hide her blood or cover her slain (Isa. 26.21). What shall we lose? A barrier of separation: for the exultant children of the resurrection find firm footing and stand together upon their heavenly sea,—bitterness and barrenness: for the pure River of Water of Life flows between banks crowned with fertility, and even now its refreshment is for whoso thirsteth and whosoever will drink (Rev. 22.1,2,17). Troubled restless waters we shall lose with all their defilement (Isa. 57.20), and with waves that toss and break themselves against a boundary they cannot overpass (Jer. 5.22), and with the moan of a still-recurrent ebb, "The sea is not full" (Eccles. 1.7). We feel at once that the sea as we know it, a very embodiment of unrest, of spurning at limits, of advance only to recede, that such a sea teaches us nothing concerning that rest which remaineth to the people of God (Heb. 4.9); who having pressed toward the mark and obtained the prize (Phil. 3.14) enjoy their final felicity in a heaven which can be no heaven at all except to persons whose wills and whose affections are at one with the Will and Love of God. "There was war in heaven" (Rev. 12.7) would be repeated to all eternity, could we conceive it otherwise.

Floods, whether defined as rain-born or snow-born torrents, noisy and destructive in their day but dwindling to nothing as time goes on, or as any river or other body of running water especially in its moments of turbulence or of overflow (as we read how "Jordan overfloweth all his banks all the time of harvest," Josh. 3.15: see also the imagery of Isa. 8.6,8; Jer. 46.7,8; 47.2), in either case some of the associations which invest the sea attach equally to floods.

"He bindeth the floods from overflowing; and the thing that is hid bringeth He forth to light. Hast thou entered into the springs of the sea? or hast thou walked in the search of the depth?" (Job 28.11; 38.16).

Beasts and Cattle.
"Behold now behemoth, which I made with thee." *Job 40.15.*

Whichever animal behemoth may be (for different theories have been propounded as to his identity) one thing, if I mistake not, is clearly conveyed to us by that vivid figure of speech, "he drinketh up a river, and hasteth not"; and that thing is the power, competence, ease, of his existence: he meets and provides for his necessities without strain of effort; he is even serenely conscious of inherent resource adequate to the supply of all his contingent wants, and "trusteth that he can draw up Jordan into his mouth."[68]

Let us take behemoth, made with us and "chief of the ways of God," as head and type of the whole brute family: and, in the entire passage which describes his endowments and habits (Job 40.15–24), there can, I think, be traced that instinctive and faultless mastery of all that irrational creatures can be called upon either to be or to do, which contrasts obviously and utterly with the birthright of fallen man; who has to undo and do, unmake, make, and become, in the very teeth (so to say) of flesh and blood and human possibility. Not so, doubtless, with Adam in his primeval righteousness; but with each one of us his children, and most of all now under the Gospel Dispensation, thus it is: "The kingdom of heaven suffereth violence, and the violent take it by force" (St. Matt. 11.12). To resist unto blood, striving against sin, seems mentioned in the Epistle to the Hebrews (12.4), as no portent, but as the matter of course lot of many a Christian. To endure unto the end is simply the qualification for salvation (St. Matt. 24.13). To overcome must precede enthronement (Rev. 3.21). The innumerable white-robed palm-bearing multitude whom St. John beheld in vision "came out of great tribulation (7.9,14). Reason and free will, those exalted gifts, may and must be a ladder leading from earth either heavenwards or hellwards; a ladder inaccessible to the beasts that perish (Ps. 49.20; Eccles. 3.21), but inevitable by man; at the outset of life man's foot is planted midway upon that ladder; and up or down it he must go, for here we have no abiding place (1 Chron. 29.15). How imminent our danger, how vast our alternatives, how critical, how momentous our position, words cannot exaggerate for they cannot even express: involuntarily we are standing in a poised balance, involuntarily we are made like a wheel (see Ps. 83.13), never continuing in one stay.

It shames us to observe how very much nearer the whole tribe of irresponsible beasts comes to the Apostolic summary of King David's career, who served his own generation by the Will of God and fell on sleep (Acts 13.36), than do a multitude of our responsible selves. We shall do wisely to study Agur's portrait of ants and conies, locusts and a spider (Prov. 30.24–28): and when we have reformed our conduct by theirs,—though truly we may find it a lifelong business to acquire the prudence, industry, and temperance of ants; the harmonious unity of locusts; the self-help and self-elevation of spiders; not to speak of the provident master-building of conies (compare St. Matt. 7.24,25),—when by these we have remodelled our doings, then we who as Christians are a nation of kings and priests (1 Pet. 2–9; Rev. 1.6), may go on to add grace and dignity to our demeanour by considering lion, greyhound, and he-goat (Prov. 30.29–31).

Beasts and Cattle correspond with our wild and domesticated animals. The duty of kindliness towards either class is enjoined in Holy Scripture not only by merciful enactments in the Mosaic Law (Exod. 20.10; Deut. 25.4), and by Solomon in his surpassing wisdom (Prov. 12.10), but most persuasively of all by examples of[69] Divine Providence such as we gather from the Books of Job (38.39–41; 39), and of Psalms (84.3; 104.10–31; 147.9). Before the Seventh Plague "destroyed" Egypt a warning was vouchsafed which ensured the safety of cattle as well as of men (Exod. 9.19; 10.7). The Prophet Joel (1.18–20; 2.21–22) noticing the poor beasts in their misery, encourages them by a promise of plenty.[70]

Of the many animals which play their part in the Old Testament history some few at least must not here be overlooked. The ram caught in a thicket by his horns, in connexion with which occurs the first mention of a lamb (Gen. 22.7,8,13). The camels which knelt while Eliezer prayed (24.11,12). Balaam's ass (Num. 22.21–33). The young lion roaring against Samson (Judges 14.5,6). The milch kine that drew the Ark and lowed as they went (1 Sam 6.7–12). The lion and bear of David's first memorable victory (xvii. 34–37). The oxen of Perez-uzzah (2 Sam. 6.6). Absalom's mule (18.9). The lion which slew the disobedient Prophet, but spared the ass (1 Kings 13.23–29). The dogs executing judgment upon Ahab (22.38), and upon Jezebel (2 Kings 9.35,36). The two she bears that avenged Elisha's insulted sanctity (2.23,24). The lions devastating Samaria (17.24,25). The horse of Mordecai's opening triumph (Esther 6.7–11). Job's riches first and last (Job 1.3; 42.12). The lions powerless against Daniel but mighty against his accusers (Dan. 6.19–24). The fasting beasts in the great national repentance of Nineveh (Jonah 3.7–8).

Every one of these creatures has a lesson for us, and divers of them set us an example. But vain it is and worse than vain to con a lesson yet not learn it, to relish an example yet not follow it. Now this is a danger to which students of the Bible are eminently exposed. The Word of God is so full of charm, so deep, so wide, so inexhaustibly suggestive, that for the mere delight's sake one may imbue oneself with its letter and sharpen ingenuity to display subtlety in its application, without a vestige of love in the heart or of grace in the soul. A thing ever so good and in itself permanently good may be wrested by men to their own ruin: the sun ceased not to shine, or the moon to walk on in her appointed brightness, despite the incense[71] of their votaries (Job 31.26–28; 2 Kings 23.5); St. Paul, a very emporium of superhuman gifts, and speaking with tongues more than the whole Corinthian Church (1 Cor. 14.18), yet avowed the necessity of standing ever on his guard lest having preached to others he himself should be a castaway (9.27). If we be Bible students we must not deem ourselves too safe to need watchful prayer against the temper of Ezekiel's hearers: "Lo, thou art unto them as a very lovely song of one that hath a pleasant voice, and can play well on an instrument: for they hear thy words, but they do them not" (Ezek. 33.32).

Spirits and Souls of the Righteous.
"Have the gates of death been opened unto thee?
or hast thou seen the doors of the shadow of death?" *Job 38.17.*

To us Christians the land of the shadow of death is no longer the dominion
of the King of Terrors, but rather a tiring-closet for the Bride of the King of
kings. There having put off the corruptible and the mortal she prepares to
put on incorruption and immortality (1 Cor. 15.52,53), meanwhile making
melody in her heart to the Lord. We seem to hear her singing a Psalm of
thanksgiving, the very Psalm of her Risen Saviour: "The lines are fallen unto
me in pleasant places. My heart is glad, and my glory rejoiceth: my flesh also
shall rest in hope. For Thou wilt not leave my soul in hell. Thou wilt shew
me the path of life" (Ps. 16.6,9–11; Acts 2.22–28).

We may still reverently ask, "I have put off my coat; how shall I put it
on?" (Song of Sol. 5.3); but it must be with the enquiring mind of faith, not
with the cavilling mind of doubt. We may search what or what manner of
time the Spirit of Christ testifies beforehand touching the Resurrection, but
it must be with the joyful confidence of Abraham, when he also heard of life
as it were from the dead: alike in laughter, he and Sarah were unlike in the
motive of their laughter (Gen. 17.17; 18.12–15; Rom. 4.18–21).

Mankind, though still no further advanced than to see through a glass
darkly (1 Cor. 13.12), may, on[72] comparing its later with its earlier generations, say thankfully, "Whereas I was blind, now I see" (see St. John 9.25).
Perhaps the tone of the Old Testament is nowhere more startling at first
sight, than in a few passages on the subject of death: for that here and there
a text does baffle interpretation and challenge faith, cannot[73] be denied:
though love even then never fails to find a clue by its own intuition of the
love of God, resting and rejoicing now in what it shall know hereafter. Thus
does deep respond to deep at the noise of the waterspouts, for "many waters
cannot quench love, neither can the floods drown it" (Ps. 42.7; Song of Sol.
8.7). If an ordinary believer trembling on the brink of the grave were now
to lament as saintly Hezekiah of old lamented (Isa. 38.10–20) it would at
the least surprise us.

But we (thank God) can never be called upon to realize what it was to precede, not to follow, Christ into the valley of the shadow of death. Once for
all our Good Shepherd has gone before His own sheep: whenever now He
puts them forth it is only to go home to Him along the very path which He
has already trodden (see St. John 10.4). Of old it was far otherwise. Think
what it may have been for Abel to pass (as it seems) first of the whole human
family into the veiled world; and after him went forth each soul in individual loneliness, much as Abraham who knew not whither he went (Heb. 11.8):
it needed a David, and him under inspiration, in such a transit to "fear no

evil" (Ps. 23.4). True it is that Moses showed at the Bush that the dead rise (St. Luke 20.37,38): but if some in Israel were slow of heart to interpret that text, what are the mass of ourselves in comprehending many another? To be alone was never indeed at any period the lot of a faithful soul; but to feel alone has been, and is, one besetting trial of man: how keen is this trial and in a sense how unsuited to our constitution we may deduce both from a Divine sentence true of Adam even in his original innocence (Gen. 2.18), and also from a Messianic psalm (88.8,18), from a Messianic prophetic vision (Isa. 63.3–5), and from words uttered by our Lord Himself in foresight (St. John 16.32) and in the crisis (St. Mark 15.34) of His atoning Passion.

Of actual glimpses into the realm of departed souls the Old Testament affords us very few. Once and once only do we behold a saint reappear from his grave: "An old man cometh up; and he is covered with a mantle. And Saul perceived that it was Samuel. . . . And Samuel said to Saul, Why hast thou disquieted me, to bring me up?" (1 Sam. 28.14,15). From these words we gather, yet at most by implication, that the elect soul was dwelling in a quiet abode and cared not to be disquieted. Thus Job (3.17–22) also spoke when he thought to rejoice exceedingly and be glad if only he could find a grave: "There the wicked cease from troubling; and there the weary be at rest." A second utterance of disembodied Samuel shows him, as in the days of his mortality, so then once again moved by the Spirit of prophecy (1 Sam. 28.19). The dead, however, are as a rule they who characteristically "go down into silence" (Ps. 115.17): not any of themselves, but Isaiah (14.9–11) and Ezekiel (32.21) only, acquaint us with that mighty stir in the underworld which greeted the fallen King of Babylon, and that voice out of the midst of Hades which spake to overthrown Egypt.

But when from the intermediate state we turn faithful eyes towards the final beatitude, all becomes flooded no longer with mist but with radiance: that which baffles our vision is not darkness but light,—light not dubious though partly undefined. Thus has it been with the Church of God from Abel downwards (Heb. 11.4–14, &c.): thus will it be to the end of time (1 Cor. 15.51–54). Full quotations become impossible by reason of abundance: but over and over again we recognise the one glorious hope of immortality persisting in Patriarchs, singing in Psalmists, rejoicing in Prophets (e.g., Job 19.25–27; Ps. 49.15; Isa. 26.19; Hos. 13.14). We know that this mortal life is the sufficient period of our probation, we know that the life immortal is the sufficing period—if we may call eternity a period—of our reward: let us not fret our hearts by a too anxious curiosity as to that Intermediate State which hides for the moment so many whom we love and whom we hope to rejoin, for even now we know that "the souls of the righteous are in the hand of God, and there shall no torment touch them" (Wisdom 3.1).

Holy and Humble Men of Heart.
"This commandment which I command thee this day,
it is not hidden from thee, neither is it far off." *Deut. 30.11.*

Thank God that in the Way of Holiness wayfaring men, though fools, shall not err (Isa. 35.8). The ground of praise we must now consider is simplicity itself, is within the reach of all, is an union of "things lovely" endeared to noble hearts (see Phil. 4.8), is an indisputable point of likeness to our Heavenly Father ("Be ye holy; for I am Holy;" 1 St. Pet. 1.16; Lev. 19.2): and to our Divine Brother ("I am meek and lowly in heart;" St. Matt. 11.29), is the key of contentment here and of exaltation hereafter.

By the word Holiness we understand two[74] things: one involuntary, the other voluntary; one accidental (so to say), the other inherent; one a privilege, the other a grace. This grace is what God requires: without it, all else which has been granted us of office, privilege, gift, will but increase our condemnation. Under the Jewish Dispensation the inferior sort of holiness was lavished on the chosen race: but the higher holiness consisted then as it remains now, as it has been and will be ever, in the voluntary harmony of each human will with the Divine Will, in (if we dare say so) the personal likeness of each human character to the Divine Character.

In the loftier sense it does not seem that even a single personage of the Old Testament is throughout the historical record pronounced holy: at least, I can recal [sic] no such instance as occurring in the Authorized Version. Of course all I mean is that the particular expletive is not used concerning individuals: for the fact of their holiness is often "fair as the moon, clear as the sun, and terrible as an army with banners" (see Song of Sol. 6.10). But the first man we find verbally designated as "holy" was that last of Jewish Saints, John Baptist (St. Mark 6.20): and in him the more than prophet (St. Luke 7.26) terminated the goodly fellowship of those prophets whose privilege was restricted to standing without while they listened for the Bridegroom's Voice, or as in the holy Baptist's unparalleled case heard it (see St. John 3.29). Noah, Ruth, Job, were just, virtuous, perfect, and upright (Gen. 6.9; Ruth 3.11; Job 1.1); but of none of them is the word "holy" used; no, nor yet of Lot, whom we know as "just Lot . . . that righteous man" (2 St. Pet. 2.7,8). Of all such terms "holy" seems the highest, the most spiritual; the rest appear to be lower steps of the same ascent: these certify the conduct, the other vouches for the heart. Perhaps without rashness we may quote Lot himself as exemplifying the inferiority of righteousness as compared with holiness. He in his own person was a good man, with so genuine a love of right and loathing of wrong, that his residence among sinners was a source of unceasing vexation to his soul: but no zeal of God's Sanctity consumed him; he remained while he loathed: and when rescued with a high hand

from imminent destruction his enthusiasm for his own salvation carried him
no further than "little" Zoar, itself all but included within the penal fire, instead of winging his feet up the appointed mountain of safety (Gen.
19.12–23). But for the verdict of an inspired Apostle I think we might have
doubted whether in very truth Lot was even so much as righteous.

For holiness we must rather look to Abraham, Moses, David, Elijah; yet
not for unflawed holiness even to them: to David perhaps least of all, yet was
he the man after God's own heart (1 Sam. 13.14), and God alone could slake
the thirst of his soul (Ps. 63.1; 143.6). Enoch stands solitary in the glory of
his acceptance (Gen. 5.24; Heb. 11.5), Melchizedek in the mystery of his
august[75] individuality (Gen. 14.18–20; Heb. 7.1–4); of these twain we
know nothing amiss; nor yet of Daniel, but for his own self-accusation
(Dan. 9.20). Still, Solomon avers that "there is no man that sinneth not" (1
Kings 8.46), and centuries later St. John instructs us how "if we say that we
have no sin, we deceive ourselves" (1 St. John 1.8): One, and One alone,
there is "Who did no sin" (1 St. Pet. 2.22).

All that is spiritual within us, that is noble, that is aspiring, yearns after holiness even while we offend seven times, yea, seventy times seven. What is the
dissatisfying element in all we have? Whence derives that recoil of pleasure
which deals a pang, that influence of beauty which steeps us in sorrow? Each
of these becomes on occasion a weapon sharper than any two-edged sword
(see Heb. 4.12): and we might almost adjure our misery in the words of Je-
remiah (47.6,7), "O thou sword of the Lord, how long will it be ere thou be
quiet? put up thyself into thy scabbard, rest, and be still;" but, "how can it be
quiet, seeing the Lord hath given it a charge?" We only can quiet it (and that
at God's time, not at man's) by first yielding ourselves to the legitimate influence of each good creature, and learning from it the lesson they all are framed
to teach. Their beauty from without rebukes us until from within ourselves
there responds to it that beauty which returns after penitence as a clear shining after rain (see 2 Sam. 23.4), "beauty for ashes" (Isa. 61.3). All creation begins by enforcing a negative lesson: "The depth saith, It is not in me:"
nevertheless in that negative is latent an affirmative: Not in me, then elsewhere. While we praise God because "He setteth an end to darkness," let us
confidently crave His Spirit in searching out all perfection (Job 28.3,14).

If Humility is before honour (Prov. 15.33), no less inevitably does it un-
derlie holiness. And here we find an accessible vantage ground on the road
heavenwards. Holiness overawes while it attracts. He Who is "Glorious in Holiness" is likewise "Fearful in praises" (Exod. 15.11): and Joshua protested
even[76] to the chosen race newly settled in the Land of Promise, "Ye cannot
serve the Lord: for He is an Holy God; He is a Jealous God; He will not forgive your transgressions nor your sins" (Josh. 24.19). Humility on the other
hand is all attraction: it is one ground of our Saviour's claim to our confidence:

"Come unto Me, . . . learn of Me; for I am meek and lowly in heart," He says and draws us to Himself (St. Matt. 11.28,29). If we cannot at once be holy, let us at once be humble: if we cannot at once be humble, let us at once aim at becoming humble. To be humble is delightful, for it is to be at peace and full of contentment: to become humble is far from delightful, but it is necessary and it is possible. If we sincerely, persistently, prayerfully, desire this good estate, humility will not be denied us; it may even be lavished upon us: but perhaps in the whole range of graces there is not one likely to be vouchsafed us by a more trying process. When we ask to be humbled we must not recoil from being humiliated: when we ask God to humble us we must not wince if His instrument of discipline be some individual no better than ourselves. Humility, like all other graces, was not fully exemplified till He assumed it Who is "the Chiefest among ten thousand" (Song of Sol. 5.10), and for whose dearest sake no height or depth ought to seem to us unattainable. Even before His Advent His saints, like dulled mirrors, shone here and there with an image of some of His virtues: thus we discern humility combined with unselfishness in Abram (Gen. 13.8,9), with magnanimity in Moses (Num. 11.27–29), with filial piety in Ruth (3.5,6), with friendship in Jonathan (1 Sam. 2.16,17), with meekness in David (2 Sam. 16.5–13). This blessed Humility is a grace specially open and adapted to us sinners: by it aged Eli, who was our warning, became also our example (1 Sam. 3.18); by it Hezekiah, having come to a better mind, refused not to be comforted under the foreseen consequences of his own folly (2 Kings 20.12–19; 2 Chron. 32.24–26,31).

"Thus saith the High and Lofty One that inhabiteth eternity, Whose Name is Holy; I dwell in the high and holy place, with him also that is of a contrite and humble spirit, to revive the spirit of the humble, and to revive the heart of the contrite ones" (Isa. 57.15).

THE SECOND SERIES: REDEMPTION.[77]

Waters above the Firmament.
"We know that all things work together for good
to them that love God." *Rom. 8.28.*

As in the former Series of Studies, so now again I reserve instances of "waters" for subsequent sections, and here take the "Firmament" as our text.

In one very solemn passage Christ Himself took it in some sort for a text. The Pharisees desired of Him a sign from heaven: and "He answered and said unto them, When it is evening, ye say, It will be fair weather: for the sky is red. And in the morning, it will be foul weather to-day: for the sky is red and lowring. O ye hypocrites, ye can discern the face of the sky; but can ye not discern the signs of the times?" (St. Matt. 16.1–3).

Thus we learn that to exercise natural perception becomes a reproach to us, if along with it we exercise not spiritual perception. Objects of sight may and should quicken us to apprehend objects of faith, things temporal suggesting things eternal. Our Just and Tender Lord Who accepts good will without regard to ability (see 2 Cor. 8.12), stands ready to sanctify and utilize every sense and faculty we possess (see Rev. 3.20). Natural gifts are laid as stepping-stones to supernatural: the nobler any man is by birth-right, if keen of insight, lofty of instinctive aim, wide of grasp, deep of penetration, the more is he able and is he bound to discern in the visible universe tokens of the Love and Presence and foreshadowings of the Will of God. It is good for us to enjoy all good things which fall to our temporal lot, so long as such enjoyment kindles and feeds the desire of better things reserved for our eternal inheritance. The younger fairer than the elder (Judges 15.2), the best wine last (St. John 2.10), these are symbols calculated[78] to set us while on earth hankering, longing, straining, after heaven.

If inherent in all beauty is a subtle influence whereby it may sadden in the very act of delighting us, this influence resides certainly not least efficaciously in beauties of the sky. We watch the ever-varying heaven overhead, and all its changes still leave it essentially unchanged and unchangeable: it seems to kiss earth and ocean at the horizon, but we know that for ever it cannot be touched, nor can the foot of the world-spanning rainbow be found amongst us. Not these, or such as these, are our real heaven, or even our bridge to reach heaven: "there is a path" but no fowl knoweth it, nor hath the vulture's eye seen it (Job 26.7).

Yet it is no lesson of "vanity of vanities," of barren dreaming or desire (see Eccles. 1.2,14) which our Divine Master draws from the sky. The Pharisees whom He is addressing made a practical use of their sky-study, and for this they are not blamed: on the contrary, they had but to take an onward and upward step, to pass from the region of sight into the region of faith, and they then would have discerned that such "a sign from heaven" as they challenged had actually been vouchsafed to them, "He that came down from heaven, even the Son of Man which is in heaven" (St. John 3.13).

What they missed we may appropriate.

"From all blindness of heart, Good Lord, deliver us."[79]

Showers and Dew.
"If any man have ears to hear, let him hear." *St. Mark 4.23.*

Leaving Dew to be considered further on, where it reappears combined with frost, I will for the present confine myself to a few remarks connected with showers.

He Who spake as never man spake (St. John 7.46) deigned many times to take for His text or illustration some common every-day object, making thereof the key to unlock a mystery or the goad to urge His hearers to a duty (see Eccles. 12.11). Thus, concerning "the face of the sky and of the earth," we find Christ appealing to an experience which men admit and act upon as convicting them of sin in remaining ignorant of matters more momentous: the shower which they foretell rebukes them for those signs of the times which they discern not (St. Luke 12.54–56).

This nineteenth century of ours seems beyond all previous centuries to be a period of running to and fro, and of increased knowledge (see Dan. 12.4). Now therefore presumably, in at any rate no less a degree than heretofore, must men be liable to the risk of at once knowing and not knowing: knowing many things, while ignoring the one thing needful (see St. Luke 10.41,42); adding knowledge to knowledge, but not as St. Peter bids us adding it to virtue, and least of all adding it through virtue to underlying faith (2 St. Pet. 1.5). And whilst the high and deep men of to-day abide pre-eminently exposed to so great a peril; lesser persons, including many nimble-witted individuals of our lesser sex, run their parallel and proportionate risk by adding flowers of superficial knowledge to a rooted ignorance, the play of a fanciful luminous iridescence to the crest of a dense mental mist.

Yet since charity always edifieth, although knowledge oftentimes puffeth up (1 Cor. 8.1), neither the least instructed person nor the most learned need miss his own appointed "showers of blessing" (Ezek. 34.26): for while knowledge is and must remain exceptional, charity lies ever accessible to us all. Our loving Master desires to add true wisdom, be it to man's knowledge or to his ignorance: whichever of the twain is ours we have but to carry it to Him; and He Whose first-called Apostles were unlearned and ignorant men (Acts 4.13), but Who afterwards elected to the same Apostleship the erudite and eloquent St. Paul,—He only and He amply is both able and willing to make us wise unto salvation. And along with heavenly wisdom all else shall in good time be added to us: that which He doeth and we know not now, we shall, please God, know hereafter (see St. John 13.7). It may never indeed in this world[80] be His pleasure to grant us previsions of seers and forecastings of prophets: but He will assuredly vouchsafe us so much foresight and illumination as should[81] suffice to keep us on the watch with loins girded and lamps burning; not with hearts meanwhile failing us for fear as we look for those things that are coming upon the earth, but with uplifted eyes and uplifted heads, because as they come to pass our redemption draweth nigh (St. Luke 12.35–38; 21.25–28).

A cloud and a shower, then, become mementoes to stir us up to spiritual alertness and discernment. Familiar objects continually set afresh before us, and once for all through association Divinely commended to our notice, they incite us not merely to study signs of yet weightier import, but also to observe modesty and accuracy in all our investigations, whether of matters momentous or trivial: for we notice how not every cloud is the cloud in question, nay, nor even every cloud in the west; it must be a rising as well as a western cloud to be the precise cloud of our Lord's discourse. And if two characteristics must tally to establish so unimportant an identity, many prayers and careful pondering, a loving fear as well as a reverent love, will do well to regulate our investigation of matters spiritual, future, eternal (consider Job 32.6,7; Ps. 131; Prov. 30.5,6; St. John 21.23; Rom. 12.3).

"If any man think that he knoweth any thing, he knoweth nothing yet as he ought to know" (1 Cor. 8.2).

Ice and Snow.

"My brethren have dealt deceitfully as a brook, and as the stream of brooks that pass away; which are blackish by reason of the ice, and wherein the snow is hid: what time they wax warm, they vanish." *Job 6.15–17.*

These words of Job, spoken in his desolation, befit a desolation yet more utter and more patient than his, even the desolation of our Lord Jesus Christ when in the Garden of the Agony all His disciples forsook Him and fled. As the troops of Tema looked and found nothing (Job 6.18,19), as David looked on his right hand and beheld, but there was no man that would know him (Ps. 142.4), so the sinless Son of David, every man being scattered to his own, was left alone (St. John 16.32; St. Mark 14.50–52). And just as ice and snow promise to thirst an intensity of refreshment beyond the refreshing virtue of mere water, so they may remind us in particular of St. Peter's protestations: "Although all shall be offended, yet will not I . . . If I should die with Thee, I will not deny Thee in any wise" (Mark 14.29,31): protestations which at first falsified attained nevertheless at last to fulfilment: "Jesus answered him, Whither I go, thou canst not follow Me now; but thou shalt follow Me afterwards" (St. John 13.36): and again after the three denials and threefold renewal of the Apostolick Commission: "This spake He, signifying by what death he should glorify God" (John 21.18,19).

Ice and snow are figures to us of evanescence, of that which passes away. If aught which endures or which is eternal be likened to snow, it is on occasion of its brief revelation to mortal eyes: thus on the Mount of Transfiguration three Apostles beheld the effulgent raiment of Christ "exceeding white as snow" (St. Mark 9.3); thus in the Isle called Patmos St. John "in the Spirit" fell as dead at the Feet of Him Whose Head and Whose Hairs "were white like wool, as white as snow" (Rev. 1.9–17; see also Dan. 7.9); thus moreover (to descend to an inferior connexion) the Roman Guard and the faithful women when gathered around the empty Sepulchre in Joseph's garden encountered an Angel whose raiment was white as snow (St. Matt. 28.1–5). That celestial sea which St. John beheld before the Throne of God, that solid sea whereon the victorious host of the elect took their stand, was "of glass like unto crystal," was "as it were a sea of glass mingled with fire" (Rev. 4.6; 15.2), but was not of ice.

Symbols, parables, analogies, inferences, may be fascinating, must be barren, unless we make them to ourselves words of the wise which are as goads (Eccles. 12.11). Let us imitate the practical example of that Virtuous Woman who "is not afraid of the snow for her household: for all her household are clothed with scarlet" (Prov. 31.10–31): and copying her we shall become trustworthy, loving, prudent, diligent; we shall go in advance of those whom we require to labour with us (consider much more the example of the Good Shepherd Himself: St. John 10.4,11); we shall demean ourselves charitably, decorously according to our station; we shall reflect honour on those from whom we derive honour; out of the abundance of our heart our mouth will speak wisdom; kindness will govern our tongue, and justice our enactments;—thus shall it be with us even now, and much more in the supreme day of rising up, the Day of Resurrection, then our nearest and dearest who never cease to love us shall bless and praise us; we shall still have somewhat in our hands, because our works have followed us (Rev. 14.13; see Acts 9.39); and being ready we shall enter with praise through the door before it be shut (St. Matt. 25.10; 1 Cor. 4.5).

Yet so long as each of us gives all diligence to make her own personal calling and election sure (2 St. Peter 1.10), it will do us no harm to recognise in this Saintly Spouse a figure of the Church: that great Mother and Mistress (Gal. 4.26) who because her whole family is washed and beautified in the Blood of Christ (Rev. 7.13,14) has no need to fear any transitory creature; who through the burden of her day of probation looks forward to the day of praise; who even now amid many sins and many shortcomings, knows that less for her love's sake than for His own the Heart of her Divine Husband safely trusts in her and accounts that she doth Him good and not evil all the days of her life (see 2 Cor. 12.9; Rev. 3.7–13).

"As in water face answereth to face, so the heart of man to man" (Prov. 27.19).

Children of Men.
"What I do thou knowest not now; but thou shalt know hereafter."
St. John 13.7.

It has been pointed out that, while marvellous are the miracles of mercy which Jesus wrought, still more marvellous are those which He wrought not. We comprehend at once that as a good tree naturally brings forth good fruit, and a sweet fountain sends forth sweet waters (St. Matt. 7.16–18; St. James 3.11,12), so Very Love must beyond all question naturally perform works of love: therefore what again and again He did to relieve human suffering is miraculous not as the outcome of His good will, but simply as a suspension or contravention of established law; what He did not is mysterious. Mysteries lie deeper than miracles: they address and they tax a higher faculty in whoso would apprehend them. Many a miracle could in its own day be estimated and attested by the senses: all mysteries ever have been and at this day continue inappreciable except by faith and love.

The secret things belong unto the Lord our God: nevertheless so far as they are revealed they belong unto us also (Deut. 29.29). They become as talents entrusted to us, and for which we shall have sooner or later to give account (see St. Matt. 18.23–25; St. Luke 12.20; 16.1,2; 19.12,13,15).

Not least mysterious among mysteries appears to us that lifelong self-restriction in observance of which our Saviour ministered almost exclusively to those of His own nation: for thus undoubtedly in the main He did. True, He was as one who hideth the ointment of his right hand, which bewrayeth itself (see Prov. 27.16); His love once and again coming out of its place (see Mic. 1.3) to bestow uncovenanted mercies, and to give unto the last even as unto the first (see St. Matt. 20.14): but His so doing was the exception, not the rule. Wherefore? Our own hearts suffice to respond with more than St. Paul's emphasis of absolute conviction: Wherefore? because He loved us not? God knoweth! (see 2 Cor. 11.11). Yet the question remains in great measure still unanswered, and must so remain. Man cannot reply to it fully, but God is able to instruct souls by their own ignorance no less efficiently than by any knowledge. When out of the Whirlwind He answered Job (28.12,28; 38.1; 40.4; 43.2,6), we cannot suppose that Patriarch to have gleaned many scientific facts till then unknown to him, and the mysterious Providence which had so searchingly tried his faith and patience remained mysterious still: but none the less did he then and there find wisdom and the place of understanding, for he learned to say: "Behold, I am vile; what shall I answer Thee?" and again, "I know that Thou canst do everything, and that no thought can be withholden from Thee. . . . I abhor myself, and repent in dust and ashes." God's Will respecting those who are outside the Church's pale has not been revealed to us who abide within: every duty of love, of intercession, of corporal or spiritual mercy, we can discharge towards them; but judge them (thank God) we may not and cannot; though not seldom their righteousness judges and shames our unrighteousness (see 1 Cor. 5.12,13; Gal. 6.10; Rom. 2.13–15,27–29).

The Gospels comfort us with most blessed instances of graces and gifts lavished in excess of any definite convenant. Vividness of faith and aptitude for love constrained the Magi to travel westward in search of the Object of their costly worship (St. Matt. 2.1–11). "Draw me," each seems to say, "We will run after Thee" (Song of Sol. 1.4): and of sweeter influence than the unbound Pleiades (see Job 38.31). "His star" drew them.[82] The Woman of Samaria, besides sharing the errors of her nation, appears to have become personally degraded: yet when to her Jesus said, "I that speak unto thee am He,"[83] she cavilled not at the word of truth; which thereupon kindled within her a flame of charity towards her own fellow-citizens; and this shining before men led some to glorify their Heavenly Father (see St. Matt. 5.16) by believing on His Christ; other converts afterwards being added to the first (St. John 4.16–42). That Centurion who loved and succoured God's chosen people and by whom a slave was most tenderly cared for, became in matters spiritual as a Roman Eagle gazing upon the unveiled sun; and attained to such a pitch of supernatural insight that Jesus "marvelled at him . . . and said . . . Verily I say unto you, I have not found so great faith, no, not in Israel. And I say unto you, that many shall come from the east and west, and shall sit down with Abraham, and Isaac, and Jacob, in the kingdom of heaven" (St. Luke 7.2–9; St. Matt. 8.10–13). Maternal love wrought up on Syrophenician Woman to such indomitable persistence, that she could bear a rebuff such as no second suppliant is recorded to have undergone: and thereby won from her Saviour not only her heart's desire and the request of her lips (see Ps. 21.2), but a word of approval which was in itself a beatification (St. Matt. 15.21–28; St. Mark 7.26). At that Feast of the Passover, to which all previous Passovers had led up, and which was itself the greatest and the last of all, certain Greek Pilgrims having come to worship with the sacred nation in their sacred city, craved to "see Jesus:"[84] and though we are not informed whether at the moment they obtained their request, it gave occasion to the Divine discourse in which the Saviour of Mankind distinctly pledged Himself to the whole human race: "I, if I be lifted up from the earth, will draw all men unto Me" (St. John 12.20–33). Last of all we read of the Centurion, who at the Crucifixion glorified God, saying, "Truly this Man was the Son of God," "Certainly this was a righteous Man." And they also that were with him feared, and confessed the Son of God (St. Mark 15.39; St. Luke 23.47; St. Matt. 27.54).

The twenty-fifth chapter of St. Matthew's Gospel consists of what is, to all appearance, one unbroken Divine discourse composed of three distinct portions. Of these the first, the Parable of the Ten Virgins, addresses with special directness such persons as practise or at the least profess a devoted life, and urges them to a constant readiness of preparation: the second, the Parable of the Talents, representing our probation under the figure of a trust used or abused, may be claimed by all alike who in any vocation are called to know and serve God, and certifies each one among us of the individual responsibility which all lie under[85] and which none can evade. The third and concluding portion of the discourse, quitting the parabolical form, speaks plainly of the judgment which overhangs the whole world; proclaims a test, tried by which the arraigned will stand finally or fall finally; and first sets the Judge before us, if so by any means we may be prepared to be set before Him in that last awful day.

In this revelation, all turns upon what each man has done or has not done: motives are not sifted, knowledge and ignorance alike seem to be beside the question; at least, no such matters are here on record as being gone into: "Ye have done[86] it," "Yet did it not," sums up all. It has been noticed that the righteous and the wicked reply in the selfsame words: "Lord, when saw we Thee . . . ?" neither class seeming to have formerly even suspected with Whom it was that in the charities of daily life they had to do. The duties alleged are moreover such as are incumbent not exclusively upon Christians as Christians, but upon all men as men: and hence it has been argued that by this portion of Holy Writ is revealed to believers God's perfect Will towards those who have not shared their privileges.

This however we know not, neither can we yet know. For the present we have nothing to do with judging those that are without: only our own selves we do well to judge (see 1 Cor. 11.31), and to judge trembling.

"For the time is come that judgment must begin at the house of God: and if it first begin at us, what shall the end be of them that obey not the Gospel of God? And if the righteous scarcely be saved, where shall the ungodly and the sinner appear?" (1 St. Pet. 4.17,18).

Holy and Humble Men of Heart.
"The Holy One and the Just." *Acts 3.14.*
"He humbled Himself." *Phil. 2.8.*

"Come unto me," says our gracious Lord: "Learn of Me; for I am meek and lowly in heart" (St. Matt. 11.28,29). The injunction, "Learn of Me," implies the promise, "I will teach;" for God accepts us according to that we have, and not according to that we have not (see 2 Cor. 8.12), and consequently demands no more than He is willing first to supply; but it does not define or limit the Divine mode of teaching, and experience attests that after divers manners does Christ instruct His disciples.

Taking Humility as our subject: He taught His blessed Mother once and again by a check (St. John 2.4; St. Mark 3.31–35),—Nicodemus by his ignorance (St. John 3.10),—the Woman of Samaria by her depravity (4.16–18),—the Sinful Woman by suffering her to be despised (St. Luke 7.39);—shallow[87] persons He taught by revealing the impartiality and inevitableness of impending judgment (13.1–5),—the Canaanitish Mother by delay, even by apparent denial and contempt (St. Matt. 15.22–26),—the Apostles collectively by pattern of a little child (18.1–4); and by His own habitual (St. Luke 22.24–27) and exceptional (St. John 13.12–17) example,—St. Peter individually by a patient prophetic warning (37,38). He likewise in abasement of pride and exaltation of humility spake two Parables; that of the Highest Room (St. Luke 14.7–11), and that of the Pharisee and Publican (18.9–14).

All these instances taken together illustrate not the necessity merely of our acquiring humility, but the painfulness of the process whereby it must be acquired. Yet surely necessity and pain fall into the background, giving place to aspiration and love, when our Master Himself first performs the task He is about to set us. As (according to a most poetical simile) a brimming cup overflows, whether a pebble or a pearl be cast into it, so does a heart full of love overflow not with pain, but with love, even if that which stirs its depths be not a pleasure but a pang.

Humility pervades the Apostolic Epistles. To take one instance only; the First Epistle of St. Peter is a study of humility, submission, patience. If in defiance of nature St. Peter, the dominant Apostle, clothed himself with humility (see 5.5), which of us need despair? Not one of us who brings to the work a spark of that love which blazed in his heart. Love, the key of all perfection, is itself that perfection whereof it is the key. Love it is which fulfils the First and Great Commandment, and the Second likewise (St. Matt. 22.37–40; Rom. 13.8–10); these two fulfilled, what room remains for transgression or defect? Yet some things, which for the present form part of our salutary discipline or our bounden duty, must at length be abolished in the Triumph of Love. "Let us fear," is our rule to-day (Heb. 4.1); but the day approaches when "perfect love" shall cast out fear; "He that feareth is not made perfect in love" (1 St. John 4.18).

We learn from the Epistle to the Hebrews (12.9–11) how God chastens us for our profit, that we may be partakers of His Holiness; and how such chastening, seeming for the present grievous, afterwards yields the peaceable fruit of righteousness. These declarations send us back to our Lord's words[88] of tender invitation: "Take My yoke upon you, and learn of Me; for I am meek and lowly in heart: and ye shall find rest unto your souls" (St. Matt. 11.29). Now if the promise of "peaceable fruit of righteousness,"[89] and of "rest unto our souls," suffice not to allure us, yet one more motive remains; for without holiness "no man shall see the Lord" (Heb. 12.14). Shall we have travelled so far, to miss the goal at last? Shall we so often have gazed on Christ with the eye of intellectual knowledge, it may be even of intellectual faith, and never behold Him face to face with the eye of love? Every eye indeed shall see Him, and they also which pierced Him (Rev. 1.7); but they only who shall be like Him shall see Him as He is (1 St. John 3.2).

"As He which hath called you is Holy, so be ye holy in all manner of conversation; because it is written, Be ye holy; for I am Holy" (1 St. Peter 1.15, 16).

From *Called to be Saints:*
The Minor Festivals
Devotionally Studied (1881)

⁓◦◦⁓

C alled to be Saints was published in the same year as *"A Pageant" and Other Poems* (1881), though it was in fact completed five years earlier. Rossetti offered the book to Alexander Macmillan in a letter of 4 November 1876: "I have by me a completed work, a sort of devotional reading-book for the red-letter Saints' Days, which of course is longing to see the light & which I shall be glad if you will consent to look at" (*RM,* 120). As with *Annus Domini,* she wishes that the Reverend Burrows might examine and "sanction" this work, originally ti-tled "Young Plants and Polished Corners." In fact, SPCK, Rossetti's usual pub-lisher, would issue the book in an extremely attractive format, with every page set out by rules (an ornamental device in each corner), and with running headlines and section titles in gothic type. There are ornamental, engraved initial letters at the beginning of each subsection, accompanied by engraved illustrations of each flower (or plant). The paper is an antique white, and the whole book is bound in dark blue, fine-ribbed buckram; the title is stamped in gold on the spine. Such care for the physical design of the book is characteristic of much Tractarian publish-ing of which *Called to be Saints* is a particularly splendid example.

Rossetti explains the plan of her book in the opening paragraphs, or "Key to my Book," a design that is essentially her own although she would have been aware of the emblematic significance of flowers, plants, stones, and of many natural objects. She must have seen such a work as Peter Parley's *Tales About Plants* (London: Tegg, 1839) or known John Gerard's celebrated *Herball or Generall Historie of Plantes*

(London: 1597, 1633, and other dates). Yet Rossetti was, in any case, fully sensitive to reading the created world as directly related to God, for she consciously discovered correspondences between all things on earth and the divine order. John
Ruskin, whom Rossetti knew, reflects the common Victorian attitude toward nature. He explained that one's surroundings are filled with hidden meaning, and that
"by rightly understanding as much of the nature of everything as ordinary watch-
fulness will enable any man to perceive, we might, if we looked for it, find in everything some special moral lesson or type of particular truth" (letter to W. J.
Stillman, in *The Works of John Ruskin*, eds. E. T. Cook and Alexander Wedderburn,
39 vols. [London: G. Allen, 1903–12], 36:123; and compare his *Proserpina* of
1875–76, vol. 35). While distinctively Rossetti's own work, *Called to be Saints*
should nevertheless be read within this large and appreciative cultural context.
Very useful discussions are by Jack Goody, "The Secret Language of Flowers," *Yale
Journal of Criticism* 3 (1990): 133–52; Sabine Haass, "'Speaking Flowers and Flo-
ral Emblems': The Victorian Language of Flowers," in *Word and Visual Imagination: Studies in the Interaction of English Literature and the Visual Arts*, eds. Karl Josef
Höltgen, Peter M. Daly, and Wolfgang Lottes (Erlangen: Universität-Bibliothek,
1988), 241–68 (with excellent illustrations); and Gisela Hönnighausen, "Emblematic Tendencies in the Works of Christina Rossetti," *Victorian Poetry* 72
(1972): 1–15 (with particular reference to *Called to be Saints*). Mary Arseneau and
D.M.R. Bentley discuss "Peter Parley and the Rossettis" in *English Language Notes*
20 (September 1993): 56–60.

Selections given here are from a copy of the first edition of 1881 in the University of British Columbia Library. The poem that ends this selection also concludes *Called to be Saints*; it subsequently appeared as one of the "Songs for
Strangers and Pilgrims" in *Verses* with the title "Whither the Tribes go up, even
the Tribes of the Lord" (*Poems*, 1979–90, 2:298).

Called to be Saints:
The Minor Festivals Devotionally Studied

The Key to my Book.

How beautiful are the arms which have embraced Christ, the hands which
have touched Christ, the eyes which have gazed upon Christ, the lips which
have spoken with Christ, the feet which have followed Christ. How beautiful

are the hands which have worked the works of Christ, the feet which treading in His footsteps have gone about doing good, the lips which have spread abroad His Name, the lives which have been counted loss for Him. How beautiful upon the mountains were the feet of them who brought glad tidings and published peace, saying unto Zion "Thy God reigneth:" how beautiful was the wisdom of those unlearned and ignorant men, whose very opponents felt that they had been with Jesus.

I will endeavour to write of the nineteen Saints commemorated by name in our Book of Common Prayer, with the Holy Innocents neither named nor numbered, with St. Michael and his cloud of All Angels, with All Saints as the stars of the firmament and as the sand by the sea-shore innumerable: and lest any one in reading what I write should condemn me as dwelling too prominently on the servant in lieu of the Master, I pray him to recall the words of Abigail, who, because she was the King's bride, protested, "Let thine handmaid be a servant to wash the feet of the servants of my lord." Or if one say, "Was Paul crucified for you?"[90] I answer that I desire to follow St. Paul not otherwise than as he bade us thus follow Christ. But if one object that many of my suggestions are exploded superstitions or mere freaks of fancy without basis of truth; and that if I have fancied this another may fancy that, and another again that, till the whole posse of idle thinkers puts forth each his fresh fancy, and all alike without basis; I frankly answer, Yes: so long as with David our musings are on God's works, among the chief whereof is His sinful Saint made perfect; and so long as with St. Timothy our meditations are on charity, faith, purity, which array the Saints of Christ in a robe more excellent than the glory of Solomon or the loveliness of a lily. And whereinsoever I err I ask pardon of mine own Master to Whom I stand or fall, and of my brother lest I offend him.

Those verses in the Book of Revelation which name the twelve apostolic foundation stones of New Jerusalem, when set against the Calendar naturally assign the jasper to St. Andrew; and thence progressing in a regular order throughout, the amethyst at last to St. Jude: according to which arrangement, in default of any clue to the contrary, I have written concerning them.

For as all virtues have one and the same root, even so does that one root shoot up into every virtue: and although on one tree of God's own planting the branch of love may overshadow its fellow branches, bearing aloft the double rose of love to God and man; while on another the lily of faith may exalt its whiteness above its fellows; and on a third every twig may be tipped with azure bells of hope which trembling make music; yet no single plant, be it lowest or loftiest, be it indomitable trunk which may break but will not bend, or frail climber clinging and mounting around another's strength, can lack the germ if no more of each grace; the least indeed may elude notice on earth, but in Paradise it shall become a thousand.

Wherefore, to quote one instance as a sample of all, I am not afraid to adorn my conception of St. Andrew with the jasper stone, or to endeavour among its characteristics to find some emblem which may befit him: for little as I know of him now, I know that he lived and died and shall wake up after the likeness of our common Lord; and much more, I know that He Who is full of grace cannot but show forth every grace when reflected in a faithful mirror, even though it be one from which many flaws have had to be abolished. Thus shall the stones also cry out Hosanna.

But precious things of the earth and of the deep are for those who are gorgeously apparelled and live delicately and are in kings' courts. I think the Gospel records more lessons drawn by our Master from a seed or a plant than from a pearl. So I will, as it were, gather simples and try to spell out their lessons: I will adorn the shrines of Christ's friends with flowers, and plant a garden round their hallowed graves. Fuller remarks of a flower: "In the morning when it groweth up, it is a lecture of Divine Providence: in the evening when it is cut down and withereth, it is a lecture of human mortality."[91] Let us learn something from the grass of the field which God clothes.

Much of my material can only be drawn from uncertain traditions: but after one protest that to such I attach no binding faith, nor even necessarily any credence, I shall not deem it incumbent upon me to guard each sentence as it occurs by a supplementary protest; nor have I hesitated partly to construct my so-called "Memorials" on a legendary foundation. Such Memorials may, I am not without hope, prove helpful towards realizing each Saint in his special Office on his appointed Day. They took their rise from my own observation of appropriate verses when I joined in our Church Service: one such association succeeded another, until it appeared to me that the Psalms of each Feast might be arranged in more or less apt connection with its special history. In the Scripture texts of the parallel column I have observed or imagined some bearing on the subject in hand, at the least either typical or suggestive: and as in every instance reference is made to chapter and verse, no misapprehension of the primary drift need ensue even where I may have strained an application.

My work is based on no text more recondite than that of the Authorized Version: nor have I supposed it either essential or edifying to dwell on alternative readings, or on many other disputed points which meet one even in preparing so slight a study. I have, however, felt at liberty to abridge the text, and to combine into one narrative the statements found in (for instance) the separate Gospels; but without verbal alteration, though not invariably without change of punctuation. The references to chapter and verse enable each clause to be traced to its source. My occasional linguistic statements are given at second-hand, as are most of the authorities I cite whether by name or anonymously. No graver slur could attach to my book than would be a reputation for prevalent originality: and I hope my here, once for all, acknowledging how deeply and widely I am indebted to the spoken or written words of many, will be accepted as sheltering me equally from charges of rashness and of plagiarism.

For the learned, then, I have no ability to write, lacking as I do learning and critical practice. But I suppose not that much mischief need accrue from my violating probability so far as, for instance, to accept the precious stones of our Authorized Version as gems now known to us under the same names. And if some points of my descriptions are rather flights of antique fancy than lore of modern science, I hope that such points may rather recall a vanishing grace than mislead from a truth. Avowing, as I must, a general ignorance of petrology, and even of botany, I ask any who turn to my nature-portraits to accept them as confessedly no more than loving studies from the outside; elaborated by one who has written partly indeed from her own observation of appearances, but mainly from a little reading; and who is quite prepared to be convicted of numerous mistakes. Nor have I attempted to select my illustrative flowers from the flora of Palestine: I even think that a flower familiar to the eye and dear to the heart may often succeed in conveying a more pointed lesson than could be understood from another more remote if more eloquent. "Consider the lilies of the field, how they grow."[92]

From *"St. Andrew, Apostle"*
30 November
THE DAISY.
We are well placed where God places us.

The daisy, scattered over many soils, blows the whole year round in genial weather, and though less plentiful in November than in milder months, its rarity may then be viewed as choiceness, for throughout November flowers are few. The daisy must almost always be precursor and companion of some blossom more gorgeous, or more beautiful, or more fragrant than itself: yet not for this does it shrink from opening wide its star towards the sky, and tipping its white disk with a pink nimbus when it expands in sunshine; even in shade it wears no sadder colour than a spotless white. Its centre, or heart, or eye, is of pure gold. Its very name, day's-eye, shows how it courts the sun, and closes against darkness. Its leaves grow habitually close to the ground, though sometimes a leaf or two unfolds along the flower-stalk: yet low-growing as they are, and springing in profusion amid the meadow grasses, a certain acridity protects them from being made havock of altogether and devoured by the grazing cattle which trample them under foot. Grass is tall enough to tower above and hide a daisy; yet the daisy will more readily spread and supersede the grass, than the grass it. Not the petals only, but the leaves also of the daisy are often tinged with pink; as though its allotted beauty and joy overflowed its capacity to hold them. Small as this plant is, it both spreads rapidly and is at the same time multiplied by seed; it is "mother of thousands of millions."[93]

God giveth it a body as it hath pleased Him, and to every seed his own body.—1 Cor. 15.38.

From *"St. Thomas, Apostle"*
21 December
IVY.
Not strong, except with a prop.

Ivy, though greenest when putting forth fresh foliage, remains green and luxuriant the whole year round. Its leaves, which are often of so crowded a growth as to overlap each other, are glossy and full-coloured on that upper surface which spreads towards the sun; duller and paler underneath where they face earthwards. Each individual leaf has its edges fashioned in special curves, or peaked with particular points, unlike the curves and points of a million others; some are boldly rounded, some notched and very delicately tapered off. Ivy flowers in October with a greenish-whitish brushy blossom, not showy but plentiful: in December it is adorned by black or deep purple berries. Its foliage is often dark and even dusky in colour, and is of a solid texture: its stems are rugged and woody, fringed in parts by a coarse shag of rootlets, like bark combed to shreds, or like hundreds of minute fingers helping to attach it here or there. On the whole, ivy wears a sober aspect, yet by an exception it will show forth a wonderful beauty and grace: its branches hanging in garlands, or creeping in exquisite traceries; its leaves decked with a delicate lacework of veins, or blushing with a rich redness, or wholly pale as if carved out of ivory; while let but the sun shine through the tangle of foliage, and it will put on a rich verdure, or a harmony of lights and shadows.

Ivy affects not to stand alone, but by clinging and clambering it will scale a lofty height till it overhangs the sustaining oak or pine. Objects which lack beauty, whether decaying trunk, ruin, or chasm, ivy will embrace or bridge over and clothe with grace and comeliness. The entire plant gives out a peculiar aroma; the old stems when bruised exude a very fragrant resin. Ivy flourishes in sunshine and in shade, it mounts skywards, it nestles in nooks, it refuses not to trail along the ground: everywhere and at all times, except by some special freak of beauty, it is green; it is sometimes more than green, but at the least it is green with an unfading greenness.

He is green before the sun, and his branch shooteth forth in his garden.—Job 8.16.

From *"St. Stephen, Deacon"*
26 December
HOLLY.
Prickles below, no prickles above.

Holly blossoms about the month of May with a white and waxy efflorescence: but the period of its chief glory occurs in the heart of winter, when, arrayed in evergreen foliage and studded with coral-like berries, it spreads a feast for birds, and is not disdained in the adornment of churches. Its leaves, of a deep glossy green, are boldly curved and twisted, stiffly angular and edged with numerous prickly corners: thus towards the ground the bush is clothed with strong defensive armour; whilst such twigs as grow high up the stem are often adorned with smooth leaves destitute of lateral prickles. The holly bush is slow of growth, and varies in scale from a shrub to a tree. Its wood is hard, white, of fine grain, and adapted to delicate workmanship. Its berries are plentiful, and usually of a rich red colour: though amongst varieties one there is which bears bright yellow berries; as also there are plants which, not through culture but naturally, have their green foliage diversified by white or yellow borders or patches.

The title of Scarlet Oak has been borne by holly; but not, perhaps, with any striking appropriateness. Let us rather dwell on its familiar name of holly as derived from holy-tree: and thus connecting it with all holy things we note how its blossom shadows forth the hue of innocence, and its leaf the flourishing of hope, and its berry the colour of the blood which is the life; its earthward side is guarded by sharpness, as of self-denial; its heavenward aspect is smooth, as by peaceful contemplation; its leaf fades not, its blossom, is comely, its fruit is the crown of its beauty.

He hath made everything beautiful in his time.—Eccles. 3.11.

From *"St. John, Apostle and Evangelist"*
27 December
THE FOURTH LIVING CREATURE.
An Eagle.

In the midst of the throne, and round about the throne, were four beasts full of eyes before and behind. And the fourth beast was like a flying eagle. And the four beasts had each of them six wings about him; and they were full of eyes within: and they rest not day and night, saying, Holy, holy, holy, Lord God Almighty, Which was, and is, and is to come.—Revelation 4.6,&c.

Of these four awful diverse living creatures the fourth has been assigned to St. John the Evangelist as his symbol. The four Gospels day and night praise without pause the great Name of God and His unutterable sanctity:

yet while in this alike, they differ from each other under many aspects. Wherefore let us consider the natural eagle, if so we may ascribe glory unto Him Who formed the eagle, and by Whose inspiration each Evangelist wrote down his own proper notes of the divine melody in harmony.

The eagle is endowed with beauty and strength; grave and royal beauty, dominant strength. His eye, sheltered by feathers, endures the blaze of the noontide sun. He is a bird of day, not of night; and delights to hunt a living prey, rather than to batten on carrion. His talons, not his beak, inflict death, clenching mechanically with a mighty pressure as he bends his legs: even so in matters spiritual bent knees are mighty towards overcoming the foe and acquiring all things. His beak, which slays not, expresses love: it calls to his mate, and in conjunction with her feeds the young hungry eaglets; these are cradled not delicately, but in a rough nest of sticks, often built on a ledge of rock. The swoop of the eagle is as a flash of lightning: his upward flight is by spiral curves without apparent movement of the wings; he ascends spire above spire dwindling to an almost invisible speck; until from the height he discerns and descends on his prey which he tears in pieces, his very name in Hebrew signifying lacerator. He gorges to the full, yet can sustain long fasts. After gorging he is loath to soar. A comparatively slight injury to the wing will disable him from darting aloft. The eagle is faithful in love, and changes not his mate except by reason of death. His age is supposed to teach or even to exceed a century.

Doth the eagle mount up at thy command, and make her nest on high? She dwelleth and abideth on the rock, upon the crag of the rock, and the strong place. From thence she seeketh the prey, and her eyes behold afar off. Her young ones also suck up blood: and where the slain are, there is she.—Job 39.27,&c.

As an eagle stirreth up her nest, fluttereth over her young, spreadeth abroad her wings, taketh them, beareth them on her wings: so the Lord alone did lead him.—Deut. 32.11,12.

They that wait upon the Lord shall renew their strength; they shall mount up with wings as eagles; they shall run, and not be weary; and they shall walk, and not faint.—Isa. 11.31.

THE THIRD FOUNDATION.
A Chalcedony.

The wall of the city had twelve foundations, and in them the names of the twelve apostles of the Lamb. And the foundations of the wall of the city were garnished with all manner of precious stones. The third, a chalcedony.—Rev. 21.14,19.

Chalcedony displays many tints, many patterns and textures so to say, many degrees of transparency or opacity. Its home is in rock, whereof it lines

or fills up cavities, becoming itself modified in accordance with their varying shapes. In hardness it exceeds flint, yet it is obedient to the graving tool.

Its colours, rather delicate than striking, are of wide range: comprising
shades of yellow, green, and blue; of grey, and brown; besides white and
black; a grey modified blue, a yellow approaching amber, an ivory whiteness.
Some Chalcedonies are uniform of hue, some are variegated; of some the
surface looks crystallized, of others dim.

The Chalcedony is neither gorgeous nor brilliant, but subdued: it is, as it
were, all made up of half tints and half degrees of beauty; invested with so
much liveliness as might serve for foil to a fuller loveliness; with so much as
may kindle joy by what it is, and quicken desire for that which it is not.

As concerns mystical virtues, Chalcedony is reputed to confer success in
lawsuits:—

And shall not God avenge His Own elect, which cry day and night unto
Him, though He bear long with them? I tell you that He will avenge them
speedily.—St. Luke 18.7,8.

MISTLETOE.
Our life is a derived life.

Mistletoe springs not straight from the earth; but striking root in some
plant nobler than itself, draws nourishment from that higher life, seldom
ceases to grow while the sustaining stock lives, but at the death of this also
dies. So keen is its craving to draw life from that only which is alive, that
though experiments have succeeded in raising Mistletoe on lifeless matter,
such as stone or dead wood, the plants thus artificially bred are but short
lived, and those alone which spring from living organisms display vigorous
vitality. Yet while the very life of the parasite depends on the life of that
from which it derives nutriment, the nobler plant bears the less noble not
without cost to itself, but is drained of the strength it imparts. Mistletoe
in its growth adheres to no one fixed characteristic direction, but assumes
any posture in compliance with the position of that whence it springs; it
droops towards the ground below, or juts out sideways, or spreads skywards indifferently: yet while almost all other plants send their roots
downwards, the Mistletoe protrudes its root first upwards, and afterward
curves it hither or thither towards its support as the situation of this latter
may entail.

The leaves of Mistletoe are evergreen and grow in pairs. Its blossom is yellow; its berry is white, shining, and in a measure translucent, yet not altogether free from speck of blackness. Though amongst ourselves no longer in
vogue as a remedy, some medicinal virtue appertains to this plant; by the
Greeks and Romans it was esteemed an antidote to poison.

Mistletoe flourishes on many different trees: in England most frequently on the apple tree.

As the apple tree among the trees of the wood, so is my Beloved among the sons.—Song of Sol. 2.3.

From *"St. Matthias, Apostle"*
24 February
BIOGRAPHICAL ADDITIONS.

Thus much and no more do the inspired Scriptures record concerning St. Matthias, though obviously he is included in all subsequent statements of what was done or suffered by the whole Apostolic body. Tradition adds to our picture of his holy life that he probably belonged in the first instance to the number of those seventy Disciples whom our Lord sent before His Face, two and two together, into every city and place whither He Himself would come; thus ordaining them His forerunners and representatives: to be, even whilst as lambs among wolves, yet conferrers of peace, worthy contented labourers, healers of the sick, preachers of God's kingdom, witnesses against rejecters of the truth; yea also dominators of devils, yet as concerning this to rejoice rather because their names were written in heaven.

After the mighty effusion of God the Holy Ghost at Pentecost, it is thought that St. Matthias was blessed with a large measure of success while, as from the first, he laboured amongst his own nation. According to one legend he finished his glorious course in Judaea, being stoned by his own countrymen. Elsewhere we read that he removed into Ethiopia or Colchis, where, proclaiming Christ, his ministrations and sufferings were prospered to the conversion of many souls. Yet from that same barbarous people to whom he preached and for whom he prayed, he won for his earthly guerdon cruel usage and death by crucifixion: even while God the Judge of all awarded to him the heavenly unfading palm branch, white robe, and crown incorruptible.

Some men's sins are open beforehand, going before to judgment; and some men they follow after.—1 Tim. 5.24.

Thus "openly" Cain, ordained a fugitive and a vagabond; Esau seeking repentance with tears, yet finding no place for it as concerned the blessing; Shechem, slain in his act of reparation; Pharaoh, foundered in the Red Sea; Moses, stopped short at Pisgah; Achan, stoned in the valley of Achor; Abimelech, struck down by a woman; Samson, having wantoned away his strength and paying the penalty; Saul, rejected from being king; Nabal, become as a stone; Michal, childless; David, fasting in vain for his firstborn by Bathsheba; Solomon, forfeiting ten tribes; the Man of God from Judah, destroyed by a lion; Ahab, requited in kind for the blood of Naboth; Gehazi, smitten with leprosy; Jezebel, devoured by dogs; Joash king of Judah, killed by his own servants; Uzziah, a leper unto the day of his death; Sennacherib, turned back by the way that he came; Zedekiah, blinded; Nebuchadnezzar, driven out from among men; Belshazzar, slain in the night; Haman, hanged on the gallows he had set up for Mordecai: thus openly all alike were these saints and sinners chastised for their transgressions. Thus last of all Judas, a hissing, an astonishment, a curse: who having gone in and out with Christ, and having in His Name wrought miracles, was yet a thief: and from being a thief went on to plot against his Master, and became a tabernacle of Satan, and sold his God for thirty pieces of silver, and betrayed the Son of Man with a kiss; and then, being eaten of remorse, did cast down the price of Innocent Blood in the Temple, and went and hanged himself.

The heart is deceitful above all things, and desperately wicked: who can know it? I the Lord search the heart, I try the reins, even to give every man according to his ways, and according to the fruit of his doings. As the partridge sitteth on eggs, and hatcheth them not; so he that getteth riches, and not by right, shall leave them in the midst of his days, and at his end shall be a fool.—Jer. 17.9,&c.

Most of all may God keep us from that more terrible judgment which followeth after; which cometh as a thief in that night when men can but stumble on the dark mountains and cannot work; which overtaketh after the long day of grace, after the long-drawn day of repentance, after the year of digging about, after the ambassage of God, after the beseechings of Christ, after the harvest, after the summer:—

The harvest is past, the summer is ended, and we are not saved.—Jer. 8.20.

Likewise also the good works of some are manifest beforehand; and they that are otherwise cannot be hid.—1 Tim. 5.36.

So it was and will be with St. Matthias: and so and not otherwise, I hope, will it turn out to have been with his competitor Joseph called Barsabas and surnamed Justus: the one exalted to be an Apostle, the other left as a simple saint; the one at once inheriting all things with persecutions, the other attaining less dignity, yet it may be with no less tribulation. If on a former day of suspense and prayer to St. Peter it was commanded "Follow Me," and to St. John "Tarry";[94] and if all these saints, each at his assigned post, ceased not to stir or to sit still according to God's appointment; then on the final supreme day of suspense and recompense (when God pity us all), to each individually yet to all alike shall the word of acceptance be spoken:—

Well done, good and faithful servant.—St. Matt. 25.23.

If one may talk of a sad festival, St. Matthias' Day is surely such an one in the Christian year; for his Feast from a different point of view may be called Judas' Fast. His light flashes from the other's darkness; he is elected an

Apostle, because the other has made himself an apostate; he is shaped and weighed as a foundation stone of New Jerusalem, because the other being weighed in the balances is found wanting. This day with its vigil falls most commonly in Lent; but whenever so, always within the period assigned to our own penitence, never within the sacred precinct of our Lord's Passion. Moreover when it thus occurs in Lent, itself or else its vigil frequently coincides with one of the three Ember days: and then with exceeding urgency, by the prick of fear alike and the pleadings of charity, is pressed home on each faithful soul the bounden duty laid upon us all of interceding for those whose special office it is to intercede for us.[95] The uplifted hands of Moses, and of Moses only, prevailed against Amalek; yet were they sustained by Aaron and Hur: which of us can be like Moses? Yea, rather, which one of us may not become like those his brethren?

Let whoso loves God's harvest-field pray Him to send forth into it labourers: to make them many and faithful, to sustain them through the burden and heat of the day, to give them hire of souls with joy in the day of account; supplying efficacy to the sacraments they administer, accepting the prayers they offer up, abiding with them in loneliness, walking with them in the furnace of persecution, covering their eyes and stopping their ears whilst they journey through this world of vanity and iniquity, guiding them with counsel, and after that receiving them with glory.

Who then is sufficient for these things? Christ, in His feeblest minister; apart from Christ, neither giant nor archangel. With His call He is ready to bestow strength superhuman, grace supernatural; without His call Paul had been impotent to plant, Apollos to water. His call implies promise of illumination, shelter as of the apple of an eye, a crown which no man shall snatch away: nevertheless it implies not a blessing by constraint, or sanctification by main force. It behoves us of the flock to pray for our pastors, and that surely not by constraint but willingly if we bear in mind their labour of love for us. For our sake they are posted in perilous places, occupying the forefront of the battle; whilst day by day they school themselves to love every soul beloved of Christ, to follow in His footsteps doing good and seeking the lost; to exercise exhaustless patience with ingenuity of winningness, to rebuke with the terrors of God, to console with His all-surpassing comfort, propping stumblers, goading laggards, awakening sleepers, signalling wanderers, leading the swift, accompanying the slow, making themselves all things to all men if by any means they may save some. Yet these who need endowments of seraphim, of cherubim, of all saints, yet these are but men, still in the flesh, still fallible: whilst of such men, fleshly and fallible, one was St. Matthias but another was Judas Iscariot. Therefore let us pray for them. Even St. Paul wrote:—

Brethren, pray for us.—1 Thess. 5.25.

Lord, teach us to pray.—St. Luke 11.1.

As with other Saints' Days the fast of this vigil leads us up to our feast of Commemoration; yet under its double aspect of bliss and woe this one Feast itself appears as the appropriate vigil of a twofold everlasting future, as a landmark where two roads separate, as a touchstone discriminating gold from dross, as a stand-point betwixt heaven and hell.

I call heaven and earth to record this day against you, that I have set before you life and death, blessing and cursing: therefore choose life.—Deut. 30.19.

A Prayer for Holy Fear.

O God of bounty, in the good pleasure of Whose Will all saints rejoice and rest;—Who passing by Joseph, didst choose St. Matthias and bless him in the forfeited apostleship and ministry of Judas; enriching him with gifts, beautifying him with graces, prospering his labours, enduing with power his words, setting his face as a flint against his adversaries; until the measure of their offence being full and his cup of suffering also full, Thou didst call him out of exile home, from death to life, from earth to heaven: grant us, I beseech Thee, holy fear, that having glorified Thee for the beatitude of St. Matthias, we may not forget Judas, but may tremble while we acknowledge Thy good gifts to us unworthy; lest any of us should out-sin Thy grace, and at the last our habitation should be desolate, and we superseded in our office, and our royal estate should be given to others that are better than we. From which ruin deliver us, for our Lord Jesus Christ's sake Who died in our stead. Amen.

HEPATICAS.
Acquiescence in change.

Cheering the late winter or early spring Hepaticas put forth single blossoms, white, or blue, or red, these last doubling under cultivation. Attractive little plants they are, rearing lowly heads in our bleak garden plats; the flower small yet conspicuous, the prettily outlined leaves grouped in clumps and of a green more dark than bright. Hepaticas favour a light soil, and love to meet the morning sun rather than to endure a more continuously sunny exposure. They do not well bear moving, or at the least they bear it not always with indifference: an instance is quoted of one changing from blue to white when transplanted, whilst on returning to its former soil the enduring plant resumed its original tint. Humble in height, the Hepatica may be termed patient in habit; for during one whole year the blossom, perfect in all its parts, lurks hidden within the bud.

This plant belongs to the family of Anemones or Wind-flowers; and, as a wind-flower, seems all the more congruous with St. Matthias; for our saint was no Apostle, neither at first was a throne prepared for him in the Sacred College; when, the lot having already fallen on him, "suddenly there came a sound from heaven as of a rushing mighty wind," that wind which "bloweth where it listeth," and on him as on the rest the Fiery Tongue of consecrating power lighted and sat.[96]

Kindly as the Hepatica thrives amongst us, it yet is no native of England, but comes to us from Switzerland. Thus if Hepaticas prefer repose, they yet submit to transference, blooming cheerfully in their allotted sphere.

Be careful for nothing.—Phil. 4.6.

From *"St. Mark, Evangelist."*
25 April
THE FIRST LIVING CREATURE.
A Lion.

In the midst of the throne, and round about the throne, were four beasts full of eyes before and behind. And the first beast was like a lion. And the four beasts had each of them six wings about him; and they were full of eyes within: and they rest not day and night, saying, Holy, holy, holy, Lord God Almighty, Which was, and is, and is to come.—Rev. 4.6,&c.

It is not by universal consent that the Lion is awarded to St. Mark for his evangelical symbol. The arrangement I am venturing to reproduce has been called in question, and much has been brought forward in favour of an order which appropriates the Lion to St. Matthew, whilst the Angel or Man to St. Mark. Thus assigned, the Lion, held to have been the standard of the royal tribe of Judah, falls to that very Evangelist who alone celebrates the homage of the wise men to the Infant King of the Jews, with the consequent jealousy of king Herod; who stands alone in using, and that three times over, the phrase "the (or this) Gospel of the kingdom;" and who in recording our Lord's prophecy of the last judgment perpetuates to us the words, "Then shall the King say unto them on His right hand."[97] Whilst in St. Mark's Gospel careful and loving study has thought to recognise an even exceptional prominence given to Christ's very and perfect Humanity, a prominence not limited to one text, but pervading the inspired narrative.

On the other hand, even a very slight amount of observation suffices to note that St. Matthew is one of the two Evangelists (the second being not St. Mark but St. Luke) who gives the table of our Lord's genealogy; St. Matthew being that one who stops at Abraham the human father of a human race; St. Luke, on the contrary, tracing back the sonship of our Lord through Adam to God Himself. With St. Luke no less, but with St. Luke only, St. Matthew shares and transmits to us the precious treasure of all we are taught concerning our blessed Saviour's veritable infancy, childhood, and early family life. While if we observe less prominent traces of Jewish royalty in St. Mark's narrative, this Evangelist stands alone in suggesting that inherent kingship over the lower animated creation, which the first Adam partly forfeited and the Second resumed: "He was there in the wilderness forty days, tempted of Satan; and was with the wild beasts."—St. Mark 1.13.

After all I do not claim to follow the more convincing line of argument, but merely perhaps the more popular impression, when I leave St. Mark in possession of his Lion. That application of the "desert voice" with which I venture to follow up the text of the ensuing little article, is one which I have met with in print.

The lion hath roared, who will not fear?—Amos 3.8.

The lion's dwelling-place is chiefly the open plain with its coverts, or the pathless desert: and thus he symbolizes that Evangelist the first verses of whose Gospel resound with "The voice of one crying in the wilderness."[98] While even as St. John Baptist gleaned sustenance from the desert products; so the lion, should water be lacking to slake his thirst, recognises and avails himself of it in the juicy substance of the water-melon, at first sight no food for him.

The Lion is our type of strength and dignity. His form is massive and stately, his colour prevalently tawny; in his neck, shoulders, and fore-limbs resides enormous strength; his sight (though not his scent, and least of all, apparently, his organ of taste) is consummately keen; his sensitiveness of touch is exquisite; the muscles of his forearm resemble the corresponding muscles in the human limb; his forehead contracts with a man-like frown. A voluminous mane accumulates mass and majesty upon his mighty presence, and rises erect with his rising wrath; his eyes beneath overhanging brows glow and flame on his prey; his tufted tail lashes his sides. By the impetus of his tremendous leap he is described as dragging down the largest elephant: yet will the buffalo frequently vanquish and sometimes gore him. His vigour is such that he can carry off prey even heavier than himself; the smaller kinds being generally flung across his shoulders. His feeding-times are chiefly at dawn and twilight; his favourite repast is chosen amongst the ruminants or some allied groups; he prowls all night, and bearing off the prey to his lair there consumes it at leisure. But if pressed by hunger he regards neither time, nor place, nor species, in seizing his quarry; though even in slaughter some allege that he obeys a law of moderation: the one victim his hunger demands, he rends and devours; the remainder of the herd go free.

The Lioness though strong is weaker than her mate, and she lacks that mane which clothes him with so special a grandeur. She brings forth from two to four cubs at a birth: and being herself an excellent nurse, is sometimes assisted in her mother-work by the Lion. Like far more familiar specimens of the same family, these mighty creatures purr in their moments of pleasure. Their cubs are born open-eyed but helpless; destitute of mane, and of tuft to the tail: after a while they become very playful. They are moreover brindled,[99] as if they would turn out tigers rather than Lions: but as they grow up this brindling vanishes, and their coat subsides into tawniness.

Amongst that group of beasts to which the Lion belongs, a group distinguished by eminent examples of speed, fierceness, grace, beauty,—amongst these, the Lion has been judged to excel in generosity, patience, grateful memory of kindness, and affection to benefactors.

There be three things which go well, yea, four are comely in going: a lion which is strongest among beasts, and turneth not away for any.—Prov. 30.29,30.

Behold, the Lion of the tribe of Juda, the Root of David, hath prevailed to open the book, and to loose the seven seals thereof.—Rev. 5.

Behold, the people shall rise up as a great lion, and lift up himself as a young lion: he shall not lie down until he eat of the prey, and drink the blood of the slain.—Num. 23.24.

From *"St. Barnabas, Apostle."*
11 June
A Prayer for Goodwill of Love.

O God of Patience and Consolation, by Whose gracious indwelling St. Barnabas became to the Church his Mother a Son of Consolation;—who having land sold it for the profit of his brethren, having insight bore witness to the sincerity of St. Paul, having knowledge preached the Gospel, having gifts used them to the glory of Christ in the edification of souls;—who being a good man full of the Holy Ghost and of faith was glad when he saw the grace of God, and being St. Paul's elder in the truth occupied the second place in serving with him, and being himself a luminary withdrew not from the other's exceeding effulgence, and who thus hath left a shining light for our guidance, even his own example for our imitation:—Give us such good will, I beseech Thee, O God All-gracious, that with free hearts we too may love and serve Thee and our brethren; Thy grace in us stirring up and not neglecting, Thy gifts to us using and not abusing, Thine appointment rejoicing in without grudging, Thy choice making our choice and Thy pleasure our pleasure; that with one voice, great and small in unison, we may praise Thee for all our higher and all our lower vocations, and having thus the mind of Christ may begin Heaven on earth, and exercise ourselves therein till that day when Heaven where love abideth shall seem no strange habitation to us. For His only sake Who for our sakes made Himself of no reputation, our Lord Jesus Christ. Amen.

HONEYSUCKLE.
Lavish sweetness.

Honeysuckle is a name of sweetness, and stands for a flower of exuberant sweetness. Its many-headed blossom groups together a number of actual honey-cups: these being elongated and narrow, it happens that sometimes a bulky bee cannot reach their store, and then other insects will puncture the tube towards its base and draw off and feast on the juice within. Delicious fragrance breathes from this plant, making sweet the noontides of its bloom and embalming the evenings after rain. Choice beauties grace it: nothing of gorgeousness or strong contrast, but tender tints of pink and straw yellow, with white for a scentless variety. Its flowers are elegant, and by combination rich: the blossom-tubes spring from a common circular base, and broaden into a fair head curving freely, light of structure and feathered with stamens. The bloom is succeeded by crowded clusters of red berries, which, harbouring no poison, afford food to birds. In size the berries differ conspicuously: sometimes one in a cluster will wax as large as a currant, its neighbours balancing such excess by their own comparative smallness.

The Honeysuckle is also called by the name of Woodbine, supposed to be derived from wood-bind; and aptly it is so designated: for while it enjoys only scant strength of its own, it spreads afar along supporting hedgerows, and mounts aloft by twining around trees, linking branch to branch and weaving isolated stems into bowers. So truly is to embrace one of its characteristic features, that its own leaf sometimes encircles the stalk from which it springs; till we cannot decide whether to clasp or to store honey be its chief gift.

What is sweeter than honey?—Judges 14.18.

From *"St. John, Baptist."*
24 June
A Prayer for Conformity to God's Will.

O God, Whose Presence is the Holy of Holies: by Whose Will, at Whose Word, made like unto the trump of the Archangel, the Voice sounded; denouncing sinners, preaching repentance and righteousness, proclaiming the Kingdom of Heaven already at men's doors, proclaiming the King standing in their midst, and the axe laid unto the root of the trees; Thine be the glory, O our God, as Thine are the gifts of this Thy Saint: for by the fiat of Thy Will St. John Baptist, prophesied of from old time, was born beyond the probability of nature, grew up in holy seclusion, lived in austere penitence, directed others to Christ, yet himself abode far off in patient obedience: Grant us, we pray Thee, after his pattern to obey Thy commandment whereunto soever Thou mayest call us; to accept what Thou bestowest, to forego what thou deniest: and thus labouring and enduring unto the end, after the weariness and painfulness of this mortal life are fulfilled, to go home as the Baptist hath gone home from promise to possession, from longing to love, from sympathy of friendship to intimacy of union, from interval of space to oneness with Jesus.

Even so on our better birthday, from prison and bondage of corruption set us also free, for Thine only Son's sake, the same our Lord Jesus. Amen.

From *"St. Matthew, Apostle and Evangelist."*
21 September
A Prayer for Use of Talents.

O God, Whose excelling glory overflowing upon the works of Thy hands invests with glory princes celestial and princes terrestrial, Angels, Apostles and Evangelists;—Who from filthy lucre didst call Matthew Thy willing Saint to a heavenly treasure, from an evil name to everlasting renown, from scorn of Israel that is in bondage to honour amongst Israelites that are free;—Who moving him by the Holy Ghost, endowedst him with the pen of a ready writer, committing unto him as unto a nursing father the Gospel of salvation, that he might feed therewith Thine infant Church and set before her things new and old:—O God, the God of the least and of the greatest, Thou Who entrustest talents unto men demanding from them increase of substance and return of thanks, grant unto each one of us so to serve Thee, that with earthly pounds we may buy of Thee gold tried in the fire, and with human faculties seek Thee where Thou mayest be found; spending, labouring, influencing others, as those who must give account not of their own souls only, but of their brother's also. And who is sufficient for these things? Of Thee, O Father, be our sufficiency, for Thy Son our Lord Jesus Christ's sake. Amen.

From *"All Saints."*
1 November
The Arbutus and Grass.
Great and small.

Even in small matters the end implies a certain solemnity; the last opportunity to be utilized or missed, the last occasion of gain or loss. Often as I have let slip what cannot be regained, two points of my own experience stand out vividly: once, when little realizing how nearly I had despised my last chance, I yet did in bare time do what must shortly have been for ever left undone; and again, when I fulfilled a promise which beyond calculation there remained but scant leisure to fulfil.

Our last Apostles might, I thought, suitably commend to us fruit rather than flowers. Our last and widest Saints' Day, embracing height and depth, honour and humility, shall put on for its garland that which is lofty entwined with that which is very lowly.

Puny in a forest, yet in a shrubbery of grand and stately presence, the Arbutus or Strawberry Tree wears all at one time the panoply of its beauties; combining the blossom of a late flowering season, with ripened fruit from the preceding autumn, and with dark rich foliage in profusion. Its so-called strawberry sprouts rather after the manner of a cherry; but a red and roughened surface invites for it the former name: like its namesake it is edible, though of a far less delicious flavour. The blossom hangs in bunches, and is of a waxen semblance, white, greenish, or pink: each individual floweret approaches certain heath blossoms in size and shape, being rounded and lipped like a minute bottle. Nor do even leaves, flowers, and fruit exhaust the simultaneous graces of the Arbutus: the tree itself branches boldly and nobly, and by a general darkness throws out the fairness of its efflorescence.

At the foot of the Arbutus and of the plant-world in general, trodden at all seasons by all feet, live and thrive the Grasses; stripped of which, earth would lack half her refreshing charm. At the tropics they often match trees in stature; in arctic regions they maintain their ground with no less persistent vitality. They compose a numerous tribe, numbered by hundreds and frequenting every latitude. Most precious of all their charms to us seems their inexhaustible verdure, parched indeed by summer drought but renewed by a shower of rain: sun they need, and air, and moisture; these given, they clothe the ground with a living carpet which snow cannot nip or tempest destroy, yet which a breeze can break up into a sea of ripples, and of which each component blade is straight-veined pointing skywards. In its modest flowering season, however, when the pointed stalk shoots up to a slim tallness and prepares to shed its harvest of seed, then Grass rallies not under trampling foot or stress of weather but is laid low by the assault of even a slight pressure.

The beauty of Grasses whether in blossom or in seed is widely varied, and in some instances truly exquisite. One like miniature barley grows a beard, another showers a weeping oat-like head, another droops a thick rose-tinted plume; one is invested with purple knops,[100] a second feathers greenly, a third displays prevalent whiteness; the leaf of a fourth hangs like a striped ribbon; and yet another, sweetened by an enduring scent, turns a hayrick into a nosegay.

All these and many more we include under the common name of Grass: but other specimens there are of more honourable standing and of yet higher service in our economy, which belong to the same tribe, and being analyzed reveal some of the same constituents. Grasses contain sugar, and the sugar-cane claims kindred with them: they are stiffened by flint, and flint imparts stiffness to the cereal straws. Rice and rye belong to the Grass connection; barley and oats recognise not mere likenesses among the Grasses, but humble kinsfolk: the very "corn of wheat" is itself the most noble member of the common family.

From the Grasses no less than from the heavenly host, from mankind at large, even from Apostles, we gather one same reiterated lesson: Angels share one nature with devils, sanctified souls with souls nigh unto cursing, St. Matthias with Judas Iscariot, the very staff of our life with the noxious darnel.[101] And thus the perfections of our Very God's very Humanity urge us to fear and hope: though we are of one blood with Him we may not be of one mind, may never become like Him, may never see Him as He is; on the other hand (blessed be God), though we languish ready to perish, yet is He our Brother Who loveth us, Who can be touched with the feeling of our infirmities, and is able to save them to the uttermost that come unto God by Him.

I will cause the shower to come down in his season; there shall be showers of blessing. And the tree of the field shall yield her fruit, and the earth shall yield her increase.—Ezek. 34.26,27.

Light is our sorrow for it ends to-morrow,
    Light is our death which cannot hold us fast;
So brief a sorrow can be scarcely sorrow,
      Or death be death so quickly past.

One night, no more, of pain that turns to pleasure,
    One night, no more, of weeping weeping sore;
And then the heaped-up measure beyond measure,
      In quietness for evermore.

Our face is set like flint against our trouble,
    Yet many things there are which comfort us,
This bubble is a rainbow-coloured bubble,
      This bubble-life tumultuous.

Our sails are set to cross the tossing river,
    Our face is set to reach Jerusalem;
We toil awhile, but then we rest for ever,
      Sing with all Saints and rest with them.

From *Letter and Spirit:*
Notes on the Commandments (1883)

*L*etter and Spirit: Notes on the Commandments was completed during the autumn of 1882 and the winter of 1883 and published in the late spring of 1883 (Marsh, 503). There is little mention of the volume in letters of this time as yet published, preoccupied as they are with the aftermath of the deaths of Dante Gabriel Rossetti and Charles Cayley. G. A. Simcox in *The Academy* (23 [9 June 1883]) praised the book's "simple and ingenious" (395) organizational scheme, a harmony of the Decalogue with Christ's two "great" commandments. However, while noting Rossetti's wit, he also remarked upon her sometimes "caustic shrewdness" and the "severity" of some judgments while disagreeing with some of her typologizing (396). Certainly she was pragmatically concerned with interpreting the meaning of the biblical commandments for her contemporaries, especially women. She examines what constitutes breaches of duty (whether filial, domestic, or marital), characterizes a series of transgressive types of sin (idleness, envy, anger, and so on), meditates on the meaning of the Fall, idolatry, and language use, and cites biblical models in describing feminine ideals of virgin and wife. As Mackenzie Bell early observed, *Letter and Spirit* often approaches "theological disquisition" (337).

There is a fair manuscript of this work in the author's hand, deposited in the Humanities Research Center, the University of Texas at Austin, but like the autograph manuscript of *Treasure-Trove* (that is, *Seek and Find*), it seems to be earlier than the printed text, with many verbal differences. The printed version frequently omits words and phrases of the manuscript, or otherwise revises passages, generally it would seem for the sake of greater clarity or economy of expression.

Yet this manuscript of *Letter and Spirit*, unlike that of *Seek and Find*, shows no sign of being compared with the final text, and one may suppose that it represents an earlier draft. The punctuation of the text appears also to have been carefully corrected; it is much heavier than in the manuscript, possibly suggesting the author's later additions. We have decided to follow the first printed edition in all respects, but give in the notes substantive variants of the manuscript. The punctuation is also that of the printed text, except where noted, with the exception of scriptural references, which we have normalized by giving standard abbreviations and arabic numerals throughout. Rossetti cites illustrative passages of Scripture with great frequency, but we have omitted most of these references. We have used the copy of the 1883 text in the University of British Columbia Library.

Letter and Spirit: Notes on the Commandments

"Hear, O Israel; The Lord our God is One Lord: and thou shalt love the Lord thy God with all thy heart, and with all thy soul, and with all thy mind, and with all thy strength."

This First, "the Great," Commandment is characterised by unity. Whatever else we find in it, this is one of its essential features, if not its leading feature. And, in fact, within this unity is bound up the entire multitude of our duties; out of this one supreme commandment have to be developed all the details of every one of our unnumbered obligations.

"Hear, O Israel; The Lord our God is One Lord." While "the Christian verity" declares to us the Mystery of the All-Holy Trinity, "the Catholic religion" asserts the inviolable Unity of the Godhead [Athanasian Creed]. And touching these two Mysteries, it seems that to grasp, hold fast, adore the Catholic Mystery leads up to man's obligation to grasp, hold fast, adore the Christian Mystery; rather than this to the other.[102] What is Catholic underlies what is Christian: on the Catholic basis alone can the Christian structure be raised; even while to raise that superstructure on that foundation is the bounden duty of every soul within reach of the full Divine Revelation.[103] In God's inscrutable Providence it has pleased Him that millions of the human race should live in unavoidable ignorance of Christian doctrine: to that fundamental doctrine of God's Unity, from which the other is developed, He has graciously vouchsafed a freer currency; so that while the Jewish Church knew it by revelation, multitudes of the Gentile world knew or at least surmised it by intellectual or spiritual enlightenment. Let us thank God that this main point of knowledge we hold in common with so vast a number of our dear human brothers and sisters, children along with ourselves of the all-loving Father;[104] let us thank Him through Jesus Christ that we Christians are instructed how thus acceptably to thank Him; let us beseech Him in that all-prevailing Name to add to each of us, whatsoever we be, every lacking gift and grace.

Whilst Unity appears the sole existence essential to be conceived, our conceiving it as separate from ourself attests[105] at once our likeness and our unlikeness to it. That which we conceive is on our own showing other than[106] ourselves who conceive it: yet to[107] conceive that which has no existence is (I reverently assume) the exclusive attribute of Almighty God, Who out of nothing created all things. To modify by a boundless licence[108] of imagination the Voice of Revelation, or of tradition, or our own perceptions, concerning the universe, its Ruler, inhabitants, features, origin, destinies, falls within the range of human faculties. And thus may not light be thrown on that mass of bewildering error (whose name is legion) which at every turn meeting us as man's invention, is after all a more or less close travestie of truth? So like in detail, so unlike as a whole, to the truth it simulates, that alternately we incline to ask: If so much is known without immediate revelation, wherefore reveal? If truth pervades such errors, if such errors can be grafted upon truth, is truth itself distinguishable, or is it worth distinguishing?

At first sight and apparently the easiest of all conceptions to realise, I yet suppose that there may in the long run be no conception more difficult for ourselves to clench and retain than this of absolute Unity; this Oneness at all times, in all connexions, for all purposes. Even if we consider Attributes, they seem to clash: while if we ascend to contemplate the Trinity in Unity, Three Persons, One God, immediately we must confer not with flesh and blood, but walk by faith in lieu of sight. Opposite errors invite us; and well will it be for us if trembling between them our magnet yet points aright: if while not tampering with the Unity, and while fully persuaded that the Father, the Son, and the Holy Ghost are Three distinct Persons in the One Only Godhead, we yet set Them not practically one against another, producing in our vain imaginations a "Trinity in dis-Unity."[109]

Nor is it possible that either error should, so to say, lie fallow: each cannot but bear its legitimate poison-crop. But for the Ever Blessed Trinity man might seem to stand aloof from the sympathy of his Maker: absolute Oneness may, but could *exclusive* Oneness have any fellow-feeling with such as we are? an ever-renewed multitude who stray like sheep and need a shepherd, who die away like foliage and need renewal, who from evening to morning are made an end of yet not done with. On the other hand, to view in fact even if not avowedly the Three Persons as Three Gods leads towards arraying them in opposition to each other: till we feel towards the Divine

Son as if He alone was our Friend, the Divine Father being our foe; as if Christ had not only to rescue us from the righteous wrath of His Father, but to shelter us from His enmity.

A self-surrendering awe-struck reverence is all that beseems us in contemplating this Mystery of Mysteries, the Trinity in Unity. Yet, perhaps, we may not unlawfully ponder whether, could the Divine Unity have existed as (so to say) an unmodified Oneness, whether such a God would (I say not could) have created this multitudinous ever-multiplying creation. For if (as I have seen[110] pointed out) God is not to be called like His creature, whose grace is simply typical, but that creature is like Him because expressive of His archetypal Attribute, it suggests itself that for every aspect of creation[111] there must exist the corresponding Divine Archetype.[112]

Nor surely is it without a practical aim that we seek (not to explain, but) to define to ourselves that only Lord God in Whom we believe. "The Lord our God is one Lord:" and every ignorance which has its origin in our own sins or negligences becomes itself a sin against Him Who has declared Himself to be "a Jealous God," One Who will not give His glory to another (Isa. 43.8); One Whom we Christians are privileged, and are therefore bound, to know and to adore as He is and by no means as He is not.

And even as our God is One, so does He summon us to become one in His service. The powers and passions of our complex nature must be concentrated in one only love of Him alone: His many gifts to us must be returned to Him in one self-exhaustive gift of all we are and all we have.

To the Jewish Church the Commandments were, in point of time, first[113] Ten (Exod. 20.1–17), subsequently Two (Deut. 6.4,5; Lev. 19.18): if, that is, we may adhere to the order in which they appear registered in the Pentateuch.[114] To the Christian Church they are, in virtue of our Lord's authoritative summary, first Two; from which Two "all the Law" has to be developed (St. Matt. 22.34–40). The Law therefore appears under the similitude of a numerous offspring of the Two united and indivisible Commandments; which two, while of equal obligation,[115] are nevertheless of unequal dignity; the First is the head, source, root; the Second, made after its likeness, derives from it authority and honour. Even could the Second be abolished, the First would remain: yet to fulfil that Second is man's only mode of making sure that he observes the First, nor can these two which God has joined together be put practically asunder. "We love Him, because He first loved us. If a man say, I love God, and hateth his brother, he is a liar: for he that loveth not his brother whom he hath seen, how can he love God Whom he hath not seen? And this commandment have we from Him, That he who loveth God love his brother also" (1 St. John 4.19–21).

The First Great Commandment, including that Second, which is its like, necessarily includes the entire Decalogue: while of the Decalogue the first four Commandments, being traceable to the First but not to the Second, become characteristically *the* substance of that First Commandment.

And being four in number, these commandments naturally range themselves (though not in exactly corresponding order) under those four powers of man (heart, soul, mind, strength),[116] which are summoned to fulfil the Great Commandment. God claims our whole selves, all we are, all we have, all we may become; and doubtless the all-important feature of the Great Commandment is that we must keep back nothing: still, it may in fact help us to keep back nothing if, so to say, we sift and sort our resources; and offer not simply *all* as a whole, but *each* one by one.[117]

Yet before we descend to classification, it is necessary to make sure that we do without evasion or abatement offer all and keep back nothing. A Jew, quoting the letter of the Decalogue, might plead that the point of his First Commandment was to "have none other gods but" the One true God. Not so a Christian, nourished "by every word that proceedeth out of the mouth of God."[118] To him—to us, the point of our First Commandment is that all we are, and all we have, must be not merely withheld from false gods, but devoted to the true God.

Of this, as of all its dependent excellences, we find but one perfect example, our Lord Jesus Christ. Of its contrary we find specimens on every hand and in endless variety.

Adam and Eve illustrate two sorts of defection (1 Tim. 2.14). Eve made a mistake, "being *deceived*" she was in the transgression: Adam made no mistake: his was an error of will, hers partly of judgment; nevertheless both proved fatal. Eve, equally with Adam, was created sinless: each had a specially vulnerable point, but this apparently not the same point. It is in no degree at variance with the Sacred Record to picture to ourselves Eve, that first and typical woman, as indulging quite innocently sundry refined tastes and aspirations, a castle-building spirit[119] (if so it may be called), a feminine boldness and directness of aim combined with a no less feminine guessiness as to means. Her very virtues may have opened the door to temptation. By birthright gracious and accessible, she lends an ear to all petitions from all petitioners. She desires to instruct ignorance, to rectify misapprehension: "unto the pure all things are pure," and she never suspects even the serpent. Possibly a trace of blameless infirmity transpires in the wording of her answer, "*lest* ye die," for God had said to the man " . . . in the day that thou eatest thereof thou *shalt surely* die:" but such tenderness of spirit seems even lovely in the great first mother of mankind; or it may be that Adam had modified the form, if it devolved on him to declare the tremendous fact to his second self. Adam and Eve reached their goal,[120] the Fall, by different routes. With Eve the serpent discussed a question of conduct, and talked her over to his own side: with Adam, so far as appears, he might have argued the point for ever and gained no vantage; but already he had secured an ally weightier than a score of arguments. Eve may not have argued[121] at all: she offered[122] Adam a share of her own good fortune, and having hold of her husband's heart, turned it in her hand as the rivers of water. Eve preferred various prospects to God's Will: Adam seems to have[123] preferred one person to God: Eve diverted her "mind" and Adam his "heart" from God Almighty. Both courses led to one common result, that is, to one common ruin (Gen. 3).

Whatever else may be deduced from the opening chapters of Genesis, their injunction[124] of obedience is plainly written; of unqualified obedience, of obedience on pain of death.

To do anything whatsoever, even to serve God, "with all the strength," brings us into continual collision with that modern civilized standard of good breeding and good taste which bids us avoid extremes. Such modern standard may be regarded as having by ancient anticipation brought King Saul into collision with the Prophet Samuel in the matter of Amalek and especially of Agag (1 Sam. 15.1–33).

———

If we may accept Adam, Eve, Saul, as illustrating defective heart, mind, strength, in loyalty to Almighty God, we seem still in search of a representative of defective "soul." But here reaching (so to say) the very throne of man's free-will service, the noblest element of his noble nature, we observe how soul-defection being the root of every defection, and in itself including all defection, expresses itself in each breach of any commandment, be that breach one of commission or of omission, yet is not itself to be expressed in any separate form: it prompts, it pervades, it incurs the guilt of every transgression; nevertheless to us creatures of sense it becomes perceptible not otherwise than through effects wrought by means of agents,—as indeed, as regards our own faculties, is the case with all causes, even with our God Himself.

———

The exceeding difficulty of laying a finger (so to say) on any distinct breach specially of the First Commandment sends us perforce to sift motives, gauge tendencies, test not conduct directly, but the standard which regulates conduct. Even virtues must be mistrusted; their root as well as their shoot must be examined, while nothing short of that mature fruit, whereby alone they "cheer God and man," can pass muster as of final account. The First Commandment, being itself framed upon a negative, invites us to study negatives in our search after all perfection. Of these one may perhaps serve as a specimen of its class, as a clue whereby each of us for himself can track home others.

DISINCLINATION may never go such lengths as to make us purposely omit a single duty, yet may it colour and dwarf our whole conception of duty. Far from breaking the box with Mary, we eke out our spikenard, and, unlike the Apostles, are more intent on rescuing the last fragments than on spreading the feast. All sorts of prudent precautions occur to us in studying Holy Scripture, and these land us occasionally in very eccentric latitudes; at least, so would persons say who merely look to the landmarks vouchsafed for our guidance. Sometimes our comment appears about as compatible with the text, as was that child's who pointed out the "niceness" of St. John Baptist's wild honey. Thus meditation on the Magi (St. Matt. 2.1–12) leads us not to any tangible offering,[125] but to the still higher truth that,

> "Richer by far is the heart's adoration,
> Dearer to God are the prayers of the poor:"

a truth adapted to the devoted missionary bishop who penned the lines, but not so obviously to the run of men.[126] Our study of Martha and Mary (St. Luke 10.38–42) assures us that the former was not wrong[127] in the main, the latter setting an example to be followed cautiously because (we flatter ourselves)[128] not applicable to all persons. Who has not seen the incident of the Young Ruler (St. Mark 10.17–27) utilized as a check to extravagant zeal? so far, that is, as a preliminary stress laid on what it does *not* enjoin can make it act as a sedative. It does not, we are assured, by any means require us to sell all; differences of rank, of position, of circumstances, are Providentially ordained, and are not lightly to be set aside; our duties lie within the decorous bounds of our station. The Young Ruler, indeed, was invited to sell all in spite of his great possessions; therefore we must never suppose it impossible that that vague personage, "our neighbour," may be called upon to do so; we must not judge him in such a case, nay, we must view it not as his penalty but rather as his privilege: only[129] we ourselves, who are bound by simple every-day duties, shall do well in all simplicity to perform them soberly, cheerfully, thankfully, not overstepping the limits of our vocation: wherefore let us give what we can afford; a pleasure or a luxury it may be well to sacrifice at the call of charity.

Yet is a caution against "righteousness overmuch" the gist of our Master's lesson? His recorded comment on the incident was "How hardly shall they that have riches enter into the kingdom of God!" which He goes on to explain as they "that *trust* in riches."[130] Is our most urgent temptation that which inclines us to do too much, or that which lulls us to do too little, or to do nothing? Is it so, that the bulk of professing Christians are likely to be dazzled by the splendid error of excessive "corban,"[131] and fairly to consume themselves by zeal? or are they not more likely so sedulously to count the cost as never to undertake building? It may be worst of all to put hand to plough and then look back: nevertheless it is no light evil so to gaze backwards as never to grasp the plough. When we detect ourselves calculating how little will clear us from breach of any commandment, and paring down our intention accordingly, we shall (I think) have grounds for searching deeper, lest already we be breaking the First Commandment.[132]

Conscientious, and more especially scrupulous, persons seem characteristically open to this sin of Disinclination, even while they toil persistently along the narrow path; Disinclination makes them (so to say) graze the hedge on one side or other at every step; thorns catch them, stones half trip them up, a perpetual dust attends their footsteps, grace and comeliness of aspect vanish. Though they dare not shut themselves up comfortably indoors with the slothful man (Prov. 22.13), they are haunted by the "lion without," and dwell on the probability of his catching them at every corner. They observe the wind even while they sow, and study the clouds while they reap; thus combining into one unseemly whole the discomforts of obedience and of disobedience.

The Bible records for our encouragement instances of persons who needed to overcome themselves in the first place: that done, their circumstances turned out favourable. Gideon had recourse to an offered omen before unsheathing the victorious "sword of the Lord, and of Gideon" (Judges 7.9–25). Nehemiah nerved himself by prayer before risking a manifestation of sorrow in the King's presence, and thereby moving him to acts of grace (Neh. 1.3–11, 2.1–8). Esther, trembling amid her fellow exiles, solemnized a three days' national fast before she faced her husband and won him to her will (Esther 4.8–17, 5.1–3).

When all due weight has been conceded to secondary motives, the paramount motive for what we do or leave undone—if, that is, we aim at either acting or forbearing worthily—is love: not fear, or self-interest, or even hatred of sin, or sense of duty, but direct filial love to God. Without this, they who shout for the battle and go forth one way will, in the end, flee five ways. Let us trace a parable in the adventure of a shepherd lost in a valley mist. No effort of his could beat that mist away: but by mounting a hill he rose above it, and discerned his path home. Our hill is communion with God. "Blessed be the God and Father of our Lord Jesus Christ, Who hath blessed us with all spiritual blessings in heavenly places in Christ. . . . And hath raised us up together, and made us sit together in heavenly places in Christ Jesus" (Eph. 1.3, 2.6).[133]

Whilst all men so far represent God to us that to wrong them is to wrong Him, and to serve them is to serve Him; certain individuals in an exceptional sense and degree, either in person or by office, sometimes under both aspects, do beyond others represent Him to each of us, not as His substitutes, but as governors appointed of the Father, as powers ordained of God, which whoso resisteth resisteth the ordinance of God.

First of all, father and mother, to be held equally sacred, equally dear; who spend and are spent for their children before these can so much as love them in return. Their love outruns the letter of any law, except indeed it be the law of the Divine example. Under the Mosaic Dispensation a son's obstinate disobedience was punishable by death at his parents' demand (Deut. 21.18–21), but no instance of such a demand is recorded in the Bible; Eli remonstrated with Hophni and Phinehas, but—alas for him and for them!—seems to have done nothing more stringent (1 Sam. 2.22–25); David interceded with his captains, and this failing half broke his heart for Absalom (2 Sam. 18. 5,32,33, 19.1–4). And it may be that Rebekah's sin, when she commanded and contrived Jacob's imposture, had no more envenomed root than an unscrupulous fondness and headstrong preference for him whom to her certain knowledge God was pleased to prefer; however this may have been, she later on paid the penalty of her error, not living to welcome her darling back from the prolonged exile into which her tardy fears had sent him (Gen. 25.21–23, 27.6–17, 41–46).

Of filial duties the earliest in date is towards father and mother. Second in date, yet not secondary in dignity, devolves upon us the duty of obedience to spiritual superiors. And at the outset one contrast between the twain is noticeable. For a while the infant abides apparently incapable of fulfilling any obligations more abstruse than those to literal father and mother; his love and obedience towards them, his confidence and delight in them, are (if no more lies within his power) beyond a doubt adequate to fulfil the filial law incumbent upon him. His parents worthy of implicit obedience, love, honour, of small self-sacrifices and self-devotion, are the appointed recipients of such at his hands; we cannot tell whether he yet enjoys faculties to realize by means of them and beyond them any conception of the Supreme Father of all, though blessed words from Christ's most blessed lips open our eyes to such a hope: "Take heed that ye despise not one of these little ones; for I say unto you, That in heaven their angels do always behold the face of My Father which is in heaven" (St. Matt. 18.10).

On the contrary, the child must have entered (however dimly) into the awful knowledge of God Himself, before he can understand any special debt to spiritual pastors and masters and to Godparents. They are to him simple channels of God's Voice and Will: they have towards him no independent personality, but are ministers and mouthpieces. His natural parents are much more than this: from them secondarily but literally he derives being, inherits nature, assumes flesh: even were the Scriptural "fool" to prove his point (Ps. 14.1) filial piety would remain to us as the last holy trace of a vanished something holier even than itself. The rule applicable to the natural and the spiritual body, "first . . . that which is natural, afterward that which is spiritual" (1 Cor. 15.46), applies equally as regards humankind to the associated kingdoms of nature and of grace: grace has to be grafted upon, not substituted for, nature. Nevertheless, as a graft supersedes the original stock, so do we observe how that second step which enters into the spiritual world is an advance beyond and above that first step which introduces into the natural world: and thenceforward, our natural duties are discharged by conscious strength of grace, and by no means our spiritual duties by strength of nature. The ascending sequence ends, however, with the second step: along the advancing years the field of duty widens, and intellectual teachers, temporal rulers, superiors of all sorts and degrees, claim reverence and obedience: but not one of them stands on a level with "ministers of Christ, stewards of the mysteries of God," "ambassadors for Christ" (1 Cor. 4.1; 2 Cor. 5.20); or engages our heart with the intact sacredness of father and mother. A wife's paramount duty is indeed to her husband, superseding all other human obligations: yet to assume this duty, free-will has first stepped in with its liability to err; in this connexion woman has to reap as she has sown, be the crop what it may: while in the filial relation all is safe and flawless, for all is of Divine ordaining.

"To the law and to the testimony: if they speak not according to this word, it is because there is no light in them" (Isa. 8.20). Old fashioned it certainly is to search the Scriptures (*see* Acts 17.10–12) for our examples and warnings; but surely the dread of appearing old fashioned is one form of that Disinclination in which already we have thought to discern a breach of the First Commandment!

Never must we forget that the Inspired Word says not *duty* but "*Love* is the fulfilling of the law" (Rom. 13.10): as the First Commandment, so also can the Fifth be fulfilled only by love.[134]

Duty to parents includes duty to all men, because we all are brethren: and tracing back to an indisputably real, however remote and unknown, pair of common ancestors, our duty to them cannot be performed except by performing also our duty to their children and children's children for ever. At the outset of the race we clearly recognise such an obligation consequent upon such a tie: Cain's crime was not more obviously an outrage against Abel, whom he murdered, than against Adam and Eve, whose son he destroyed. Again, Joseph, whose filial affection withstood the encroachments of absence, exile, adversity, prosperity, was by that very affection bound hand and foot from taking vengeance on his brethren (Gen. 1.15–21). And by this process of tracking reciprocal duties back to a common fountain-head we perceive how the obligations of parents towards children, of all superiors to all inferiors, cannot but be included in the brief formula of the Fifth Commandment: something of which train of thought may perhaps be traced in Laban's noble valedictory charge to Jacob (Gen. 31.43–53).

If we ascend a step and trace second sources back to their first source, we behold the same truth built on a yet broader and more impregnable foundation. The Fifth Commandment is swallowed up in the First, for "God is greater than our heart;" and because One is our Father which is in heaven, therefore all we are brethren (*see* St. Matt. 23.8,9).

It is perhaps easier to quote from the Old Testament history than from the New, examples of relative duties fulfilled; and this not merely because of the copiousness of the former text as compared with the latter, but, possibly, from a deeper and dearer cause. Christ deigns to claim each obedient disciple as His own "brother and sister:" He therefore cannot be less than such to anyone of us who walk in His ways, and we become privileged to do to Himself what we do to even the least of His and our brethren. The two motives harmonize together and co-operate, yet one supersedes the other; as voices of praise and love soar beyond, and, as it were, silence the accompanying undertone of instruments: and saints are what they are primarily towards "Him Whom their soul loveth," secondarily towards one another; what they do towards men, they do "as to the Lord, and not unto men" (*see* Col. 3.23). Around that loveliest and closest relation to the Incarnate Son of God, bone of Whose Bone we are, and flesh of Whose Flesh, group themselves all close and lovely human relationships, casting down their crown before Him that was dead and is alive for evermore, and saying: "Not unto us, O Lord, not unto us, but unto Thy Name give glory."

———

Scriptural Husbands and Wives, many and various, invite our study. To begin with Adam and Eve; one is so accustomed to contemplate the Fall as well-nigh simultaneous in both, that perhaps the subsequent Christ-likeness of Adam, presumably in forgiving and cherishing, certainly in retaining, the wife who had cost him life and all things, may pass unnoticed. That Eve responded to his love and patience we need not doubt. Nor need we attempt to settle which (if either) committed the greater sin; Adam's faithful love (at the very lowest as a probable conjecture) remains in any case. Sarah (vouched for by an Apostle as our wifely model, 1 St. Peter 3.1–6) illustrates that blemishes must be looked for even in the excellent of the earth (Gen. 18.12–15, 20.16; perhaps also 16.6). Deborah startles us both by her official dignity and her personal prominence; for although she is defined as "wife of Lapidoth," after-ages only know of his existence as husband of Deborah (Judges 4.4,5). The rule is prominence for the husband, retiredness for the wife; nevertheless, the Source and Author of all rule once emphatically declared, "Many that are first shall be last; and the last first,"[135] which authoritative declaration has already even in this world oftentimes been verified. Again: between Manoah and his wife, the wife appears the quicker-sighted in matters spiritual (Judges 13.22,23). Elkanah and Hannah exhibit that mutual paramount affection which befits the conjugal relation. Peninnah, more tried herself, it may be, by being the less beloved wife than was her rival, by being the childless wife, may remind us how happy are we in the restrictions as well as in the privileges of Christian marriage (1 Sam. 1.1–8). Vashti we may hesitate to condemn. Esther, in her humble reverent demeanour and prayerful policy towards her husband, modern wives would do well to copy. The force of the example is enhanced by (in this instance) the husband's essential inferiority, by no one more inevitably known or more fully understood than by a wife of the still sacred though enslaved race (Esther 1.10–12, 4.10–17, 5.1–8, 7.1–4, 8.3–6).

Jacob, however, of all the Old Testament personages is pre-eminently the representative Husband. His engrossing love for Rachel made toil light to him, delay short, wrongs endurable. Her children became apparently the dearest of his children, her memory remained indelible. He and she exemplify to us that where love reigns any and all faults will be forgiven. "Many waters cannot quench love, neither can the floods drown it."[136] To form our estimate of Jacob and of his two wives their history should be studied at large, not from a few scattered references.

Rachel stands for our picture of the triumphant Wife, whose sway over her husband's heart is legitimate and supreme, who knows that thus it is, and who says and does very much as she pleases. Leah "hated," secondary, ever haunted it may well have been and ever humiliated by the fraud to which she owed her position, yet as it would seem loving her alienated husband with inalienable tenderness, and exulting in her sons as so many links attaching him to her, represents another and not rare class of wives. Perhaps Jacob's deliberate and solemn choice of a grave for himself where he "buried Leah" and not beside the cherished dust of unforgotten Rachel, may have arisen if chiefly from knowledge of our Lord's predestined descent from Leah, yet in part from some gratefully affectionate, not to say remorseful feeling, towards the distasteful wife who had lavished her heart on him.

As Priest, despite more than one glaring flaw, we recognise Aaron: most of all at that critical moment when at Moses' word he "ran into the midst of the congregation; and, behold, the plague was begun among the people: and he put on incense, and made an atonement for the people. And he stood between the dead and the living; and the plague was stayed" (Num. 16.46–48). For then he threw himself into the path and forefront of destruction, and made himself the shield of his people: thus prefiguring that "High Priest for ever,"[137] Who not in will or symbolic act merely, but in very deed and truth gave His life a ransom for many.

———

Now as we found that Disinclination vitiates if it does not nullify any observance of the First Commandment, so I think we may remark that a subordinate species of Distaste will inevitably nullify, or, at the least, vitiate our observance of the Fifth Commandment: I mean DISTASTE for our own relative posture towards any individual contemplated; akin to which is all false shame as to circumstances, position, calling, family, or any other personal concern.

For frequently it is scarcely either positive fault or positive weak point which grates upon us at every turn; let our neighbour undergo the very same trial and we feel at once how lofty and imperturbable a sweetness befits him, and how unreasonable is his resentment of mere passing trifles and matters of taste. But ourselves touched, we wince; we even think well of ourselves if we do not kick and rebel. In fact we do kick and rebel a hundred times under cover of silence, too often of sullen or contemptuous silence. We contemplate our elders and betters not to learn but to criticise,—they speak and we wish they would be quiet; their manners are old fashioned, their taste is barbarous, their opinions are obsolete, their standard is childish, they know nothing available, they do not even aim at knowing any person or any thing worth knowing. We stand habitually in an attitude of endurance or of self-defence, we are censors not children, at best we tolerate what we cannot reform! Bystanders may see ever so clearly that our father's little finger outweighs our whole self, but we see nothing of the sort: "No doubt but we are the people, and wisdom will die with us;" "We are they that ought to speak, who is lord over us?"[138] Intensify and render habitual such Distaste as I am thinking of, and it inevitably breeds its own punishment; it embitters with an utterly futile bitterness the unalterable course of life. No syllable of disrespect may find vent, no form of respect be omitted; but under all forms will burrow an envenomed root of bitterness which must infect and slay the spiritual life, except it be itself extirpated. Nor is our own day exempt from even an exceptional temptation to this sin of Distaste; for now it is common enough in some ranks for children to be better taught than their parents, and for the young to outrun the old in intellectual exercises; and those who acquire that dangerous thing, a little learning, are more likely to be puffed up by the little they know than ballasted by the much they know not; conceit spurns at reverence and submission, and the undermining of natural piety is too often followed by the repudiation of spiritual loyalty. Alas, if the last step be taken and the final result achieved: "Even as they did not like to retain God in their knowledge, God gave them over to a reprobate mind" (Rom. 1.28).

The First Commandment of the Decalogue deals with principle, the Second Commandment with practice. The first binds all creatures without exception, its negative form including even irrational nature in some sort within the pale of its obedience; and was assuredly broken by Satan and his angels when they rebelled, whether or not their spiritual essence exempted them from certain forms of temptation which beset ourselves. The Second Commandment is adapted especially to man as compounded of soul and body, both of which God claims for His own exclusive homage; to "bow down" is simply a corporeal act; to "worship" (in the sense here indicated and as regards ourselves in this present life) is mainly an act of the will and the intention corporeally expressed; neither act must be addressed to idols; both by implication are constituted our bounden duty and service towards our Maker.

As any direct breach of the Second Commandment consists in part of a bodily act, so we observe that this same commandment confines itself to such temptations as address us through our senses. Descending from the First and Great Commandment to the Second its like,—from these twain to the Decalogue,—from the First and Fifth of the Decalogue which embody the principle, to such consequent commandments as prescribe details,—ever thus descending we narrow and once more narrow the field of discussion while we multiply the points under discussion.

I think we may venture to consider not merely that each infringement of the Second Commandment must necessarily (so to say) have its bodily as well as its spiritual characteristic, but that all temptations whatsoever which harass us through our senses and could obtain no access to us at all except through our sensual side,—that all such temptations may be classed as warring against the Second Commandment; and that all and any yielding to such temptations involves a breach of that same Second Commandment. This assumed, the Sixth, Seventh, and Eighth Commandments appear as correlatives of the Second Commandment.

Allowing thus much, it follows that our breach of the Second Commandment consists in substituting in our affections and homage something, any thing for God: and not only this, but in substituting it for Him under that very aspect according to which its created nature has nothing in common with His all-perfect Divine Nature. Very early traces of corrupt religions appear to illustrate this. Underlying their corruptions we recognise man's sense of sin, helplessness, dependence, his clogged aspirations, his half-blind gropings after light and goodness, his terrors, his desires insatiable unless they find out God. He pleads piteously: "Behold, I go forward, but He is not there; and backward, but I cannot perceive Him: on the left hand, where He doth work, but I cannot behold Him: He hideth Himself on the right hand, that I cannot see Him."[139] Man burdened by the unbearable burden of self grows wearied in the greatness of his way, his strength and his weakness alike rise in rebellion, he stoops to sensible encouragements and has recourse to vivid symbols, oftentimes at the outset being fully convinced "that an idol is nothing in the world, and that there is none other God but One."[140] Yet sooner or later the symbol supersedes that which it symbolizes; at first among foolish and ignorant apprehensions; afterwards the wise themselves become taken in their own craftiness; till tribes, races, nations, all go astray together, and speak lies and love and make lies. The Word of Inspiration itself tells us: "God is light," "Our God is a consuming fire," "The Lord is a man of war;"[141] but that Word is spiritual. Man, on the other hand, is carnal; his unaided meditations debase their object, and his grasp defiles. St. Paul teaches us what were the downward steps of man's career:—"For the wrath of God is revealed from heaven against all ungodliness and unrighteousness of men, who hold the truth in unrighteousness; because that which may be known of God is manifest in them; for God hath shewed it unto them. For the invisible things of Him from the creation of the world are clearly seen, being understood by the things that are made, even His eternal power and Godhead; so that they are without excuse: because that, when they knew God, they glorified Him not as God, neither were thankful; but became vain in their imaginations, and their foolish heart was darkened. Professing themselves to be wise, they became fools, and changed the glory of the uncorruptible God into an image made like to corruptible man, and to birds, and four-footed beasts, and creeping things" (Rom. 1.18–23).

Such errors avenge themselves. Nature worshipped under divers aspects exacts under each aspect her victims; or rather, man's consciousness of guilt invests her with a punitive energy backed by a will to punish greater than he can bear. We read in the Prophet Micah (6.5–8) how Balak, appealing to Balaam, was fain to propitiate "the High God" with burnt offerings, calves of a year old, thousands of rams, ten thousands of rivers of oil; nor with these only, but even with his firstborn for his transgression, the fruit of his body for the sin of his soul. To him the answer was vouchsafed: "He hath shewed thee, O man, what is good; and what doth the Lord require of thee, but to do justly, and to love mercy, and to walk humbly with thy God?"

But few were they who found even such a prophet as Balaam to answer them.

Left to themselves, to their own appetites, fears, caprices, imaginations, men made originally capable of discriminating truth from falsehood sought out many inventions. Sun, moon, and stars, from being accounted symbols came to be rated as gods; rivers were deified; beasts, birds, fishes, reptiles, all were adored: trees waxed oracular, mountain-heads grew sacred, light and darkness engrossed each its representative deity, fire had its own formidable divinity, and the world of the dead its own. Mere attributes, mere operations, became embodiments capable of undergoing invocation and receiving worship; and destruction claimed its horrid ritual of human sacrifice, and fruitfulness was adored with such rites as it is a shame even to speak of.

Each race of mankind seems to have materialized and enshrined its own characteristic tendencies and gifts: so, at least, it strikes a surface observer who does not aim at unravelling possible complications introduced by changes of dynasty or of national preponderance.[142] Egypt loaded the world with massive monuments of long-drawn-out dominion, its gods or deified kings, smooth-faced and passionless, seeming by their colossal scale to express the immeasurable serene remoteness whence they contemplated that enslaved herd whose bondage they made cruel, and whose lives they lavished. Centuries and solid earth have disgorged in the human-headed winged Bulls of Nineveh types of all-mastering might. Greece, keen and subtle of intellect, was content to petrify and adore its own birthright-beauty heightened and refined to a superhuman exquisiteness, and constituted the shrine and vehicle of elaborate conceptions. Wisdom, power, arts, sciences, all assumed outward semblances of more or less beauty and dignity; winds, woods, streams, seas, teemed with quaint or lovely inhabitants; the dayspring and the rainbow entertained each its goddess. Rome, when it in turn had superseded all nations as regent of the world, was allured by the supreme intellect and loveliness of fallen Greece to adopt Greek myths and the Greek pantheon in lieu of its own traditional cult; meanwhile by such an apparent cession expressing (it may be) its own paramount claim to appropriate earth and her fulness. According to Roman estimate, the whole world was simply Rome; Rome and the slaves of Rome made up the entire world.

If thus may be deciphered the broad intention (so to say) of each well-defined group of idols, a further idea suggests itself: because besides the genuinely independent individuality ascribed or appertaining to every god or deified personage, each national family of divinities became unmistakably stamped with the national characteristics of its votaries; therefore every pantheon was in fact and to a great extent a reproduction, exaltation, exaggeration, of its worshippers: man reversed the process of creation, and making gods after his own likeness adored himself in them.

No wonder that breaches of the Second Commandment, heinous according to the Divine standard, are even, according to an elevated human standard, oftentimes base and worthy of abhorrence. No wonder that breaches of the Sixth, Seventh, and Eighth Commandments (if these may be classed as answering on a lower level to the Second) strike at the root of human society and tend towards the bringing on of social chaos. The idolater substitutes in his heart and worship something material in lieu of God; and as being material, akin to himself and unlike God: the murderer, the sensualist, the thief, substitutes for his neighbour or for the well-being of that neighbour some personal indulgence or acquisition of his own: each postpones God or man to self.

To ignore God, to obliterate Him (so far as on the contrary remembrance and observance can figuratively be said to retain Him there), to obliterate Him from His own universe by absolute disregard or by distinct denial of His existence, to flee from Him in will, to hate Him; these, and such as these, seem sins against God which correspond with the Sixth Commandment.

Studying our subject we clearly, I think, trace at any rate in the majority of cases, that man's hatred or negation of his Creator by no means limits itself to pure hatred or simple negation: for the hated he substitutes a something beloved, for the denied a something implicitly or explicitly acknowledged. Such a result is apparently inevitable according to the constitution of his nature: anything may, something must, become to him an object of worship.

With direct hatred of God in His own Person stands connected all worship of Him by acts of hatred and not of love, such as would be any endeavour at the cost of others to propitiate Him towards ourselves: for St. John (1 John 4.20) argues: "He that loveth not his brother whom he hath seen, how can he love God Whom he hath not seen?" By such acts the Second and Sixth Commandments are broken together. First we falsify God, substituting for Him a being of our own devising; and this done, we approach the creation of our fear or fancy not otherwise than in accordance with the promptings of our baser self. Sometimes indeed it would seem that into a vacant shrine of man's construction, swept and garnished but devoid of the Real Presence, the personal unclean spirit intrudes himself, and actual devil-worship ensues avowedly or unavowedly.

The meanness as well as the heinousness of sin is illustrated by Adam's apparent effort to shelter himself at the expense of Eve: "The woman whom Thou gavest to be with me, she gave me of the tree, and I did eat" (Gen. 3.12). Which primitive instance serves as specimen of that law of sin, diametrically opposed to the Divine law, by which the strong inflict vicarious suffering on the weak. It is the Good Shepherd Who in unapproachable love lays down His life for the sheep: in emulation of Whose pattern one Apostle prescribes how "we ought to lay down our lives for the brethren" (1 St. John 3.16), while another avers: "We then that are strong ought to bear the infirmities of the weak, and not to please ourselves" (Rom. 15.1).

It is, I suppose, a genuine though not a glaring breach of the Second Commandment, when instead of learning the lesson plainly set down for us in Holy Writ we protrude mental feelers in all directions above, beneath, around it, grasping, clinging to every imaginable particular except the main point.

Take the history of the Fall. The question of mortal sin shrinks into the background while we moot such points as the primitive status of the serpent: did he stand somehow upright? did he fly? what did he originally eat? how did he articulate? Or again, man's overwhelming loss ceases to be the chief concern, when at the gate of Paradise our eye lights upon the flaming sword. How about that sword? was it a sword as we understand a sword? was it a blade flashing and swaying towards each point of the compass, or was it rather a blazing disk to be flung with rotatory motion against the foe? Once more, as to Cain and Abel. An Apostle simplifies Cain's motive for murdering Abel into the bare statement that "his own works were evil, and his brother's righteous:"[143] not so we. What was amiss with Cain's offering? did he substitute inferior for superior produce? did he by his unbloody sacrifice evince disbelief of the Atonement? was his non-acceptance evidenced by the flame not kindling (supposing, that is, his offering to have been made by fire), or by the smoke recoiling upon himself, or how otherwise? what was the mark set upon him? At every turn such questions arise. What was the precise architecture of Noah's Ark? Were the Cherubim of the Tabernacle, of the first Temple, and of the second Temple, of similar or of diverse aspects? Clear up the astronomy of Joshua's miracle. Fix the botany of Jonah's gourd. Must a pedestal be included within the measurement of Nebuchadnezzar's "golden image"? In the same vein we reach at last the conjecture which I have heard quoted: In which version was the Ethiopian Eunuch studying Isaiah's prophecy when Philip the Deacon met him? "By these, my son, be admonished: of making many books there is no end" (Eccles. 12.12).

A heart divorced from its Maker breaks the Second Commandment; a divided heart breaks it no less grievously. Perhaps we may even say *more* grievously, when we recall our Master's awful message to the Church of Laodicea:

"I know thy works, that thou art neither cold nor hot: I would thou wert cold or hot" (Rev. 3.15). Divided allegiance is no true allegiance, as our Lord's words elsewhere recorded certify: "No man can serve two masters: for either he will hate the one, and love the other; or else he will hold to the one, and despise the other" (St. Matt. 6.24). And once more He saith, "He that is not with Me is against Me" (St. Matt. 12.30).

It is well and best to be ruled by the highest motive, yet is it not necessarily evil to be influenced by lower considerations. St. Paul speaks of one who "doeth well," even when naming another who "doeth better." In the same context he tells us: "The unmarried woman careth for the things of the Lord, that she may be holy both in body and in spirit: but she that is married careth for the things of the world, how she may please her husband" (1 Cor. 7.34,38). These two contrasted figures (the married woman and the virgin) may, I think, be studied as illustrative of the First and Second Commandments.

She whose heart is virginal abides aloft and aloof in spirit. In spirit she oftentimes kneels rather than sits, or prostrates herself more readily than she kneels, associated by love with Seraphim, and echoing and swelling the "Holy, Holy, Holy,"[144] of their perpetual adoration. Her spiritual eyes behold the King in His beauty; wherefore she forgets, by comparison, her own people and her father's house. Her Maker is her Husband, endowing her with a name better than of sons and of daughters. His Presence and His right hand are more to her than that fulness of joy and those pleasures which flow from them. For His sake rather than for its own she longs for Paradise; she craves the gold of that land less because it is good than because it is His promised gift to her. She loves Him with all her heart and soul and mind and strength; she is jealous that she cannot love Him more; her desire to love Him outruns her possibility, yet by outrunning enlarges it. She contemplates Him, and abhors herself in dust and ashes. She contemplates Him, and forgets herself in Him. If she rejoices, it is on spiritual heights, with Blessed Mary magnifying the Lord; if she laments, it is still on spiritual mountaintops, making with Jephthah's daughter a pure oblation of unflinching self-sacrifice. The air she breathes is too rare and keen for grosser persons; they mark the clouds which involve her feet, but discern not those early and late sunbeams which turn her mists to rainbows and kindle her veiled head to a golden glory. Her heart talks of God; "Seek ye My Face—Thy Face, Lord, will I seek;"[145] until truly her danger in the Day of Judgment would rather seem that she should not have recognised Christ's brethren to whom she ministered, than that she should have overlooked Him in them.

The Wife's case, not in unison with that other, yet makes a gracious harmony with it. She sees not face to face, but as it were in a glass darkly. Every thing, and more than all every person, and most of all the one best beloved person, becomes her mirror wherein she beholds Christ and her shrine wherein she serves Him. Her vocation is composed of indulgences and privileges as well as duties; yet being her vocation, she religiously fulfils it "as to the Lord, and not unto men."[146] Her earthly love and obedience express to her a mystery; she takes heed to reverence her husband, as seeing Him Who is invisible; her children are the children whom God has given her, the children whom she nurses for God. She sits down in the lowest place, and is thankful there. She is faithful over the few things, and not impatient to rule over the many things; she is faithful in that which is another man's, and can wait patiently for that which is her own. As the Cloudy Pillar deigned indifferently to head the Exodus or to bring up the rear of the children of Israel, so she leads or follows; and is made all things to all her own, if by any means she may save some; while like that sacred Symbol she also veils her perfections from alien eyes, reserving the luminous fire of her gifts and graces to him most of all whose due they are, and in him to the Maker of them both (see Exod. 14.19,20).

And we may trace no less clearly the correspondence (if I may call it so) of these two "holy estates" with the First and Second Commandments, by weighing and sifting the characteristic temptation of each vocation: the Virgin tends to become narrow, self-centered; the Wife to worship and serve the creature more than the Creator.

Thus does our Blessed Master in His Sermon on the Mount by promises incite us to observe the Sixth Commandment, and by threats deter us from its breach. The case of Cain (Gen. 4.1–16) the second man and (so far as we know) the first murderer appears, in part by contrast and in part by congruity, closely to correspond with this passage.

Cain's anger was unjust, provoked by Abel's righteousness and acceptableness with God as set against his own sin and rejection: and although we know not what conversation passed between them, we may fairly surmise that the enraged elder brother lapsed from bad to worse in speech before proceeding to extremity in act. In his doom two of the Beatitudes quoted above are pointedly forfeited: driven out from the face of the earth, he becomes a fugitive and a vagabond; hidden from the Face of the Lord and going out from His Presence, he is no longer reckoned among God's children, and becomes an occasion of enmity and not of peace. Yet there remains that third Beatitude already referred to; and from this, unless by his own obstinacy he is not finally excluded, even if those others should continue on this side of the grave irrecoverable. "Thou hast destroyed thyself; but in Me is thine help:"[147] the All-Merciful shows uncovenanted mercy to him who showed no mercy, and so far mitigates Cain's sentence as to insure to him time for repentance.

Anger, Envy, Pride, Lust, Avarice, Gluttony, Sloth. In this ghastly catalogue of the seven deadly sins (arranged in the above order simply for convenience) the last two, except indirectly, are not likely to lead to any flagrant breach of the Sixth Commandment. The first two are notoriously liable to end in such a heinous[148] extreme.

Yet between Anger and Envy there remains an essential distinction. Anger may on occasion be innocent; "Be ye angry, and sin not," says St. Paul (Eph. 4.26): it may even be virtuous; for we read how once Christ Himself looked round about Him with anger, being grieved for the hardness of men's hearts (St. Mark 3.5). Envy, on the contrary, never can be anything but vicious, venomous, abominable. And by general instinct and common consent this distinction seems to be practically recognised: for one person who will plead guilty to envy, hundreds will, I suppose, readily and sometimes lightly own to faults of temper.

The Angry Man is not all anger or always angry. He and his enjoy respites, at times long truces, from their scourge. He is often warm-hearted and affectionate, anxious to make friends again, frank in apology: some specimens of him are even peculiarly amiable when not perturbed. Often moreover his provocation is genuine, although his rage is disproportionate: in a sense he has right on his side at the very moment that he is glaringly in the wrong. His sin appals us when it intensifies into malice or deepens into revenge: it disgusts us when it lapses into crossness or sullenness: it stings us beyond all endurance (except Christian endurance) when it becomes coldly aggravating: it too often lashes others into corresponding fury, or else cows them, when its own fury approaches frenzy: yet as a threefold cord is not quickly broken, so an honest homely love—I am not now thinking of supernatural Christian love—made up, for instance, of the tie of blood, or friendship, or marriage, long-endeared habit, and personal fondness, will resist the strain put upon it by repeated outbursts of temper; so that Jacob and Rachel (Gen. 30.1,2), Job and his friends, Naaman and his servants, will remain faithful to the end.

Not so the Envious Man. His sin is no mere surface deformity, but rankles deep within: it may never even appear on the surface, but may leave him outwardly attractive as a whited sepulchre[149] or a well-fleeced wolf. Envy has pride for its root; pride not puffed up by endowments too keenly relished, but depressed and soured by grudging consciousness of gifts withheld. Self-exaltation is a poor bubble to aim at, yet Envy aims lower and is content with the abasement of others. Envy revels in spreading an evil report, and yet more perhaps in crediting one. It cheerfully points out the mote in a brother's eye, but would by no means pull it out. Spots in the sun, thorns to the rose: such are its congenial parables of nature. It can scarcely fail to be hypocritical, knowing itself scorned even by sinners and loathsome even among vices. It tends and it desires to make the victims who fall within its blight miserable: while with absolute certainty and tenfold virulence it makes miserable the wretch whose heart cherishes it. It is like jaundice, discolouring every object; like blood-poison, transmuting life into death: so that the man who does not by grace expel envy from his heart, and hate the very heart spotted by it, must rest content to gaze upon a world of distorted semblance and hideous gloom, and to entertain a creeping dissolution gaining ground within him. Thus in this world: and after this life he may look forward to hell and its society as, at the worst, less excruciating than a new heaven and a new earth wherein, beyond any possibility of two opinions, will dwell righteousness.

Hence I venture to infer that one legitimate mode of treating our present subject, and it may be not the least profitable mode, is to turn our hearts and thoughts away from it. "Blessed are the pure in heart:"[150] but how shall a heart preserve its purity if once the rein be given to imagination; if vivid pictures be conjured up, and stormy or melting emotions indulged? This, surely, were to commit sin already in the heart, and to act in direct defiance of God Who in this matter hath plainly charged us, and Who, being greater than our heart, knoweth all things. Purity is like snow which a warm contact diminishes if it does not actually sully. Purity is like a bubble, which a touch demolishes, and of which light (never darkness) augments the beauty by play of tints all alike celestial. Purity is like silence, destroyed by discussion. "Unto the pure all things are pure: but unto them that are defiled and unbelieving is nothing pure; but even their mind and conscience is defiled" (Titus 1.15); a warning we do well to keep in view even when studying Holy Scripture itself.

Blessed indeed are the pure in heart, for they shall see God. With such a beatitude in view, with so inestimable a gain or loss at stake, with such a prize of our high calling in Christ Jesus to yearn for,[151] all we forego, or can by any possibility be required to forego, becomes—could we but behold it with purged impartial eyes—becomes as nothing. True, all our lives long we shall be bound to refrain our soul and keep it low: but what then? For the books we now forbear to read, we shall one day be endued with wisdom and knowledge. For the music we will not listen to, we shall join in the song of the redeemed. For the pictures from which we turn, we shall gaze unabashed on the Beatific Vision. For the companionship we shun, we shall be welcomed into angelic society and the communion of triumphant saints. For the amusements we avoid, we shall keep the supreme Jubilee. For the pleasures we miss, we shall abide, and for evermore abide, in the rapture of heaven. It cannot be much of a hardship to dress modestly and at small cost rather than richly and fashionably, if with a vivid conviction we are awaiting the "white robes" of the redeemed.[152] And indeed, this anticipation of pure and simple white robes for eternal wear may fairly shake belief in the genuine beauty of elaborate showiness even for such clothes as befit us in "the present distress;" Solomon in all his glory was outdone by a lily of the field,[153] and all his glory left him a prey to sensuality: and this launched him into shameless patronage of idol-worship; until the glory of his greatness and the lustre of his gifts, combined with the heinousness of his defection, have remained bequeathed to all ages as an awful warning beacon.

The phraseology of the Old Testament systematically connects idolatry with breaches of the Seventh Commandment. Both subjects should prudently and (at least by many individuals) charily be approached, in deference to the spirit of Moses' enactment: "The graven images of their gods shall ye burn with fire: thou shalt not desire the silver or gold that is on them, nor take it unto thee, lest thou be snared therein: for it is an abomination to the Lord thy God. Neither shalt thou bring an abomination into thine house, lest thou be a cursed thing like it: but thou shalt utterly detest it, and thou shalt utterly abhor it; for it is a cursed thing" (Deut. 7.25,26).

The Seventh Commandment forbids by analogy, though not verbally, the over-indulgence of any bodily appetite: thus, gluttony and drunkenness range under this Commandment: moreover, experience teaches us that such gross gratifications, and even that wealth, ease, luxury, unchastened by almsgiving and self-denial,[154] predispose frail humankind towards further sensual excesses. . . .

But if "not with observation,"[155] is it therefore no kingdom at all, merely a kingdom by courtesy and a well-sounding figure of speech? Nay, on the contrary, it is the sole kingdom reigned over by man; for he who is not Christ's freeman is Satan's slave, and the master not the slave possesses all things. The heart which is one with Christ shares His dominion, first over itself and afterwards over all else. He whose Head reigns, himself reigns: he whose Representative is king, is himself royal. Nor does such an one lack guard and retinue, for the Angels, excellent in strength, are God's servants who do His pleasure; and that gracious pleasure ordains them ministering spirits, and sends them forth to minister for the heirs of salvation.

This kingdom, then, which is our own if we adhere to that elect company whom the first Beatitude pronounces blessed (for the qualification for[156] the eighth Beatitude is not here in question), is clearly one without temporal pomp, or parade, or homage. "My son, give Me thine heart," says to each of us our Heavenly Father; and man freely giving his heart therewith transfers his whole treasure to heaven, for his heart and his treasure abide inseparable (*see* St. Matt. 6.19–21). The heart once divorced from earth, the things of earth dwindle to pettiness; we possess our souls in patience, and await that day when the righteous shall shine forth as the sun in the kingdom of their Father. Meanwhile luxuries enhance the ensnaring influence of the world, and therefore almsgiving is eagerly substituted for luxury: personal comforts are like locked-up capital bearing no interest; and therefore they who desire at the last Day of Reckoning to receive their own with usury pare down comforts, clipping off one here, another there, according as vividness of faith, hope, love, urge them in the direction of selling all, and spending themselves and being spent in obedience to the Divine precept already quoted: "Give to him that asketh thee, and from him that would borrow of thee turn not thou away."[157]

But what we may lawfully clip, pare, stint, is our own provision; the unique person whom we have a right to grind is ourself. A munificent giver must not be a fraudulent acquirer, or here niggardly and there lavish; or open-handed in response to calls upon generosity, while lax or evasive when justice puts in a claim. Even unselfish persons, if they permit themselves to be generous at the cost of justice, substitute the kind of luxury they relish for another kind which they care not for: generosity is *their* luxury; yet if incompatible with justice it must be foregone. Charities in debt exhibit a dubious side as well as an edifying one; and if charities, how much more the common run of debtors.

From the noble desire to give, springs that apparently alien and by comparison mean virtue, Economy: for no revenues, however vast, can be administered to advantage while sapped by waste. Economy is oftentimes a shamefaced virtue; more prone to blush when to keep clear of dishonesty poverty practises it by constraint, than when ample means are voluntarily husbanded for the sake of some unselfish purpose. On the contrary, when economy lapses into stinginess it frequently parades itself with brasen effrontery, visibly hugging itself and despising its betters.

The sordid Economist walks the world unabashed, and says her say complacently in company. She keenly realises and relishes the distinction between eleven pence three farthings and one shilling, and ignoring all claims of neighbourhood, however struggling and meritorious the neighbour, frequents remote shops in honour of this distinction. Her remarks turn on prices, and linger in the store-room or the coal-cellar. She gossips about the extravagance of this dinner-giver, and the wastefulness of that household, frittering away her own and her neighbour's time, not to speak of her neighbour's patience. To save a halfpenny she will squander time recklessly, that priceless, irrecoverable treasure time. Her tastes, aims, contemplations, standard, are of the earth, earthy.

The heavenly-minded Economist reflects how when our Lord bade "Gather up the fragments that remain, that nothing be lost" (St. John 6.5–13), it was after feeding a multitude to the full; therefore fragments become precious to her for her own consumption, because thus she can succour the larger number of her brethren, and yet more, because thus she imitates Christ. "She looketh well to the ways of her household, and eateth not the bread of idleness;"[158] and this by no means grudgingly or of necessity, but by free-will of love, enabling herself the more abundantly to stretch out her hand to the poor, yea, both hands to the needy. Her diet approaches the dinner of herbs with love: her own dress is plainer than the letter of the apostolic injunction prescribes, "not with gold, or pearls, or costly array;"[159] yet may she find scarlet for her household, wine for her friends (*see* 2 St. John 2.1–11), or if not wine, at least a cup of cold water sweetened by sympathy. Meanwhile she tests her ways by the sentence of Solomon: "There is that scattereth, and yet increaseth; and there is that withholdeth more than is meet, but it tendeth to poverty" (Prov. 11.24): wherefore if ever the balance trembles doubtfully between gift and thrift, her glad preference weights the scale of gift and sends thrift flying upward. All the same, she wastes nothing; nothing either literally or figuratively on inferior bags, insecure property, or perishable goods (*see* St. Luke 12.32–34). She "considers" a field before buying it, and counts the cost before beginning to build Church or Hospital, or (far behind these) her own house[160] (*see* St. Luke 14.28–30).

If Dishonesty is uninteresting among vices, so it would seem is Honesty among virtues. Even religious people appear[161] at a pinch hazy as to its requirements. I remember an instance of (as I believe) such an individual remonstrating on a receipt stamp being defaced in accordance with the law,—"Better drop the penny into the Offertory." Surely not, when it was due to the Government. Another, whose standing was I think of the same sort, kept one more dog than he paid duty upon. Such practices are explicable enough among the *ordinary* class of respectable people, but among the *extraordinary* one might hope for a stricter rule. Yet no; Church goers and Bible readers may be found who seem never to have observed that plain text, "Render therefore to all their dues: tribute to whom tribute is due;

custom to whom custom" (Rom. 13.7). On the other hand, I recollect once reading of an exemplary Christian woman who used to transmit to some Government department an annual sum as conscience-money for infringements of law.

⁓

These passages, besides condemning prevaricating oaths and (at the very least) oaths on trivial occasions, open our eyes to the dignity of creation in general, and consequently to the reverence which should pervade and check our speech. For not only "heaven" and "Jerusalem;" "earth" also and our own "head" must not be lightly invoked. In every creature is latent a memorial of its Creator. Throughout and by means of creation God challenges each of us, "Hath not My hand made all these things?"[162] Our prevalent tone of mind should resemble that of the Psalmist when he proclaimed: "The heavens declare the glory of God; and the firmament sheweth His handywork;" saying[163] elsewhere in the same vein, "When I consider Thy heavens, the work of Thy fingers, the moon and the stars, which Thou hast ordained; what is man . . . ?" Nay, more, we should exercise that far higher privilege which appertains to Christians, of having "the mind of Christ;"[164] and then the two worlds, visible and invisible, will become familiar to us even as they were to Him (if reverently we may say so), as double against each other; and on occasion sparrow and lily will recall God's Providence, seed His Word, earthly bread the Bread of Heaven, a plough the danger of drawing back; to fill a bason and take a towel will preach a sermon on self-abasement; boat, fishing-net, flock or fold of sheep, each will convey an allusion; wind, water, fire, the sun, a star, a vine, a door, a lamb, will shadow forth mysteries. Versed in such trains of thought the mind becomes reverential, composed, grave; the heart imbued with such associations becomes steadied and ennobled; and out of the abundance of such a heart the mouth impulsively speaks that which is good and edifying; not corrupt communications, or foolish talking and jesting which are not convenient, or idle words whereof an account will have to be given. A Christian is one whose smooth fair outer surface of manner covers and reveals a transparent depth of character, and whose hidden man of the heart is fairer than are any outward features; he puts away childish things, and that foolishness which is bound up in the heart of a child; he keeps his tongue from evil and his lips that they speak no guile, and because he is privileged to name the Name of Christ he departs from iniquity.

What is it literally to take God's Name, any name, "in vain"? I suppose the primary meaning of the phrase points to indifferentism at least as obviously as to antagonism. "In vain" suggests not irreverence merely, but voidness, nothingness, the bringing in for no cause but to round a sentence or fill up a gap, that Name which was proclaimed before Moses in Majesty and Mercy (Exod. 34.4–8); to utter simply for the sake of saying something, that Name which Isaiah (30.27) foresaw as coming from far burning with Divine anger. It is to pronounce the Name as though it were a mere word, not standing for any person; to bring It in where another word would actually serve our purpose as well; to speak as though God Omnipresent were one of those "vanities of the Gentiles," those "nothings in the world" (*see* 1 Cor. 8.4) which have ears and hear not. Nevertheless "He that planted the ear, shall He not hear?"[165] To swear deceitfully may be more heinous, but to swear idly is almost more foolish: just as to exchange a soul for the whole world, would be a less absurd transaction than to throw one away gratuitously.

Perhaps more generally distasteful than the command to work, is the command to rest: at first sight a monstrous proposition, yet not so when sifted. For man calls work, or at any rate absorbing occupation, what God calls evil work or else idleness; thus man may be accounting himself a worker, at the very same moment that God's judgment overhangs him as at the best a cumberer[166] of the ground. Even good done at an unlawful time becomes, so far, evil: as we see illustrated of old. It is good to set store by God's gifts: but not to hoard them perversely, as certain Israelites reserving manna until the morning found worms and corruption (Exod. 16.19,20). It is good to confront and fight God's enemies: but not after the unalterable word ominous of overthrow has been pronounced, "Go not up, for the Lord is not among you" (Num. 14.40–45).

Men of pleasure and men of business who during six days have neither interest nor occupation in common, harmonize on the seventh day so far as to repudiate the intolerable burden of its hallowed rest. Some other style of rest they will adopt, but by no means that style. They will lie late, or go holidaying, or doze in pew or armchair, or smoke. The idler will idle on. The drudge will (sometimes, not always) indulge in the unwonted luxury of idleness. Such "rest" deserves not the name of rest, when tried by the sacred standard of God's Fourth Commandment.

Toil, not repose, is fallen man's birthright: "In the sweat of thy face shalt thou eat bread."[167] Repose has a solemn, in a sense an unnatural side to it. Our ordinary night's rest breaking off work for the time being, rehearses that rest in the grave which will break off our work finally. And as each night's sleep prefigures the sleep of death, so does each hallowed day of repose prefigure the eternal repose of heaven. But which of us in the sweet familiar aspect of sleep loves to discern a dim forshadowing of the veiled face of death? Alas, our fondness for rest too often stops short at "sleep and slumber and folding of hands to sleep;"[168] and a relish of physical enjoyment or relaxation is no help at all towards any longing after heaven; and therefore is equally no help towards a welcoming of the hallowed day of rest which prefigures heaven, or of the unknown sleep of death which precedes heaven.

"Remember that thou keep holy the Sabbath Day." This unique verbal form suggests that our liability to transgress the command is increased by a danger of its slipping our memory. Not that the day itself is likely to elude observation: on the contrary, temporal affairs are in Christian lands regulated and modified in reference to its recurrence. But we must not merely start in the morning under a conviction that Sunday is Sunday: we must bear the circumstance in mind all day long, doing or not doing in intentional subordination to that dominant circumstance, or else we shall not hallow the hallowed day. Wandering thoughts and a wandering heart desecrate it. Heart and thoughts must be concentrated and consecrated in loving, conscious, sustained observance of that day which we are bound not to call merely, but thankfully to esteem "a delight, honourable."[169]

This reason for consecrating a Sabbath holding good from the foundation of the world, is quite independent of the added emphasis with which the same Festival was enforced at the period of the Exodus.

Presumably those only who work heartily and well are those who will even feel predisposed to rest heartily and well. For—if without irreverence we may append words and thoughts of our own to the inspired record— "God . . . rested on the seventh day from all His work which He had made," because then looking back, "God saw every thing that He had made, and, behold, it was very good" (Gen. 2.2, 1.31).

Two sorts of persons appear, by inference, likely to transgress the Fourth Commandment: the Idler and the Money-grubber.

The Idler has a standing quarrel with time. Punctuality would be his bugbear if he did not ignore it. He likes indeed, in a certain sense, to bestir himself: he may become a busybody, yet notwithstanding all his occupations, little or nothing will he have to show at the close of day. Sometimes he wastes time frankly by doing nothing, sometimes by misappropriating to a favourite avocation the period due to another he relishes less. He is systematically behindhand, and would be perpetually running after his work in the vain endeavour to overtake it, if only he would either run or work. He is not likely to be an early riser: the day which should commence at eight, dawns not perhaps before ten. Half-a-dozen desultory acts and interests wile away the first hour or two; his vessel buoyant, because without ballast, gets (so to say) underweight towards noon. But time and tide alike wait for no man, and the occupation our Idler is commencing is the very one he ought then to be leaving off. He has not leisure to be thorough, neither has he energy to be prompt. Whether his lot be to labour for a livelihood, or—not less awful—simply so to labour that at the final reckoning his day's work may pass muster, he falls short of both the earthly and the heavenly standard, and his wages are contempt from earth and from heaven. He who will not exercise so much self-discipline as to map out his six days with tolerable accuracy, is the last man to draw an unswerving line of sacred demarcation around the seventh day. His mind is lax; his habits are unstable as water, dribbling out in this direction, overflowing in that, running short somewhere. It is out of the question that once a week he should gird himself to worship with zeal, to teach the ignorant with perseverance, to shut his mental door peremptorily against the lounging concourse of every-day interests which keep it on the jar, or even to rest throughout and not beyond the enjoined period of rest. Six consecutive days enervate him, and the seventh cannot brace him mechanically as clocks are wound up once a week; in fact, if he resembles any clock (and few may those clocks be which resemble him!) it is one with a light-weight pendulum, fussing along in an unmeaning hurry, and marking no particular time; or one which proceeds by jerks, and stops irrespective of the solar system. Everywhere and always, whether or not they drop into Church, Idlers and Pleasure-seekers, as such, are conspicuously indisposed towards observing a set day of religious retiredness: cares of this life may not choke their souls, but riches and pleasures do. Even the woman—let alone the man—"that liveth in pleasure is dead while she liveth."[170]

The Money-grubber repudiates Sunday from far different motives. Six days are all too brief for his engrossing toils; the seventh day cannot be sacrificed to a mere imaginative punctilio.[171] It may not answer to outrage popular opinion; so in some places (alas! not in all, even in Christendom) shops, counting-houses, business quarters in general, are closely shuttered during one day in seven, outsides are whited over and garnished, while within ledgers and such like unfold fascinating pages. Or if not literally thus, if importunate decency transports our Money-grubber into his pew on Sunday morning, then before his mental eyes ledgers and their kin flaunt themselves, where neighbours only discern Bibles, Prayer-books, Hymn-books, on the desk. His bales of goods, cattle, hay-ricks, would be no more out of place in Church than is he himself; his money-bag would occupy a seat as worthily; they would put full as much heart into their attendance, and full as much spirituality. Indeed, in one sense they are present, he is absent; for he carries them in his heart into the holy place, while yet all the time his heart tarries outside among them.

Indifference, then, is the proper soil of covetousness, which need not be malicious but must be more or less callous. And herein, I think, resides its efficacy as test-commandment of the Second Table. *Self*-love is a natural healthy constituent of human nature, not reprehensible at all unless—as, alas! it is very likely to become—disproportioned and domineering. What standard of *neighbourly* love does the Bible itself set up? "Thou shalt love thy neighbour as thyself:" it demands no more, and this it is which St. Paul enlarges upon and enforces:—"Owe no man anything, but to love one another: for he that loveth another hath fulfilled the law. . . . Love worketh no ill to his neighbour: therefore love is the fulfilling of the law" (Rom. 13.8–10). The vicious form of self-love is selfishness: but this may be refined, ennobled, sanctified, spiritualized, until it becomes no grosser sentiment than that which made the Apostle of the Gentiles all things to all men that by all means he might save some; which made him count all things loss if so he might win Christ.

Nevertheless, as regards love it is possible to deceive oneself; mistaking flights of fancy, or an emotional temperament, or constitutional good nature, for that "one thing needful:"[172] a ruinous self-deception, to unmask which no anguish or humiliation were too keen. Then as the touchstone detects base metal, covetousness or envy tracked home to the heart reveals the hollow sham. For these two evil tempers are alike in presenting no good side, and in being incapable of reform: for both of them the sole remedy is extirpation. Neither the good seed nor the good soil accounts for these, "an enemy hath done this;" if these "fell by the wayside, the fowls of the air"[173] would be far too wary to devour them. Covetousness is and must abide incompatible with any love worthy of the name. If consciously and deliberately we would fain supplant our neighbour in small matters, so (presumably and granted the temptation) would we in great: if in that which he has, so also in that which he is. And thus does our secondary circle of duty become full rounded: the Tenth Commandment tests and certifies our fulfilment of the Fifth Commandment.

And now since one example is worth a world of precepts, let us briefly contemplate the winning Perfection of our dear Lord: Who while going in and out among his fellow-men condescended to fulfil before their eyes and in their ears the Law of Love; making Himself, as it were, God's Epistle written in our very hearts, known and read of all Christians to all generations.[174]

From *Time Flies:*
A Reading Diary (1885)

First published in 1885 and reprinted several times, *Time Flies: A Reading Diary* is the most accessible of Christina's volumes of devotional prose. Mackenzie Bell described it as a "kind of spiritual autobiography" that contains "more frequent personal references than any other of her books" (*Christina Rossetti: A Biographical and Critical Study* [Boston: Roberts Brothers, 1898], 338). Many of these personal allusions were identified by Christina's marginal annotations in a copy of the book now held by the Harry Ransom Humanities Research Center, the University of Texas at Austin. These annotations are identified in the notes by the use of quotation marks and the initials CGR.

The text is that of the first edition, published by SPCK in 1885, from the copy in the University of British Columbia Library.

Time Flies: A Reading Diary

January 2.

1.

A certain masterly translator[175] has remarked that whatever may or may not constitute a good translation, it cannot consist in turning a good poem into a bad one.

This suggestive remark opens to investigation a world-wide field. Thus, for instance, he (or she) cannot be an efficient Christian who exhibits the religion of love as unlovely.

Christians need a searching self-sifting on this point. They translate God's law into the universal tongue of all mankind: all men of all sorts can read them, and in some sort cannot but read them.

Scrupulous Christians need special self-sifting. They too often resemble translations of the letter in defiance of the spirit: their good poem has become unpoetical.[176]

They run the risk of figuring as truthful offensively, conscientious unkindly, firm feebly, in the right ridiculously. Common sense has forsaken them: and what gift or grace can quite supply the lack of common sense?

Reverently I quote to my neighbour (and to *myself*) the grave reproof of St. James: "My brethren, these things ought not so to be."[177]

Stars, like Christians, utter their silent voice to all lands and their speechless words to the ends of the world. Christians are called to be like stars, luminous, steadfast, majestic, attractive.

January 3.

2.

Scrupulous persons,—a much tried and much trying sort of people, looked up to and looked down upon by their fellows.

Sometimes paralysed and sometimes fidgeted by conscientiousness, they are often in the way yet often not at hand.

The main pity is that they do not amend themselves. Next to this, it is a pity when they gratuitously attempt what under the circumstances they cannot perform.

Listen to an anecdote or even to a reminiscence from their lips, and you are liable to hear an exercise on possible contingencies: a witticism hangs fire, a heroic example is dwarfed by modifying suggestions. Eloquence stammers in their mouth, the thread even of logic is snapped.

Their aim is to be accurate; a worthy aim: but do they achieve accuracy? Such handling as blunts the pointed and flattens the lofty cannot boast of accuracy.

These remarks have, I avow, a direct bearing on my own case. I am desirous to quote here or there an illustrative story or a personal reminiscence: am I competent so to do? I may have misunderstood, I may never have understood, I may have forgotten, in some instances I cannot recall every detail.

Yet my story would point and clench my little essay.

So here once for all I beg my readers to accept such illustrations as no more than I give them for; true or false, accurate or inaccurate, as the case may be. One perhaps embellished if I have the wit to embellish it, another marred by my clumsiness.

All alike written down in the humble wish to help others by such means as I myself have found helpful.

January 11.

Example kindles enthusiasm, enthusiasm aspires to emulate.

But unfortunately pseudo-aspiration often selects points impossible to be emulated, and overlooks at least some one point within the boundary of possible imitation.

How great a dignity, how great a happiness, to have been one of the Magi!

This, however, we cannot be. Our Saviour no longer dwells in a small humble house; ready to be worshipped with men's hands as though He needed anything. Neither does any star traverse heaven as our guide. Neither does any dream enable us to mock the counsels of a king.

Nevertheless as those Wise Men offered their treasures to the Visible Presence, so can we offer ours to the Invisible.

Not frankincense or myrrh, necessarily: nay, nor gold either, necessarily. Yet such as they are, our treasures.

And though not to Christ Whom mortal eyes can look upon, yet as truly to Christ unseen in His Temple or veiled in His poor.

If not gold, then silver; if not silver, then copper.

Yet if our hearts were set on reproducing the Magi in some one particular, I suppose many of us could find gold (though it were only the *least* gold coin) for our Epiphany offering.

Perhaps many have tried to do so and have succeeded.

Perhaps not one has tried to do so and has failed.

January 27.

1.

"Nemico del bene è il meglio" (Better is foe to well).

Much good work has been hindered by such an anxiety to do better as deters one from promptly doing one's best.

Acquiescence in remediable shortcoming degrades: resignation to unavoidable shortcoming ennobles.

When we so set our hearts on doing well that practically we do nothing, we are paralysed not by humility but by pride. If in such a temper we succeeded in making our light to shine, it would shine not in glorification of our Heavenly Father but of ourselves.

Suppose our duty of the moment is to write: why do we not write?—Because we cannot summon up anything original, or striking, or picturesque, or eloquent, or brilliant.

But is a subject set before us?—It is.

Is it true?—It is.

Do we understand it?—Up to a certain point we do.

Is it worthy of meditation?—Yes, and prayerfully.

Is it worthy of exposition?—Yes, indeed.

Why then not begin?—

"From pride and vain glory, Good Lord, deliver us."[178]

January 28.

2.

Patience! At any rate let us enquire what we propose to do instead of grappling with that distasteful duty.

Are we inclined to pray?—No, for that would end in our having to set about the evaded task.

Or to praise and give thanks?—No, for we have not put on our armour, much less are we taking it off.

Or to meditate?—No, for meditation would harp on the silenced string.

What then?—It is vain saying "what" in particular. Centuries ago an inspired Apostle summed up all alternatives for duty in a brief quotation: "Let us eat and drink, for to-morrow we die."

"From sudden death, Good Lord, deliver us."

January 31.

A friend[179] once put it to me that the choice of each man's free will must be unknown beforehand even to God Omniscient Himself. To foreknow would involve to preordain, and that which is ordained is not free:—so, I suppose, my friend might have gone on to argue, handling a mystery far beyond my comprehension.

Yet one thing I seem to comprehend clearly. Either we must accept God's Omniscience as compatible with man's freedom of choice, or else we in truth set human free will as a limit of Divine Omniscience.

Limited Omniscience is a contradiction in terms.

A being any one of whose attributes is limited, cannot be our Infinite Lord God.

February 3.

Feast of St. Blasius or Blaise, Bishop and Martyr.

This Saint was Bishop of Sebaste, a city of Cappadocia, and whilst fulfilling his episcopal duties found leisure for much devout retirement. Under Diocletian, his eminent position, Christian work and contemplative piety

naturally led him up to the glory of martyrdom which glory he attained at
an uncertain date early in the 4th century.

Now it was a hill to which St. Blaise was used to resort for holy privacy:
and we may contemplate him as "set on a hill"[180] for our edification. Or
again, if we view him as an elevated candle showing light to all the household, this figure falls in with the fact that tapers and bonfires belonged of
yore to the observance of his festival.

This connexion of fire with St. Blaise is not, it seems, accounted for: the fact
however remains certain. A pun on his name of "Blaise" has been suggested as
the connecting link, but only to be branded as "absurd" by at least one author
of repute. Yet let us hope that this particular pun if baseless is also blameless.

Can a pun profit? Seldom, I fear. Puns and such like are a frivolous crew
likely to misbehave unless kept within strict bounds. "Foolish talking" and
"jesting," writes St. Paul, "are not convenient."[181] Can the majority of puns
be classed as *wise* talking?

February 8.

1.

A Heaven of ceaseless music,—a monotonous heaven, a heaven of ceaseless
endless weariness, say some.[182]

Yet surely this heaven of music (if for argument's sake we may so define
the Christian heaven of the Beatific Vision) is obviously and characteristically otherwise.

For is music monotonous? On the contrary, a monotone is not music.

No single note, however ravishing, amounts to music: musical it may be,
but not music.

How is it to become an element of music? By forming part of a sequence.
Change, succession, are of the essence of music.

Therefore, when our Christian heaven is by condescension to man's limited conceptions represented as a heaven of music, that very figure stamps it
as a heaven, not of monotony, but of variety.

For in music one sound leads unavoidably to a different sound, one harmony paves the way to a diverse harmony.

A heaven of music seems rather a heaven of endless progression, of inexhaustible variety, than a heaven of monotony.

February 9.

2.

If music, because opposed to monotony, typifies celestial ever fresh delight;
vocal music, as the highest form of so high an art, exhibits special apposite-
ness in illustration of heaven.

For the voice is inseparable from the person to whom it belongs. The voice which charms one generation is inaccessible to the next. Words cannot describe it, notes cannot register it; it remains as a tradition, it lingers only as a regret: or, if by marvellous modern appliances stored up and re-uttered, we listen not to any imitative sound, but to a reproduction of the original voice.

In St. John's vision we read of "the harps of God":[183] but the human voices worthy of such accompanying instruments are the actual voices of the redeemed who sing the new song.

The song indeed is new: but those singing voices are the selfsame which spake and sang on earth, the same which age enfeebled and death silenced.

"And I look for the Resurrection of the Dead."[184]

February 10.

Perhaps one reason why music is made so prominent among the revelations vouchsafed us of heaven, is because it imperatively requires living agency for its production.

For I think that from this connection music produced by mere clockwork is fairly excluded: ingenious it may be, but inferior it cannot but be.

Music, then, demands the living voice for its utterance, or, at the least, the living breath or the living finger to awaken a lifeless instrument.

Written notes are not music until they find a voice.

Written words are words even while unuttered, for they convey through the eye an intellectual meaning. But musical notes express sound, and nought beside sound.

A silent note, then, is a silent sound: and what can a silent sound be?

The music of heaven, to become music, must have trumpeters and harpers as well as harps and trumpets, must have singers as well as songs.

"Glorious things are spoken of thee, O city of God. . . . As well the singers as the players on instruments shall be there."[185]

February 13.

Tact is a gift: it is likewise a grace. As a gift it may or may not have fallen to our share: as a grace we are bound either to possess or to acquire it.

Tact has, as all human good things have, a weak side open to temptation. Its love of conciliation and abhorrence of jars too readily incline it to over-step the boundary of truth, or at the least to curve that straight line of limitation.

Yet we can scarcely overstate the daily practical value of tact, if only kept pure from insincerity. Take a story in illustration:—

A certain man on being challenged to fight a duel became, of course, entitled to choose his weapon. "Javelins," said he. "But whoever heard of such a weapon?"—"Well, that is mine." And the duel never came off.[186]

February 18.

"What a good thing my feet are large, for so anyone can wear my boots:" such a remark I once heard made by one of the kindest-hearted of my friends.[187]

A quaint remark and humourous, as she uttered it. I do not think she entertained an idea that she was propounding any high or deep or spiritually helpful truth.

Yet such surely we may find it to be: a key at least in part to the why and the wherefore of some irremediable blemishes, a comfort under the depression of lifelong inferiority.

For oftentimes our disadvantage promotes the welfare of others, or our weak-point nerves them to endure their own.

If really and truly we loved our neighbour as ourself, such aspects of our sorry plight would brighten its gloom and blunt its sting.

If only we could and would estimate every blameless blemish in ourselves, not as a personal hardship, but as a helpful possibility; as, so to say, large feet in doubly available boots!

February 20.

A great many years ago, I do not recall how many, I visited a large waxwork exhibition brilliant with costumes, complexions, and historical effigies.[188]

And entering that gorgeous assembly I literally felt shy!

The real people present did not abash me: it was the distinguished waxen crowd which put me out of countenance.

Now looking back I laugh at my own absurdity. Why then recount it? Because it seems to furnish a parable of many passages in many lives.

Things seen are as that waxwork, things unseen as those real people. Yet over and over again we are influenced and constrained by the hollow momentary world we behold in presence, while utterly obtuse as regards the substantial eternal world no less present around us though disregarded.

Will we not rise above an awe of waxwork?

February 21.

1.

"A square man in a round hole,"—we behold him incompatible, irreconcileable, a standing incongruity.

This world is full of square men in round holes; of persons unsuited to their post, calling, circumstances.

What is our square man to do? Clearly one of two things: he must either get out of his round hole, or else he must stay in it.

If he can get out by any lawful exit, let him up and begone, and betake himself to a square habitat.

But for one cubic man who can shift quarters, there may be a million who cannot. And this notwithstanding that many such ought never to have stepped into a circular hole at all: once in, therein they must abide.

Our permanent square tenant, then: what shall he do to mitigate the misfit which cannot be rectified?

He can turn that very misfit to account by sitting loose among his surroundings. If it brings home to him daily that "this is not our rest"[189] it will be blessed to him. If so uneasy a present "city" moves him to seek "one to come"[190] blessed will be his lot.

In one sense we are all alike square people in round holes, inasmuch as we are made less for our actual environment of earth and time than for heaven and eternity. Thus it appears that the main change must, after all, be wrought not in our surroundings but in ourselves: for the circle symbolizes eternity; and to fit into any round, any square must sacrifice its angles.

February 22.

2.

Or to reverse the figure. Let our man be round and let him occupy a square hole.

Let man thus appear to us as in truth he is, primarily tenant not to a finite "square" but to an infinite "circle."

He feels ill at ease in his square: or thus, at least, he ought to feel.

He abides cramped, dwarfed; he cannot expand evenly and harmoniously in all directions with perfect balance of parts. Wherever he expands he is liable to graze and get jammed against prison confines.

Ought he to feel habitually comfortable? He ought to be incessantly thankful, contented, joyful, hopeful: scarcely, perhaps, prevalently comfortable.

We do not expect a caged eagle to look comfortable. We rather expect him to exhibit noble indignant aspiration and the perpetual protest of baulked latent power.

February 26.

Sloth does not at a first glance seem the deadliest of the seven deadly sins, yet under one aspect it can fairly be reckoned such. The others may consist with energy, and energy may always be turned to good account.

Sloth precludes energy.

Sloth may accompany a great many amiable tempers and skin-deep charms: but sloth runs no race.

And a race is the one thing set before us. We are not summoned to pose picturesquely in *tableaux vivants,* or die away gracefully like dissolving views.[191]

We are called to run a race, and woe is us if we run it not lawfully, and with patience and with pressing toward the mark.

Sloth tends to paralyse the will. Blessed are those merciful who labour to help the self-helpless slothful, and betimes to arouse him.

It is never too early to fight against sloth in one committed to my charge,—or in myself. It is never too early, but ere long it may be too late.

February 28.

The difference between heaven and human attempts at describing heaven may, I think, be illustrated by the difference between pure colour and pigments or dyes.

Such colour as is cast by a prism is absolutely pure, intangible, incapable (it would appear) of analysis. It is not so much as a film: it is, so to say, a mode, a condition.

Far otherwise is it with dyes and pigments. These exhibit colour, while their substance is by no means colour, but is merely that field upon which light renders visible one or other of its component tints. Animal, vegetable, or mineral, the substance may be; oily, gummy, watery, simple, compound; however dense or however translucent, equally an appreciable body.

Now just as prismatic hues take no hold of aught on which they fall, but like the pure light which is their parent are shifting, evanescent, intangible; while dyes seize on what they come in contact with and affect it permanently: so any literal revelation of heaven would appear to be over spiritual for us; we need something grosser, something more familiar and more within the range of our experience.

The heavenly symbol attracts: what will be the heavenly reality?

It was blessed to know Christ on earth: what will it be to know Him not as mortal eye hath seen, or mortal ear heard, or mortal heart conceived?

March 4.

My first vivid experience of death (if so I may term it) occurred in early childhood in the grounds of a cottage.[192]

This little cottage was my familiar haunt: its grounds were my inexhaustible delight. They then seemed to me spacious, though now I know them to have been narrow and commonplace.

So in these grounds, perhaps in the orchard, I lighted upon a dead mouse. The dead mouse moved my sympathy: I took him up, buried him comfortably in a mossy bed, and bore the spot in mind.

It may have been a day or two afterwards that I returned, removed the moss coverlet, and looked . . . a black insect emerged. I fled in horror, and for long years ensuing I never mentioned this ghastly adventure to anyone.

Now looking back at the incident I see that neither impulse was unreasonable, although the sympathy and the horror were alike childish.

Only now contemplating death from a wider and wiser view-point, I would fain reverse the order of those feelings: dwelling less and less on the mere physical disgust, while more and more on the rest and safety; on the perfect peace of death, please God.

March 6.

In a certain little nest, built almost if not quite upon the grassy ground, having a sheltering bush behind it, and not far in front a railing, I one day saw three naked young birds consisting mainly of three gaping beaks.[193]

Neither father nor mother in sight, there sat the three wide open birds and beaks handy and prompt in case anything edible should drop in.

There seemed a thousand chances that these particular nestlings should never attain to feathers and years of discretion; for like their own beaks their nest spread wide open, and any passing cat might in a moment "finish the birds with the bones and the beaks." Occasional cats were known to haunt those grounds.

Yet feather by feather the three became fledged; until deserting their nest they fluttered, perched, made merry, among the world-wide family of birds.

Part of all this I saw, part was told me. I had felt in doubt about the three and their prospects: but as it turned out I had better have learnt a lesson they were teaching me open-beaked.

With well-placed blind confidence they sat ready and adapted to be fed. No visible agency did *I* discern at the moment, yet *they* gaped on unabashed and unwearied. They settled themselves and persevered in the attitude of recipients, and they lacked nothing.

I might well have recalled (though I did not) that familiar verse of the Psalm: "Open thy mouth wide, and I shall fill it."

"Ask now . . . the fowls of the air, and they shall tell thee."[194]

March 13.

1.

Can false etymology ever be of use? I think in one instance it has been of use to me.

"Lent." Good as it is to understand one's own language, I feel neither incited nor helped to observe Lent by being referred to a German root.

But when once (however erroneously) I connect the word with "a loan": that which is lent, that which being lent, not bestowed, will some day be withdrawn: then it sounds an alarm in my ears.

Forty chances to be used or abused.

Forty appeals to be responded to or resisted.

Forty battles to be lost or won.

Forty days to be utilized or wasted.

And then the account to be closed, and the result registered.

March 14.

2.

Or again, and yet more solemnly.

Lent: a loan of forty days: but such a loan as is terminable at the pleasure of the Lender.

Lent: a loan of unguaranteed duration: the beginning, by God's mercy, ours; the end not assured to us.

Lent: a period set us wherein specially to prepare for eternity: forty days long at the longest: can forty days be accounted long when eternity is at stake?

"In the Day of Judgment, Good Lord, deliver us."

March 28.

Is it any disadvantage when the performance of duty is attended by unavoidable pain or difficulty, and so by an involuntary tinge of disrelish?

Not necessarily a disadvantage. Grievous besetments may turn to our greater edification and profit, so long as we guard against difficulty breeding discontent, or pain a grudge.

Such a point was once illustrated to me in conversation:—[195]

A vigorous man strolls a couple of miles along country lanes to call on an acquaintance: the act is friendly, and as such it is accepted. The same man, grown gouty, hobbles his two miles on tortured feet, reluctant, yet eager, because he "loveth at all times."[196] Which walk gives the higher proof of love? Which will most endear him to his friend?

March 30.

1.

Once in Scotland, while staying at a hospitable friend's castle,[197] I observed, crossing the floor of my bedroom, a rural insect. I will call it, though I daresay it was not one in strictness, a pill millepede.

Towards my co-tenant I felt a sort of good will not inconsistent with an impulse to eject it through the window.

I stopped and took it up, when in a moment a swarm of baby millepedes occupied my hand in their parent's company.

Surprised, but resolute, I hurried on, and carried out my scheme successfully; observing the juniors retire into cracks outside the window as adroitly as if they had been centenarians.

Pondering over this trifle, it seems to me a parable setting forth visibly and vividly the incalculable element in all our actions. I thought to pick up one millepede, and behold! I was transporting a numerous family.

If thus we cannot estimate the full bearing of action, how shall we hope to estimate the full extent of influence? I thought to catch one millepede, and an entire family lay at my mercy!

March 31.

2.

In that self-same bedchamber I used to answer matutinal taps,[198] supposing myself called: and lo! it was only a tapping of jackdaws or of starlings lodged in the turrets.

Winged creatures they were, but neither angel visitants nor warning summoners. How many fancied calls or omens are in fact no more significant than jackdaws or starlings?

On the other hand: to him "that hath ears to hear,"[199] any good creature of God may convey a message.

April 2.

I have an impression (for I will not relate my adventure quite positively) that in my youth, being at that time too ignorant to appreciate such a rarity, in one of my country walks I found what I can only call a four-leafed trefoil.[200]

Perhaps I plucked and so destroyed it: I certainly left it, for most certainly I have it not.

Not that I thought nothing of it: I thought it curious, pointed it out, I daresay, to my companion, and left it.

Now I would give something to recover that wonder: *then,* when I might have had it for the carrying, I left it.

Once missed, one may peer about in vain all the rest of one's days for a second four-leafed trefoil.

No one expects to find whole fields of such: even one, for once, is an extra allowance.

Life has, so to say, its four-leafed trefoils for a favoured few: and how many of us overlook once and finally our rare chance!

Well, whether literally or figuratively, but one thing then remains for us to do: to walk humbly and thankfully among this world's whole fields of three-leafed trefoil.

April 10.

One day long ago I sat in a certain garden by a certain ornamental water.[201]

I sat so long and so quietly that a wild garden creature or two made its appearance: a water rat, perhaps, or a water-haunting bird. Few have been my personal experiences of the sort, and this one gratified me.

I was absorbed that afternoon in anxious thought, yet the slight incident pleased me. If by chance people noticed me they may have thought how dull and blank I must be feeling: and partly they would have been right, but partly wrong.

Many (I hope) whom we pity as even wretched, may in reality, as I was at that moment, be conscious of some small secret fount of pleasure: a bubble, perhaps, yet lit by a dancing rainbow.

I hope so and I think so: for we and all creatures alike are in God's hand, and God loves us.

April 11.

Among duties which are characteristically Christian there is not one more plainly prescribed than the love of enemies. Moreover, this duty once laid down commends itself forthwith to man's noblest sympathies: it appears ravishingly lovely, irresistibly attractive, to eyes inured to gaze on Christ.

Most people, I assume, have no private and personal enemies of their own: but so long as they themselves are ranged on God's side, God's enemies become theirs.

All sinners, all shortcomers, all criminals, all are to be beloved, if not as friends then as enemies.

But which of us is the lover and which the beloved in this connexion? The best of us is a sinner, the worst of us may become a saint.

If we love all, we shall be the less likely to class erroneously either ourself or our neighbour.

April 17.

"Our soul loatheth this light bread."—(Numbers 21.5)
"Is there any taste in the white of an egg?"—(Job 6.6)

That first is the speech of certain carnal Israelites concerning the Manna: that last, of one sorely tried Saint concerning the natural food in question.

Manna, we know on Divine authority, is a type of the Blessed Sacrament of Christ's Body and Blood (*see* St. John 6.26–58). An egg (though not by revelation) is one commonly accepted symbol of the Resurrection. Thus both combine in bearing a reference to the same life-sustaining Sacrament.

And, alas! If the two symbols bear such a reference, so also do the two murmurs. Still the natural man craves not for spiritual nourishment of his spiritual self, but rather for gross relishing bodily indulgence: and still many a harassed saint feels in silence—God grant to us all the grace at least of *silence*—that there is no "taste"[202] for him in "the Life of the world."[203]

Let us turn to a different discouragement: perhaps one may throw light upon the other.

I suppose I do not stand alone in feeling (at least on unreasoning impulse) as if our Blessed Lord in the days of His mortality, whilst man's eyes could look upon and his hands handle that living and breathing "Word of Life,"[204] appeared more winningly accessible, less awe-striking, less overwhelming than He does now. The element of doubt was in great measure excluded from Face to face intercourse with Him. Men, women, children could see and hear, and in some degree could estimate His inviting Aspect, His gracious Voice: when He said "Come unto Me," "Follow Me,"[205] His Will and pleasure were spoken plainly and not in parables.

We ourselves, on the contrary, look forward to never beholding Him until He comes "to be our Judge,"[206] revealing that Face from which earth and heaven shall flee away. Meanwhile we approach His Altar in dimness: our own sinfulness comes home to us by every channel of conviction; "Him we see not."[207]

O Lord, make us even as those Thy beloved blind men who first beheld Thy Face of Love when their eyes were opened, but on whom Thy Face of Love was also bent while they beheld it not. Amen.

April 21.

Once in conversation I happened to lay stress on the virtue of resignation, when the friend I spoke to depreciated resignation in comparison with conformity to the Divine Will.[208]

My spiritual height was my friend's spiritual hillock.

Not that he reproved me: standing on a higher level he made the way obvious for others also to ascend.

Now he was a man in continual pain, hindered and hampered in his career by irremediable ill-heath. And moreover he was in occasional social intercourse one of the most cheerful people I ever knew.

If only we—if only I were as *resigned* as he was *conformed!*
And why not?

April 22.

One of the most genuine Christians I ever knew, once took lightly the dying out of a brief acquaintance which had engaged her warm heart, on the ground that such mere tastes and glimpses of congenial intercourse on earth wait for their development in heaven.[209]

Then she knew Whom she trusted: *now* (please God) she knows as she is known.

> Lord, I had chosen another lot,
> But then I had not chosen well;
> Thy choice and only Thine is good:
> No different lot, search heaven and hell,
> Had blessed me, fully understood;
> None other, which Thou orderest not.[210]

April 28.

1.

A friend[211] once vividly described to me how in a country walk he had re-marked cobwebs shaped more or less like funnels or tunnels, one end open to the road, while deep down at the other end lay in wait the spider.

I walked a little about the same country, and failed to observe the spider. Fortunately for me I was not a fly.

The spider was on the alert in his sphere, my friend was on the alert in his higher sphere; I alone, it would seem, was not on the alert in either sphere.

If we turn all this into a parable, and magnify the spider to human or su-perhuman scale, what must become of the wayfarer who strolls along not on the alert in any sphere?

April 29.

2.

That funnel web seems to me an apt figure of the world.

It exhibits beauty, ingenuity, intricacy. Imagine it in the early morning jewelled with dewdrops, and each of these at sunny moments a spark of light or a section of rainbow. Woven, too, as no man could weave it, fine and flex-ible, frail and tenacious.

Yet are its beauties of brilliancy and colour no real part of it. The dew evaporates, the tints and sparkle vanish, the tenacity remains, and at the bottom of all lurks a spider.

Meanwhile a fly has been tempted in through the wide mouth of easy access: a fly who returns no more. What becomes of the fly takes place (happily) out of sight: the less seen of that fly the better.

Or suppose that a pitiful passer by stops and stoops to rescue the fly in mid funnel before the spider clutches it. Out it comes alive indeed, but to what a life!

If its wings are not left behind, they are swathed around it as by a mummy cloth; and if its legs remain, so also are they.

Fine and flexible, frail and tenacious, the web clings to the fly, although the fly clings not willingly to the web.

At the worst, it must lie immovable and starve. At the best, it must live an uncouth, hampered, degraded life, at least for a time.

And this creature that can scarcely, or that cannot crawl, is a creature endowed with wings!

May 7.

A lovely young woman[212] (not then of my acquaintance) went one evening to a concert, her face swollen and bound up, observing that she went not to be seen but to hear.

She had, I believe, a methodical brain in that charming head of hers. Certainly on this occasion she drew the line accurately between what is and what is not essential to a listener. Thus, despite her swollen face, she went with a fair prospect of enjoyment.

Half the mortifications of life (many of them lifelong mortifications) spring from a confusion in our own minds as to what the particular occasion, connexion, circumstance, demands of us.

We insist on being attractive, when all that is required of us is to be attracted, edified, or it may be merely entertained. It is not our neighbour's standard but our own we fall short of, if our utmost efforts leave us unsightly, uninteresting.

Our neighbour, according to his (or her) gift, sings, listens, looks beautiful, simply and contentedly.

If only we too would adorn ourselves with simplicity and contentment, at the worst we could sit listening with pleasure and profit. Meanwhile it is very likely that a cheerful, radiant heart would light up even our faces with some charm we hanker after and miss.

A corrosive mind gives plain features no chance.

May 15.

I have long remembered a story I was once told as a party of us sat at luncheon.

The speaker, a General,[213] had had a pet robin, a tame wild robin if I may call it so, a free familiar bird, fed and cared for by him and his.

One day coming home from shooting he aimed his last random shot at a speck in the sky. No startling result ensued: what should ensue from a shot aimed at such a safe altitude?

Alas, a presumable result did ensue, not visible, but unalterably invisible.

The tame robin never came again: and the soldier who loved it, and as he believed shot it, could not, when I listened to him, tell the story without emotion.

How many of us in heedlessness or in haste have ere now wounded some affection dear to us as our own heart. Perhaps a friend would pardon so grave an offence the more readily did he but realise how much sorer in such a case must be the offender's own wound than any other. Let us have mercy on each other and forgive: even a wronged robin's silence and absence were hard to bear.

May 22.

An English tourist in Sicily relates how he met with general kindness and hospitality. At one single house, however, the tone, though not the broad basis of hospitality, changed.

The family did not come forward to welcome him, but a depressed staff of domestics received and waited on him.

He lacked nothing, save a welcome. Arriving one day and departing the next, unwelcomed he arrived, and unwelcomed he departed.

This treatment left upon him a gloomy impression. How should meat, drink, shelter suffice and solace an unwelcomed guest?

Yet afterwards he saw cause to revise and reverse his estimate becoming aware that the undemonstrative family who had harboured him laboured at that very time under the anxiety of a bitter grief. Rejoice with him they could not, burden him with a share of their own misery they would not; all that they had to give they gave, and hid from their guest an irremediable sorrow.

How often we judge unjustly when we judge harshly. The fret of temper we despise may have its rise in the agony of some great, unflinching, unsuspected, self-sacrifice, or in the sustained strain of self-conquest, or in the endurance of unavowed, almost intolerable pain.

Whoso judges harshly is sure to judge amiss.

"Judge not, and ye shall not be judged: condemn not, and ye shall not be condemned."[214]

May 31.

A civilized man complaining of having little time, an uncivilized man, who heard him, retorted that he supposed he had all there was to be had. So runs the story.

That savage taught not his hearer only, but me also.

Each of us, then, possesses all the time there is for any one: an obvious truth, but one which never struck me so forcibly before.

What is meant by "want of time?" What do I mean by the words?

It seems that I must mean one of two things: either that I lack time for duties because I devote it to non-duties, or that, devoting it to duties, I feel discontented at lacking leisure for non-duties.

Non-duties may be attractive; they may even appear on occasion heroic or self-devoted: but we may be sure they are not duties so long as there honestly is not time for them.

On the contrary, taking the place of duties, they would degenerate into offences.

If we are bound to pronounce ourselves "unprofitable servants,"[215] even when "we have done that which was our duty to do," what are we to be called when we have *not* done so? when we have done something else? or when we have done nothing?

June 3.

"The bottomless pit"[216] mentioned several times in the Apocalypse is not (I believe) named in any other Book of Holy Scripture. To us Christians it is revealed "for our admonition, upon whom the ends of the world are come."[217]

Whatever other idea we may form of the bottomless pit, whatever other feature we may think to detect within its undefined horror, two points stand out unmistakably: as a *pit* it is a place into which to fall; as *bottomless*, it appears to be one within which to fall lower and lower for ever and ever.

Herein lies one distinct thought for ourselves: an awful thought. A deep fall, indefinitely deep, so long as any bottom at any depth underlies the lapser, must at length be arrested and must stop. However mangled or shattered, and on whatever floor landed, the wretch cannot cease there to lie: self-destroyed, indeed, yet accessible to Mercy and Help if these deign to look so low, and lift with recovering hands, and carry home on shoulders rejoicing.

But in the *bottomless* pit I see a symbol of that eternal antagonism and recession by which created free will seems able to defy and baffle even the Almighty Will of the Creator. At a standstill anywhere, though on the extreme boundary of time or space, the sinner might be overtaken by the pursuing Love of God: but once passing beyond those limits, eternity sets in; the everlasting attitude appears taken up, the everlasting recoil commenced.

Beyond the grave no promise is held out to us of shipwreck, great fish, dry land, to turn us back towards the Presence of God from our self-chosen Tarshish.[218]

June 13

1.

Years ago a small part of us crossed the Alps into Italy by the Pass of Mount St. Gotthard.[219]

We did not tunnel our way like worms through its dense substance. We surmounted its crest like eagles.

Or, if you please, not at all like eagles: yet assuredly as like those born monarchs as it consisted with our possibilities to become.

To act like an eagle is so far to emulate an eagle. To act by preference like a worm, is voluntarily to discard any shadow of resemblance to its betters.

Better be the last of eagles than the first of worms.

June 14.

2.

At a certain point of the ascent Mount St. Gotthard bloomed into an actual garden of forget-me nots.

Unforgotten and never to be forgotten that lovely lavish efflorescence which made earth cerulean as the sky.

Thus I remember the mountain. But without that flower of memory could I have forgotten it?

Surely not: yet there, not elsewhere, a countless multitude of forget-me-nots made their home.

Such oftentimes seems the principle of allotment (if reverently I may term it so) among the human family. Many persons whose chief gifts taken one by one would suffice to memorialise them, engross not those only but along with them the winning graces which endear. Forget-me-nots enamel the height.

And what shall they do, who display neither loftiness nor loveliness? If "one member be honoured, all the members rejoice with it."[220]

Or, if this standard appears too exalted for frail flesh and blood to attain, then send thought onwards.

The crowning summit of Mount St. Gotthard abides invested, not with flowers, but with perpetual snow: not with life, but with lifelessness.

In foresight of the grave, whither we all are hastening, is it worth while to envy any? "There is no work, nor device, nor knowledge, nor wisdom, in the grave, whither thou goest."[221] "Grudge not one against another, brethren, lest ye be condemned: behold, the Judge standeth before the door."[222]

June 26.

If ever I deciphered a "Parable of Nature" surely I did so one summer night at Meads.[223]

The gas was alight in my little room with its paperless bare wall.

On that wall appeared a spider, himself dark and defined, his shadow no less dark and scarcely if at all less defined.

They jerked, zigzagged, advanced, retreated, he and his shadow posturing in ungainly indissoluble harmony. He seemed exasperated, fascinated, desperately endeavouring and utterly helpless.

What could it all mean? One meaning and one only suggested itself. That spider saw without recognising his black double, and was mad to disengage himself from the horrible pursuing inalienable presence.

I stood watching him awhile. (Presumably when I turned off the gas he composed himself.)

To me this self-haunted spider appears a figure of each obstinate impenitent sinner, who having outlived enjoyment remains isolated irretrievably with his own horrible loathsome self.

And if thus in time, how throughout eternity?

June 27.

A Bishop's Pastoral Staff has two quaint likenesses among natural objects: a curled-up elephant's trunk, and a young budding frond of fern.

There is a theory that the soul within moulds the outer frame. Hence surface similarity suggests a corresponding similarity underlying the surface.

Whence—at least as a harmless fancy—I infer that the Staff may advantageously study an elephant's trunk as a pattern of delicately discriminating tact, copying its nicety of touch in minute matters and its vigorous hold on things broad and weighty.

While the frond will teach ways of bowing gracefully, of being pliant without weakness, of profiting by light and not losing ground in darkness, of bearing storms from any quarter.

. . . But Bishops should write for me, not I for Bishops!

For my own behoof therefore I wind up by reflecting that every Christian is constituted "king and priest"[224] in our Father's kingdom: that in consequence some grade of pastoral work devolves on each of us, if not as a dignity yet as a responsibility: and that as regards every soul within reach of our influence we all are in truth our "brother's keeper."[225]

So that we all may meditate profitably on a Pastoral Staff.

July 4.

Feast of the Translation of St. Martin, Bishop of Tours.

(This saint we shall meet with again, and in person, on November 11.)

As a general proposition, it surely is most pious and most reverential to leave the dead at rest in their graves.

Often, moreover, as in the case of this St. Martin, holy men have loved and observed an ascetic retirement which seems doubly indisposed towards posthumous translation.

Had this well-meant rite been more charily practised, such reticence might at least in some measure have checked that scandalous multiplicity of relics, which has assigned duplicate heads and an overplus of members to the same Saint in the face of abashed Christendom.

Not but what some exhumations for honourable enshrinement may have been praiseworthy: amongst which let us hope this of St. Martin ranks. Indeed, as a case more or less in point and "written for our learning,"[226] we read in Genesis how "Joseph took an oath of the children of Israel, saying, God will surely visit you, and ye shall carry up my bones from hence:"[227] which oath being observed, the Patriarch's remains were transported out of Egypt into the holy Land of Promise. But as bearing on ourselves and on our own practice, surely all Christendom *is* "holy ground."[228]

Now if I have betrayed prejudice, I beg my reader's pardon. Meanwhile I well remember how one[229] no longer present with us, but to whom I cease not to look up, shrank from entering the Mummy Room at the British Museum under a vivid realisation of how the general resurrection might occur even as one stood among those solemn corpses turned into a sight for sightseers.

And at that great and awful day, what will be thought of supposititious heads and members?

July 6.

Two frogs I met in early childhood have lingered in my memory: I frightened one frog, and the other frog frightened me.[230]

The frightened frog evinced fear by placing its two hands on its head: at least, I have since understood that a frog assumes this attitude when in danger, and my frog assumed it.

The alarming frog startled me, "gave me quite a turn," as people say, by jumping when I did not know it was near me.

My fright was altogether without justifying cause. Not so the first frog's: for presumably my warm finger made the cool creature uncomfortable. Besides, how could it tell what was coming next? although in truth I meant it no harm.

I wish that as regards their intention as much could nowadays be certified for some of the wisest of this world, and that every scared frog were like my scared self, unreasonable.

But seeing that matters are as they are—because frogs and such like cannot in reason frighten us now,—is it quite certain that no day will ever come when even the smallest, weakest, and most grotesque, *wronged* creature will not[231] in some fashion rise up in the Judgment with us to condemn us, and so frighten us effectually once for all?

July 13.

1.

Let none despair of any grace, however remote from their original lot.

I once looked over a fine collection of old Venetian glass vessels.[232]

By no means, I suppose were any two of these precisely similar, not a mould from without but a breath or a blast from within having shaped them.

Some perhaps might be described as quaint, others certainly as elegant, many, if not all, as beautiful.

But the point of beauty which astonished me was that one or more of the specimens had caught, as it were, a momentary grace such as charms us in many flowers. Such a contour, a curve, an attitude if I may so call it, did here or there one of these old glasses exhibit, as a petrified blossom bell might retain, or as flexibility itself or motion might show forth if these could be embodied and arrested.

Inert glass moulded from within caught the semblance of such an alien grace.

Now God's grace moulds us from within.

July 14.

2.

In the same collection of glass, but not among the Venetian specimens, stood two antique Greek vases, mended, I believe, though to all intents flawless, portly and oxydised.

What words can describe their beauty? Placed as they were aloft in my friend's drawing-room, one might stand for sunrise, the other for moonrise.

Sunrise was brilliant as the most gorgeous pheasant; *moonrise* exquisite as the most harmonious pigeon. But, as I said before, words do not describe them: I cannot exaggerate, I can only misrepresent their appearance.

Well, with these unrivalled vases vivid in my memory, I one day rescued from an English roadside ditch a broken bottle: and it was also oxydised![233] So, at least, I conclude: for in a minor key it too displayed a variety of iridescent tints, a sort of dull rainbow.

Now my treasure-trove was nothing to those others: yet could not their excess of beauty annul its private modicum of beauty.

There are, I presume, many more English ditches than Greek Islands, many more modern broken bottles than antique lustrous vases. If it is well for the few to rejoice in sunrise and moonrise, it is no less well for the many to be thankful for dim rainbows.

July 17.

1.

To this hour I remember a certain wild strawberry growing on a hedgerow bank,[234] watched day by day while it ripened by a little girl[235] and by my yet younger self.

My elder instructed me not to pluck it prematurely, and I complied.

I do not know which of us was to have had it at last, or whether we were to have halved it. As it was we watched, and as it turned out we watched in vain: for a snail, or some such marauder, must have forestalled us at a happy moment. One fatal day we found it half-eaten, and good for nothing.

Thus then we had watched in vain: or was it altogether in vain? On a very lowly level we had obeyed a counsel of prudence, and had practised self-restraint.

And shall the baulked watches of after-life prove in vain? "Let patience have her perfect work."[236]

July 18.

2.

"Half-eaten and good for nothing," said I of the strawberry. I need not have expressed myself with such sweeping contempt.

Some snail may have been glad to finish up that wreck. Some children might not have disdained the final bite.

Yet to confine my reflections to snails and their peers: why should not they have a share in strawberries?

Man is very apt to contemplate himself out of all proportion to his surroundings: true, he is "much better than they,"[237] yet have they also their assigned province and their guaranteed dues.

Fruits for man, green herb for other living creatures, including creepers on the earth, is the decree in Genesis. Thus for the Garden of Eden: and why not thus, as regards the spirit of the decree, here and now?

But man, alas! finds it convenient here to snap off a right and there to chip away a due. Greed grudges their morsel to hedgerow birds, and idleness robs the provident hare of his winter haystack, and science pares away at the living creature bodily, "And what will ye do in the end thereof?"[238]

July 27.

1.

> "Simon, Simon, behold, Satan hath desired to have you, that he may sift you as wheat."—(St. Luke 22.31.)

These words of our Blessed Lord, spoken in the first instance to one Apostle, have ever since warned, and still cease not to warn, each Christian soul.

For though an ordinary Christian is no conspicuous prey, like the College of Apostles, yet Satan deems him well worth a shake of the sieve.

The warning conveyed by our Lord's words is awful: for our "adversary the devil, as a roaring lion, walketh about, seeking whom he may devour."[239] A flesh and blood lion is appalling to human flesh and blood: how tenfold appalling is a spiritual roaring devouring lion to man's spirit.

But the encouragement in those same precious words rings through and above the alarm they sound. "Satan hath desired"[240] to have us: but of whom? Of Him to Whom we are as the apple of the eye.

And wherefore does he desire to have us? That he may sift us as wheat. We are certified as good seed by Satan's desiring permission to sift us: for who ever heard of his desiring to sift tares?

As to tares, Satan is quite satisfied so long as they grow unmolested, ripen, shed seed, propagate, flourish until the harvest.

Wheat only does he reckon worth his sifting: therefore whatever he sifts is wheat.

July 28.

2.

Temptation is Satan's sieve: and a wonderful sieve-maker is Satan.

For he can ply as sieves advantages, gifts, even graces.

More than this: he can turn what we have not into an exceptionally searching sieve.

In one case pride, vanity, self-confidence, contempt of others, are likely to come to the surface. In the other case discontent, envy, rebellion. All alike hideous blotches, eating ulcers.

Nevertheless, it is at his own cost that he sifts, and not necessarily at all at ours; although for the time being it cannot but be at our deadly peril.

For he can never carry his point and destroy us, unless we first make a convenant with death and an agreement with hell: whereas we shall infallibly save our souls alive, if holding fast our profession and our patience, we are careful to maintain good works.

Meanwhile he is doing us an actual service by bringing to the surface what already lurked within. However tormenting and humiliating declared leprosy may be, it is less desperate than suppressed leprosy.

Or rather, nothing is desperate which can and will turn to Christ:—

"There came a leper to Him, beseeching Him, and kneeling down to Him, and saying unto Him, If Thou wilt, Thou canst make me clean. And Jesus, moved with compassion, put forth His Hand, and touched him, and saith unto him, I will; be thou clean. And as soon as He had spoken, immediately the leprosy departed from him, and he was cleansed."[241]

August 4.

When I was in north Italy, a region rich in sunshine, heat, beauty, it struck me that after all our English wild scarlet poppies excelled the Italian poppies in gorgeous colour.[242]

I should have expected the direct contrary; the more sunshine, surely the more glow and redness: yet it appeared otherwise when I came to look.

Perhaps sheer stress of sunshine tended to bleach as well as to dye those poppies.

And if so, they aptly symbolize those "always rejoicing"[243] Christians who are, notwithstanding, so sorrowful during the present distress.

For on earth souls need bleaching as well as developing and embellishing. Only in heaven will the sun cease to smite on the just made perfect, and the vehement east wind cease to beat on them.

August 20.

1.

Interruptions are vexatious.

Granted. But what is an interruption?

An interruption is something, is anything, which breaks in upon our occupation of the moment. For instance: a frivolous remark when we are absorbed, a selfish call when we are busy, an idle noise out of time, an intrusive sight out of place.

Now our occupations spring? . . . from within: for they are the outcome of our own will.

And interruptions arrive? . . . from without. Obviously from without, or otherwise we could and would ward them off.

Our occupation, then, is that which we select. Our interruption is that which is sent us.

But hence it would appear that the occupation may be wilful, while the interruption must be Providential.

A startling view of occupations and interruptions!

August 21.

2.

Ah but, that which is frivolous, selfish, idle, intrusive, is clearly not Providential.

As regard the doer, no: as regards the sufferer, yes.

I think we often quite misconceive the genuine appointed occupation of a given moment, perhaps even of our whole lives. We take for granted that we ought to enjoy a pleasure, or complete a task, or execute a work, or serve some one we love: while what we are really then and there called to is to forego a pleasure, or break off a task, or leave a cherished work incomplete, or serve some one we find it difficult to love.

Interruptions seem well nigh to form the occupation of some lives.

Not an occupation one would choose; yet none the less profitable on that account.

How would saints speak of interruptions? One might remark, "To me they are not grievous:" and another, "For me they are safe." But would any saint observe, "Interruptions are vexatious," and there stop?[244]

August 25.

> "Rooms shalt thou make in the ark"—(Gen. 6.14): but the literal Hebrew (see margin of Authorised Version) says not "rooms" but "nests."

Now without for one moment calling in question that these particular "nests" were rooms, the special word employed does yet suggest a special train of thought.

The Ark: the Church. Destruction without, safety within. "A dispensation of the Gospel"[245] is vouchsafed to man, and woe is us if we accept not the offered salvation.

We do (please God) accept it. However unworthily, we occupy rooms in the spiritual Ark: there we live, and there we hope to die.

The rooms being commodiously and thoroughly furnished unto good works, the tenants are thereby invited to perform such good works as belong to their several vocations.

So to do becomes our duty. And it is constituted no less our privilege, seeing that to crown all it has promise of a reward.

Christian duties, Christian privileges: some honest Christians do much, and upbraid themselves for not doing more. They labour and are heavy laden, they are careful and cumbered; making a task of duty, a task of privilege, a task of life, and a most formidable task of death.

The vastness and still more the loftiness of their "room" overwhelms them: "Who is sufficient for these things?"[246] is their prevalent forlorn feeling. At times they would almost be ready (if they dared) to say: "It were better to dwell in a corner of the housetop."[247]

They comport themselves as if too little for their own greatness. They appear like savage man consumed and dwindling away in the face of a civilisation too high for him.

But wherefore contemplate their allotted room as a lofty and vast palace of well-nigh uninhabitable grandeur: as this, and as nothing more?

Our room, as God builds and makes it for us, is likewise our nest: and a nest is surely the very homeliest idea of a home.

August 31.

It was once pointed out to me that in countenance a grey parrot and an elephant resemble each other.[248]

But presumably the creatures themselves remain to this day unconscious of their common type, and inhabit pastures or trees or caravans or cages without a notion that each is (with limitations) the other's looking-glass; thus living and thus dying as utter aliens even when brought face to face.

"Know thyself" is an old-established injunction, and conveys a hint that probably we do *not* know ourselves.

It is startling to reflect that you and I may be walking about unabashed and jaunty, whilst our fellows observe very queer likenesses amongst us.

Any one may be the observer: and equally any one may be the observed.

Liable to such casualties, I advise *myself* to assume a modest and unobtrusive demeanour.

I do not venture to advise *you*.

September 2.

1.

I am told of certain birds which for protection take up their abode beneath wasps' nests. How it happens that they (as I assume) escape being strung, I do not know; but one sees at once that outside enemies might thus be kept at bay.

A wasps' nest for a canopy; wasps for neighbours: clearly in itself no attractive neighbourhood. Yet better than the alternative, death, or deadly bereavement. So those birds are wise which, preferring of two evils the less, contrive of stings a shelter.

Similarly those persons are wise who amongst evils choose the less rather than the greater.

Why not accept all our trials as beneficial wasps and wasps' nests?

What is most irritating teaches patience, if we will be taught: what is most overbearing teaches humility, if we will learn.

Patience and humility predispose to faith, hope, charity: and where these are, there is safety.

September 3.

2.

I said "I do not know" how birds dwelling near wasps' nests escape stinging. Second thoughts show me that I do know.

God's Providence keeps them safe.

In the same sense as young ravens cry to God, we may think of all other feeble instinctive creatures as trusting in Him:—"Thou wilt keep him in perfect peace, whose mind is stayed on Thee: because he trusteth in Thee."[249]

Even so the rose dwells amidst a guard of thorns, and stands alone in her loveliness.

Surely the rose, our own cherished rose, would lose a fine finishing touch of grace and beauty if divorced from her thorns.

And cannot we, who are so much better than bird or flower, take courage to trust our Heavenly Father implicitly? saying and feeling that if only we are such as love Him, our "wasps" and "thorns" alike are ordained for good; inasmuch as "all things work together for good to them that love God."[250]

September 4.

3.

Indeed, I think we may proceed a step further, and reflect that any who like us like us as we are and not as we are not.

The person with the blemishes which are ours, and the weak points which are ours, is the person that those who love us love.

And conversely we may surely admit that (sin excluded) we also love our own beloved without on the whole wanting them to be different.

They are themselves, and this suffices.

We are quite ready to like something superior, but it contents our hearts to love them.

And when once death has stepped in, dividing as it were soul from spirit, the friend that is as one's own soul from oneself, then half those vanished peculiarities put on pathos. We remain actually fond of the blameless oddities, the plain face abides as the one face we prefer.

Now if persons as imperfect as ourselves can secure a permanent place in the affection of their fellows (of which everywhere and always we behold proofs), our "vale of misery"[251] turns to a perennial well of very sweet and refreshing water and it becomes us to be thankful.

September 5.

4.

Not that human affection, excellent as it is, suffices: only it illustrates and certifies to us beyond a doubt the corresponding Divine Affection.

This it does, even if we receive not its testimony. It is like the celestial luminaries which discourse without speech: its sound is gone out into all lands, and its words unto the ends of the world, declaring the Glory of God.

Nevertheless, as sun, moon and stars have had their worshippers, so human love has engrossed its idolatrous votaries.

It, indeed, is ready to "bless with the spirit,"[252] but those others are not edified.

Christ keep us or deliver us from worshipping and serving the creature more than the Creator, Who is Blessed for ever. Amen.

September 9.

"An alabaster box of ointment of spikenard very precious."—(St. Mark 14.3).

I have read that both the precious spikenard and an inferior quality of perfume are yielded by the same plant.

The commoner sort is extracted by art. The choicer kind consists of such balsam as exudes from the untouched plant.

One resembles a tax, the other a gift.

Thus, by a figure, even a vegetable demonstrates how much nobler is voluntary than compelled service. For love alone genuinely gives: love turns a levied tax into a free gift, whereas a servile gift dwindles in essence to a mere tax.

Nor least so, in things spiritual. Love transmutes bounden duty into freewill oblation: constraint other than love transmutes even unprescribed offerings into taxes.

September 10.

1.

I have read of an elephant who was set to move an enormous weight, which it behoved him to do by sheer force of his mighty head.

But not even his mighty head could stir it.

This his overseer perceived, whereupon other elephants were summoned to assist.

Then the first elephant seeing them approach, and being bent on carrying his point by himself, put forth so desperate an exertion of strength as fractured his skull.

As an elephant I greatly admire him.

Yet a man moulded on his model would, I fear, turn out a failure. He would be too independent to accept help, or to be set right, and he would sacrifice his cause rather than his pride.

September 11.

2.

Meanwhile there appears a heroic and exemplary side, as well as a warning side to our elephant.

He stands as a figure of one who prefers his work to himself, his duty to his life.

A somewhat comical figure of a hero, yet none the less pathetic.

Not to be laughed at, but looked up to by such persons as have ever postponed work to self, duty to life.

I, for one, must not laugh at him.

September 16.

Once as we descended a mountain[253] side by side with the mountain torrent, my companion saw, while I missed seeing, a foambow.

In all my life I do not recollect to have seen one, except perhaps in artificial fountains; but such general omission seems a matter of course, and therefore simply a matter of indifference. That single natural foambow which I might have beheld and espied not, is the one to which may attach a tinge of regret; because, in a certain sense, it depended upon myself to look at it, yet I did not look.

I might have done so, and I did not: such is the sting to-day in petty matters.

And what else will be the sting in matters all important at the last day?

September 23.

1.

I have read that such plants as produce a cruciform flower are all alike free from poison.

Life has its blossoming season preparatory to its season of fruit.

And many lives by bereavement, disappointment, pain, hope deferred, blossom, so to say, with crosses.

A choice and blessed blossom, if it correspond with nature's emblem and harbour no venom. For one day the cross petals will drop off, and only the good fruit remain.

September 24.

2.

Christ, "for the joy that was set before Him, endured the cross, despising the shame, and is set down at the right hand of the Throne of God."[254]

For our sakes the cruciform blossom of His mortal life was agony and shame: for our sakes the salutary fruit of His life immortal is glory and grace.

And now He looks down from heaven, from the habitation of His holiness and of His glory, if so be He may in us see of the travail of His Soul and be satisfied.

Once He looked, and there was no man. Once He looked, and one penitent went out and wept bitterly.

Now He looks on you, on me.

October 3.

I have noticed in cold weather how many days a rose will linger in the bud, quarter blown, half blown. When at length, if ever, it expands fully, it will probably not be the most beautiful of roses: still, if far below the finest blossoms at their best moment, it has, on the other hand, lasted longer than they.

Superiority in one point may fairly be set against inferiority in another: duration against quality.

And if this is equitable in estimating flowers, it is no less equitable in estimating people.

Many lives pass in chills and in shadows which preclude certain fine finishing touches of loveliness: their resource will be to excel in endurance.

And in the long run surely the livers of such lives will be ready to sing with David: "The lot is fallen unto me in a fair ground:" for "he that shall endure unto the end, the same shall be saved."[255]

October 12.

A good unobtrusive Christian[256] of my own intimate circle told me that in her worried life—and a worried life it has been—she has derived comfort from the reflection that no day lasts longer than twenty-four hours.

To a good worried Christian this certainty affords legitimate comfort.

But, as it cannot certify comfort to all classes of worried persons, it seems safe for most of us not to wish time shortened.

If time is short, many tempers are yet shorter.

Even a Psalmist prays: "O spare me a little, that I may recover my strength: before I go hence, and be no more seen."[257]

And most of us have very much besides strength to recover.

October 14.

A sensual Christian resembles a sea anemone.

In the nobler element, air, it exists as a sluggish unbeautiful excrescence.

In the lower element, water, it grows, blows and thrives.

The food it assimilates is derived not from the height, but from the depth.

It possesses neither eyes nor ears, but a multitude of feelers.

It squats on a tenacious base, gulps all acquisitions into a capacious chasm, and harmonises with the weeds it dwells amongst.

But what will become of it in a world where there shall be no more sea?[258]

October 20.

1.

As I am nothing of an ornithologist, any small outdoor bird with forked tail and black and white plumage may pass with me as a swallow or as a martin. When mud nests are not in sight, then it becomes a swallow.

Once at the seaside[259] I recollect noticing for some time a row of swallows perched side by side along a telegraph wire. There they sat steadily. After a while, when some one looked again, they were gone.

This happened so late in the year as to suggest that the birds had mustered for migration and then had started.

The sight was quaint, comfortable looking, pretty. The small creatures seemed so fit and so ready to launch out on their pathless journey: contented to wait, contented to start, at peace and fearless.

Altogether they formed an apt emblem of souls willing to stay, willing to depart.

Only I fear there are not so many "willing" souls as "willing" swallows.

October 21.

2.

That combination of swallows with telegraph wire sets in vivid contrast before our mental eye the sort of evidence we put confidence in and the sort of evidence we mistrust.

The telegraph conveys messages from man to man.

The swallows by dint of analogy, of suggestion, of parallel experience, if I may call it so, convey messages from the Creator to the human creature.

We act eagerly, instantly, on telegrams. Who would dream of stopping to question their genuineness?

Whilst often we act reluctantly, often we act not at all, on the other sort of messages. We dwell anxiously on the thousand contingencies of life, tremblingly on the inevitable contingency of death. We call everything in question, except the bitter certainty of suffering, the most bitter certainty of death.

Who, watching us, could suppose that the senders of telegrams are fallible; and that the Only Sender of Providential messages is infallible?

November 2.

"Unstable as water,"—(or according to an alternative rendering)—"Bubbling up as water, thou shalt not excel." (Gen. 49.4)

These prophetic words of doom spoken against one such individual seem to apply to all persons of the "watery" type: to such persons, that is, as are born unstable and excitable.

So far, of course, as the mere natural disposition goes, no fault attaches to them. Only they will have to work under the condition of (at the least) a predisposition towards inferiority.

Which predisposition invites the virtue of humility.

Now where humility lays deep the low-lying foundation, the superincumbent structure can safely and permanently tower aloft unto heaven.

Whence we perceive how by God's grace a predisposition towards inferiority may be reclaimed as a vantage ground for the achievement of excellence.

November 7.

One of the dearest and most saintly persons[260] I ever knew, in foresight of her own approaching funeral, saw nothing attractive in the "hood and hatband" style towards which I evinced some old-fashioned leaning. "Why make everything as hopeless looking as possible?" she argued.

And at a moment which was sad only for us who lost her, all turned out in harmony with her holy hope and joy.

Flowers covered her, loving mourners followed her, hymns were sung at her grave, the November day brightened, and the sun (I vividly remember) made a miniature rainbow in my eyelashes.

I have often thought of that rainbow since.

May all who love enjoy cheerful little rainbows at the funerals of their beloved ones.

November 9.

A covetous, grasping Christian is like a quicksand: the surface smooth, the depth unceasingly on the suck and gulp.

Everything goes down, nothing comes up again: yet is the quicksand apparently none the fuller, neither does it cease from engulphing.

In fact—whether or not one may attribute ideas to a quicksand—it seems at any rate to entertain no idea of ever becoming satisfied. Its aim appears to be not to attain repletion, but to exercise an unbounded swallow.

In this world, crews, cargoes, ships, waifs and strays, respond to the "Give, give" of the quicksand; while objects of proportionate bulk and quality often respond to the unuttered "Give, give" of the covetous man.

Thus in this present world, both; but how in the next world, either?

December 4.

I once heard an exemplary Christian[261] remark that she had never been accused of a fault without afterwards recognising truth in the accusation.

And if she, how not I?

At the least her words should make me cautious not to rebut any charge in anger or in haste.

And if me, why not you?

December 10.

"If any man will do His Will, he shall know of the doctrine, whether it be of God,"[262] said Jesus Christ our Lord.

Blessed on all sides is this infallible promise.

It assures us that, at least in the long run, we shall by working faithfully get clear of doubt and darkness.

Obedience, then, is the key of knowledge.

That was a masterstroke of guile by which the serpent cajoled Eve into believing disobedience to be the key of knowledge.

Disobedience may (indeed and alas!) be the key to many of our own beliefs and opinions. Yet even thus, if we will, we can turn it into a genuine though base-metal key of knowledge.

For that which disobedience teaches us is false, either in its essence or in its aspect as regards ourselves.

Wherefore since disobedience unlocks not truth, whatsoever it unlocks is thereby certified as falsity.

For each key fits its own lock and no other.

From *The Face of the Deep: A Devotional Commentary on the Apocalypse* (1892)

⁓❧⁓

Estimations about how long Christina worked on this final, massive prose volume (about 550 octavo pages) are varied: Sandars (p. 214) and Eleanor Thomas (p. 115) say three years, Battiscombe (p. 196) and Jones (p. 216) suggest seven years, while Bell (p. 310) speculates two and a half ("or perhaps three years"). Remarks Christina made in a letter to Theodore Watts-Dunton on 22 November 1886, support the longer estimates: "All I am doing is reading and thinking over part of the New Testament, writing down what I can as I go along. I work at prose, and help myself forward with little bits of verse" (*The Life and Letters of Theodore Watts-Dunton*, eds. Thomas Hake and Arthur Compton-Rickett [London: T. C. & E. C. Jack, Ltd., 1916], 2:47).

First published in 1892, *The Face of the Deep* went through seven editions. Rossetti was not, however, pleased with the accuracy of the first printing. Writing to William on 20 May 1892, she refers to a list of errata she had sent to Mr. McClure of the SPCK after the book's publication. Two months later, writing to Frederic Shields on 15 July 1892, about *The Face of the Deep* (Troxell, 179), she tells him that "All too late I discovered several grave mistakes (some my own, some I think the printer's) which had escaped me. . . ." The modest list of nine errors she enclosed in another copy of the book sent to Miss Henrietta Rintoul is included in the Troxell Collection, Princeton University Library, and it demonstrates the scrupulous care with which she prepared her books for the press. The second edition of 1893 included her corrections, "much to my satisfaction" she told William (*FL*, 192). Five years after Rossetti's death, W.M.L. Jay mixed to-gether a variety of prose meditations and verse in his *Reflected Lights from "The Face of the Deep"* (New York: E. P. Dutton & Company, 1899) to form a curious an-thology. The editor's sole aim in this compilation was to "inspire and comfort" the reader (preface, iv).

The selections given here are taken from a copy of the first London edition of 1892 in the University of British Columbia Library.

The Face of the Deep: A Devotional Commentary on the Apocalypse

Prefatory Note.

If thou canst dive, bring up pearls. If thou canst not dive, collect amber. Though I fail to identify Paradisiacal "bdellium," I still may hope to search out beauties of the "onyx stone."[263]

A dear saint—I speak under correction of the Judgment of the Great Day, yet think not then to have my word corrected—this dear person once pointed out to me Patience as our lesson in the Book of Revelations.

Following the clue thus afforded me, I seek and hope to find Patience in this Book of awful import. Patience, at the least: and along with that grace whatever treasures beside God may vouchsafe me. Bearing meanwhile in mind how "to him that knoweth to do good, and doeth it not, to him it is sin."[264]

Now if any deign to seek Patience in my company, I pray them to re-member that One high above me in the Kingdom of Heaven heads our pil-grim caravan.

> O, ye who love to-day,
> Turn away
> From Patience with her silver ray:
> For Patience shows a twilight face,
> Like a half-lighted moon
> When daylight dies apace.
>
> But ye who love to-morrow,
> Beg or borrow
> To-day some bitterness of sorrow:
> For Patience shows a lustrous face
> In depth of night her noon;
> Then to her sun gives place.[265]

From **CHAPTER 1**

3.   Blessed is he that readeth, and they that hear
the words of this prophecy, and keep those things which
are written therein, for the time is at hand.

"Understandest thou what thou readest?" asked Philip the Deacon of the Ethiopian Eunuch. And he said, "How can I, except some man should guide me?"[266] Whereupon flowed forth to him the stream of light, knowledge, and love. Yet not then did his illumination commence: it already was his in a measure to enjoy, respond to, improve, even before his father in God preached Christ unto him. What could he do before that moment? He could study and pray, he could cherish hope, exercise love, feel after Him Whom as yet he could not intelligently find.

So much at least we all can do who read, or who hear, this Book of Revelations: thus claiming, and by God's bounty inheriting, the covenanted blessing of such readers and hearers. Any who pray and love enjoy already no stinted blessing. Even the will to love is love.

A reader and hearers stand in graduated degrees of knowledge or of ignorance, as the case may be. The reader studying at first hand is in direct contact with God's Word: hearers seek instruction of God through men. The reader requires most gifts: hearers may exercise fully as much grace. Most of us are hearers: having performed conscientiously the duty of hearers, we shall be the less prone to make mistakes if ever providentially promoted to be readers. Our dearest Lord, Who deigned to become the pattern of every grade of aspirant, as a Boy showed hearers how to hear (St. Luke 2.46,47); and as a Man showed readers how to read (St. Luke 4.16–27).

> Lord, I am feeble and of mean account;
> Thou Who dost condescend as well as mount,
>   Stoop Thou Thyself to me
> And grant me grace to hear and grace to see.
>
> Lord, if Thou grant me grace to hear and see
> Thy very Self Who stoopest thus to me,
>   I make but slight account
> Of aught beside wherein to sink or mount.[267]

It suffices not to read or to hear the words of this prophecy, except we also "keep those things which are written therein." How keep them? One part in one way, another part in another: the commandments by obedience, the mysteries by thoughtful reception; as blessed Mary, herself a marvel, kept mysterious intimations vouchsafed to her, and pondered them in her heart.

Yet never had she gone on in pursuit of all mysteries and all knowledge if she had not first answered in simple obedience: "Behold the handmaid of the Lord; be it unto me according to thy word."[268]

O bountiful Lord, to Whom they who do the will of God are as brother and sister and mother, number us in that blessed company, that here we may obey and suffer as Thy patient exiles, and hereafter rule and rejoice as Thy nearest and dearest.

"Blessed are they . . . for the time is at hand." Even now, eighteen centuries later, we know not when that cry shall be made, "Behold, the Bridegroom cometh; go ye out to meet Him."[269] Nevertheless the time was then at hand, for so the Bible certifies us, and still must it be at hand. What time? Doubtless the time of fulfilment after fulfilment until all be fulfilled. Likewise also that (so to say) secondary time when each one of us, having done with mortal life and probation, shall await judgment. For truly the end of all flesh is at hand, whether or not we possess faith to realize how a thousand years and one day are comparable in the Divine sight.

"A thousand years in Thy sight are but as yesterday when it is past, and as a watch in the night."[270]

Blessed are the wise virgins whose lamps burn on unto the endless end. "Blessed are those servants, whom the Lord when He cometh shall find watching." "If ye know these things, happy are ye if ye do them."[271]

"The time is at hand," ever at hand; yet it waits long for us: "Who knoweth if he will return and repent?" But if we will not return or repent, "iniquity shall be to you as a breach ready to fall . . . whose breaking cometh suddenly at an instant."[272]

O Lord God of time and eternity, Who makest us creatures of time to the end that when time is over we may attain to Thy blessed eternity; with time, Thy gift, give us also wisdom to redeem the time, lest our day of grace be lost. For our Lord Jesus' sake. Amen.

> Astonished Heaven looked on when man was made,
>   When fallen man reproved seemed half forgiven;
> Surely that oracle of hope first said
>   Astonished Heaven.
>
> Even so while one by one lost souls are shriven,
>   A mighty multitude of quickened dead;
> Christ's love outnumbering ten times sevenfold seven.
>
> Even so while man still tosses high his head,
>   While still the All-holy Spirit's strife is striven;—
> Till one last trump shake earth, and undismayed
>   Astonished Heaven.[273]

8. *I am Alpha and Omega, the beginning and the ending,*
saith the Lord, which is, and which was, and which
is to come, the Almighty.

"I am Alpha and Omega."—thus well-nigh at the opening of these mysterious Revelations, we find in this title an instance of symbolical language accommodated to human apprehension; for any literal acceptation of the phrase seems obviously and utterly inadmissible. God condescends to teach us somewhat we can learn, and in a way by which we are capable of learning it. So, doubtless, either literally or figuratively, throughout the entire Book.

Such a consideration encourages us, I think, to pursue our study of the Apocalypse, ignorant as we may be. Bring we patience and prayer to our quest, and assuredly we shall not be sent empty away. The Father of lights may still withhold from us knowledge, but He will not deny us wisdom. "Open Thou mine eyes, that I may behold wondrous things out of Thy law."[274]

If a letter of the alphabet may be defined as a unit of language, then under this title "Alpha and Omega" we may adore God as the sole original Existence, the Unit of Existence whence are derived all nations, and kindreds, and people, and tongues; yea, all other existences whatsoever.

This title derived from human language seems to call especially upon "men confabulant" for grateful homage. As said of old the wise son of Sirach: "The Lord hath given me a tongue for my reward, and I will praise Him therewith." Or as the sweet Psalmist of Israel declared: "I will sing and give praise with the best member that I have."[275]

Alas! That men often pervert their choicest gifts to their soul's dire destruction. For St. James bears witness against the tongue: "The tongue is a little member, and boasteth great things. Behold, how great a matter a little fire kindleth! And the tongue is a fire, a world of iniquity: so is the tongue among our members, that it defileth the whole body, and setteth on fire the course of nature; and it is set on fire of hell. . . . The tongue can no man tame; it is an unruly evil, full of deadly poison."[276]

O Lord Jesus Christ, Wisdom and Word of God, dwell in our hearts, I beseech Thee, by Thy most Holy Spirit, that out of the abundance of our hearts our mouths may speak Thy praise. Amen.

From **CHAPTER 2**

1. *Unto the angel of the Church of Ephesus write;*
These things saith He that holdeth the seven stars in His right
hand, Who walketh in the midst of the seven golden candlesticks.

"He telleth the number of the stars; He calleth them all by their names."[277]

Concerning Himself God Almighty proclaimed of old: "I AM THAT I AM," and man's inherent feeling of personality seems in some sort to attest and correspond to this revelation: I who am myself cannot but be myself. I am what God has constituted me: so that however I may have modified myself, yet do I remain that same I; it is I who live, it is I who must die, it is I who must rise again at the last day. I rising again out of my grave must carry on that very life which was mine before I died, and of which death itself could not altogether snap the thread. Who I was I am, who I am I am, who I am I must be for ever and ever.[278]

I the sinner of to-day am the sinner of all the yesterdays of my life. I may loathe myself or be amazed at myself, but I cannot unself myself for ever and ever.

"O Lord, I am oppressed; undertake for me."[279]

There is no refuge, no hiding-place in multitude. The associated stars and candlesticks conceal not nor shelter that one star and one candlestick which God bringeth into judgment. Yet whilst no man may deliver his brother, there is dignity, joy, comfort, a present blessing and a future beatitude in the Communion of Saints.

> Lord, make me one with Thine own faithful ones,
>   Thy Saints who love Thee and are loved by Thee;
>   Till the day break and till the shadows flee
> At one with them in alms and orisons:
> At one with him who toils and him who runs
>   And him who yearns for union yet to be;
>   At one with all who throng the crystal sea
> And wait the setting of our moons and suns.
> Ah, my beloved ones gone on before,
>   Who looked not back with hand upon the plough!
>   If beautiful to me while still in sight,
>   How beautiful must be your aspects now;
>   Your unknown, well-known aspects in that light
> Which clouds shall never cloud for evermore.[280]

6. But this thou hast, that thou hatest the deeds of the Nicolaitanes, which I also hate.

"Ye that love the Lord, hate evil; He preserveth the souls of His saints."[281]

Good it is to hate what Christ hateth; better still to love what He loveth, and what He is. If hatred be our strongest feature of Christ-likeness, well may we betake ourselves to dust and ashes, to repentance and first works; for without love, to hate even the same object is to hate it out of a far different heart. Pride may hate much that is contemptible, fastidiousness much that is foul, softness much that is cruel; but what has pride or fastidiousness or sensual softness in common with Christ? If all human virtues are to be mistrusted, sifted, tested, not least that virtue of hatred which has for counterfeit a deadly sin.

Nevertheless Christ clearly commends hatred, and what He commends we are bound to aim at. For great saints there may be a direct royal road thither, for ordinary sinners a circuitous path may possibly prove safer if not shorter.

Extremes meet; therefore let us work our way round to hatred by way of love. A long road perhaps, but an absolutely safe one. Were we even to die in mid-pilgrimage we might hope to be accepted according to that we had, if not according to that we had not.

Moreover, however slowly, yet surely, love does infallibly breed a hatred akin to the Divine hatred. Such hatred absolute, unqualified, irreconcilable, is restricted to the one odious object. To love involves of necessity the capacity for hatred; how shall we not hate that which may sever ourselves from the supreme desire of our hearts, or may destroy others whom we love as ourselves?

And when we have learned so much of the science of love and hatred, we shall be ready to add: How much more shall we not hate that which doeth despite to the God of all goodness? Which solitary odious thing is sin.

The difficulty of hating aright is intensified by our predisposition towards hating amiss.

Lord of all power and might, bestow upon us, I beseech Thee, both love and hatred; but only that hatred which is a form and fruit of love. For Jesus Christ's sake. Amen.

"The deeds of the Nicolaitanes."—Commentators explain that the Nicolaitanes (*see also* ver. 15) were misbelievers of impure life. A suggestion which brands as their founder Nicolas of Antioch, seventh on the catalogue of the first-ordained seven deacons (Acts 6.5,6), is not to my knowledge supported by historical proof.

Whoever was their founder, their deeds and doctrines were hateful to Christ, Who is both righteousness and truth. St. John instructs us how "he that doeth righteousness is righteous"; thus doing, we shall keep free from the guilt of the Nicolaitanes; moreover thus doing we shall escape the contamination of their doctrines, in right of our Lord's own comforting declaration: "If any man will do His will, he shall know of the doctrine, whether it be of God."[282]

To avoid the contagion of their example is the essential point. If still we feel curious to ascertain what the Nicolaitanes actually professed and did, although clearly such knowledge is not necessary to our salvation, let us rather ponder the words of St. Paul on a congruous subject: "It is a shame even to speak of those things which are done of them in secret,"—lest we should degrade ourselves like any against whom elsewhere he bears witness: "Unto them that are defiled and unbelieving is nothing pure; but even their mind and conscience is defiled."[283]

Ignorance is often a safeguard and a privilege.

> Lord, make me pure:
> Only the pure shall see Thee as Thou art,
>   And shall endure.
>   Lord, bring me low;
> For Thou wert lowly in Thy blessed heart:
>   Lord, keep me so.[284]

From CHAPTER 3

10.   Because thou hast kept the word of My patience,
I also will keep thee from the hour of temptation,
which shall come upon all the world, to try them that
dwell upon the earth.

So far as I am aware the word *patience* is exclusively a New Testament word, although *patient* and *patiently* occur in both Testaments. Not that the virtue so named waited for these last days for illustration: on the contrary, St. James cites the Prophets and Job as examples of patience.[285] Yet because patience in perfection was not found on earth until Christ trod our weary ways, it wakes a harmonious chord in our hearts to observe that till His blessed human lips spake the word, that word was not (unless I mistake) recorded in the Scriptures of Truth.

Once in the days of His mortality He had said to His disciples, "In your patience possess ye your souls;" but now in His glorious immortality He so far unites His suffering Church with Himself as to say, "Because thou hast kept the word of My patience."[286]

O kind Lord, Who so identifiest Thy Church with Thyself that what Thou art she is accounted, and what she is Thou takest upon Thyself, grant that as Thy Desire is unto her, so her whole desire and longing may be unto Thee purely and without distraction, for ever and ever.

Patience goes with sorrow, not with joy. And by a natural instinct sorrow ranges itself with darkness, joy with light. But eyes that have been supernaturalized recognize, not literally only, but likewise in a figure, how darkness reveals more luminaries than does the day: to the day appertains a single sun; to the night innumerable, incalculable, by man's perception inexhaustible stars.

This is one of nature's revelations, attested by experience. God grant us to receive the parallel revelation of grace: then whatever tribulation befalls us will by His blessing work in us patience, and our patience will work experience, and our experience hope; "and hope maketh not ashamed; because the love of God is shed abroad in our hearts by the Holy Ghost which is given unto us."[287]

What those saints kept was not patience merely, but "the word" of Christ's patience. At His word they kept patience; they kept it because of His will toward themselves, and subject to each jot and tittle of His revered law. He was their pattern and text-book of patience; because He bore contradiction of sinners, so did they; because He, when He was reviled, reviled not again, neither did they; because He prayed for His enemies, they likewise prayed for theirs.

Of these unknown, unrecorded Philadelphians do we then really and truly know such great things? Yea, such things as these, inasmuch as we are certified that they kept the Word of Christ's patience.

"As unknown, and yet well known."[288]

> Patience must dwell with Love, for Love and Sorrow
>   Have pitched their tent together here:
> Love all alone will build a house to-morrow,
>   And sorrow not be near.
>
> To-day for Love's sake hope, still hope, in sorrow,
>   Rest in her shade and hold her dear:
> To-day she nurses thee; and lo! to-morrow
>   Love only will be near.[289]

Patience is its own reward. It preoccupies the soul with a sort of satisfaction which suppresses insatiable craving, vain endeavour, rebellious desire. It keeps the will steadfast, the mind disengaged, the heart quiet. Patience having little or having nothing yet possesses all things; for through faith and patience the elect inherit the promises.

God reserves many ways within His limitless resources whereby either from or under temptation to rescue as He pleases any soul He pleases. Death is one of His blessed ways: "The righteous perisheth, and no man layeth it to heart: and merciful men are taken away, none considering that the righteous is taken away from the evil to come. He shall enter into peace: they shall rest in their beds, each one walking in his uprightness."[290] (Let us not then mourn inconsolably for our own "not lost, but gone before.") Or He can with a stroke fortify that weak point which would facilitate a given temptation, as blindness or deafness seals up eye or ear against pollution. Or He can deaden our faculty of enjoyment, and therewith our inclination to parley. Or He can replace an expelled vice by its antagonistic virtue, so that seven or seven times seven wicked spirits moaning and gibbering around our swept and garnished house should find no entrance there.

Nor can we while wheat and tares grow together foresee which ears quickly ripened and spared the brunt of wind and rain, will be garnered betimes as firstfruits of a multitudinous harvest. Not even their mother presenting her petition for the sons of Zebedee can have calculated that St. James would head the noble army of martyred Apostles, whilst St. John, the last survivor of their glorious company, would come to his grave in a full age, like as a shock of corn cometh in, in his season.

"The hour of temptation, which shall come upon all the world, to try them that dwell upon the earth."—The surface of the universe, or to bring my remark within a less unmanageable area, the surface of familiar nature and of society, presents incalculable if not infinite variety. Light stands out against darkness, growth against decay; the contrast of wedding and funeral stares us in the face. Divergences are the order of our day; insomuch that it even has been alleged that no two leaves can be found alike; and I for one am ready to believe it.

Yet the more we think over these diversities and such as these, the more (I suppose) we may discern something common underlying all that is individual. To take an instance: at one moment a wedding appears all life, a funeral all death; at another, both are perceived to be equally and at once an end and a beginning.

A step further, and I recognize that during this probational period not some influences only, but all influences as they touch us become our trials, tests, temptations; assayed by which we stand or fall, we are found wanting or not wanting, as genuinely as will be the case with us in the last tremendous Day of account.

Therefore while fear is quickened because of constant peril, any sort of unreasoning horror is abated, inasmuch as even the great last Judgment though supreme and final will not stand unprecedented and alone: over and over again we have been judged and condemned, or else acquitted; over and over again have fallen or stood to our own Master.

O my God, grant us the uprightness of saints, or at the least only such falls as they arise from. For Jesus Christ's merits' sake. Amen.

This "hour of temptation" was ordained to overtake all the world. Is it already past, is it passing, or is it still to come? To ourselves it may be present, or it may be future: it were rash to reckon any temptation assuredly past, whilst the liability to all temptation remains. The "old man"[291] dies slowly, tediously, painfully: death-stricken by our Mighty Avenger of Blood, his life is indeed but death and corruption, yet "while there is life there is fear."[292]

"To try them that dwell upon the earth."—All alike must be tried: not all alike will meet and pass through the trial. The qualification for trial is dwelling upon the earth: they who are least of the earth earthy will presumably fare best; inasmuch as this trial is not in order to confirm man upon the earth that now is, but to fit him for translation to that new heaven and new earth wherein shall dwell righteousness.

Foothold we must needs have, at least until we be made equal unto the angels; but let us pray against roothold. A foot may spurn the ground it cannot choose but tread; a root grasps and holds fast the soil whence it sucks subsistence, and whence it oftentimes cannot be wrenched except to die.

Sparrows and swallows are alike safe when once they have become denizens of the amiable tabernacles. But on earth, which is at best heaven's ante-chamber, it is wiser to construct a one-season's nest than a house for prolonged residence: the swallow of this generation is wiser than the sparrow.

> Wisest of sparrows that sparrow which sitteth alone
> Perched on the housetop, its own upper chamber, for nest;
> Wisest of swallows that swallow which timely has flown
> Over the turbulent sea to the land of its rest:
> Wisest of sparrows and swallows, if I were as wise!
>
> Wisest of spirits that spirit which dwelleth apart
> Hid in the Presence of God for a chapel and nest,
> Sending a wish and a will and a passionate heart
> Over the eddy of life to that Presence in rest:
> Seated alone and in peace till God bids it arise.[293]

Will the trial last for ever?—No, for some period which an hour represents. "Couldest not thou watch one hour?"

Will it overwhelm us?—No, for the promise is unto us and to our children: "God is faithful, Who will not suffer you to be tempted above that ye are able; but will with the temptation also make a way to escape, that ye may be able to bear it."

When will it befall us?—"Of that day and hour knoweth no man . . . Watch therefore."

We fear. "He that feareth God shall come forth of them all."

We hope. "It is good that a man should both hope and quietly wait for the salvation of the Lord."[294]

"And who is he that will harm you, if ye be followers of that which is good? But and if ye suffer for righteousness" sake, happy are ye: and be not afraid of their terror, neither be troubled; but sanctify the Lord God in your hearts: and be ready always to give an answer to every man that asketh you a reason of the hope that is in you with meekness and fear: having a good conscience."[295]

12.   *Him that overcometh will I make a pillar in the temple of My God, and he shall go no more out: and I will write upon him the Name of My God, and the name of the city of My God, which is new Jerusalem, which cometh down out of Heaven from My God: and I will write upon him My new Name.*

13.   *He that hath an ear, let him hear what the Spirit saith unto the churches.*

"I will write upon him the Name of My God, and the name of the city of My God, which is new Jerusalem, . . . and I will write upon him My new Name."

Children bear their father's name, a wife her husband's. Thus the Divine Father bestows His own Name on His adopted children, and thus the Divine Bridegroom on His purchased bride; and this to all eternity, as we see in the text.

But Christian Baptism is Baptism in the Name of the Most Holy Trinity, of Father, of Son, and of Holy Ghost. All through mortal life regenerate man bears that Sacred Name in Its fulness: God forbid that he who finally perseveres unto salvation, should then cease to bear It in unabated fulness of Perfection. (I write under correction: I repudiate my own thoughts if erroneous.)

Wherefore I humbly ponder whether "the name of the City of God, which is new Jerusalem," may hide at once and reveal the Supreme Name of that Divine Most Holy Spirit Who deigns to inhabit her. "In His temple doth every one speak of His glory";[296] and she is that Temple built of living stones; which stones are men, of whom each one severally is constituted a Temple of the Holy Ghost consecrated to worship God in spirit and in truth.

If such a train of thought be lawful, it seems to illustrate the Inscrutability of the Third Person of the Ever Blessed Trinity: a sacred Inscrutability of Mystery in the revelation to man of God the Holy Spirit, beyond what invests the corresponding revelation of God the Father or of God the Son. Even natural instinct attests as true the revelation of One Divine, universal Father: the heart's desire of all nations heretofore thirsted for, and now in some measure acknowledges, the revelation of God the Son. But Christ Himself said in reference to an operation of God the Holy Spirit, "The wind bloweth where it listeth, and thou hearest the sound thereof, but canst not tell whence it cometh, and whither it goeth"; and we are ready to answer: "Lo, He goeth by me, and I see Him not: He passeth on also, but I perceive Him not."[297]

I think that a devout contemplation of our most approachable Master may help us to perceive and adore our "Other Comforter." During His earthly life Jesus engaged few followers; and these in varying degrees of knowledge or of ignorance apprehended or apprehended not His Divinity; but after His Resurrection, and again in greater splendour after His Ascension, light sprang up. Thus so long as eyes could see and ears hear and hands handle the Word of Life, Christ abode for the most part unseen, unheard, untouched; but when a cloud had received Him out of sight, then it became possible for mankind at all times and in all places to behold Him with the eye of faith, listen to Him with the ear of hope, hold Him fast and not let Him go with the clasped hands of adoring love. So long as His Tabernacle was mortal it obscured the indwelling Deity: when His mortal put on immortality it revealed what till then it had veiled.

For more than these eighteen hundred years past it has pleased the Holy Spirit by choosing mortal men as His temples to dwell in houses made of dust and which must return to dust. The evidence He vouchsafes of His Presence consists in the supernatural endowments of His saints. Holy men, holy women, holy children, act like prisms to exhibit His Light: they are not that Light, but bear witness of that Light. Their love, joy, peace, longsuffering, gentleness, goodness, faith, meekness, temperance, bear witness to Him: these are His fruits, and the fruits declare the tree.

Now if Christ's mighty works, perfection of grace, unmeasured plenitude of the Spirit, did not to the universal apprehension announce His Godhead so long as this was enshrined in a mortal though ever-immaculate Body,—no wonder is it that the Presence of God the Holy Ghost, in shrines so narrow, frail, flawed, polluted as are ordinary human hearts which have still to die, is often overlooked or denied: no wonder that His very Being should be denied by some who look for judgment, but behold oppression; for righteousness, but behold a cry.

An awful responsibility devolves on each Christian soul. You, I, are summoned and constituted to bear witness to the Person and Work of Almighty God the Holy Spirit; to be in some degree His evidence, His illustration, His proof. "O God, Thou knowest my foolishness; and my sins are not hid from Thee . . . Let not those that seek Thee be confounded for my sake, O God of Israel."

The saints are God's epistle known and read of all men: "tables of testimony . . . written with the finger of God."[298]

"New Jerusalem, which cometh down out of heaven from My God."—Wherefore cometh she down? and whither cometh she down?

It seems to be the reverse of what our Redeemer spake concerning Himself: "No man hath ascended up to heaven, but He that came down from heaven, even the Son of Man which is in heaven."[299]

He first descended, then ascended. His followers one by one slowly, painfully, precariously toil up from earth to the better country. And then after all we read that the New Jerusalem will come down!

Now if for the present this scarcely sounds to us like any phase of beatitude, it may prove to us none the less profitable: by setting us on our guard against fancying we know and comprehend what we neither know nor comprehend; by inviting us to trust God implicitly, and not to lean to our own understanding; by bringing home to us that God's perfect Will and not our own desire or imagination is the standard of beatitude.

O our God, teach us so to trust Thee that knowledge and ignorance may be alike welcome to us when of Thine appointing. What we know we know only in part; what we know not Thou knowest altogether. The darkness and light to Thee are both alike: therefore under the shadow of Thy wings will we rejoice. Through Jesus Christ our Lord. Amen.

"My New Name."—O Lord Whom we have loved as God, as Man, as Son of God, Son of Man, Son of David, Son of Mary, as Christ, as Jesus, what is that New Name, under which Thine own shall one day love Thee? I ask not to know it while It is secret. I ask that with all my brethren and all my sisters in Thee I may know, adore, love Thee under that New Name and under every Name through all eternity: for ever following on to know Thee; ever learning, and coming to the knowledge of the truth, and learning still for ever.

> O Lord, I am ashamed to seek Thy Face
>   As tho' I loved Thee as Thy saints love Thee:
>   Yet turn from those Thy lovers, look on me,
> Disgrace me not with uttermost disgrace;
> But pour on me ungracious, pour Thy grace
>   To purge my heart and bid my will go free,
>   Till I too taste Thy hidden Sweetness, see
> Thy hidden Beauty in the holy place.
> O Thou Who callest sinners to repent,
> Call me Thy sinner unto penitence,
>   For many sins grant me the greater love:
>   Set me above the waterfloods, above
> Devil and shifting world and fleshly sense,
> Thy Mercy's all-amazing monument.[300]

From **CHAPTER 4**

1. After this I looked, and, behold, a door was opened in heaven: and the first voice which I heard was as it were of a trumpet talking with me; which said, Come up hither, and I will shew thee things which must be hereafter.

"After this I looked, and, behold . . ."—Let us too look, even if we should not behold. "Mine eyes fail with looking upward: O Lord, I am oppressed; undertake for me." "Then I saw that wisdom excelleth folly, as far as light excelleth darkness."[301]

Far be it from me to think to unfold mysteries or interpret prophecies. But I trust that to gaze in whatever ignorance on what God reveals, is so far to do His will. If ignorance breed humility, it will not debar from wisdom. If ignorance betake itself to prayer, it will lay hold on grace.

As children may feel the awe of a storm, the beauty of sunrise or sunset, so as least I too may deepen awe, and stir up desire by a contemplation of things inevitable, momentous, transcendent. "Consider the work of God: for who can make that straight, which He hath made crooked? In the day of prosperity be joyful, but in the day of adversity consider."[302]

The eagle strengthened with might gazes full at the sun. Glory be to God for all His gifts to all His creatures.

But God has not bidden us be mighty as eagles, but be harmless as doves. I suppose a dove may be no more fit than myself to look steadily at the sun: we both might be blinded by what would enlighten that stronger bird. The dove brings not much of her own to the sun, yet the sun caresses and beautifies her silver wings and her feathers like gold: it would be a sore mistake on the dove's part were she to say, Because I am not the eagle I am not a sun bird, and so were to cut herself off from the sun's gracious aspect.

And since five sparrows are sold for two farthings, and not one of them is forgotten before God, even the least and last of *birds* may take courage to court the light-giving, life-giving, munificent sun.

"After this,"—after, that is, a revelation, an alarum, a Great Voice of praise and rebuke, hope and fear. Rebuke and fear should not paralyse us: they should rather rouse us to instant exertion, instant obedience, instant prayer.

O Lord our God, deliver us, I beseech Thee, from idle tremblings and abject fear. It is Thou: give us grace not to be afraid, except with the fear of those who always fearing are happy. For Jesus Christ's sake. Amen.

"I looked,"—If we will not look, we should not behold even though a door were opened in heaven for our enlightenment.

This Apocalypse is a celestial door opened to us: let us not, until we have looked, despair of seeing somewhat. Having looked, we shall not despair.

What shall we see? As it were the company of two armies; life and good, death and evil. Wherefore choose life.

7.   *And the first beast was like a lion, and the second beast like a calf, and the third beast had a face as a man, and the fourth beast was like a flying eagle.*

Tradition assigns these four Living Creatures to the four Evangelists. St. John that Son of Thunder illuminated and unconsumed by "the Fire of God"[303] inherits the sun-facing Eagle. St. Luke with his revelation of reconciling Love, the sacrificial Calf. The Lion and the Man remain for St. Matthew and St. Mark; of whom each sometimes takes one, sometimes the other: reasons have been alleged for either arrangement. If the Man is attributed to the St. Matthew, we may connect it with his table of our Lord's Human genealogy: while St. Mark's Lion may remind us how he alone notices that it was "with the wild beasts"[304] that our Lord sojourned during Forty Days in the wilderness. Reversing the position (and not to enumerate other points), the Lion of the royal tribe of Judah befits St. Matthew in virtue of his unique narrative of the Adoration of the Magi when they worshipped Christ as King: the Man harmonizes with that special prominence of the Very Manhood which it has been thought characterizes St. Mark's Gospel.

Yet this venerable scheme need not (I hope) exclude the view that in these august Living Creatures; the Cherubim apparently of Ezekiel's visions; the Chariot of the Almighty Himself, whence the Psalmist sings, "He rode upon a Cherub, and did fly,"[305]—that in them is perpetuated a sort of summary and memorial of those good gifts which God has lavished on man indeed pre-eminently, but likewise in varying degrees and after various fashions on beast, bird, and every inferior creature that hath life; all which creatures at the first were beheld to be very good. St. Paul writes: "The earnest expectation of the creature waiteth for the manifestation of the sons of God. For the creature was made subject to vanity, not willingly but by reason of Him Who hath subjected the same in hope, because the creature itself also shall be delivered from the bondage of corruption into the glorious liberty of the children of God. For we know that the whole creation groaneth and travaileth in pain together until now. And not only they, but ourselves also, which have the firstfruits of the Spirit, even we ourselves groan within ourselves, waiting for the adoption, to wit, the redemption of our body":[306]— thus opening our eyes to a mysterious element in those lower existences so familiar and often so friendly to us. We think of them in relation to man: yet surely the unnumbered multitudes of them which live, propagate, die "on the earth, where no man is; on the wilderness, wherein there is no man,"[307] may have some purpose independent of direct human profit, discipline, convenience. "O Lord, how manifold are Thy works! in wisdom hast Thou made them all."[308]

Sacred association makes reverend to us lamb, lion, sheep (*see* Isa. 53.7), dove, eagle (*see* Deut. 32.11,12), even leopard and bear (*see* Hos. 13.7,8): and endears to us on inferior grounds hart, stork and sparrow, owl and pelican. All sentient creatures have a claim on us: and well may we admit and honour their claim, when we recollect Who vouchsafed to have respect to the much cattle of Nineveh.

O Good God, Who permitting to every man his temptation preparest for him a way of escape, and hast constituted the present age a period of knowledge and of thirst after knowledge; give us grace never to pursue knowledge by avenues of cruelty or impurity, but keeping innocency to take heed to the thing that is right; lest headstrong lust of good and evil mislead us to choose the evil and refuse the good. Which God forbid, for His All Holy Son's sake. Amen.

If Cherubim transcendent in knowledge and accounted second in the ninefold celestial hierarchy exhibit any likeness to man's inferiors, well may I be contented to learn of these humble brethren. The serpent can teach me wisdom, the dove harmlessness, the ant prudent industry, the coney adaptability to circumstances, the locust self-government, the spider resource; lions and young ravens set me, in some sort, an example of prayer; dog and sow scare me from relapses into sin.

A Psalm asserts: "O Lord, Thou preservest man and beast"[309]; or according to the Prayer-book version: "Thou, Lord, shalt save both man and beast." It were unwise to reflect on no statement besides "the beasts that perish"[310]; or so to exalt man's spirit which goeth upward, over the beast's which goeth downward, as practically to ignore that the beast is endowed with any spirit at all. Land may cry out against an unrighteous owner, and furrows complain: how much more the moving creature that hath life.

From CHAPTER 5

6.   And I beheld, and lo, in the midst of the Throne and of the four beasts, and in the midst of the elders, stood a Lamb as it had been slain, having seven horns and seven eyes, which are the seven Spirits of God sent forth into all the earth.

If the preceding chapter (4) unfolds a vision of the Creator surrounded and worshipped by His creation, this present chapter appears more particularly to set before us in vision the Redeemer, always well pleasing to God His Father, and to Whom is given all power in Heaven and in earth.

Doubtless a thread of perfect sequence runs throughout Divine Revelation, binding it into one sacred and flawless whole. But not so do feeble eyes discern it. I can but study piece by piece, word by word, unworthy even to behold the little I seem to observe.

Much of this awful Apocalypse opens to my apprehension rather a series of aspects than any one defined and certified object. It summons me to watch and pray and give thanks; it urges me to climb heavenward. Its thread doubtless consists unbroken: but my clue is at the best woven of broken lights and shadows, here a little and there a little. As when years ago I abode some while within sight of a massive sea rock, I used to see it put on different appearances: it seemed to float baseless in air, its summit vanished in cloud, it displayed upon its surface varied markings, it passed from view altogether in a mist, it fronted me distinct and solid far into the luminous northern summer night, still appearing many and various while all the time I knew it to be one and the same,—so now this Apocalypse I know to be one congruous, harmonious whole, yet can I read it only as it were in disjointed portions, some to myself inexplicable, some not unmistakably defined; all nevertheless, please God, profitable to me for doctrine, for reproof, for correction, for instruction in righteousness.

From CHAPTER 8

2.   *And I saw the seven angels which stood before God; and to them were given seven trumpets.*

Recalling the seven trumpets of rams' horns sounded by the seven priests on seven successive days, whereby was announced and achieved the overthrow of Jericho.

The seven priests blew their trumpets together, the seven Angels one by one; the seven priests thus appearing as it were equivalent to the single angel; in accordance with St. Peter's declaration: "Angels, which are greater in power and might."[311] And as the agency is greater, so apparently the series of events is greater and the result greater; harmonizing with Isaiah's prophecy, when after foretelling "the day of the great slaughter, when the towers fall,"—he adds: "Moreover the light of the moon shall be as the light of the sun, and the light of the sun shall be sevenfold, as the light of seven days."[312]

Jericho, the outpost of the Promised Land; the earthly Israel shouting and going up straight before them: a figure of the spiritual Israel going out with joy and led forth with peace into the heavenly Canaan.

The destruction of Jericho and entering in of the chosen race, whether considered from the historical or from the emblematical view-point, encourages us to face hopefully the awful unprecedented blast of the seven angelic trumpets. Then the Ark of the Lord encamped before Jericho among the thousands of Israel: and Christ our true and sole Ark of Safety has promised His Church: "Lo, I am with you alway, even unto the end of the world."[313]

His Presence ensures safety and every blessing. Yet it may be—and if such be His Will, Christ grant it may be even so to you, to all, to me—it may be that one day It will ensure these by taking the place to us of any other safety and of every other spiritual blessing. For instance: of old He pronounced, "The Sabbath was made for man, and not man for the Sabbath," upholding its pious though not its superstitious observance; and again He tenderly bade His disciples, "Pray ye that your flight be not . . . on the Sabbath-day."[314] The Sabbath ranks amongst venerable and immutable Divine institutions, dating back to unfallen man in the Garden of Eden; yet may it be reft from us as regards its outward national observance, though never from the faithful as regards its inward hallowing. Already in England (not to glance at other countries) the signs of the times are ominous: Sunday is being diverted by some to business, by others to pleasure; Church congregations are often meagre, and so services are chilled. Our solemn feasts languish, and our fasts where are they? Yet each for himself, and God for us all, we can if we choose "remember the Sabbath-day, to keep it holy";[315] jealous of its essentials, not wedded to its accidents.

So Joshua and his host when summoned to storm Jericho day after day for seven days, must amongst those days have kept one unexampled Sabbath, if not in the letter yet in the spirit.

From **CHAPTER 9**

1. And the fifth angel sounded, and I saw a star fall from heaven unto the earth: and to him was given the key of the bottomless pit.

The Revised Version has: "I saw a star from heaven fallen unto the earth,"—not seeming necessarily to imply that St. John witnessed its downfall; but perhaps that he discerned the star, that (so to say) it only then came to light, being *already* fallen.

If such a suggestion may be entertained, then the office assigned to this fallen star may possibly brand it as being one of the rulers of the darkness of this world; once superhuman, but now of its own free choice a subhuman wandering star to whom is reserved the blackness of darkness for ever. "How art thou fallen from heaven, O Lucifer, son of the morning!"[316]

Whatever the star be, one thing is evident: its function is assigned to it; it is not an independent agent, still less an independent potentate. If it be a malevolent power rejoicing in iniquity, yet has it no power at all except under constraint or by sufferance; any more than the sea can overpass its decreed place, or behemoth evade the sword of Him that made him.

A fallen star, not otherwise an outcast star; a self-made outcast. Whoso turns his back on heaven may propose to stop short at earth: but next below yawns the pit. The outcasts of the final day who depart into outer darkness will all be self-made outcasts.

> Oh fallen star! a darkened light,
>   A glory hurtled from its car,
> Self-blasted from the holy height:
>   Oh fallen star!
>
> Fallen beyond earth's utmost bar,
> Beyond return, beyond far sight
>   Of outmost glimmering nebular:
>
> Now blackness, which once walked in white;
>   Now death, whose life once glowed afar;
> Oh son of dawn that loved the night,
>   Oh fallen star![317]

Self-conceit blinds, self-will destroys; self-oblation consecrates, self-sacrifice saves: for once our Master taught His disciples: "If any man will come after Me, let him deny himself, and take up his cross daily, and follow Me. For whosoever will save his life shall lose it: but whosoever will lose his life for My sake, the same shall save it."[318]

The bottomless pit preaches a sermon. It has a lid: which keep shut, and the pit's bottomlessness remains neutral. But lift the lid, and none can calculate the volume of deathly outcome from a fathomless abyss, or the depth of a fall into it.

If God permits the lid of evil to be lifted as a test or as a punishment, the key remains in His hand to secure that lid again when He will. But if I lift any lid of evil, I have no power to shut off the dire escape from myself or from others: death and defilement I may let loose, but I cannot recapture. Solomon gives us a sample of such deeds and their consequences: "The beginning of strife is as when one letteth out water": followed by a precept: "therefore leave off contention, before it be meddled with,"[319]—the precept in spirit though not in the letter being applicable to all "touching of pitch."

20.   *And the rest of the men which were not killed by these plagues yet repented not of the works of their hands, that they should not*

worship devils, and idols of gold, and silver, and brass, and stone,
and of wood: which neither can see, nor hear, nor walk:

21.   Neither repented they of their murders, nor of their sorceries,
nor of their fornication, nor of their thefts.

These two verses by giving a summary of the Ten Commandments remind us that God's Will changes not; that even "if we believe not, yet He abideth faithful: He cannot deny Himself."[320] As St. John points out to the disciples of his day: "Brethren, I write no new commandment unto you, but an old commandment which ye had from the beginning. The old commandment is the word which ye have heard from the beginning."[321]

Whoever worships devils transgresses glaringly the First Commandment, and less obviously that Fourth Commandment which appropriates or hallows the whole of time either to sanctioned labour or to enjoined rest. Certain heathens formally and of set purpose do, as we are assured, worship devils. This literal gross act is not perhaps likely to tempt nineteenth century Christians; or even others who, without being personally Christian, have been born and bred where in a certain sense the world itself is Christian as well as civilized. Wherefore, not so much looking at my remote neighbour, I consider myself; lest I also be tempted, although by means modified to assail my own particular weak points.

PLEASE GOD. I will have nothing to do with spiritualism, whether it be imposture or a black art; or with mesmerism, lest I clog my free will; or with hypnotism, lest wilful self-surrender become my road to evil choice, imagination, conduct, voluntary or involuntary. Neither will I subscribe to any theory which would pursue knowledge by cruel or foul methods; or do evil that good may come.[322] Neither will I either in jest or in earnest tamper with fortune-telling or any other fashion of prying into the future. Moreover, I will aim at avoiding both in speech and in correspondence such expressions as by good luck, or, there seems a spell against us. In performing my daily duties I must strive against the spirit of a frightened slave (which so far as it goes is the spirit of a devil worshipper), and must aim instead at the conformed will of a loving child: I ought to shrink from sin more sensitively than from punishment. In all my dealings temporal and spiritual I must adhere to a just weight, a just measure, even balances, a superhuman standard. I must set conscience above convenience, and Divine law above worldly conventions. I cannot have two masters. I cannot serve God and Mammon. "I have set the Lord always before me," sings David.[323]

The Second Commandment is obviously broken by worshipping idols of any sort, and the mention of their inability to "hear" suggests without stating that kindred breach of the Third Commandment which is involved in misdirected prayer, praise, deprecation, thanksgiving. Studying my own more probable temptations, I pass over idols of brass, stone, wood, to dwell rather upon those of gold and silver. A molten and graven image of gold or of silver is strictly and literally reproduced nowadays and for us moderns, although in altered guise, in the current coin of the realm: it depends on myself whether to make it my minister or my idol. Demas is a warning beacon:[324] set up against him for our encouragement and emulation stands St. Peter, who silver and gold had none. Since I cannot avoid continual contact with that which has the material and make of an idol, I must take good heed that it become not to me an idol. The "almighty dollar" seems to me a phrase simply (however unintentionally) blasphemous: in my mouth it would be blasphemy. May such an estimate of money be far from Christian tongues, and farther from Christian hearts.

Of the other sins enumerated (murders, sorceries, fornication, thefts) three more or less flagrantly transgress the Fifth, Sixth, Seventh, and Eighth Commandments, all belonging to the Second Table (unless so far as the Fifth is concerned, of which I have seen the position discussed). Sorceries alone, at least at first sight, might appear to fall exclusively under the ban of the First Table. But if sorceries, while insulting the Divine Majesty, be regarded as likewise seducing, hoodwinking, misleading, entrapping man; then we recognize in it a distinct breach of the Ninth Commandment: it becomes a fatal false witness borne against our neighbour. One Commandment, the Tenth, remains: and this being spiritual, covetousness may be viewed as underlying and prompting the infractions of the preceding Five. For covetousness, preferring as it does self-interest to alien interest, whether or not co-extensive with selfishness, does at any rate so far as it goes cover the same ground; and is directly contrary to love, which, working no ill to its neighbour, is therefore the fulfilling of the law.

Yet the desperate element as regards these sinners against their own souls was not that they had sinned, but that they did not repent. Repentance would have bleached their scarlet to snow, their crimson to wool. It would have made them like unto ancient Israel when "Samuel said unto the people, Fear not: ye have done all this wickedness: yet turn not aside from following the Lord, but serve the Lord with all your heart; and turn ye not aside: for then should ye go after vain things, which cannot profit nor deliver; for they are vain. For the Lord will not forsake His people for His great Name's sake; because it hath pleased the Lord to make you His people."[325]

All is promised to the penitent, but repentance is not promised to any individual sinner.

Tortures and terrors cannot do the work of love. Nay, more: Love from without cannot accomplish its own work, unless there be some response from love within.

The proportion of men is one taken, two left: and the two repent not. I who write, any who read, are for the present left: God vouchsafe to all, vouchsafe to me, repentance unto amendment of life, for Jesus Christ's sake.

And this thought, that two are as it were "left" even though in such extremity, brings home to all who are not reprobate certain inspired words redolent of hope: "Two are better than one; because they have a good reward for their labour. For if they fall, the one will lift up his fellow: but woe to him that is alone when he falleth; for he hath not another to help him up . . . And if one prevail against him, two shall withstand him."326

If then I be one of twain I must comport myself accordingly: be it in labour and in hope of reward; in falls, in arisings, in helps; in contest, in alliance, and in victory; I must as much as in me lies impart to him that hath not, and bear my neighbour's burdens.

Lord Jesus, Thou becamest Man thereby to become One of twain, Thyself and Thy Bride the Church. Thou hast laboured for her; and labourest with her, and sharest with her Thy reward. If she fall Thou liftest her up: happy she who is never alone when she falleth. If the battle go sore against her, yet with Thee she discomfiteth a host: happy she whom Thou hast joined unto Thyself.

Because the Church is moulded after Thy likeness, her least and last member is thus moulded. Lord, give me grace ever thankfully to account myself one of twain; humbly receiving help from my superiors, and myself helping any Thou empowerest me to help. Thou Who createdst all things out of nothing, lay help even on me, making my influence tend to good. Turn, I beseech Thee, my sins to repentance, my repentance to amendment, my amendment to a shining light. Even so of Thy Goodness perfect all and perfect me. Amen.

From **CHAPTER 10**

6.   And sware by Him that liveth for ever and ever, Who created heaven, and the things that therein are, and the earth, and the things that therein are, and the sea, and the things which are therein, that there should be time no longer:

"And sware by Him that liveth for ever and ever . . . that there should be time no longer."—*Delay* has been proposed instead of *time*. As this alternative word would have to do with the interpretation of the sense, not with simple meditation, I leave it to my betters.

Studying the Authorized Version as it actually stands, a contrast is suggested between "for ever and ever" and "time." He that liveth for ever and ever inhabiteth eternity; His works (enumerated by the angel) are creatures of time. Eternity is duration which neither begins nor ends; time is duration which both begins and ends: the mystery of eternity seems to be its having no beginning; the obscure point of time its having an end.

What is time? It is not subtracted from eternity, which if diminished would fall short of being eternal: neither is it substituted awhile for eternity, which thus would assume both end and beginning: neither is it simultaneous with eternity, because it is in Him Who inhabiteth eternity (not time) that we ourselves day by day live and move and have our being. Perhaps I shall not mislead my own thoughts by defining to myself time as that condition or aspect of eternity which consists with the possibility of probation.

If such indeed be time, then in part I understand how at length there shall be time no longer. The words, "Their time should have endured for ever" (Ps. 81.15), suggest that no break will occur between time and eternity.

> Time seems not short:
>   If so I call to mind
>   Its vast prerogative to loose or bind,
> And bear and strike amort
>   All humankind.
>
> Time seems not long:
>   If I peer out and see
>   Sphere within sphere, time in eternity,
> And I hear the alternate song
>   Cry endlessly.
>
> Time greatly short,
>   O time so briefly long,
>   Yea, time sole battleground of right and wrong;
> Art thou a time for sport
>   And for a song?[327]

From CHAPTER 12

1.   And there appeared a great wonder in heaven; a woman clothed with the sun, and the moon under her feet, and upon her head a crown of twelve stars:

The Preacher, the son of David, King in Jerusalem, has left on record: "I know that, whatsoever God doeth, it shall be for ever: nothing can be put to it, nor anything taken from it; and God doeth it, that men should fear before Him. That which hath been is now; and that which is to be hath already been; and God requireth that which is past."[328] Thus the past which we know, presages the future which we know not.

And Greater than that King and Wiser than that Preacher, our Lord Himself said to His disciples: "Have ye understood all these things? They say unto Him, Yea, Lord. Then said He unto them, Therefore every scribe which is instructed unto the kingdom of heaven is like unto a man that is an house-holder, which bringeth forth out of his treasure things new and old."[329] Now as every Christian "is instructed unto the kingdom of heaven," he cannot be destitute of a treasure whence to bring forth somewhat; new it may be, old it cannot but be.

Of this Apocalypse the occult unfulfilled signification will be new; the letter is old. Old, not merely because these eighteen hundred years it has warned us to flee from the wrath to come; but also because each figure appeals to our experience, even when it stands for some object unprecedented or surpassing.

A rose might preach beauty and a lily purity to a receptive mind, although the ear had not yet heard tell of the Rose of Sharon and Lily of the Valleys.

"A woman clothed with the sun, and the moon under her feet, and upon her head a crown of twelve stars."—Whatever else may here be hidden, there stands revealed that "great wonder," weakness made strong and shame swallowed up in celestial glory. For thus the figure is set before our eyes. Through Eve's lapse, weakness and shame devolved on woman as her characteristics, in a manner special to herself and unlike the corresponding heritage of man.

And as instinctively we personify the sun and moon as *he* and *she,* I trust there is no harm in my considering that her sun-clothing indicates how in that heaven where St. John in vision beheld her, she will be made equal with men and angels; arrayed in all human virtues, and decked with all communicable Divine graces: whilst the moon under her feet portends that her sometime infirmity of purpose and changeableness of mood have, by preventing, assisting, final grace, become immutable; she has done all and stands; from the lowest place she has gone up higher. As love of his Lord enabled St. Peter to tread the sea, so love of the same Lord sets weak woman immovable on the waves of this troublesome world, triumphantly erect, despite her own frailty, made not "like unto a wheel,"[330] amid all the changes and chances of this mortal life.

Eve's temptation and fall suggest the suitableness and safety of much (though by no means of all) ignorance, and the wholesomeness of studying what is open without prying into what is secret. We have no reason to doubt that the forbidden fruit was genuinely "pleasant to the eyes":[331] as such she might innocently have gazed upon it with delight, and for that delight might profitably have returned thanks to the Author and Giver of all good. Not till she became wise in her own conceit, disregarding the plain obvious meaning of words, and theorizing on her own responsibility as to physical and intellectual results, did she bring sin and death into the world. The Tree of the Knowledge of Good and Evil was as it were a standing prophet ever reiterating the contingent sentence, Thou shalt surely die.[332] This sentence, plain and unmistakable, she connived at explaining away, and being deceived, was undone.

Eve exhibits one extreme of feminine character, the Blessed Virgin the opposite extreme. Eve parleyed with a devil: holy Mary "was troubled"[333] at the salutation of an Angel. Eve sought knowledge: Mary instruction. Eve aimed at self-indulgence: Mary at self-oblation. Eve, by disbelief and disobedience, brought sin to the birth: Mary, by faith and submission, Righteousness.

And yet, even as at the foot of the Cross, St. Mary Magdalene, out of whom went seven devils, stood beside the "lily among thorns,"[334] the Mother of sorrows: so (I humbly hope and trust) amongst all saints of all time will stand before the Throne, Eve the beloved first Mother of us all. Who that has loved and revered her own immediate dear mother, will not echo the hope?

Again and eminently, the heavenly figure under consideration presents an image of the Church: "the King hath brought me into His chambers."

"Who is she that looketh forth as the morning, fair as the moon, clear as the sun, and terrible as an army with banners?"[335] All glorious she is within by the Indwelling of the Holy Spirit, and effluent glory envelopes her as with the sun for a garment. The moon, set below, may never again eclipse the sun; yet inasmuch as the perfect life had to be developed out of the imperfect, the unchangeable out of the changeable, therefore the moon abides underlying that consummated glory. Twelve stars compose her crown, a twelvefold splendour. I have seen the Twelve Apostles suggested as the interpretation of this symbol; and well may it direct our thoughts to their glorious company, the illumination of their doctrine, the shining light of their example. Perhaps there will be no harm in an additional gloss. The eternal state of the Church Triumphant is expressed by her sun-vesture; the moon beneath her feet memorializes her temporal probation while militant in this world; the twelve stars may—may they not? for earth's day is as night when compared with heaven's day—may remind us of those twelve hours in the day during which she was bound to walk and work in accordance with our Lord's own words and practice. Thus her probation issues in glory, a glory all the more glorious because of that probation. "Give her of the fruit of her hands; and let her own works praise her in the gates."[336] Or if *stars* seem too incongruous an emblem of any *daylight* hours; I call to mind both that there shall be no night there, and that certain benefactors have for their allotted dignity to shine as the stars for ever and ever: whereby stars take rank in the everlasting day.

Or rather, what real connection is there between stars and night more than between stars and day? Earth's shadows approach them not in their high places; nor so far as we can trace, affect them in any way, or do aught in their regard beyond revealing them to mortal ken. Our perception varies, not their lustre.

From **CHAPTER 13**

2. And the beast which I saw was like unto a leopard, and his feet were as the feet of a bear, and his mouth as the mouth of a lion: and the dragon gave him his power, and his seat, and great authority.

This Apocalyptic beast combines in its one aspect features of three distinct and successive beasts of Daniel's vision [Rossetti quotes Dan. 7.2–8].

Daniel's vision has been expounded as concerning the successive empires of Babylon, Persia, Greece; personified respectively as lion, bear, leopard. The fourth yet more mysteriously appalling beast stands over to what was then and may still be the future. St. John's vision may haply already concern ourselves, or at any rate will concern others like us. Its lesson is for all and is for me.

Whatever this Apocalyptic beast may prove in fulness of time, it exhibits some likeness to that world, flesh, devil, which are my daily antagonists; of which I must daily, hourly, momentarily beware.

The world is like a leopard. Beautiful but spotted; soft, graceful, sportive, yet a devourer, a destroyer. "A leopard shall watch over their cities." Nor can the leopard change his spots. "Love not the world, neither the things that are in the world. If any man love the world, the love of the Father is not in him. For all that is in the world, the lust of the flesh, and the lust of the eyes, and the pride of life, is not of the Father, but is of the world. And the world passeth away, and the lust thereof: but he that doeth the Will of God abideth for ever."[337]

The flesh is like a bear. Its hug is deadly. "How long wilt thou sleep, O sluggard? when wilt thou arise out of thy sleep? Yet a little sleep, a little slumber, a little folding of the hands to sleep: so shall thy poverty come as one that travelleth, and thy want as an armed man."[338] The bear treads with his whole foot upon the earth, and his gross aspect is prominently of the earth earthy.

The devil is like a lion: as a roaring lion he walketh about seeking whom he may devour. He is as a lion's whelp lurking in secret places. "Rescue my soul from their destructions, my darling from the lions."[339]

World, flesh, devil, comprise all sources and varieties of my temptations. Repelling these three wherever found, I shall not fail to repel them even if in my own mortal day they appear concentrated into one ghastly head, one obscene monster.

On the other hand: if I succumb to them separately, how shall I cope with them should they rise up against me as one?

But that word *the world* is frequently used to denote a great portion of the human race. How little must I love the world? How much may I love it?—Love it to the fulness of thy heart's desire, so thou love it with self-sacrifice; for thus to love it is after the Mind of God, the Pattern of Christ: "God so loved the world, that He gave His Only Begotten Son, that whosoever believeth in Him should not perish, but have everlasting life. For God sent not His Son into the world to condemn the world; but that the world through Him might be saved."[340]

> Love is alone the worthy law of love:
>   All other laws have pre-supposed a taint:
>   Love is the law from kindled saint to saint,
> From lamb to lamb, from tender dove to dove.
> Love is the motive of all things that move
>   Harmonious by free will without constraint:
>   Love learns and teaches: love shall man acquaint
> With all he lacks, which all his lack is love.
> Because Love is the fountain, I discern
>   The stream as love: for what but love should flow
>   From fountain Love? not bitter from the sweet!
>   I ignorant, have I laid claim to know?
>   Oh teach me, Love, such knowledge as is meet
> For one to know who is fain to love and learn.[341]

This world is not my orchard for fruit or my garden for flowers. It is however my only field whence to raise a harvest.

What is the world? Wherein resides its harmfulness, snare, pollution? Left to itself it is neither harmful, ensnaring, nor polluting. It becomes all this as the passive agent, passive vehicle if I may so call it, of the devil, man's outside tempter, and of the flesh, man's inside tempter. There is no inherent evil in cedar and vermilion, horses and chariots, purple and fine linen; nay, nor in sumptuous fare, in down, silk, apes, ivory, or peacocks. St. Peter himself objects not to hair, gold, apparel, but to women's misuse of them. An alabaster box of precious ointment becomes good or bad simply according to the use it is put to. Through envy of the devil death came into the world, and man hath sought out many inventions; but the heavens and the earth, and all the host of them when made and finished were beheld to be "very good."[342]

Lord Jesus, everywhere and always inspire us to refuse the evil and to choose the good; and I beseech Thee, give us grace never to judge our neighbour rashly, whilst one by one we ourselves endeavour to learn and perform Thy Will.

Christ exchanged heaven for earth to enable man to exchange earth for heaven. Hast Thou done that for me, and will I not do this for Thee?

"The dragon gave him his power, and his seat, and great authority"— constituting him, so to say, diabolical viceroy. The flesh is even now such a viceroy, having the world for a throne, while the devil keeps out of sight ruling by deputy.—Or the world is a stage, the flesh an actor, the devil prompter and scene-shifter.

From **CHAPTER 14**

8.   And there followed another angel, saying, Babylon is fallen, is fallen, that great city, because she made all nations drink of the wine of the wrath of her fornication.

Some have thought to identify the site and structure of a local "Babylon." As to me, who can by no means identify them, I think not I need therefore miss my practical lesson from her greatness and her fall.

Wherefore fell she? The Angel declares, because of what she did; not otherwise because of what she was. Let me (if I may) consider her as that World, which in some sort seems to form common ground, a point of contact, a link, a conductor, between flesh and devil.

Long ago Satan boasted to Christ's very Face that "all the kingdoms of the world, and the glory of them"[343] were delivered unto him; nor did the Truth then and there give the lie to the father of lies. If, then, we may assume an ingredient of truth in the assertion, that element of truth supplies a clue to the fascination and domination of the world; a fascination which is deadly, a domination which is tyrannous. For Satan is the showman of her goodly show: he who can himself appear as an angel of light understands how to inflate her scale, tint her mists and bubbles with prismatic colours, hide her thorns under roses and her worms under silk. He can paint her face, and tire her head, and set her on a wall and at a window, as the goal of a vain race, and the prize of a vain victory. David, superb in his kingliness, made to himself instruments of music; and so has she her men singers and women singers, her brazen wind instruments and her hollow drums. She spreads a feast: first her best, afterwards that which is worse; apples of Sodom to follow forbidden fruit. And as to her cup, "all nations" have not unwarned drunk of it: "Look not thou upon the wine when it is red, when it giveth his colour in the cup, when it moveth itself aright. At the last it biteth like a serpent, and stingeth like an adder. Thine eyes shall behold strange women, and thine heart shall utter perverse things."[344] If this be true of earth's vintage, how tenfold true of the world's!

The City and Woman appear so indistinguishable in the Apocalyptic vision as to justify (I trust) my confusion of personification. Temptation, by a common instinct, seems to be personified as feminine: let us thence derive courage; the symbol itself insinuating that as woman is weaker than man, so temptation is never so strong as the individual assailed. "There hath no temptation taken you but such as is common to man: but God is faithful, Who will not suffer you to be tempted above that ye are able; but will with the temptation also make a way to escape, that ye may be able to bear it."[345]

We daughters of Eve may beyond her sons be kept humble by that common voice which makes temptation feminine.

Woman is a mighty power for good or for evil. She constrains though she cannot compel. Potential for evil, it becomes her to beware and forbear; potential for good, to spend herself and be spent for her brethren. In the Bible the word *tempt* (or its derivatives) is used in a good or in an evil sense, according to the agent or to the object aimed at.

The wisest of three wrote: "Women are strongest"; and said: "Many also have perished, have erred, and sinned, for women."[346]

"Babylon is fallen," saith the Angel: he saith not, Is cast down. Though she be cast down, yet is the impulse of her casting down in herself; she hath undermined herself. Sin is the essential destroyer: the sinner is self-destroyed. Drunkenness especially sets this truth as in a picture before our eyes; drunkenness being the example of a general rule, not its exception.

Taking physical corruption as the foul image of sin, we see how it consists not with stability, permanence; but dissolves, disintegrates its prey. It turns bone to dust, muscle as it were to pulp: we loathe to look upon it in a body; who shall bear to look upon it in a soul?

From **CHAPTER 17**

*1.   And there came one of the seven angels which had the
seven vials, and talked with me, saying unto me, Come hither;
I will shew unto thee the judgment of the great whore that
sitteth upon many waters:*

*2.   With whom the kings of the earth have committed fornication,
and the inhabitants of the earth have been made drunk with the
wine of her fornication.*

As to its subject, the vision of this chapter [17] does not in order of time appear to follow passages which more or less remotely precede it; but rather to be at least partially simultaneous, elucidatory, and so to say parenthetical. The very words "Babylon is fallen" (chap. 14.8), "Great Babylon came in remembrance" (chap. 16.19), show that her existence antedates either mention of her. So far then it becomes conjecturable that this present chapter will exhibit a traceable connection with previous portions of the Apocalypse; will, as it were, fit into what we have already studied.

Lord, Who by Thy Most Holy Spirit hast inspired Thy Prophets to speak and to write Thy word, grant us by help of the Same Spirit to study that blessed word which for each of us contains an individual lesson. Give us one by one grace to learn our own lesson, neither vexing nor envying one another; but so imbued with wisdom that we may become pure, peaceable, gentle, easy to be intreated, full of mercy and good fruits, void of partiality and hypocrisy, sowing righteousness in peace while we make peace. For our Peacemaker's sake, Jesus Christ. Amen.

Isaiah instructs us how profitably to contemplate God's judgments, while putting our whole trust in Him and honouring His Holy Name and His word: "Thou wilt keep him in perfect peace, whose mind is stayed on Thee: because he trusteth in Thee. Trust ye in the Lord for ever: for in the Lord Jehovah is everlasting strength. For He bringeth down them that dwell on high; the lofty city, He layeth it low; He layeth it low, even to the ground; He bringeth it even to the dust. . . . Yea, in the way of Thy judgments, O Lord, have we waited for Thee; the desire of our soul is to Thy Name, and to the remembrance of Thee. With my soul have I desired Thee in the night; yea, with my spirit within me will I seek Thee early: for when Thy judgments are in the earth, the inhabitants of the world will learn righteousness."[347]

Far from being necessarily an insurmountable disadvantage, I think that ignorance of the historical drift of prophecy may on occasion turn to a humble but genuine profit. Such ignorance entails (or wisely utilized might entail) that a general lesson, a fundamental principle, essence not accident, will be elicited from the abstruse text. Further:—instead of attention being directed to the ends of the earth, our eye must be turned within; elsewhere at a future moment additional light will doubtless be vouchsafed, but for the present the message is delivered pointedly to ourselves; as when "there fell a voice from heaven, saying, O king Nebuchadnezzar, to thee it is spoken";—and could no more be evaded than could that other message; "I have an errand to thee, O captain. . . . Unto which of all us? . . . To thee."[348]

Wherefore "one of the Seven Angels" talks with me, saying: "Come hither; I will shew unto thee. . . ." And what he shows me (at any rate) amounts to the vileness and ruinousness of idolatrous defection in every form subtle or gross. Assume what shape it may, its nature remains the same: kings may idolize all the kingdoms of the world and the glory of them; whilst subjects bow down to wealth, influence, fame, genius, beauty, or even to success. But under one aspect or other the sin infects "kings of the earth" and "inhabitants of the earth"; and whilst mighty men shall be mightily tormented, the meaner sort cannot go unpunished.

The First and Second Commandments concur to forbid idolatry: misplaced preference breaks the First, misdirected worship the Second. The first holds out neither threat nor promise, neither reward nor punishment: it is one, simple, featureless, absolute; and being equally incumbent upon all rational beings, addresses man on his spiritual side, not taking account of the earthy. The Second commands, but it also reasons: it sets before man his own interest, adjures him for his children's sake, deters him by a threat, allures him by a promise; remembers whereof he is made, and appeals to him both as flesh and as spirit. Perhaps even the Fifth Commandment is less persuasively formulated than the Second: the Fifth guarantees a contingent blessing to ourselves, the Second to our cherished "thousands." And even in the appalling entail of contingent judgment "upon the children, unto the third and fourth generation,"[349] a door of hope, howbeit of a trembling hope, remains open, when we turn to a Divine exposition of mercy and judgment; for by the mouth of Ezekiel the Lord God deigned to refute the Jewish proverb, "The fathers have eaten sour grapes, and the children's teeth are set on edge," and to declare concerning a hypothetical heinous offender: "Now, lo, if he beget a son, that seeth all his father's sins which he hath done, and considereth, and doeth not such like, that . . . hath executed My judgments, hath walked in My statutes; he shall not die for the iniquity of his father, he shall surely live."[350] Thus the second generation can by righteous obedience in some measure retrieve the error of the first, thereby recovering mercy as an inheritance to his posterity; so that (may we not hope?) even the visiting upon them of their more remote forefathers' sins will be so far reversed as to help them, if they choose, to walk humbly. To the next of kin appertained a twofold office: as avenger of blood he executed judgment, as nearest in blood he filled the vacant place. Moreover though the fathers may not, yet may the children take courage and rejoice in their grievous liability because of Christ-likeness: for Christ was born for this very end, that on Him might be visited the iniquity of father Adam and of all mankind.

I suppose it is no exaggeration to say that every sin, fleshly or spiritual, is a sin of idolatry, inasmuch as it is the preference of some object tangible or intangible to God All Good: indeed further reflection recognizes sin as simply the preference of *self* to God; self-pleasing, self-will, self-indulgence, self in a word, being the universal lure. St. Paul brands covetousness as idolatry: thus the First, Second and Tenth Commandments concur in forbidding idolatry; whilst to break any of the remaining seven involves a breach of the spirit common to all.

From **CHAPTER 18**

*15.   The merchants of these things, which were made rich by her,
shall stand afar off for the fear of her torment, weeping and wailing,*

*16.   And saying, Alas, alas, that great city, that was clothed in fine
linen, and purple, and scarlet, and decked with gold, and precious
stones, and pearls!*

*17.   For in one hour so great riches is come to nought. And every
shipmaster, and all the company in ships, and sailors, and as many
as trade by sea, stood afar off,*

This desolation which we have not yet seen must one day be seen. Meanwhile we have known preludes, rehearsals, foretastes of such as this: so that looking back through the centuries we may take up our lamentation and say:—

Alas Sodom once full of bread! From empty fulness, Good Lord, deliver us.

Alas Tyre whose merchants were princes! From riches but not toward God, Good Lord, deliver us.

Alas the man whose barns sufficed not! From heart and hands shut close, Good Lord, deliver us.

Alas Dives clothed in purple and fine linen! From remediless destitution, Good Lord, deliver us.

And looking forward we may say:—

Alas any whom the unknown day and hour find unprepared! From the folly of the foolish virgins, Good Lord, deliver us.

And looking around us trembling we needs must say:—

Alas England full of luxuries and thronged by stinted poor, whose merchants are princes and whose dealings crooked, whose packed storehouses stand amid bare homes, whose gorgeous array has rags for neighbours! From a canker in our gold and silver, from a moth in our garments, from blasted crops, from dwindling substance, from righteous retribution abasing us among the nations, Good Lord, deliver us. Amen.

From **CHAPTER 19**

*6.   And I heard as it were the voice of a great multitude, and as
the voice of many waters, and as the voice of mighty thunderings,
saying, Alleluia: for the Lord God Omnipotent reigneth.*

Hearken to music of the deaf whose spirit was not deaf, and a song of the dumb whose heart was not dumb; for in this chorus all the redeemed, whatever their sometime gift or blemish, sing together. Deafness, dumbness, every imperfection has been left behind with the dust of death; and God hath put a new song into all mouths, even a thanksgiving unto our God. "Many shall see it, and fear; and shall put their trust in the Lord."[351] (Lord, so be it for Jesus' sake.)

May I be one of those wise master singers! If *then* I would be so, *now* I must become so. The talents vouchsafed me I must use and improve thankfully; the gifts withheld I must forego ungrudgingly and thankfully.

O Lord my God the Omnipotent, Who searchest all hearts; Who knowest my heart through and through; Who in many hearts discernest lifelong disappointment, mortification, aching rankling soreness; O Lord our God, grant us such grace that Thy Will may be to us glory and Thine award satisfaction; so in our solitary place shall we be glad, awaiting that day of days when patient mourners shall come forth in the dances of them that make merry. Amen, for the honour of Jesus Christ, Who for our sake exhausted human bitterness.

If reverently I may say so:—In the Bible God condescends to employ multiform overtures of endearing graciousness, wooing, beseeching, alluring, encouraging. We love beauty; He lavishes beauty on the sacred text. We desire knowledge; He tells us much, and promises that one day He will tell us all. We are conscious of feelings inexpressible and as yet insatiable; He stirs up such feelings, at once directing them and guaranteeing their ultimate satisfaction. He works upon us by what we can and by what we cannot utter; He appeals in us to what we can and to what we cannot define.

Whence it seems to ensue that not only words and thoughts compose such a commentary on Revelation as may lawfully be brought by man for his offering of firstfruits; but that painting, sculpture, music, all are sources capable of swelling that store.

Without cavilling or doubt then let us worship God in wordless aspiration aroused by any form of beauty, let us praise Him in musical yearnings and ecstasies. Or if not thou, at least I; who remember how one highly endowed by nature and by grace and by me ever to be venerated, was affected by one movement in the overwhelming harmony of the Hallelujah Chorus.

> When wickedness is broken as a tree
> 　　Paradise comes to light, ah holy land!
> 　　Whence death has vanished like a shifting sand
> And barrenness is banished with the sea.
> Its bulwarks are salvation fully manned,
> 　　All gems it hath for glad variety,
> 　　And pearls for pureness radiant glimmeringly,
> And gold for grandeur where all good is grand.

An inner ring of saints meets linked above,
And linked of angels is an outer ring:
For voice of waters or for thunders' voice
Lo! harps and songs wherewith all saints rejoice,
And all the trembling there of any string
Is but a trembling of enraptured love.[352]

From **CHAPTER 20**

2.   And he laid hold on the dragon, that old serpent, which is the Devil, and Satan, and bound him a thousand years,

3.   And cast him into the bottomless pit, and shut him up, and set a seal upon him, that he should deceive the nations no more, till the thousand years should be fulfilled: and after that he must be loosed a little season.

Truly a joyful day when these "former things"[353] shall come to pass. Meanwhile if it was not for Apostles to know the times and the seasons which the Father hath put in His own power, how much less for me!

The date is hidden, the event revealed: the date therefore concerns me not at present, the event concerns me at once.

But what? must we fall a helpless prey to the strong raging dragon, the insinuating serpent, until an angel secure him with chain and seal and the lid of hell? Not so. Even now already thou hast thy chain at hand, my brother, my sister: I, if I will, have mine.

"Satan trembles when he sees
The weakest saint upon his knees."[354]

Prayer is a chain apt presently to bind him, and which he cannot snap; prayer which links earth to heaven, human weakness to Divine Strength, me (if I will), even me to my Redeemer. Though the great and wide sea be Leviathan's playground, yet to him and to his habitation alike God hath assigned a bound by a perpetual decree so that neither can pass over it.

Lord Jesus, Who Alone makest our prayers acceptable to the Father, shelter us under prayer, hide us in prayer, give us breathings of prayer wherewith to quench the fiery breath of the dragon, wisdom of prayer whereby to silence the lying subtilty of the serpent. Amen.

Not dragon simply, or serpent simply; but serpent-dragon to be fled from when met raging, and still more to be feared when gliding unobtrusively. Not a novice, but an "old serpent," surpassingly subtil when Eve encountered him, and having now the accumulated experience of thousands of years and millions of victories.—Good Lord, deliver us.

"A seal upon him, that he should deceive the nations no more, till. . . ."—If upon *himself,* Cain's mark as it were. If upon his *prison,* then we are reminded of the irreversible act of Darius: "A stone was brought, and laid upon the mouth of the den; and the king sealed it with his own signet, and with the signet of his lords; that the purpose might not be changed."[355]

Hell has no bottom, but has a lid: I need not fall in. Hell has indeed no bottom, yet has it one only exit and that upwards. A figure to me of the folly of piling sin on sin in hopes of self-extrication. To cover one lie by a second lie thickens the lid over me.

> Lord, grant us wills to trust Thee with such aim
>> Of hope and passionate craving of desire,
>> That we may mount aspiring, and aspire
> Still while we mount; rejoicing in Thy Name
> Yesterday, this day, day by day the Same:
>> So sparks fly upward scaling heaven by fire,
>> Still mount and still attain not, yet draw nigher
> While they have being to their fountain flame.
>> To saints who mount, the bottomless abyss
>> Is as mere nothing: they have set their face
>> Onward and upward toward that blessed place
>>> Where man rejoices with his God, and soul
> With soul, in the unutterable kiss
>> Of peace for every victor at the goal.[356]

"The thousand years . . . a little season."—I can compute a *thousand,* but not *a little.* The thousand years I might call long: the little season I incline to figure to myself as much shorter. Either would appear brief if compared with the whole of time; and time from beginning to end would itself dwindle to mere brevity if set against eternity. Nevertheless eternity hangs on time. "Behold, how great a matter a little fire kindleth!"[357]

The thousand years of exemption are to be "fulfilled." We read not that the little season of final horror is to be *fulfilled.* Perhaps Divine Compassion may cut it short; if so, it appears in harmony with Christ's promise: "For the elect's sake those days shall be shortened."[358]

"He must . . ."—What is to be understood by this *must?* an irresponsible, inflexible fate overbearing the Will of the Almighty?—Not so: it expresses to us the fiat of that Almighty Will.—*Shall* would have conveyed the same without ambiguity.—Possibly so: and if so, a surface ambiguity is here superadded for my profit.—How should it profit one?—By pressing home upon me to acquiesce in any case and to trust in every case. By practising me in discerning truth and eschewing error.—But suppose the other should be the true sense?—I cannot suppose what contradicts everything I know.—But suppose it for argument's sake.—I will not even for argument's sake suppose that to be true which I know to be a lie.

12.   *And I saw the dead, small and great, stand before God; and the books were opened: and another book was opened, which is the book of life: and the dead were judged out of those things which were written in the books, according to their works.*

> On the dead for whom once Thou diedst, Lord Jesus, have mercy.
> On the living for whom Thou ever livest, have mercy.
> Thou Who wast arraigned before a corrupt judge, O Incorruptible Judge, have mercy.
> Thou Who knowest what is in man, O Son of Man, have mercy.
> Thou Whose works were all good, have mercy.
> Thou Whose life, in the sight of the unwise, once hung in suspense before Pilate, have mercy.
> Thou Who Thyself ever knowest what Thou wilt do, have mercy.
> On the small, mercy.
> On the great, mercy.
> Thou Who art unlike us in Thy sinlessness, on us sinnners have mercy.
> Thou Who are like us in Thy Humanity, on us Thy brethren and Thy sisters, have mercy.
> Blot out our evil works from Thy Book of Works, and have mercy.
> Write our names in Thy Book of Life, and have mercy.
> Blot not out our names, but have mercy.
> Give us tears from the Fountain of Thy Mercy.
> Store our tears in Thy bottle, with Thine own tears shed for us in pure mercy.
> And whatever we lack let us not lack Thy mercy. Amen.

"Stand before God"—past kneeling, past praying; not to be converted, but sentenced. *Now,* not *then,* is the day of salvation: not *then* except for the already saved.

My page in the Book of Works is to me awful: the contents are my own, the record is not my own. It is my life's record without oversights, without false entries or suppressions: any good set down accurately as good; all evil, unless erased by Divine Compassion, set down accurately as evil. Nothing whatever is there except what I have genuinely endeavoured, compassed, done, been: I meant it all, though I meant not to meet it again face to face.

It is as if all along one had walked in a world of invisible photographic cameras charged with instantaneous plates.

The Book of Life may seem yet more awful, kept secret as it has been from the foundation of the world in the knowledge of God Omniscient.

Yet is it really so? It is in fact no independent statement, but appears to be essentially an index or summary of the other. I who composed although I compiled not my Book of Works, I myself virtually entered or entered not my name in the corresponding Book of Life: to dread this beyond the other, is to dread a sum total rather than those very items which produce the total.

For whilst we read that "the dead were judged out of those things which were written in the Books," it was none the less "according to their works."

From CHAPTER 21

24.   *And the nations of them which are saved shall walk in the light of it: and the kings of the earth do bring their glory and honour into it.*

Experience worketh hope. As yet my own experience attests nothing whatever as to "nations" of the saved. To have known here one and there another individual self-evidently rich in grace and goodness has, however, been my happy lot: so that experience has actually already familiarized me with samples of elect communities, units of the sum-total which no man can number.

Patience it is which works experience: no wonder that a vast amount of human experience is limited. To stint patience stints hope at one remove.

Patience is irksome, experience tedious; but then without hope which is their result life were a living death. Every course of life at any level affords scope for patience. Let us not despond if destined to stick fast in patience and there come to an end; the fault is mine if my patience shoot not up into experience, or if my experience bud and blossom not into hope.

When past history strikes us as a tissue of crimes, and present history as a tangle of unrighteousness; when a backward glance scares, and a forward glance scares yet more; then the word of this sure prophecy revives a comfortable hope: "The kings of the earth do bring their glory and honour into it." Not kings of a new creation, of a superior dynasty, but literal kings of this literal earth. From their palaces of pomp, from their giddy pinnacles of dominion, they too have gone up on high and have led their captivity captive; as Barak son of Abinoam from his high places, or as Deborah wife of Lapidoth from palm tree of earth to palm trees of heaven.

If hard it is for any rich man to enter into the kingdom of heaven, how hard must it be for those royal rich men to whom tribute, custom, fear, honour, are due it may be from subject millions. Wise indeed was Agur when he prayed, "Remove far from me vanity and lies: give me neither poverty nor riches"[359]—wiser, so far, than wisest Solomon who lost himself in luxuries and pleasures for a while, if not (as God forbid!) for ever.

Every man's vocation exhibits a twofold aspect. Primarily, it is allotted to him for himself, that therein he may glorify God and save his own soul; secondarily, it is allotted to him for his brethren, that therein he may serve them and promote their salvation.

Children, servants, subjects, exist in right of parents, masters, monarchs; and *vice versâ;* each equally in right of the other, each complementarily to the other. I see this at once as to parents and children: I accept it readily as to monarchs and subjects: I must take heed to admit it practically as to superiors and inferiors, employers and employed.

O Perfect Lord Jesus, Who being the Creator wert pleased to abase Thyself to become a Creature, and amongst creatures a dutiful Son, a submissive Subject, and though not a servant of men yet toward Thine own as he that serveth; grant us a faint shadow of Thy humility whereby we too may become dutiful, submissive, serviceable. Make us in our several stations affectionate, loyal, helpful, to one another; and in and above all earthly ties, absorb us in self-devotion to Thyself, the Source of our life, the King of our race, the Master to Whom we must stand or fall. For none of which things are we sufficient, but our sufficiency is of Thee. Make us as Mary when she turned and said Rabboni.

> Bring me to see, Lord, bring me yet to see
>   Those nations of Thy glory and Thy grace
>   Who splendid in Thy splendour worship Thee.
> Light in all eyes, content in every face,
>   Raptures and voices one while manifold,
>   Love and are well-beloved the ransomed race:—
> Great mitred priests, great kings in crowns of gold,
>   Patriarchs who head the army of their sons,
>   Matrons and mothers by their own extolled,
> Wise and most harmless holy little ones,
>   Virgins who making merry lead the dance,
>   Full-breathed victorious racers from all runs,
> Home-comers out of every change and chance,
>   Hermits restored to social neighbourhood,
>   Aspects which reproduce One countenance,
> Life-losers with their losses all made good,
>   All blessed hungry and athirst sufficed,
>   All who bore crosses round the Holy Rood,
> Friends, brethren, sisters, of Lord Jesus Christ.[360]

From **CHAPTER 22**

9.   Then saith he unto me, See thou do it not: for I am thy fellowservant, and of thy brethren the prophets, and of them which keep the sayings of this book: worship God.

"For I am . . ."—All is in the present: by no means ended and consigned to the past. The speaker (apparently a deathless Angel) not merely *was* but *is* St. John's fellowservant, of his brethren the prophets, of them who keep the sayings of this Book. Thus are the lives of any such twain lovely and pleasant, being such as neither immortality nor mortality shall divide.

We too, O too, the first of us and the last, may aspire to the same blessed fellowship. By *service,*—spending and self-spending for God: by *prophecy,*—illustrating in our daily life the pleasantness of His ways and peace of His paths: by *keeping the sayings,*—watching, praying, obeying, in preparation for the day of the consummation of all things. This we can do: this will we not do?

For our all is at stake: and that which momentarily draws nearer and nearer to us is inevitable, be it gain or loss, salvation or ruin. Let us worship God by consecrated life and offered substance; by will, desire, affection; not grudgingly or of necessity, for He loveth a cheerful giver. Martyrs have worshipped Him exultant in torture, Confessors unashamed in shame, lofty Saints in self-sacrifice, lowly Saints in self-discipline. All Saints have worshipped, are worshipping, will worship Him for ever and ever. This we also can do: and this will we not do?

"The Grace of our Lord Jesus Christ, and the Love of God, and the Fellowship of the Holy Ghost, be with us all evermore. Amen."[361]

I suppose that no insight or profundity of mortal man ever has been adequate to the full exploration of this Apocalypse. I feel certain that no natural shallowness need render it a dead letter to man, woman, or child. We may wonder in vain over the personality of the Angel and over his vocation, but his practical precept is as clear as day: "Worship God."

Indeed all through the Book of Revelation lessons enforcing what we must or must not do or be, are as clear and as definite as in the rest of Holy Writ. What can be easily understood furnishes occupation for a lifetime: "The wayfaring men, though fools, shall not err therein." But this promise can be claimed only by wayfarers along "the Way of Holiness":[362] neither by standers-still in that way, nor by vagrants along any other way, can it be claimed.

To study the Apocalypse out of idle curiosity would turn it, so far as the student's self were concerned, into a branch of the Tree of the Knowledge of Good and Evil. And what came of Eve's curious investigation of the original Tree we all know.

Obey to the limit of knowledge, and in all probability obedience may extend knowledge.

10. *And he saith unto me, Seal not the sayings of the prophecy of this book: for the time is at hand.*

Once more it appears as if the Personality of the Speaker may have changed, inasmuch as this verse seems to form one unbroken sequence with those which immediately follow.

If eighteen hundred years ago the time was "at hand," how urgently at hand must it now be! If then it behoved disciples to read, mark, learn, and inwardly digest the prophecy, how urgently now! If then it was of the Divine Grace and Mercy that the Book was left unsealed, still is it of the Divine Grace and Mercy that it continues unsealed to our own day. If then it was high time to awake out of sleep, truly is it so now.

> The night is far spent, the day is at hand:
>   Let us therefore cast off the works of darkness,
>   And let us put on the armour of light.
>   Night for the dead in their stiffness and starkness!
>   Day for the living who mount in their might
> Out of their graves to the beautiful land.
>
> Far far away lies the beautiful land:
>   Mount on wide wings of exceeding desire,
>   Mount, look not back, mount to life and to light,
>   Mount by the glow of your lamps all on fire,
>   Up from the dead men and up from the night.
> The night is far spent, the day is at hand.[363]

A disobedient and gainsaying people withstood the stretched forth Divine hands. A blinded people rejected the sheltering wing of Divine Love.

Alas for the disobedient, gainsaying, blinded multitude before whom the Book now stands open! Alas for them: and what for ourselves?

Our eyes we can open or shut; but the opened Book never can we shut. Whom it cannot instruct it must judge.

O Lord our only Saviour, we cannot bear alone our load of responsibility: upbear us under it. We look without seeing unless Thou purge our sight: grant us sight. We read without comprehending unless Thou open our understanding: give us intelligence. Nothing can we do unless Thou prosper the work of our hands upon us: oh prosper Thou our handiwork. We are weak: out of weakness make us strong. We are in peril of death: come and heal us. We believe: help Thou our unbelief. We hope: let us not be disappointed of our hope. We love: grant us to love much, to love ever more and more, to love all, and most of all to love Thee.

Notes

~~~~~~

Introduction

1. See R. W. Crump, ed., *The Complete Poems of Christina Rossetti: A Variorum Edition,* 3 vols. (Baton Rouge: Louisiana State University Press, 1979–1990); Georgina Battiscombe, *Christina Rossetti: A Divided Life* (New York: Holt, Rinehart and Winston, 1981); Kathleen Jones, *"Learning not to be first": The Life of Christina Rossetti* (New York: St. Martin's Press, 1991); Frances Thomas, *Christina Rossetti* (Hanley Swan, Worcester: The Self Publishing Association, Ltd., 1992; London: Virago Press, 1994); Jan Marsh, *Christina Rossetti: A Literary Biography* (London: Jonathan Cape, 1994); Antony H. Harrison, ed., *The Letters of Christina Rossetti,* 4 vols. (Charlotte: University Press of Virginia, 1997–). Also, *Christina G. Rossetti: The Poems,* ed. Betty Sue Flowers, is forthcoming from Penguin (1998).
2. Nina Auerbach and U. C. Knoepflmacher, eds., *Forbidden Journeys: Fairy Tales and Fantasies by Victorian Women Writers* (Chicago: University of Chicago Press, 1992); Crump, *Maude;* Elaine Showalter, ed., *Maude by Christina Rossetti and* "On Sisterhoods" *and* A Woman's Thoughts About Women *by Dinah Mulock Craik* (New York: New York University Press, 1993). Another example is R. Loring Taylor, ed., *Sing-Song, Speaking Likenesses, Goblin Market* (New York: Garland, 1976).
3. Criticism on the prose has been, until recently, minimal. See, for example, P. G. Stanwood, "Christina Rossetti's Devotional Prose," in David A. Kent, ed., *The Achievement of Christina Rossetti* (Ithaca, N.Y.: Cornell University Press, 1987), 231–47; Antony H. Harrison, "Christina Rossetti and the Sage Discourse of High Anglicanism," *Victorian Sages and Cultural Discourse: Renegotiating Gender and Power,* ed. Thais E. Morgan (New Brunswick, N.J.: Rutgers University Press, 1990), 87–104; Linda Palazzo, "The Prose Works of Christina Rossetti" (Ph.D. diss.: University of Durham, 1992); Joel Westerholm, "'I Magnify Mine Office': Christina Rossetti's Authoritative Voice in Her Devotional Prose," *Victorian Newsletter* 84 (Fall 1993): 11–17; and Colleen Hobbs, "A View from 'The Lowest Place': Christina Rossetti's Devotional Prose," *Victorian Poetry* 32.3–4 (Autumn-Winter 1994): 409–28.

4. For Rossetti's contributions to "The Bouquet from Marylebone Gardens," see Marsh, 131–35. Jones notes (p. 6) that Rossetti's first stories, "Dervise" and "Retribution," were written for her family members and were contained in a family magazine called the *Hodge Podge* and later the *Illustrated Magazine.*

5. On Yonge, see Battiscombe, 32–33 and 198, and Jones, 18. For those who do not see the importance of Maude's reluctance to take communion in Rossetti's story, Yonge's *The Castle-Builders; or, The Deferred Confirmation* (1854) is a useful contemporary example. See Robert Lee Wolff, *Novels of Faith and Doubt in Victorian England* (New York: Garland, 1977), 121–26. As Palazzo notes (p. 9), William Michael Rossetti's introduction to the 1897 publication places *Maude* in the tradition of Yonge and Hesba Stretton. Palazzo herself links Rossetti's religious tale to the evangelical stories published by the Religious Tract Society. In his sermon "Blessings turned into Curses," Henry W. Burrows (Rossetti's rector at Christ Church) reminds his listeners of injunctions in the Book of Common Prayer that to take communion "unworthily" was to risk "condemnation" (*Parochial Sermons,* 3rd series [London: William Skeffington, 1872], 267).

6. "Nick" appears to be the earliest of the tales. Dante Gabriel Rossetti's efforts to find a publisher for it are mentioned in a letter of 30 September 1853 (*LDGR,* 1:156).

7. See John Dixon Hunt, *The Pre-Raphaelite Imagination 1848–1900* (London: Routledge & Kegan Paul, 1968), 224, and Christopher Ricks, "Christina Rossetti and Commonplace Books," *Grand Street* 9.3 (Spring 1990): 194. Ricks is almost the only critic to address Rossetti's prose as prose. He praises her "precise syntactical notation" in the passage in *Commonplace* describing the London railroad station: "The art is all in the eight commas, and in the suspension of the final phrase so that it comes upon us too an instant after. . . . [T]he sentence is exactly embodied, a feat of syntactical balancing which is alive if we will only let ourselves realize it. It is this corporeal susceptibility which animates the prose of *Commonplace.*"

8. U. C. Knoepflmacher, however, describes these stories as "anti-Carrollian" and her relationship with Lewis Carroll as one of "creative resistance." See "Avenging Alice: Christina Rossetti and Lewis Carroll," *Nineteenth-Century Literature* 41.3 (Dec. 1986): 307, 301.

9. Palazzo summarizes (p. 39) the less favorable responses of readers as diverse as John Ruskin and a *TLS* reviewer in 1959.

10. The phrases are from reviews in *London Quarterly Review* 36 (April 1871): 259; by G. A. Simcox in *The Academy* 1 (9 July 1870): 252; and in "Miss Rossetti's Short Tales," *The Spectator* 43 (29 October 1870): 293. In her later years, Rossetti apparently did not think highly of this volume for she described it in 1891 as "Out of print and not worth reprinting" (see Mackenzie Bell, *Christina Rossetti: A Biographical and Critical Study* [Boston: Roberts Brothers, 1898] 310).

11. Review of *Time Flies: A Reading Diary* in *The Book Buyer* (New York), n.s. 3.27 (Feb. 1886): 27. Rossetti's labors on *Called to be Saints* were also much

earlier than the publication of the book (1881) would suggest. The volume had been written before 1876 when it was turned down by Macmillan (Packer, 328).

12. This volume has not hitherto been identified, but John Murray mentions his need to find a translator in a letter of 14 August 1866, to W. M. Rossetti (*RP,* 205; see also 214). According to William's diary (11 April 1867), she was eventually paid £21 (Odette Bornand, ed., *The Diary of W. M. Rossetti* [Oxford: Clarendon Press, 1977], 229). There is no reference in the work itself to Rossetti as the translator: *The Terra-Cotta Architecture of North Italy. XIII-XV Centuries. Portrayed as Examples of Imitation in other Countries . . . ,* ed. Lewis Gruner (London: John Murray, 1867). Compare to *Letters,* 1:217 (7 January 1865, from CGR to Macmillan).

13. The title of the story was "Case 2: Folio Q"; see Marsh, 255–56.

14. George Moberly, *Sermons on the Beatitudes,* 3rd ed. (Oxford: James Parker, 1870). Among the few other writers she cites in her devotional prose are S. Baring-Gould (1 March entry in *TF*), Thomas Fuller (*CS,* xvi), Richard Hooker (the epigraph to *CS*), and Jeremy Taylor (19 August entry in *TF*).

15. A convenient summary of the controversy surrounding *Essays and Reviews* can be found in Owen Chadwick, *The Victorian Church,* 2nd ed. (London: Adam & Black, 1972), 2:75ff. He also discusses the influence of historical criticism and textual study on attitudes toward the Bible, the various biographies of Jesus that were published, as well as the emergence of the revised version of the Bible in 1883 (see 2:31–109).

16. On Christina's friendship with Richard Littledale, see Marsh, 416–17. Palazzo identifies Williams as an important influence on Rossetti's attitudes to Scripture on pps. 125–26 of her dissertation.

17. See the very long and important Tracts 80 and 87 by Isaac Williams "On Reserve in Communicating Religious Knowledge" (1838 and 1840), and Keble's equally weighty Tract 89 (1840), separately printed but collected in 6 volumes (London: Rivington, 1840). See G. B. Tennyson, *Victorian Devotional Poetry: The Tractarian Mode* (Cambridge, Mass.: Harvard University Press, 1981), esp. pps. 44–48 and 52–56.

18. In support of his approach, Joel Westerholm gives several examples of Rossetti's rejection of conventional biblical interpretations, particularly her rehabilitation of Eve through a rereading of the Fall (pps. 15–16). Certainly, Westerholm is right in insisting that the prevailing view was that only the clergy were the "authorized interpreters" of Scripture. See, for example, the Reverend George Townsend, *The New Testament Arranged in Chronological & Historical Order,* 2 vols. (London: Rivington, 1825), 1:iii (introduction). Jacqueline Rose has also maintained that Rossetti in her religious prose "made her most explicit bid for hermeneutic freedom, her boldest defences of readings that follow the heart." See "Undone, Defile, Defaced," review of *Christina Rossetti* by Jan Marsh, in the *London Review of Books,* 19 October 1995, p. 16. For a feminist reading of Rossetti's life and work, see Sharon Leder with Andrea Abbott, *The Language of Exclusion:*

The Poetry of Emily Dickinson and Christina Rossetti (New York: Green-wood Press, 1987).

19. See Horton Davies, *Worship and Theology in England from Newman to Martineau, 1850–1900* (Princeton: Princeton University Press, 1962), esp. chap. 5, "The Catholic Trend of Anglican Worship," and the brief but very useful description (with further references) to the newly formed religious communities for women (pps. 131–35). See also Diane D'Amico, "'Choose the stairs that mount above': Christina Rossetti and the Anglican Sisterhoods," *Essays in Literature* 17 (1990): 204–21.

20. See Eric Griffiths, "The Disappointment of Christina G. Rossetti," *Essays in Criticism* 47 (April 1997): 107–42: "The belief that there is something especially female about idiolectal features is groundless; the relation presumed between literary and social conventions does not exist, and, even if it did, it would not follow that a literary variation from the conventional entails a critique of the convention—artists vary on the past of their arts for many reasons, including a desire to refresh the conventional and keep it alive. What is traditional in Rossetti's poetry is quite as much hers, and hers as a woman, as is her re-inflecting of the tradition" (p. 119). Griffiths comments also on the significance for Rossetti of the new sisterhoods.

21. The quotation from Watts-Dunton is from *Old Familiar Faces* (New York: E. P. Dutton, 1916), 199. Burrows is quoted from two different sermons in his *Parochial Sermons,* cited in note 5. The first is from sermon 4, on "Stars," for the first Sunday of the Epiphany, on Dan. 12.3. Burrows calls also for "mission women, and sisters of charity in a degree" (p. 39). The second appears in a Lent sermon (number 7, "Sin, the Waste of God's Gifts in Nature and in Grace," on Luke 15.13), whose stirring words might well have reinforced and inspired Rossetti's sense of her life's purpose. The person with poetic power "touches many hearts, his sympathies are wider than those of other men, the passion of the age is concentrated in him; . . . he is sent into the world God's own work to do on earth; he has the vision and the faculty divine" (p. 62). Not to use those powers is to poison the world.

    See Antony H. Harrison, *Christina Rossetti in Context* (Chapel Hill: University of North Carolina Press, 1988), 98–101, for an analysis of St. Augustine's influence on Rossetti's idea of vocation.

22. See MacDonald's *England's Antiphon* (London: Macmillan, 1868), 3. Isaac Williams's "Advertisement" to his multivolume "Devotional Commentary on the Gospel Narrative" describes that enterprise as "intended rather for devotional than critical use," in contrast to his earlier study of *The Apocalypse* (1841, 1852). Williams's commentary includes citations of church fathers but also digressive meditations, conversational reflections, and (though rarely) quotations from hymns. The validity of Rossetti's heterogeneous commentary may have been suggested by Williams's work. As W. M. Rossetti observed, Christina had a "marked liking" for Williams's writings. She cites Williams in the opening of *Seek and Find* (p. 3), and she is known to have owned his *A Harmony of the Four Evangelists* (1850), given to her by her

mother in 1878. See Henry Sotheran, "The Rossettis," Catalogue #827 (1931), p. 178.

23. Review of *The Face of the Deep: A Devotional Commentary on the Apocalypse,* in *The Independent* 44 (27 October 1893): 1524. The reviewer elaborates as follows: "The book is not a commentary in any sense recognized hitherto among the makers of that kind of sad colored literature. Possibly in the sense of some transformation of the letter into spirit, or of a poetic mind sanctified and inspired to reveal the deep things of God, this may be a commentary, tho made of stuff that poets only know how to weave."

24. Richard Littledale's *A Commentary on the Song of Songs from Ancient and Medieval Sources* (London: Joseph Masters, 1869) reiterates similar values, affirming the "inspired character of the book" (p. xii) and insisting that his commentary was "not designed for critical purposes, but of a purely devotional character" (p. viii). Rossetti undoubtedly would have read and been affected by essays he published in the *Contemporary Review,* especially "The Religious Education of Women," 20 (1872): 1–26, and "The Pantheistic Factor in Christian Thought," 30 (1877): 642–60.

25. The Bible Rossetti used (given to her by her father in 1836) was printed at the Pitt Press in Cambridge in 1835 and is now in the Janet Camp Troxell Collection at Princeton University Library. While Rossetti understandably made no marginal notes in it, she fastidiously did make four corrections of typographical errors.

26. These phrases are from "On the Divine Inspiration of the Holy Scriptures," one of the "Essays on the most Important Subjects in Religion," *The Theological Works of the Rev. Thomas Scott* (London: Allan Bell, 1839), 164, 165.

27. In his "Devotional Commentary on the Gospel Narative," Williams similarly points out that the "signs and emblems" of Scripture represent "things spiritual and invisible" and also "form a system" (p. 267). In such "sacred expressions" we should expect "a depth of type and analogy" (p. 258).

28. In another of his *Parochial Sermons,* Burrows utters identical sentiments: "Remember the mischief that your written or spoken words may do. When once they have left you, they are beyond your control, you cannot tell how they will be taken up, misunderstood, or misrepresented" ("Government of the Tongue," p. 47).

29. Faulty exegesis is itself a serious violation. "It is, I suppose, a genuine though not a glaring breach of the Second Commandment, when instead of learning the lesson plainly set down for us in Holy Writ we protrude mental feelers in all directions above, beneath, around it, grasping, clinging to every imaginable particular except the main point" (*LS*, 85).

30. Rossetti's emphasis is certainly not entirely otherworldly. In *Letter and Spirit,* for example, she offers much practical advice for daily living and comments on a wide variety of matters, including controversial issues of her day.

31. The phrase is from Mary Arseneau and Jan Marsh, "Intertextuality and In-
    tratextuality: The Full Text of Christina Rossetti's 'Harmony on First
    Corinthians XIII' Restored," *Victorian Newsletter* 88 (Fall 1995): 21.
32. Antony H. Harrison gives some good examples of how passages in the de-
    votional prose may be helpful in interpreting Rossetti's poetry (see *Christina
    Rossetti in Context*, esp. pps. 51, 55, and 59–60).

Part 1: Fiction

Maude: Prose & Verse

Words of the text in this edition are given at the left of the bracket; Rossetti's cancelled manuscript variations appear at the right of the bracket. Editorial comments are not bracketed but marked "ed."

1. When his wife died in 1862, Dante Gabriel Rossetti placed his manuscript
   poems in the coffin with her; he later exhumed them and published them as
   Poems in 1870. For the Townsends, see *Letters,* 1:46 n.3; William Holman
   Hunt (1828–1907); Walter Howell Deverell (1827–54); for the Potters, see
   FL, 11 (ed.).
2. sonnet] careless sonnet
3. lives] states
4. the time till dinner] till dinner
5. nosegay] bouquet
6. start] operations
7. a] her
8. remains . . . seen] the course of my tale will show
9. In the drawingroom] On descending to the drawingroom
10. set in order] arrange
11. presents received] presents which she had received
12. a handsomely] There was a handsomely
13. cornelian heart] Faith, Hope and Charity
    Cornelian, also carnelian, is a dark red, semi-precious stone, a variety of
    chalcedony, used in jewelry (ed.).
14. pretty trifles] abundances of pretty trifles
15. arrangements and re-arrangements] her alterations and improvements
16. quiet colours] quiet nun-like colours
17. so much alike] so greatly resembling each other
18. prompt] dictate
19. Maude is referring to several games popular in the mid-nineteenth century.
    In her edition of *Maude,* Crump cites *The American Girl's Book; or, Occupa-
    tion for May Hours,* by Eliza Leslie (New York: R. Worthington, 1880), and
    describes the games mentioned here (85):

    "Proverbs" is a game in which one player tries to guess a
    proverb that the others have chosen. The player askes questions
    and finds one word of the proverb in each answer. In "What's
    my thought like" the members of the company sit in a row; the

one at the head of the row thinks of a word and then asks the others, "What is my thought like?" The others, who do not know the word, reply at random. When all have made their replies, the head player proclaims the thought, and then the others must give reasons why their answers resemble the thought. Whoever is unable to find a reason must pay a forfeit. In "How do you like it" one person leaves the room while the others choose a word with two or more meanings. The absentee then returns and asks each of the others "How do you like it?" The answers must refer to one of the meanings of the word. The person whose response enables a correct guess is the next to go out. "Magic music" is a game in which one player leaves the room while the others decide on something to be done by her when she returns. The player returns and tries to discover the task by attempting whatever she thinks most probable. One of the other players strikes a piano key or a bell slowly as long as the experiments go wrong, and rapidly as the player succeeds in performing the correct action. [ed.]

20. three girls] three young girls
21. This proposal . . . Agnes.] *cancelled in MS, then restored by the author*
22. such heroic] heroic
23. metre] correct metre
24. "Indeed . . . sonnet:] *cancelled in MS, then restored by the author*
25. fishing for a] holding a poor
26. "Well, Agnes . . . listen:] *cancelled in MS, then restored by the author*
27. niggard] sparing
28. renewed.] renewed with fresh vigour.
29. such] such a depth of
30. certainly] certainly singularly
31. And] And then
32. mother] Mamma
33. go near] nurse
34. all paragons] all such paragons of perfection
35. by your diligence] *deleted, then marked for reinsertion*
36. prefer] love
37. Lynch-law. "The practice of inflicting summary punishment upon an offender, by a self-constituted court without legal authority" (*Oxford English Dictionary*) (ed.).
38. made tea] presided at the tea table
39. powers] capabilities
40. a reply] an answer
41. things, or something.] things.
42. district. That is, an area of the neighborhood (ed.).
43. hers] *MS reads* her's
44. says you are to get] tells Mamma that she would like you to supply

45. things] wardrobe
46. get] replenish
47. *The MS omits the following sentence:* The language is so against us; "so full of cramped vowels and consonants."

   St. Andrew's Church, Wells Street, one of the leading Tractarian churches in London, was a chief center of the choral revival during the 1840s and early 1850s. See Bernarr Rainbow, *The Choral Revival in the Anglican Church (1839–1872)* (New York: Oxford University Press, 1970), 169 ff. and 276 ff. See Crump, *Maude*, p. 89 (ed.).
48. rummage] long rummage
49. take] escort
50. raged] progressed
51. went to her room] was permitted to retire to her own apartment
52. good] pure
53. harmless] innocent
54. sleepy] wearied and sleepy
55. music.] music, and Maude sat up to listen. waits.] Like carollers, a group of singers and musicians who go through the sheets at Christmas time performing songs (ed).
56. that] informing her that
57. will come] will be prevailed upon to come
58. tomorrow] this
59. finally] formally
60. Sisters of Mercy is a general name given to the early religious orders for women in the Anglican communion. The first of these sisterhoods was established in Christina Rossetti's parish of Christ Church in 1845. Christina's own sister Maria entered the novitiate of All Saints Sisterhood in 1873. There are useful discussions of the establishment of these religious communities in S. L. Ollard, *A Short History of the Oxford Movement* (London: A. R. Mowbray, 1915), 244–47, and in Davies, 1962, 123, 131–35 (ed.).
61. two] many
62. both] all the
63. broken] fractured
64. Epithalamium. A poem in celebration of a marriage (ed.).
65. hers] *MS reads* her's
66. "This heart sighs, and I know not why." The second and third "song" (referring to the heart) declare "It may be sighing for love, but to me it says not so"; and "Answer me, my heart, why do you sigh? It responds: I want God, I sigh for Jesus" (ed.).
67. The note is Christina Rossetti's. The quotation is from Elizabeth Barrett Browning's "Catarina to Camöens (Dying in His Absence Abroad, and Referring to the Poem in Which He Recorded the Sweetness of Her Eyes)" (1844). See *The Complete Works of Elizabeth Barrett Browning*, eds. Charlotte Porter and Helen A. Clarke (New York: Thomas Y. Crowell, 1900), 3:124–29, and accompanying annotations (ed.).

68. an emotion] a warmth of pleasure
69. will not repeat] ought not to repeat

Commonplace, and Other Short Stories

70. Bradshaw. *Bradshaw's Railway Guide,* a comprehensive timetable for British trains, first appeared in 1839. Brompton itself is a village a few miles west of Scarborough, a principal resort on the Yorkshire coast to which the fictional "Brompton-on-Sea" might bear some resemblance.
71. Indian army-surgeon. A surgeon attached to the British army in India.
72. Mrs. Grundy. Synonymous with narrow conventionality or prudery. From a character in Thomas Morton's comedy, *Speed the Plow* (1798), who never appears but who is constantly referred to by a rival farmer's wife ("What will Mrs. Grundy think?").
73. cracker. A little paper roll containing candy or various trinkets that explodes when the ends are pulled, common at parties and festive occasions.
74. Notting Hill. Part of the borough of Kensington, with the kind of large houses fashionable in the mid-Victorian period.
75. petted. To treat as a pet, spoil, indulge.
76. *"Se non è vero è ben trovato."* "If it isn't true, it's certainly a good story."
77. antimacassar. A covering to protect the back or arms of a chair or sofa.
78. Hone. William Hone (1780–1842) was a reformer, writer, and bookseller. In one of his compilations, *The Every-day Book* (1826), Christina first read Keats's poetry.
79. *tableaux vivants.* A static depiction usually presented on a stage with costumed characters.
80. Crystal Palace. Constructed largely of glass and iron, this elaborate structure cost £1,500,000 to build and was originally the home of the Great Exhibition (1851). It was later removed to Sydenham where it served as a museum until damaged by fire in 1936.
81. Love-apple. The fruit of the tomato.
82. Boreas. God of the north wind but also, here, a pun.
83. Athenian owl. The owl was sacred to Athena, patroness of Athens and Greek goddess of wisdom. The Romans identified her as Minerva, their goddess of arts and crafts. The scene portrayed refers to the Judgment of Paris. See note 113.
84. cadets. That is, the younger sons in a gentlemen's family, who lack the patrimonial inheritance.
85. propitiated. That is, to cause to become favorably inclined.
86. Bluebeard. The fairy-tale character who married and murdered six wives.
87. dog-cart. A small, light open carriage, generally two-wheeled.
88. Rocky Drumble. Drumble is an important town in Elizabeth Gaskell's *Cranford* (1853). Christina never met Mrs. Gaskell, although they had friends in common, but Mrs. Gaskell did meet Dante Gabriel and makes some amusing remarks about him in a letter (see Frances Thomas, 119–20). The review

of *Commonplace* appearing in *The Atheneum* (4 June 1870, p. 735) compliments the novella by citing its similarity with *Cranford*.

89. Cooee. A signal call used by Australian aborigines and adopted by British colonists; for the nonce. For this particular occasion.

90. *vis-à-vis.* Sitting face-to-face, and therefore improperly close.

91. Honiton lace. Honiton, in Devonshire, is a type of lace that featured designs of foliage, figures, or flowers and was popular for wedding dresses.

92. "*Quel che piace giova.*" What delights is useful.

93. seeing Naples together. The reference recalls the expression, "see Naples and die."

94. moire. Watered or clouded silk.

95. drumbles. Dialect variant of dumble or dimble; that is, a shady dell or hollow.

96. cuttle-fish. Ten-armed marine mollusk.

97. Bosphorus. That is, Bosporus, the strait between the Sea of Marmara and the Black Sea, and the location of Istanbul (Constantinople).

The Lost Titian

98. *colorito.* Manner of using color.

99. *evviva.* Hurrah.

100. Argus-eyed. Argus is a mythological figure with many eyes, some of which are always open.

101. *solitario passero.* Solitary sparrow.

102. *amico mio.* My friend.

103. *Benvenuto Cellini* (1500–71). Sculptor, metalsmith, and author of a famous autobiography.

104. Giorgione . . . Tintoret. Giorgione (1478–1510) was, like Titian, a student of Giovanni Bellini (1430–1516). Tintoretto (1518–94) apparently was a student of Titian but his abilities were supposed to have provoked his teacher's jealousy.

105. Bevilacqua Mangiaruva. According to Marsh, "a satirical name for a landlord, signifying 'drink water, eat coarse fare.'" See *Christina Rossetti: Poems and Prose*, ed. Jan Marsh (London: Everyman, 1994), 453.

106. Lupo Vorace of the *Orco decapitato*. "Ravenous wolf" of the "headless ogre."

Nick

107. pet. Childish sulking.

108. turnpike. A road on which a toll is collected at a toll booth or gate.

Pros and Cons

109. Zenana. The reference is to the apartments of an Eastern house in which the women of the family are secluded. This Islamic custom was introduced into

India and was adopted by the Indus; Japanese . . . happy despatch: Jocular reference to hara-kiri, a ritual form of suicide by disembowelling that was practised voluntarily from a sense of shame; Bushman: The San (or hunter-gatherers), indigenous people of the southern half of Africa, were reduced in numbers and dominance after the twelfth century by other tribes and European settlers. In South Africa, Boer-organized commandos virtually exterminated the San by the end of the nineteenth century.

110. throb. Pulsation of the heart.
111. flunky. Menial attendant or liveried manservant; clodhopper: Agricultural labourer.
112. Mr. Stone is concerned over certain of the ceremonial and liturgical reforms of the Oxford Movement, which were deeply resented by many ordinary English parishioners used to traditional practices.

Speaking Likenesses

113. Apple of Discord. A subject of dissension. The famous golden apple bore the inscription "To the fairest"; Hera (Juno), Athena (Minerva), and Aphrodite (Venus) each claimed the prize for herself. Paris awarded it to Aphrodite, thus incurring the wrath of the others; his decision, known as the "Judgment of Paris," was the beginning of the trouble that led to the Trojan War.
114. Les Grâces. Game in which a player holds a hoop on a pair of rods, and by drawing one rod rapidly across the other impels the hoop into the air.
115. *Nowhere* was the original title of *Speaking Likenesses* (see *RM*, 100). The nightmarish quality of the first of these repulsive "games," notes McGillis, "treats human beings as objects, things without feeling or dignity; it reverses the fairy tale convention of imagining inanimate objects as human" (Kent, 227). The second game of "Self Help" is a "bloodsport" in which Rossetti is satirizing the whole notion of self-help, popularized in the mid-nineteenth century by Samuel Smiles's *Self-Help* (1859).
116. goffer. To crimp or make wavy by using a heated iron (or similar instrument); flute: To make grooves in.
117. syllabub. Frothy dessert made with milk or cream; lunns: Cakes or raisin buns.
118. fagot. Bundle of sticks or twigs tied together as fuel.
119. scudded. Dart nimbly.
120. glutinous. Sticky.
121. hunch. A think piece.
122. carnelian. Variant of cornelian. See note 13.

True in the Main: "Two Sketches"

123. gruel. Oatmeal or similar food boiled in water.
124. charing. The household chores of a domestic servant.
125. See 1 Cor. 4.5.

126. See Eph. 6.2.
127. See 2 Kings 4.26.

Part 2: Miscellaneous Prose

"Dante, An English Classic"

1. "Honor the highest poet."
2. Rossetti is recalling 1 Cor. 2.9, itself a recollection of Isa. 64.4: "For since the beginning of the world men have not heard, nor perceived by the ear, neither hath the eye seen, O God, beside thee, what he hath prepared for him that waiteth for him."

"Dante: The Poet Illustrated Out of the Poem"

3. tyros. Novices or beginners.
4. Gabriele Rossetti, *Comento Analitico* (1826–27); Maria Francesca Rossetti, *A Shadow of Dante* (1871); Dante Gabriel Rossetti, *The Early Italian Poets* (1861); William Rossetti, trans., *Inferno* (1865).
5. Henry Wadsworth Longfellow (1807–82), popular American poet, published his translation of Dante's *The Divine Comedy* in 1865–67.
6. lusters. A luster is a period of five years. (Spelled "lustre" in *A Shadow of Dante*).
7. See William Michael Rossetti, ed., *The Collected Works of Dante Gabriel Rossetti,* 2 vols. (London: Ellis and Elvery, 1890), 2:66–67.

"The House of Dante Gabriel Rossetti"

8. Roman-cement centre. Roman cement is made by adding limestone and clay to sand, lime, and water. *Centre* is an architectural term that denotes a temporary framework supporting any superstructure. Rossetti's consciousness of architectural detail may be connected with translation work she had done many years before: *The terra-cotta architecture of North Italy,* ed. Lewis Gruner (London: J. Murray, 1867).
9. various creatures . . . unknown to me. Rossetti does not mention peacocks, a small Brahmin bull, or the armadillos that at one time or another were also residents of this garden. Nor does she refer to the parrots and monkeys that could be found indoors among decorated mirrors and Chinese panels. In fact, the reader is never taken inside the house where, perhaps, less happy memories resided.

    The wombat is a shy, nocturnal marsupial about three feet long and native to Australia and Tasmania. In his notes (*PW,* 494) to the poem, William Michael Rossetti observes, "As a motto to these verses Christina wrote an English distich: 'When wombats do inspire / I strike my disused lyre.'"

10. "Irsuto e tondo." Reprinted in *Poems,* 1979–90, 3:336. "O Wombat / nimble, joyous, / How you are made / smooth and plump! / Oh don't run away / what a vagabond, / Don't disappear / burrowing the world: / The scales indeed / Of a hemisphere / not light in weight" (our translation). Christina says that she altered line 4 to "Irsuto e tondo," that is, "hairy and round."

11. photographed . . . garden. The Reverend Charles Dodgson (Lewis Carroll) photographed the Rossettis in the autumn of 1863. See Marsh, 300–2.

Part 3: Devotional Prose

Annus Domini

1. See Rom. 8.22: "For we know that the whole creation groaneth and travaileth in pain together until now." Here as in many other instances, Christina Rossetti introduces a word or an idea drawn from the vocabulary of the Bible or the *Book of Common Prayer,* for she is very deeply—sometimes almost unconsciously—immersed in their thoughts and terms.

2. "The bottomless pit" occurs several times in Revelation: chap. 9.1–2 and 11; 11.7; 17.8; 20.1–3.

3. In the *Book of Common Prayer,* the versicles in Morning and Evening Prayer include the petition "Endue thy ministers with righteousness," with the response "And make thy chosen people joyful."

4. On forgiveness, Jesus says to Peter that one should forgive one's brother "seventy times seven" (Matt. 18.22).

5. This last sentence is quoted from Isa. 59.19.

6. On Esau, who "despised his birthright" and gave it up to Jacob, see Gen. 25.29–34. Pharaoh is frequently characterized as having a heart that was "hardened" (see, for example, Exod. 8.19). "The besom [that is, broom] of destruction" refers to Isa. 14.23.

7. See the General Thanksgiving in the *Book of Common Prayer:* "We beseech thee, give us that due sense of all thy mercies, That our hearts may be unfeignedly thankful, And that we shew forth thy praise, Not only with our lips, but in our lives. . . ."

8. Thus Rossetti frequently responds to the "new" science and to Victorian scepticism and doubt, and strikes one of the regular themes of *Annus Domini.* Compare 234, where she prays that we not be seduced by "miscalled reason."

9. See Ps. 42.1, which is echoed here.

10. See 1 Cor. 6.19: "Know ye not that your body is the temple of the Holy Ghost which is in you . . . ?"

11. Another common theme in these prayers is that of "fallen women" who are yet saved. See Gen. 38.6–24; Josh. 2–6; 2 Sam. 11–12 (and compare to David's penitence supposedly expressed in Ps. 51.1).

12. Compare to Ps. 17.15: "I will behold thy face in righteousness: I shall be satisfied, when I awake, with thy likeness."

13. See Isa. 30.21. "Follow me"—the familiar command of Jesus: see for example John 10.27 and 2 John 1.6.
14. that our prayer . . . sacrifice. See Ps. 141.2.
15. "And he said to the woman, Thy faith hath saved thee; go in peace" (Luke 7.50). Luke does not name the woman.
16. Compare to Luke 1.35 where Mary receives the news from the angel who foretells her conception: "The Holy Ghost shall come upon thee, and the power of the Highest shall overshadow thee."
17. inherit . . . world. See Matt. 25.34.
18. earth . . . sea. See Isa. 11.9 and compare with Hab. 2.14.
19. Rossetti skillfully merges several texts, including 1 Cor. 15.45, "The first man Adam was made a living soul; the last Adam was made a quickening spirit"; Micah 7.8, "When I sit in darkness, the Lord shall be a light unto me"; Eph. 5.14: "Awake thou that sleepest, and arise from the dead, and Christ shall give thee light."
20. tears . . . book. See Ps. 56.8: "Thou tellest my wanderings: put thou my tears into thy bottle: are they not in thy book?"
21. See the Baptismal Office in the *Book of Common Prayer* in which the priest prays that the child "shall not be ashamed to confess the faith of Christ crucified, and manfully to fight under his banner, against sin, the world, and the devil."
22. See the meeting of Jesus with the woman of Samaria at Jacob's well in John 4 (especially verse 10).

Seek and Find

Substantive readings of the manuscript of "Treasure-Trove" are given in the notes following the square bracket, and identified by "MS." To the left of the bracket is the reading of the printed text as it appears in this edition.

23. Isaac Williams (1802–65), who was drawn into the Tractarian Movement through John Keble's influence, wrote the famous Tract 80 on "Reserve in Communicating Religious Knowledge." Rossetti refers to his *Harmony of the Four Evangelists* (1850).
24. based . . . Margin] taken from some external source; mainly from the Margin *MS*
25. life like his own] life *MS*
26. Wise . . . felt] A different aspect of the same fundamental truth was recognised by those wise ancients who felt *MS*
27. could be] were *MS*
28. self: . . . not.] self. *MS*
29. imparted beauty] all things beautiful *MS*
30. imparted life . . . imparted goodness] all things living . . . all things good *MS*
31. signification] intention *MS*
32. Wisdom] wise Will *MS*
33. reveals] has revealed *MS*

34. in conformity] in the conformity *MS*
35. the sentence] all *MS*
36. fidelity] conduct *MS*
37. rather than] not *MS*
38. See . . . trust.] *In the manuscript, Rossetti encloses this statement in square brackets.*
39. One] The one *MS*
40. one] the other *MS*
41. reach] grasp *MS*
42. to stand aloof] *delete MS*
43. time] sense *MS*
44. madest] *The text corrects the manuscript reading of* makest.
45. Electricity . . . intelligence.] This interesting paragraph has undergone considerable revision, for the manuscript reads as follows: "Electricity: the dangerous element of the storm, invisible, inaudible, Swifter than light or sound: the lightning flash which is simultaneous with it, lags behind it in reaching our sight; the thunder clap born with both is more tardy than either in arriving within range of our perception. Electricity of strength to rend trees, shatter rocks and destroy life, has yet become man's servant; available in the Battery for the cure of disease, and in the Telegraph for the communication of intelligence." Samuel F. B. Morse demonstrated the practical use of the telegraph in 1844, while Alexander Graham Bell displayed the first use of the telephone in 1876. Rossetti's aunt Charlotte had benefitted from medical treatment involving galvanism. To Christina, all of these inventions indicated divine grace (Marsh, 463).
46. us to transfer] *delete MS*
47. to temperate zones, and to make fruits ripen] to inhabit the temperate zones, and to make fruits to ripen *MS*
48. planets escape not . . . circuits] stars fall not *MS*
49. forces] laws *MS*
50. originally] *deleted MS*
51. matters] great matters *MS*
52. they] *omit MS*
53. yet] *omit MS*
54. to others] to any other man *MS*
55. exists] *omit MS*
56. telleth] knoweth *MS*
57. a] the *MS*
58. thus . . . virtue.] *omit MS*
59. in the Inspired Text, to be or to represent a weapon] to represent in the Inspired Text a weapon *MS*
60. is its aspect] equally *MS*
61. a] the *MS*
62. that] that one *MS*
63. If the weapon . . . smitten.] *This paragraph appears only in the printed text.*
64. These . . . of] This which St. Paul tells us is the case with *MS*

65. seem . . . also] seems no less to be the case with the Sea *MS*
66. obliterated] vanished *MS*
67. at foresight of] for *MS*
68. See Job 40.23.
69. of] of the *MS*
70. Christina Rossetti was always generous and sympathetic toward animals and an early and vigorous supporter of antivivisection, a cause to which she remained committed throughout her life (see Marsh, 433–35).
71. incense] worship *MS*
72. on] by *MS*
73. cannot] cannot perhaps *MS*
74. two] two distinct *MS*
75. august] *omit MS*
76. even] *omit MS*
77. The second part of *Seek and Find* begins here, with Rossetti repeating the same headings—or objects of praise—in her "double series" of studies of the Benedicite, but in this second half of the book, concern is for the redemptive (as opposed to the creative) signs of holiness.
78. calculated] *omit MS*
79. The last statement appears near the beginning of the Great Litany in the *Book of Common Prayer:* "From all blindness of heart; from pride, vain-glory, and hypocrisy; form envy, hatred, and malice, and all uncharitableness, *Good Lord, deliver us.*"
80. world] life *MS*
81. should] will *MS*
82. See Matt. 2.2.
83. See John 24.26.
84. See John 12.21.
85. lie under] share *MS*
86. have done] did *MS* For the quotation, see Matt. 25.37–44.
87. shallow] self-complacent *MS*
88. Lord's words] Lord's own words *MS*
89. See Phil. 1.11.

Called to be Saints

90. See 1 Sam. 25.41 and 1 Cor. 1.13.
91. Rossetti refers to Thomas Fuller (1608–1661), author of *The Worthies of England* (1662), who writes of flowers in his description of Norwich (under the heading "Natural Commodities"): "In the morning when it groweth up, [the flower] is a lecture of Divine Providence. In the evening, when it is cut down withered, it is a lecture of human mortality" (ed. John Freeman [New York: Barnes & Noble, 1952], 419).
92. See Matt. 6.28.
93. See Gen. 24.60.

94. See Matt. 4.19 and Mark 14.34.
95. The Ember Days occur in four groups each of three days in the church year, namely the Wednesday, Friday, and Saturday after St. Lucy (13 December), after the first Sunday in Lent, after Pentecost, and after Holy Cross Day (14 September). They have traditionally been observed as days of fasting or special penitence in the Anglican church, but now they are associated with the ordination of the church's ministers. Rossetti refers particularly to the Lenten Ember Days.
96. See Acts 2.2 and John 3.8. Rossetti is citing the events of Pentecost.
97. Gospel of the Kingdom. See Matt. 4.23, 9.35, and, for "*this* Gospel," see Matt. 24.14 and also Mark 1.14. The further reference to "His right hand" occurs in Matt. 25.34.
98. See Mark 1.3.
99. brindled. Streaked.
100. knops. A flower-bud.
101. darnel. A grass that grows commonly in cornfields.

Letter and Spirit

As with "Treasure-Trove," substantive readings of the manuscript are given in the notes following the square bracket, and identified by "MS." The first reading, to the left of the bracket, is of the text in this edition.

102. And touching . . . the other.] And if we dare even in the First and Great Commandment to discriminate between degrees of incumbency I think we may infer that to grasp, hold fast, adore the Catholic mystery must necessarily take precedence of man's obligation to grasp, hold fast, adore the Christian Mystery. *MS*
103. raised; even . . . Revelation] raised. *MS*
104. Father] all-Father *MS*
105. as . . . attests] attests *MS*
106. on our own . . . other than] self-evidently other than *MS*
107. it: yet to] it. To *MS*
108. license] play *MS*
109. *MS note:* Quoted from a sermon I heard preached by the Revd. J. E. Snowden, Incumbent of Hammersmith.
110. as I have seen] as has been *MS*
111. not to be called . . . creation] not like His creature because of its typical grace, but it is like Him because of His archetypal Attribute, it suggests itself that for every phrase and form of creation *MS*
112. *The manuscript includes here the following paragraph:* "If without presumptuous fancifulness we may venture to lay stress on the form of those figures O Δ which express to us Unity & Trinity, we observe that the figure of utmost possible capacity O is that which stands for Unity, the figure of straitest possible area Δ symbolizes Trinity: thus harmonizing with the wider diffusion of the one truth than of the other, pressing home upon us that our perception

of the Trinity must never warp us from apprehending the all-embracing Unity, making us jealous over our own hearts lest by any means they should go astray from the simplicity of truth."

113. were, in point of time, first] were first *MS*
114. if . . . Pentateuch] *omitted MS*
115. obligation] incumbency *MS*
116. (heart . . . strength) *omitted MS*
117. *each* one by one] one by one *each MS*
118. See Deut. 5.7 and Matt. 4.4.
119. Eve, equally . . . castle-building spirit] Eve appears to have indulged sundry refined tastes and aspirations, a castle-building spirit *MS* castle-building spirit. Compare to "A Castle-Builder's World" (*Poems*, 1979–90, 2:314). It is significant that this poem was first published as the entry for 1 April in *Time Flies*. Furthermore, Rossetti describes Eve's susceptibility to Satan in terms of her "castle-building spirit" in a later instance of *Letter and Spirit* (1883, p. 17; not given here).
120. goal] self-chosen goal *MS This manuscript reading replaces "fatal"; the original word is illegible.*
121. may not have argued at all] did not argue *MS*
122. she offered] she merely offered *MS*
123. seems to have] *omitted MS*
124. injunction] lesson *MS*
125. "Suggested to me" (CGR's *MS* note)
126. The missionary bishop referred to here is Reginald Heber (1783–1826), bishop of Calcutta; the hymn quoted is from "Brightest and Best of the Sons of the Morning" (reprinted in *The New English Hymnal* [Norwich: Canterbury Press, 1986], no. 49).
127. not wrong] right *MS*
128. (we flatter ourselves)] *omitted MS*
129. only] but *MS*
130. which . . . riches."] *omitted MS*
131. corban. In Hebrew antiquity, an offering given to God, especially in performance of a vow (*Oxford English Dictionary*).
132. Omitted here are comments on Balaam (Num. 22–24) as an example of apparently faultless behavior. Additional examples of disinclination are cited: Gen. 19.15,16,26; Exod. 4.10–14; Judges 4.6–9; Ruth 1.6–15; Mark 6.20,26,27; John 18.33–40, 19.1–16; Acts 24.25–27.
133. When all . . .] *This paragraph appears only in the printed text.*
134. Never . . . by love.] *omitted MS*
135. See Mark 10.31.
136. See Song of Sol. 8.7.
137. See Heb. 6.20.
138. See Job 12.2; Ps. 12.4 (*Book of Common Prayer*).
139. See Job 23.8–9.
140. See 1 Cor. 8.4.

141. See 1 John 1.5; Heb. 12.29; Exod. 15.3.
142. who . . . preponderance] *omitted MS*
143. See 1 John 3.12.
144. See Rev. 4.8.
145. See Ps. 27.9 (*Book of Common Prayer*).
146. See Col. 3.23.
147. See Hos. 13.9.
148. heinous] guilty *MS*
149. See Matt. 23.27.
150. See Matt. 5.8.
151. yearn for] strain after *MS*
152. See Rev. 6.11, 7.9.
153. "See a sermon I heard preached by the Revd. H. W. Burrows, B. D., Canon of Rochester, and which has also been published." (Rossetti, in her manuscript note, apparently is referring to Burrows's *Parochial Sermons,* sermon 23, pp. 229–40: "Consider the Lilies" [preached on the Fifteenth Sunday after Trinity, on Matt. 6.28,29]). Burrows writes that our Lord "has stepped out of the way to give us a judgement on what might have been otherwise thought a matter of opinion or a question of taste. He affirms that even a Solomon, in all his glory, was not arrayed like one of the lilies of the field. . . . Solomon's glory had been continually surpassed by the lilies" (235, 238).
154. and even . . . self-denial,] *omitted MS*
155. From Luke 17.21, just quoted.
156. qualification for] subject of *MS*
157. See Matt. 5.42.
158. See Prov. 31.27.
159. See 1 Tim. 2.9.
160. or . . . house] how much more her own house *MS*
161. appear] seem *MS*
162. See Acts 7.50.
163. saying] and *MS*
164. See Ps. 19.1; Ps. 8.3; 1 Cor. 2.16.
165. See Ps. 94.9.
166. cumberer. Hindrance, inconvenience.
167. See Gen. 3.19.
168. See Prov. 6.10 and 24.33.
169. See Isa. 58.13.
170. See 1 Tim. 5.6.
171. punctilio. A trifle.
172. See Luke 10.42.
173. See Matt. 13.28 and Matt. 4.4.
174. *Letter and Spirit* ends here, but Rossetti has appended a "harmony" on 1 Cor. 13. It first appeared in a church magazine, *New and Old,* 7 (January 1879): 84–89. Rossetti states there that "1 Cor. 13 with illustrative texts was

suggested to me as an exercise last Lent. The *Chapter* I thought of myself; the particular treatment was suggested in part or wholly to me." Rossetti revised the harmony for inclusion in *Letter and Spirit*. For the original version and a detailed assessment, see Arseneau and Marsh.

Time Flies

Annotations identified with the initials "CGR" are Rossetti's comments in a copy of the book at the University of Texas at Austin.

175. "Gabriel" (CGR).

176. For the sieve image used here and in the July 27 and 28 entries below, see Eccles. 27.4–7, Isa. 30.28, and Luke 22.31. Rossetti also alludes to Milton's dictum about the true poet himself being a "true Poem, that is, a composition, and patterne of the best and honourablest things" in *An Apology Against a Pamphlet*, in *Complete Prose Works of John Milton* (New Haven: Yale University Press, 1953), 1. 890.

177. See James 3.10.

178. A partial quotation from the Great Litany in the *Book of Common Prayer* (as with the concluding quotations in the entries for January 28 and March 14).

179. "W. Garrett Horder" (CGR): editor of the popular *Poets' Bible* and other anthologies, to which he persuaded Rossetti to contribute (Marsh, 497–98).

180. See Matt. 5.14.

181. See Eph. 5.4. Among the prose fragments in the Troxell Collection, Princeton University Library, are some unpublished notes apparently intended for a possible new edition of *Time Flies*. One set, for January 18 (Feast of St. Prisca), revises and elaborates the original entry, dramatizing the martyr's experience and moralizing at greater length on the theme of innocence. The second set of notes for February 3 (Feast of St. Blaise) is transcribed below. Certainly Christina's interest in the welfare of animals is prominent in the proposed revision, but there is also a greater seriousness of both tone and intention evident.

> Feb.3. Feast of St. Blaise Bp. & Martyr. St. Blaise Bp. of Sebaste suffered for the Faith early in the 4th century, being decapitated in the persecution by Licinius (?) perhaps in the year 316. He is described to us as a lover of solitude, frequenting a hill for devout privacy, inhabiting a cave as his home. Yet was not his solitude altogether solitary or divorced from daily sympathy & charities. It is related how when Agricola Governor of Cappadocia & Lesser Armenia sent to arrest him the messengers found him in a cave of Mount Argus surrounded by wild animals his voluntary companions. Such creatures are said to have resorted to him for cure of their ailments, on which occasions if they found the Saint at his devotions they awaited his leisure.
>
> A beautiful picture is thus set before us, an acted parable for our instruction, a model for our imitation.
>
> Those good irrational creatures of God flocking round the Saint composed as it were a humble school of disciples. They

reverence in him the higher functions which they could not share, postponing their own urgent need to his piety: they looked up to him for help, and being helped they consorted with him gratefully and affectionately. Let us learn from them to revere & to esteem very highly in love those spiritual physicians who watch for our souls as they who must give account.

And looking higher what may we learn from St. Blaize himself? In general to be full of kindness, helpfulness, sympathy: to feel how that cannot be genuine sympathy which does not impel to acts of kindness & helpfulness. And in particular let us reflect on our duties & privileges towards dumb animals. Our love draws out their love, our sympathy their sympathy. It is no trivial boon to be loved by any love capable creature whatever its degree: a dog's fidelity through life until & beyond death shames many a human friend & lover.

Troxell Collection, folder 27. Reprinted with the permission of Princeton University Libraries.

182. Speculations about the future life in the later Victorian period ranged from the deeply theological and philosophical to the more popularly religious. See, for example, Geoffrey Rowell, *Hell and the Victorians: A Study of the Nineteenth-Century Controversy Concerning Eternal Punishment and the Future Life* (Oxford: Clarendon Press, 1974), 4.

183. See Rev. 15.2.

184. "And I look for the Resurrection of the dead, And the Life of the world to come": the final statement of the Nicene Creed (in the rite of Holy Communion in the *Book of Common Prayer*).

185. See Ps. 87.3; 68.25.

186. "Heard from Gabriel at Birchington" (CGR).

187. "Mrs. Catterson" (CGR): not traced.

188. "Mme Tussaud's" (CGR).

189. See Mic. 2.10.

190. See Heb. 13.14.

191. See Heb. 12.1. *Tableaux vivants:* cited in *Commonplace*, n. 78.

192. "Holmer Green" (CGR): Grandfather Polidori's cottage was thirty miles from London. See Marsh, 8–11.

193. "At Penkill" (CGR): Rossetti first visited Alice Boyd's small Scottish castle in 1866 in the company of Letitia Scott (see Marsh, 349–52).

194. See Ps. 81.10; Job 12.7.

195. By Dr. Littledale" (CGR): Anglo-Catholic priest and controversialist who became a life-long friend after meeting Christina through the Scotts.

196. See Prov. 17.17.

197. "Alice Boyd of Penkill" (CGR).

198. matutinal. Early morning; "at Penkill" (CGR).

199. See Matt. 11.15.

200. "At Frome" (CGR): a small town in Somerset where Rossetti and her mother unsuccessfully tried to establish a school in 1852.

201. "Botanical Gardens Regents Park" (CGR).
202. See Ps. 34.8.
203. See John 6.51.
204. See 1 John 1.1.
205. See Matt. 11.28; Matt. 4.19, and so on.
206. A phrase from the Te Deum Laudamus ("We believe that thou shalt come: to be our Judge"), the first of the canticles in the office of Morning Prayer in the *Book of Common Prayer.*
207. See Luke 24.24.
208. "Dr. Littledale" (CGR).
209. "Maria" ("one" is underscored); "with J. Ruskin" ("brief acquaintance" is underscored) (CGR).
210. See *Poems,* 1979–90, 2:299 where this short lyric forms the third stanza of "What is that to thee? follow thou me" in "Songs for Strangers and Pilgrims," the eighth section of *Verses* (1893).
211. "F. J. Shields at Birchington" (CGR): a pious and devout Christian painter (1833–1911) who became a family friend during Dante Gabriel's final years.
212. "Rosetta Wood" (CGR). A Mrs. Wood was a neighbor of the Rossettis in Charlotte Street, and "neighbour" is mentioned later in this entry. However, Bell (p. 62) identifies her as one of Maria's students in Italian.
213. "At Hastings," "General Ludlow" (CGR): He was brother-in-law to Barbara Bodichon (née Smith). See Marsh, 333, 148–54, and other mentions.
214. Bell (p. 154) believes that the English traveler in this entry was Edward Lear (1812–88). For the closing quotation, see Luke 6.37.
215. See Luke 17.10.
216. See Rev. 9.1,2,11; 11.7; 17.8; 20.1,3.
217. See 1 Cor. 10.11.
218. Tarshish. A place associated with precious metals or a refinery, but its location is unknown. Jonah (1.3, 4.2) sailed for Tarshish and believed he was leaving his God behind. This latter sense appears to be Rossetti's intention.
219. "Mamma, William + I" (CGR). Compare to Sonnet 22 in "Later Life" (*Poems,* 1979–90, 2:147–48).
220. See 1 Cor. 12.26.
221. See Eccles. 9.10.
222. See James 5.9.
223. "All Saints Convalescent Hospital" (CGR).
224. See Lam. 2.6.
225. See Gen. 4.9.
226. See Rom. 15.4.
227. See Gen. 50.25.
228. See Exod. 3.5 or Acts 7.33.
229. "Maria" (CGR).
230. "At Holmer Green" (CGR).
231. Christina has deleted "not" in her annotations.
232. "belonging to the Tebbes" (CGR). Henry Virtue Tebbs (d. 1899) was an art collector, friend of the Rossetti brothers, and brother-in-law to John Seddon

(1827–1906), an admirer of Dante Gabriel Rossetti. He acted as legal advisor in the exhumation of Elizabeth Siddal's coffin in Highgate Cemetery in 1869. Siddal, Dante's wife, died in 1862, and the bereaved husband had buried his manuscript poems with her.

233. "Cheltenham" (CGR).
234. "At Holmer Green" (CGR).
235. "Maria" (CGR).
236. See James 1.4
237. See Matt. 6.26; Luke 12.24.
238. See Jer. 5.31 or Amos 8.10.
239. See 1 Pet. 5.8.
240. See Luke 22.31.
241. See Mark 1.40.
242. Christina, William, and their mother traveled to Italy in 1865 (May 22 to June 26).
243. See 2 Cor. 6.10.
244. In Christina's copy "conclude" is inserted for "stop."
245. See 1 Cor. 19.17.
246. See 2 Cor. 2.16.
247. See Prov. 2.9; 25.24.
248. "by Gabriel" (CGR).
249. See Isa. 26.3.
250. See Rom. 8.28.
251. See Psalm 84.6 (*Book of Common Prayer*). Battiscombe believes that Charles Cayley inspired the reflections about "the friend" in this entry (p. 189).
252. See 1 Cor. 14.16.
253. "The Splügen" (CGR): Christina, William, and their mother crossed the Alps by the Splügen Pass when returning to England from Italy in 1865.
254. See Heb. 12.2.
255. See Matt. 24.13 and Mark 13.13.
256. "Aunt Eliza" (CGR): Eliza Harriet Polidori (1810–93).
257. See Ps. 39.13.
258. See Rev. 21.1.
259. "Walton on the Naze" (CGR): Resort in Essex where the Rossetti women vacationed in 1878.
260. "Maria" (CGR).
261. "Aunt Charlotte" (CGR): Charlotte Polidori (1803–90).
262. See John 7.17.

The Face of the Deep

263. See Gen. 2.12.
264. See James 4.17.
265. See *Poems,* 1979–90, 2:248–49.
266. See Acts 8.30–31.

267. See *Poems,* 1979–90, 2:255.
268. See Luke 1.38.
269. See Matt. 25.6.
270. See Ps. 90.4.
271. See Luke 12.37; John 13.17.
272. See Joel 2.14; Isa. 30.13.
273. Titled "Her Seed; It shall bruise thy head" in "Songs for Strangers and Pilgrims" in *Verses.* See *Poems,* 1979–90, 2:295.
274. See Ps. 119.18.
275. See Ecclus. 51.22 and Ps. 108.1 (*Book of Common Prayer*).
276. See James 3.5–6,8.
277. See Ps. 147.4.
278. Compare to the sequence "The Thread of Life" (*Poems,* 1979–90, 2:123), especially the conclusion to the second sonnet: "I am not what I have nor what I do; / But what I was I am, I am even I." There may be an echo of Coleridge's remarks on the imagination. See *Biographia Literaria* in *The Collected Works of Samuel Taylor Coleridge,* vol. 7 (Princeton: Princeton University Press, 1983), chap. 12, p. 275 and chap. 13, p. 304; but Packer is sceptical about Rossetti's knowing Coleridge's prose (p. 232). Compare to Exod. 3.14: "And God said unto Moses, I AM THAT I AM."
279. See Isa. 38.14.
280. Compare to *Poems,* 1979–90, 2:187–88.
281. See Ps. 97.10.
282. See 1 John 3.7 and John 7.17.
283. See Eph. 5.12 and Titus 1.15.
284. Compare to *Poems,* 1979–90, 2:254.
285. See James 5.10–11.
286. See Luke 21.19 and Rev. 3.10.
287. See Rom. 5.5.
288. See 2 Cor. 6.9.
289. Compare to *Poems,* 1979–90, 2:253.
290. See Isa. 57.1–2.
291. See Eph. 4.22 and Col. 3.9.
292. We have been unable to identify this quotation.
293. Titled "Yea, the sparrow hath found her an house" in "Songs for Strangers and Pilgrims" in *Verses.* Compare to *Poems,* 1979–90, 2:332–33.
294. See Mark 14.37; 1 Cor. 10.13; Matt. 24.36,42; Eccles. 7.18; Lam. 3.26.
295. See 1 Pet. 3.13–16.
296. See Ps. 29.9.
297. See John 3.8 and Job 9.11.
298. See Ps. 69.5–6 and Exod. 31.18.
299. See John 3.13.
300. Compare to *Poems,* 1979–90, 2:183.
301. See Isa. 38.14 and Eccles. 2.13.
302. See Eccles. 7.13–14.

303. See 2 Kings 1.12 and Job 1.16.
304. See Mark 1.13.
305. See Ps. 18.10.
306. See Rom. 8.19–23.
307. See Job 38.26.
308. See Ps. 104.24.
309. See Ps. 36.6.
310. See Ps. 49.12,20.
311. See 2 Pet. 2.11.
312. See Isa. 30.25–26.
313. See Matt. 28.20.
314. See Mark 2.27 and Matt. 24.20.
315. See Exod. 20.8.
316. See Isa. 14.12.
317. Titled "O Lucifer, Son of the Morning!" in "The World. Self-Destruction" in *Verses*. Compare to *Poems, 1979–90,* 2:263.
318. See Luke 9.23–24.
319. See Prov. 17.14.
320. See 2 Tim. 2.13.
321. See 1 John 2.7.
322. As Packer notes in her biography (p. 212), both of Christina's brothers were interested in spiritualism and at times attended seances. One "theory which would pursue knowledge by cruel or foul methods" was vivisection, the surgery on a living animal for scientific research. Christina strongly disapproved of this practice and contributed to the antivivisection movement in the 1870s that resulted in the Cruelty to Animals Act (1876). See Marsh, 433–36.
323. See Ps. 16.8.
324. See 2 Tim. 4.10.
325. See 1 Sam. 12.20–22.
326. See Eccles. 4.9–10,12.
327. Compare to *Poems, 1979–90,* 2:273.
328. See Eccles. 3.14–15.
329. See Matt. 13.52.
330. See Ps. 83.13 (*Book of Common Prayer*)
331. See Gen. 3.6.
332. See Gen. 2.17.
333. See Luke 1.29.
334. See Song of Sol. 2.2.
335. See Song of Sol. 1.4, 6.10.
336. See Prov. 31.31.
337. See Jer. 5.6 and 1 John 2.15–17.
338. See Prov. 6.9–11.
339. See Ps. 35.17.
340. See John 3.16–17.

341. Titled "Quinquagesima" in "Some Feasts and Fasts" in *Verses*. Compare to *Poems, 1979–90*, 2:220–21.
342. See Gen. 1.31.
343. See Matt. 4.8.
344. See Prov. 23.31–33.
345. See 1 Cor. 10.13.
346. We have not been able to identify this reference and quotation.
347. See Isa. 26.3–5,8–9.
348. See Dan. 4.31 and 2 Kings 9.5.
349. See Exod. 34.7.
350. See Ezek. 18.14,17.
351. See Ps. 40.3.
352. Compare to *Poems, 1979–90*, 2:280–81.
353. See Rev. 21.4.
354. This couplet is so far unidentified.
355. See Dan. 6.17.
356. Titled "As the sparks fly upwards" in "Out of the Deep Have I Cried Unto Thee, O Lord" in *Verses*. Compare to *Poems, 1979–90*, 2:182–83.
357. See James 3.5.
358. See Matt. 24.22.
359. See Prov. 30.8.
360. Titled "The General Assembly and Church of the Firstborn" in "New Jerusalem and Its Citizens" in *Verses*. Compare to *Poems, 1979–90*, 2:189–90.
361. The concluding prayer ("the Grace") for both Morning and Evening Prayer and for the Litany in the *Book of Common Prayer*, from 2 Cor. 13.14.
362. See Isa. 35.8.
363. Titled "Awake, thou that sleepest" in "Divers Worlds. Time and Eternity" in *Verses*. Compare to *Poems, 1979–90*, 2:270.

Selected Bibliography

Addison, Jane. "Christina Rossetti Studies, 1974–1991: A Checklist and Synthesis." *Bulletin of Bibliography* 52.1 (March 1995): 73–93.

Arseneau, Mary and D.M.R. Bentley. "Peter Parley and the Rossettis." *English Language Notes* 20 (September 1993): 56–60.

———— and Jan Marsh. "Intertextuality and Intratextuality: The Full Text of Christina Rossetti's 'Harmony on First Corinthians XIII' Restored." *Victorian Newsletter* 88 (Fall 1995): 17–26.

Battiscombe, Georgina. *Christina Rossetti: A Divided Life.* New York: Holt, Rinehart and Winston, 1981.

Bell, Mackenzie. *Christina Rossetti: A Biographical and Critical Study.* Boston: Roberts Brothers, 1898.

Bornand, Odette, ed. *The Diary of W. M. Rossetti.* Oxford: Clarendon Press, 1977.

Calmet's Dictionary of the Holy Bible. Revised by Edward Robinson. Boston: Crocker and Brewster, 1832.

Chadwick, Owen. *The Victorian Church.* 2 vols. 2nd ed. London: Adam & Black, 1972.

Crump, Rebecca W. *Christina Rossetti: A Reference Guide.* Boston: G. K. Hall, 1976a.

————, ed. *Maude: Prose and Verse by Christina Rossetti.* Hamden, CT: Archon Books, 1976b.

————, ed. *The Complete Poems of Christina Rossetti: A Variorum Edition.* 3 vols. Baton Rouge: Louisiana State University Press, 1979–1990.

D'Amico, Diane. "Christina Rossetti's *Maude*: A Reconsideration." *University of Dayton Review* 15 (1981): 129–42.

————. "Christina Rossetti's Christian Year: Comfort for 'the weary heart.'" *Victorian Newsletter* 72 (1987): 36–42.

————. "Christina Rossetti's 'From Sunset to Star Rise': A New Reading." *Victorian Poetry* 27 (1989): 95–100.

————. "'Choose the stairs that mount above': Christina Rossetti and the Anglican Sisterhoods." *Essays in Literature* 17 (1990): 204–21.

————. "Christina Rossetti's 'Helpmeet.'" *Victorian Newsletter* 88 (Spring 1994): 25–29.

Davies, Horton. *Worship and Theology in England from Newman to Martineau, 1850–1900.* Princeton, NJ: Princeton University Press, 1962.

Doughty, Oswald and J. R. Wahl, eds. *The Letters of Dante Gabriel Rossetti.* 4 vols. Oxford: Clarendon Press, 1965–67.

Gilbert, Pamela K. "'A Horrid Game': Woman as Social Entity in Christina Rossetti's Prose." *English* 41 (Spring 1992): 1–23.

Griffiths, Eric. "The Disappointment of Christina G. Rossetti." *Essays in Criticism* 47 (April 1997): 107–42.

Harrison, Antony H. *Christina Rossetti in Context.* Chapel Hill: University of North Carolina Press, 1988.

———. "Christina Rossetti and the Sage Discourse of Feminist High Anglicanism." In *Victorian Sages and Cultural Discourse: Renegotiating Gender and Power,* ed. Thais E. Morgan, 87–104. New Brunswick, NJ: Rutgers University Press, 1990.

———, ed. *The Letters of Christina Rossetti.* 4 vols. Charlotte, VA: University Press of Virginia, 1997–.

Hobbs, Colleen. "A View from 'The Lowest Place': Christina Rossetti's Devotional Prose." *Victorian Poetry* 32.3–4 (Autumn-Winter 1994): 409–28.

Hönnighausen, Gisela. "Emblematic Tendencies in the Works of Christina Rossetti." *Victorian Poetry* 10 (1972): 1–15.

Jones, Kathleen. *'Learning not to be first': The Life of Christina Rossetti.* New York: St. Martin's Press, 1991.

Kent, David A., ed. *The Achievement of Christina Rossetti.* Ithaca, NY: Cornell University Press, 1987.

Knoepflmacher, U. C. "Avenging Alice: Christina Rossetti and Lewis Carroll." *Nineteenth-Century Literature* 41 (1986): 299–328.

Leder, Sharon, and Andrea Abbott. *The Language of Exclusion: The Poetry of Emily Dickinson and Christina Rossetti.* Contributions in Women's Studies, 83. Westport, CT: Greenwood Press, 1987.

McGann, Jerome J. "The Religious Poetry of Christina Rossetti." *Critical Inquiry* 10 (1983): 127–44.

Marsh, Jan. *Christina Rossetti: A Literary Biography.* London: Jonathan Cape, 1994.

Marshall, Linda. "What the Dead Are Doing Underground: Hades and Heaven in the Writings of Christina Rossetti." *Victorian Newsletter* 72 (1987): 55–60.

Merwin, Dorothy. "Heroic Sisterhood in 'Goblin Market.'" *Victorian Poetry* 21 (1983): 107–18.

Packer, Lona Mosk. *Christina Rossetti.* Cambridge: Cambridge University Press, 1963a.

———, ed. *The Rossetti-Macmillan Letters.* Berkeley: University of California Press, 1963b.

Palazzo, Linda. "Two Forgotten Sketches." *Notes and Queries* 37 (1990): 38–39.

———. "The Prose Works of Christina Rossetti." Ph.D. diss., University of Durham, 1992.

Peattie, Roger W., ed. *Selected Letters of William Michael Rossetti.* University Park: Pennsylvania State University Press, 1990.

Ricks, Christopher. "Christina Rossetti and Commonplace Books." *Grand Street* 9.3 (1990): 190–98.

Rosenblum, Dolores. *Christina Rossetti: The Poetry of Endurance*. Carbondale: Southern Illinois University Press, 1986.

Rossetti, Christina. *Commonplace, and Other Short Stories*. London: Macmillan, 1870.

———. *Annus Domini: A Prayer for each day of the year, founded on a text of Holy Scripture*. London: James Parker, 1874a.

———. *Speaking Likenesses*. London: Macmillan, 1874b.

———. *Seek and Find: A Double Series of Short Studies of the Benedicite*. London: SPCK, 1879.

———. *Called to be Saints: The Minor Festivals Devotionally Studied*. London: SPCK, 1881.

———. *Letter and Spirit: Notes on the Commandments*. London: SPCK, 1883.

———. *Time Flies: A Reading Diary*. London: SPCK, 1885.

———. *The Face of the Deep: A Devotional Commentary on the Apocalypse*. London: SPCK, 1892.

———. *Verses*. London: SPCK, 1893.

Rossetti, Maria Francesca. *A Shadow of Dante: Being an Essay Towards Studying Himself, His World, and His Pilgrimage*. London: Longmans, Green, and Co., 1894.

Rossetti, William Michael, compiler. *Rossetti Papers*. 1903. New York: AMS Press, 1970a.

———, ed. *Some Reminiscences of William Michael Rossetti*. 2 vols. 1906. New York: AMS Press, 1970b.

———, ed. *The Family Letters of Christina Georgina Rossetti*. London: Brown, Langham and Company, 1908.

Sandars, Mary F. *The Life of Christina Rossetti*. London: Hutchinson, 1930.

Showalter, Elaine, ed. Maude *by Christina Rossetti and* "On Sisterhoods" *and* A Woman's Thoughts About Women *by Dinah Mulock Craik*. New York: New York University Press, 1993.

Smulders, Sharon. *Christina Rossetti Revisited*. New York: Twayne, 1996.

Soulenn, Richard N. *Handbook of Biblical Criticism*. Atlanta: John Knox Press, 1976.

Tennyson, G. B. *Victorian Devotional Poetry: The Tractarian Mode*. Cambridge, MA: Harvard University Press, 1981.

Thomas, Eleanor F. *Christina Georgina Rossetti*. New York: Columbia University Press, 1931.

Thomas, Frances. *Christina Rossetti*. Hanley Swan, Worcester: The Self Publishing Association, 1992; London: Virago Press, 1994.

Troxell, Janet Camp, ed. *Three Rossettis: Unpublished Letters to and from Dante Gabriel, Christina, William*. Cambridge, MA: Harvard University Press, 1937.

Westcott, Right Reverend B. F. *An Appreciation of the late Christina Georgina Rossetti*. London: SPCK, 1899.

Westerholm, Joel. "'I Magnify Mine Office': Christina Rossetti's Authoritative Voice in her Devotional Prose." *Victorian Newsletter* 84 (Fall 1993): 11–17.

Williams, Reverend Isaac. *The Apocalypse, with Notes and Reflections*. 1841. London: Francis and John Rivington, 1852.

———. *Thoughts on the Study of the Holy Gospels*. London: Rivington, 1876.

Index